LITERATURE ON TRIAL: THE EMERGENCE OF CRITICAL DISCOURSE IN GERMANY, POLAND, AND RUSSIA, 1700–1800

S.D. CHROSTOWSKA

Literature on Trial

The Emergence of Critical Discourse in Germany, Poland, and Russia, 1700–1800

UNIVERSITY OF TORONTO PRESS
Toronto Buffalo London

Toronto Buffalo London
www.utppublishing.com

ISBN 978-1-4426-4356-7 (cloth)

Library and Archives Canada Cataloguing in Publication

Chrostowska, S.D. (Sylwia Dominika), 1975–
Literature on trial : the emergence of critical discourse in Germany, Poland, and Russia, 1700–1800 / S.D. Chrostowska.

Includes bibliographical references and index.
ISBN 978-1-4426-4356-7

1. Criticism – Germany – History – 18th century. 2. German literature – History and criticism – Theory, etc. 3. Criticism – Poland – History – 18th century. 4. Polish literature – History and criticism – Theory, etc. 5. Criticism – Russia – History – 18th century. 6. Russian literature – History and criticism – Theory, etc. I. Title.

PT78.C57 2012 801′.95094309033 C2012-900561-4

This book has been published with the help of a grant from the Canadian Federation for the Humanities and Social Sciences, through the Aid to Scholarly Publications Program, using funds provided by the Social Sciences and Humanities Research Council of Canada.

University of Toronto Press acknowledges the financial assistance to its publishing program of the Canada Council for the Arts and the Ontario Arts Council.

Canada Council for the Arts Conseil des Arts du Canada

University of Toronto Press acknowledges the financial support of the Government of Canada through the Canada Book Fund for its publishing activities.

Contents

Preface

This book is a comparative study of the genres of literary criticism in the eighteenth century, a time when modern criticism, its fortunes intertwined with emerging national literatures, was just coming into its own. More generally, it is a history of the rules of literature in the broad sense and, by the same token, of the discourse (literary criticism) that both followed them and codified them for literature in the narrow sense. Criticism emerged as the literary rule-making and assessment that itself followed literary rules, by overlapping with, and carving for itself a space within, or on the margins of, the literary. It took shape as a rule-based discursive practice by creating an object within the broad field of 'letters,' an object still known as 'literature,' and by subjecting it to judgment. But because it is still intimately connected to literature, criticism is not in the position of absolute arbiter that escapes all the laws to which it submits the literary. My approach was, accordingly, to draw attention to it as a rule-bound practice, subjecting the history of criticism – a discourse of judgment according to literary rules – to a set of these very rules, *the rules of genre.*

As for the choice of texts, I relied on the history to suggest what was worth looking at. The corpus, in other words, was chosen according to the literary-critical canon as it came to be. But my interest gravitated to those texts that were not simply typical representatives of a genre, but that worked – and played – at the borders of existing genres, occasionally flirting with literary ones. They can be called 'transgressive,' because they did something new. But as creative 'exceptions' that lay at the felt limits of the emerging discourse (when these limits were hazy and in flux), these samples served to codify the new institution/discipline, to set its generic standards. In sum, the project involved looking at canonical texts that reflexively formed the critical (not to mention the literary) canon, particularly texts that do not fit in the now-standard genres, that do not follow their rules (though they helped lay them down and have become part of the canon), but that, historically and now, render the distinction between literature and criticism problematic.

Of broadest interest, I think, will be the theoretical introduction, which lays out a framework for understanding discursive practices through genre. While criticism as a discipline appears at first to be an anomaly insofar as its arises by defining itself vis-à-vis a (changing) category of texts, which it aims to sort through, to reflect on and interpret, and finally to judge – is this not also true of the discourses of history, anthropology, sociology, political theory, and related sciences? And are not the theoretical and philosophical approaches *within* (as well as *to*) these disciplines a result of textual reflection and criticism by their practitioners, who labour ceaselessly to define them, to reinvent them, to compensate for their blind spots, and to respond to various 'crises' they face? Indeed, I would contend that the separation of the evaluative function from the literary evident in the present study not only produced the distinction between literature and literary criticism, it also made criticism the growth factor of most modern knowledge discourses. To look at these disciplines in their evaluative mode would mean considering writing in more or less established yet dynamic forms, obeying specific conventions and standards. So, while specific, the genre approach employed in this volume can be extended as a method of study to other fields of knowledge.

I would like to thank the following individuals and institutions for supporting me in this project: Professors Wladimir Krysinski, Kenneth Lantz, Michał Paweł Markowski, Peter Nesselroth, John Noyes, Brian Stock, Sarah Young, Michael R. Borkowski, Danuta and Bogusław Chrostowscy, and, more recently, James D. Ingram, as well as the Joseph Bazylewicz foundation and the University of Toronto for their financial generosity in the years 2001–2006.

LITERATURE ON TRIAL: THE EMERGENCE OF CRITICAL DISCOURSE IN GERMANY, POLAND, AND RUSSIA, 1700–1800

Introduction

The history of criticism should not be a purely antiquarian subject but should, I believe, illuminate and interpret our present situation. It will, in turn, become comprehensible only in the light of a modern literary theory.
(René Wellek, *A History of Modern Criticism, 1750–1950*)[1]

1 Genre, Discourse, History

The historiographic experiments of decades past have given us numerous ways of writing the history of discourses and disciplines. If historians remain on the lookout for new methodological directions, it is not, at least not principally, from a need for a definitive approach or variety for its own sake, or from any perception of oversights in contemporary scholarship. The main reason for this search, in my view, lies elsewhere, in one of the implications of methodological pluralization: that to 'always historicize' we need fresh modes of inquiry into the planes and dimensions particular to each discourse's internal and external organization. Such, at least, was my own sense as I set out to study a comparatively neglected field: the literary criticism that emerged over the course of the eighteenth century in parts of Central and Eastern Europe, in what is now Germany, Poland, and Russia.[2]

Major correctives to historical research subscribe, in one way or another, to a basic incommensurability between past and present. Thus, it is said that a constructive, durable bridge between outmoded and outgrown approaches, or the spirit of a whole discipline, and approaches or programs valid today is merely a Piranesian fiction for the confinement of new thought – that such a bridge, in short, is an epistemic impossibility. In this view, whatever vestigial connection does exist is merely nominal and deleterious – a bridge to be burned after it has been crossed. Yet even when as basic a concept as the *text* is called into question and effectively reconfigured, historians in particular continue to draw tenuous, subconscious, but nonetheless real and productive lines to findings obtained by the biased or otherwise flawed methods of earlier paradigms, in which the traditional notion of a text as a written artefact went unchallenged. To historians of discourse, critical discourse analysts, and even rhetorical critics these may be unwelcome ties precisely because of a suspicion of sweeping institutional narratives that precede the linguistic and rhetorical 'turns' and pantextualism, or the claim that everything knowable is textual. The tradition of rhetoric, for one thing, had been fractured with the proclamation of a 'new' rhetoric; continuity between the prescriptive rhetorical theory and practice of old and the study of practical rhetoric that got underway in the 1970s and 1980s was provisional and insubstantial. Many trends in late-twentieth-century humanities were predicated, after all, on a decisive break with event- and individual-centred models, whose fabled humanistic 'unities' overarched the night of knowledge like stellar constellations with the reassuring glimmer of meaning. A consistent commitment to mobile local research agendas and system-wide scrutiny of the discursive power/knowledge nexus labour against the *doxa* of earlier scholarship. This brand of intervention is justified variously as a post-objectivist, post-positivist, de-centring, self-critical work of edification, which ensures the continuity of academic authority while methodically undermining its concrete manifestations. At issue, then, is the curious case of an anti-paradigmatic paradigm and the dangers it engenders. For once a generative connection to and respect for past authority are lost, intellectual labour in these bleachfields is left without one of the most valuable resources for self-transformative critique. A structure that links in memory what is already separated in time need not be the Achilles heel of vanguard knowledge; it can offer a commanding view of our progress through the maze of ideas. The more fantastic its architecture, the more liberating become the 'other' spaces of thought.

Although not unsympathetic to those who prefer a clean break with past method, I am about to argue for a historical approach to discourse which actively connects and builds on findings obtained through older approaches – chief among them formal and stylistic analyses. Despite many commonalities, this method cannot be equated with historical study of the 'grammar' or conditions of possibility of discourses (Foucauldian archaeology), cultural stylistics, the rhetorics of inquiry, the ideological/social aspects of discourse, or the epistemic orders and objects it produces (as in various functionalist, sociological, or social constructionist perspectives). It is an approach that, while departing radically from the traditional focus on the epistemic contents of discourse, calls for a critical reappraisal of older studies of individual texts, styles, terminologies, and genres. It does so in an attempt to isolate so-called formal features that bear the modes of reasoning and conceptual-analytic techniques – in a word, the knowledge – of a given discourse. (While the traditional distinction between form and content facilitates such refocusing, the point of this effort at reappraisal is to further problematize that distinction, without suggesting it should be done away with altogether.) In keeping with this, the objective of a comparative, regional study of a discourse like literary criticism would be to juxtapose the ways in which linguistically distinct cultural systems have come to *formulate* the practical/applied and theoretical elements of the modern critical knowledge of literature.

Far from divorcing them from the ideational and social registers of discourse, the historical study of discursive forms – and, by implication, of written genres – must be a study of the manifestations of social and intra-/intercultural developments. These include (but are not limited to) the initial deployment of discursive practices and their subsequent adjustment to changing socio-cultural, political, and economic conditions, institutional structures, paradigms, doctrines, ideologies, ethoses, and moral and aesthetic values. Traditional histories of criticism tracked the development of contents (concepts, figures, theories, methods) but generally neglected to analyse them in relation to their diverse forms of expression or their social and other correlatives. The challenge when analysing genres is to avoid mirroring this neglect – on the rationale that the ideas of criticism have already been dealt with – or, for that matter, conflating form and genre. That being said, it is not so much the contents as the modes of discourse and their formal regulation – the recognized, ritualized, and codified forms of discursive materialities – that bring into focus and enable access to their socio-cultural configuration as a discourse. I contend, in other words, that analyses of generic aspects of literary-critical writing can yield a deeper understanding of the emergence of criticism *qua discourse* (as opposed to, primarily, a system of ideas and criteria persisting through time and projective of a consensus-based science of literature, abstracted from their discursive existence). Given this departure from methodological convention – that is, the shift away from ideas – I did not expect to collect anything more than fragments of insight from older scholarship. (Reference to ideational material was warranted only insofar as it rendered visible the correlation between conceptual transformations in literary judgment and transformations in its discursive form.) Where my inquiry took me, there could be no question of retreading familiar territory, nor even so much as a beacon – for where was that systematic history of general and specific forms of criticism or, for that matter, of any other knowledge discourse, when one needed it?[3]

My purpose here is to lay the theoretical groundwork for just such a history, advancing genre as a prism through which to view other discursive features. As one of the complex rules for the formation, organization, relation, and transformation of discourse, genre wields the power of discursive law. Its observance indicates consistency, as much as its breach does discursive change. A major generic shift is tantamount to a transformation of a discourse in its other registers. Every formal upheaval entails an adjustment, whereby a discourse maintains continuity, merges with or is absorbed by another, or else dissolves or disintegrates. The process of realignment and stabilization is similar at the emergence of discourses and disciplines: through consistent appearance in a set of altered or markedly new forms, formulations acquire coherence as texts, texts acquire uniformity as discourses, and discourses attain regularity as disciplines and professional praxes.[4] The codification of generic choices can thus be said to correspond to the crystallization and articulation of epistemic standards – thus contributing to a discourse's legitimacy and overall stability. Further, if differences in forms of communication reflect differences in experience, understanding, and reasoning, then formal distinctions among parallel discourses in different cultures, as well as between texts within each discourse, translate into epistemic distinctions. My argument rests on the proposition that each critical genre corresponds to specific evaluative methods and criteria and to specific conceptions of literature and criticism alike. It follows that significant change in the forms (variety, complexity, or function) of criticism indicates significant change in the praxis, function, and value of literature, and hence also in literary-critical methods and principles. In short, formal differences do make, or mark, a difference.

The approach just outlined takes up a challenge presented by, among others, the 2007 papers in *Poetics Today* devoted to philosophical genres and John Frow's contribution in the *PMLA* issue of the same year – namely, to raise critical attention to genre to the rank of a method for the historical study of discourses that can yield insights into their emergence and development. It advances a theory of discourse that uses formal discursive conventions as its analytical lens. This means that, on the level of genre (of formal generalization), correspondences between a discourse's form and content regularly constrain it just as they make it distinct, and that these general correspondences are significant for the production of knowledge associated with that discourse – indeed, can tell us how the association was formed and sustained (or not). Genre is central to understanding how nascent discursivities stake their claims to a given object, making it into an object of knowledge, and how they shape this knowledge-object after securing their right to (and power over) it.

A history adopting genre as a gauge of discourse formation and transformation is tenable only if it refuses analogies customary to the history of ideas – in particular, an evolutionary, orthogenetic perspective on generic change. It takes looking at genres not as natural kinds, but as non-discrete, relational systems within a larger genre system: kaleidoscopic, evincing in every phase a particular 'internal' power dynamic as well as 'external' relations with genre systems in adjacent discourses. This perspective on genre is inspired by the first cohesive theoretical statement on the reconcilability of hitherto dissociated conceptual systems, literature, and language: 'The history of a system is in turn a system … The opposition between synchrony and diachrony was an opposition between the concept of system and the concept of evolution; thus it loses its importance as soon as we recognize that every system necessarily exists as an evolution, whereas, on the other hand, evolution is inescapably of a systemic nature.'[5] 'Evolution' is here understood not in a biological sense (to which Russian formalism was a reaction); it is not to be associated with phylogenetic classifications of genres qua genera after the manner of Ferdinand Brunetière and others.[6] Yet even as we distance ourselves from organicism, we must also admit that biological metaphors like 'hybridization' or the 'survival of the fittest' could prove useful in a genre-based discourse history, provided that we do not find ourselves looking for a genetic basis for genre behaviour.

My working hypothesis, then, is the possibility of historically systematizing a discourse in its genres. Although not itself of Bakhtinian provenance, the crux of historical genre systematics[7] was framed in the Russian theorist's celebrated essay on speech genres. 'Each separate utterance [oral and written] is individual, of course, but each sphere in which language is used develops its own *relatively stable types* of these utterances,' reflective of habits of experience and understanding.[8] Bakhtin clearly saw these types as neither the bedrock of utterances nor merely their static products. The above hypothesis is premised on every discursive formulation being made in connection to or within stabilized generic categories, be they pure or impure. In the case of literary criticism, they shade into those of the literary medium itself – significantly more than do the formal conventions of other knowledge discourses (this premise leads us, below, to speak of the *crisical* effect of such shading). Like many other textual domains, modern criticism has an early history of comparatively loose generic organization. That is to say, 'its' genres – those in which it gradually came to be articulated and apprehended – were not all or always typified and binding.

The challenge, then, lies in representing a dynamic, culturally and historically specific system of codified formal features and discursive strategies (modes), both of which enable – and are themselves underwritten by – legible methodological and ideological praxes exercised with varied competence as well as a differentiated conception of the discursive object (e.g., the literary text). The category of *mode* supplies the functional link between utterance and genre. A set of modes (many of which are carryovers, following genres appropriated or adapted from other discursive contexts) demarcates a discourse and permeates its established genres. Some examples of modes active in literary-critical discourse are: evaluative, normative, prescriptive, narrative, interpretive, explicative, descriptive, impressionistic, analytic, synthetic, and self-reflexive.[9] By emphasizing the interaction (or 'textual hylomorphism')[10] of mode, genre, formulation, and idea, we avoid giving causal weight to either form or content.

In practice, a historical concern with discourse through 'the eye of genre' requires examining texts with different relationships to contemporary generic categories. Some texts will be found to conform to one genre, others will overflow the generic category they ostensibly identify with, while still others will accentuate or flaunt their hybridity, undermining or rejecting specific generic labels or even generic categorization as such. Attention to genre must also be informed and tempered by the realization that many generic categories existed and were in use before being mobilized for the discourse in question. In criticism, this applies to the commentary, the dialogue, the essay, the letter, the notice, the poetics, the preface, and the review. Their earlier career (whether ancient or modern) may or may not be relevant to their introduction into critical discourse. However, many such pre-existing forms proved transitional; of those just named, only the critical commentary, essay, notice, preface, and review became permanently associated with literary criticism. To make matters still more complicated, the same genres could also define criticism's contemporary neighbours, most notably philosophy.[11]

The task of examining a discourse's 'beginnings,' as I set out to do, need not entail establishing, reaffirming, or disputing its textual and generic canons. The eighteenth-century critical texts I worked with, far from obscure and minor, are by and large considered canonical, in the sense of being historically widely recognized as seminal for discursive standards.[12] They do not, however, always or exclusively fall into canonized *genres* – sometimes because the question of canonicity was not explicitly raised with regard to discursive genres, sometimes because the erstwhile repertoire of literary-critical forms exceeded what has since become the discourse's genre canon. In order to speak of a 'canon' of genres in the first place, we must bear in mind the word's meaning as 'a general rule or fundamental principle governing the systematic treatment of a subject.' A genre canon (one of several canons for any given discursive practice) standardizes a discourse's generic attributes, those which compose its genre system. The genres in the generic canon of literary criticism, for example, would contain the general conceptual-methodological code for the critical treatment of literature. If Dominick LaCapra's proposal was to read a (literary) canon non-canonically, so as not to fall into the trap of elitism or uncritical populism,[13] mine is to read it through an alternate sense of 'canonicity,' giving us insight into the selective process of formation and transformation of a discourse's architecture, function, ideology, and institutional profile.

In writing of the emergence of a discourse, few today would be tempted by traditional 'history of origins' (*Entstehungsgeschichte*). Nor would they likely profit from historicizing this discourse's formation as an institution (genre is both in excess and in deficiency of the institutional framework of discourse; the institutional aspect certainly enters the discussion, though not as the overriding problem). Instead, I set out to trace the formation, transformation, and codification of its formal features. My ultimate aim, however – and all the more reason to speak of a 'genre genealogy' – is to uncover the specific generic relations that exist between a discourse and its object(s) of knowledge: in the present case, relations of formal determination, reciprocity, and antagonism –

enabling, structuring, unifying, diffusing, limiting, and hindering – in the transactions between critical and literary phenomena.[14]

Qualifying my application of genealogical analysis to modern literary criticism is, thus, an inquiry into the latter's generic development. My interest lay, first, in the status of different genres within a changing generic hierarchy and within the consecutive genre systems in criticism's formative stages. The central question here was, What led to the privileging of some genres as the bearers of the discourse, supporting the intelligibility of its statements? Second and more concretely, I became interested in the contemporary generic status of texts (and formulations within them) that, to a greater or lesser extent, were recognized as part of the emerging discourse. Here the main question was, What weight did these texts' genre status carry in the early definition and institutionalization of criticism? The answers to these and related issues could be framed in terms of the dominance ('appropriateness') of certain genres over others as effects of discursive power relations – 'internal' and 'external' relations that reproduced or disrupted existing epistemic paradigms and ideologies, their corresponding institutional disposition, and patterns of socio-political domination. Consequently, the object of inquiry became the emerging, dynamic, local, and extra-local jurisdiction of a set of (frequently hybrid) generic forms and their systematic dissemination in a discourse, or else their dissipation.

Looking at discursive 'beginnings' cannot, in this case, be detached from looking at 'endings,' particularly if we wish to contribute something to the 'history of the present.'[15] We find ourselves returning to beginnings at the sign of crisis because the process of a discourse's emergence, during which it asserted itself ideationally/formally as an active confrontation and amalgam of pre-existing discourses, can shed light on the dialectical process of its 'degeneration,' when it loses its position against them. Nowhere perhaps is this more apropos than in the case of literary criticism. The formal condition of academic criticism under the sign of postmodern theory has, for some three decades now, existed in a heightened, invigorating state of crisis that, to varying degrees, affects the humanities at large. (Most developments suggest that intellectuals embattled in these disciplines have lost ground to the sciences and that their activity is actually a sign of imminent collapse.)[16] In order to maintain its place within the academic milieu, from about 1965 onwards criticism has waxed conspicuously autotelic, functioning *crisi*cally – that is to say, by reference to and interrogation of its own *raison d'être*, epistemic limits, professional identity, social purpose, role, and status – where it ought, in order to fulfil its mandate, to function critically – that is, by focus on an object other than itself (including texts from the borderline between criticism and literature).[17] In North America, the analytical model of humanistic inquiry and the changing face of higher education have done their share to erode the credibility of literary criticism, putting it on the defensive for having become 'its own worst enemy'[18] – overly crisical and not positive enough. Its high-theoretical phase was perceived as discursive self-alienation. On the Continent, by contrast, criticism's crisical turn followed a philosophical and theoretical ferment which, for a time, seemed only to reinforce its discursive position (public and academic alike) as both discourse and metadiscourse. That this extended crisis was not, until not long ago, as real a threat to critical practices in West Germany, for example, may partly be attributed to the long-established division of intellectuals into thoroughbreds and scholars/academics.[19] Also, one should not underestimate the deeply dissenting and traditionally crisis-oriented (as such also more resilient) intellectualism in areas long subject to foreign occupation and the Soviet regime, which forced academic critics to double as political journalists.

Two possible causes of the shift in balance from the critical to the crisical are theoretical in nature: the universalization of textuality (culminating in Derrida's '*il n'y a pas de hors-texte*')[20] and radical revisions to the literary canon. And if that new balance seems to have held, it may be because, on the one hand, the once potentially boundless textuality seems to have been mapped and its exploration to have plateaued, while, on the other hand, a de-canonizing, de-centring/regional approach to the curriculum has gained wide acceptance across North American sites of higher learning. But the main factor in a continued crisical orientation may be the growing pressure to defend and reaffirm criticism's practical value for a society whose readership is dwindling or relocating online, as more media reckon with a paperless future.[21]

A history that bases itself on the study of eighteenth-century critical genres in three cultures naturally cannot claim to be more than a fragment-sketch for a history of the current worldwide crisis in criticism, whose generic values are surely just one of many sides to the story. Put differently, complementary outlines and full studies would be needed to attend to the discourse's conceptual, institutional, socio-cultural, and political frameworks. Such a work cannot, furthermore, seek to explain directly the specific causes of the current formal condition, only to think it through as a historical parallel. In the eighteenth century, critical discourse similarly manifested a strong crisical disposition; however, this does not imply that the eighteenth century 'anticipated' the twentieth, or that the twentieth 'recapitulated' the eighteenth, or again, that there is any inevitability of such 'repetition' under comparable formal conditions. It might be objected that a broadly formal inquiry into critical genres cannot accommodate inquiry into such (epiphenomenal?) manifestations of discursive crisis as crisicality. Indeed, on an empirical level, we can do little more than *critically register* the crisical mode in criticism from the ideational level, without delving into crisical formulations as such. But we can also make inferences about this mode's formal conditions and generic basis. We can attempt to establish some of the earlier formal predicates of *crisique,* as a discursive function always integral to *critique* and the necessary converse of its heterotelic orientation (a relationship substantiated by their common Greek root, *cri-*: 'to judge,' 'to decide'). We are one step away from seeing criticism as a discourse in chronic crisis, as the crisis-discourse of letters, punctuated by periodic flare-ups and revolutions in language, to say nothing of economic and political crises.[22]

If a preliminary comparison of the eighteenth century with the present is to yield any formal generalization at all, it is that criticism seems to be pushed into crisical overdrive whenever its and/or its object's parameters become indeterminate (one indeterminacy often abetting the other), whether this is because its forms coincide too overtly with those of literature, or because boundaries within the larger discursive milieu are, for one reason or another, being redrawn. The crisical disposition of eighteenth-century criticism could therefore be ascribed to its still incomplete comportment as a discourse with relative autonomy – in part due to its incomplete formal separation from literature (then a more inclusive concept, synonymous with 'letters' – the sum of writings produced in a given period or area). This might suggest something like an immanent logic to all critical discourse, be it concerned with literature, society, or other areas of human activity. As soon as it diverts from this modus operandi, losing sight of its historically 'proper' object (indexed by its various qualifiers: 'literary,' 'social,' and so on), critical discourse begins to turn on itself, becomes consumed with itself, in danger of consuming itself. But this (self-reflexive, self-conscious) crisical attitude – in which the discourse suspends its own identity and stands as if outside itself, calling into question its autonomy, value for the present, and historical situation (what is this time which makes critique less than given, which forces it to seek anew its reason?) – this crisicality that marks a turning point is the source of critical dynamism and acumen, generating its most far-reaching contributions to letters, arts, and society. Times of crisis renew criticism's enduring attention to limits and contingency, alternately drawn or transgressed – a quality brought out most remarkably during the French and, later, German Enlightenment.

Wherever it develops, literary criticism enters into a generative interrelation with its object. It must, therefore, be seen as directly or indirectly responsible for literary innovation. The opposite also being true, literature impels criticism to reshape its own idiom and function. A historical study of critical discourse needs to note the concrete sociocultural processes affecting literature that effectuate criticism's modal/generic change: rises in literacy, consolidation of public readership, organization of literary activity, growth of intellectual and academic centres, development of print media. These processes, implicated to different degrees in other contemporary 'discursive formations,'[23] are tied in turn to each culture's political and economic conditions, its languages and lexicons, techniques for the dissemination of writing, as well as various means of discursive control (access, application, circulation, commission, delimitation, distribution, legitimation, and regulation of texts, e.g., in response to censorship). In other words, we must resist the temptation to study the form of discourses solely in relation to discursive objects or the institutions from which they issue.

Granted some thematic positivity and modal continuity, every discourse is comprised of statements of kinship, opposition, or telling indifference towards discursive phenomena (its own included). It 'takes effect indirectly through its relation to, its address to, another discourse.'[24] Interdiscursive power relations – conflicts as much as alliances – thus have a constitutive and cumulative effect on discursive practices – affecting, among many other things, their formal condition. As other, both newly emergent and more entrenched, domains of knowledge lend a nascent discourse their discursivities (without serving directly as models), they help to define and refine it thematically, theoretically, terminologically, stylistically,[25] and, of course, generically. Likewise, new entries in the discursive fold ripple across its surface.

Individual discourses are defined, therefore, not only by what they reject, but also by what they assimilate, from other discourses. A formally and functionally comprehensive study of a discourse such as literary criticism, one that would distinguish between its at times divergent, at times convergent, praxes – book reviewing and academic criticism – requires a working definition, restrictive and flexible in equal measure, of criticism as a discourse its own right. If I identify *critical*, that is, *evaluative* engagement with literature as the defining element, it is because this seems to be both the common functional denominator and the dominant mode of writing placed under the rubric of literary criticism. Despite a workable delineation of criticism's discursive field, we must remember that it is workable primarily for the core rather than the peripheries. We should also keep in mind that literary-critical acts are multimodal as well as 'multifunctional (and ambiguous)';[26] their various functions can be in competition within a single text, and sometimes a relation between them cannot even be established (for example, as competitive or complimentary). Critical texts, while presenting judgments on literary phenomena (specific works, literature in general, literary movements, or events like theatrical performances), are also spun from literary-theoretical, literary-historical, or metacritical (auto-critical and auto-theorizing) material in varied proportions. These other modes may come to the fore at different points in the history of a text's reception. We must, therefore, make allowances for varying historical readings and alternate discursive groupings of such works within their discursive formation. But, at least where canonical literary-critical texts are concerned, the criterion of evaluation is discernible in them regardless of the passage of time, independently of the validity or invalidity of specific judgments. Even a text not primarily evaluative of literature, but which, according to historical sources, once fulfilled a literary-critical function by extension or cross-application, has a place in this study if the existing (and, in parts, necessarily hazy) textual canon of criticism is to hold. A work of literary history that appears as a straightforward account of literary schools, authors, works, and their historical interpretations may not count as a work of criticism; but if evaluation is detected as its pervasive undercurrent, the piece deserves to stand alongside a book review as part of the literary-critical corpus. In academic criticism, evaluation tends to be implicit, buried in layers of interpretation or historical commentary, while in journalistic criticism it is as a rule explicit.

It is important, at this juncture, to address the problem of different praxes within one discourse that might further complicate my historiographic project. The main types of criticism – literary scholarship (including academic literary criticism) and applied (journalistic) literary criticism – notwithstanding their claims in a history of critical discourse, did not always run side-by-side and were not always grouped within one discursive formation. The dissociation, in nineteenth-century Germany, between literary scholarship as a whole (*Literaturwissenschaft*) and journalistic criticism (*Literaturkritik* or *literarische Kritik*) perpetuated a dichotomy between literary studies and literary criticism well into the twentieth century that led to a narrowing of both types. Wellek explains the dissociation by the rise to academic prominence of philosophical aesthetics and poetics, combined with the establishment of a specialized, predominantly historiographic, literary scholarship (*Literaturgeschichte*) divorced from contemporary literature, which was left to popular journalists.[27] The term *Literaturkritik* thus came to be reserved for day-to-day pronouncements on almost exclusively new works, whose role was to mediate between them and the contemporary audience. As in Poland, so in Russia during this period, the terms *krytyka literacka* and *literaturnaia kritika* (respectively) denoted an area of investigation greater than its German cognate, but less than what we understand by *literary criticism* in English and less still than the all-inclusive English *literary scholarship*.[28] Here, literary scholarship (Polish *literaturoznawstwo, wiedza*, or *nauka o literaturze*; Russian *literaturovedenie*) distinguished itself through scholarly erudition, yet still remained close to, often coincident with, the everyday practice of reviewing. In light of such culturally specific demarcations, the synchronic and diachronic aspects of criticism's formal/generic development must be correlated with its elaboration as a branch both of learning and of journalism, and with its later consolidation as a self-regulating scholarly discipline (institutionalized in literature departments) and an autonomous professional practice. A form-bound discourse history must therefore take into account and offer insight into the changing profile of a discourse – its degree of consolidation within the larger institutional spheres of academic, journalistic, or any other discursive praxis over a given period of time – from less formalized to downright formulaic.

In proposing an alternative analysis of a modally and functionally related group of texts, I am proposing no more, and no less, than an alternative approach to the problem of discursive change. The choice of genre and its components as the frame through which to study successive phases in a discourse's history requires us to historicize genre as a regulating idea. Here understanding is guided by historicity and *periodicity* (i.e., cycles of emergence, domination, stabilization, and/or decline). A comparative study of discursive forms sees genres cutting casually across not just different linguistic cultures but also identifiable cultural periods, owing to their 'capacity for dispersion (among diverse cultures) and for spontaneous recurrence (without the stimulus of a tradition, revival, or "retro" style)' – a 'historical rhythm' rather than the resurfacing of timeless, transhistorical ideas or natural kinds.[29] That a genre such as the critical essay qualifies as cross-historical in this way does not have bearing on its discursive future, much less necessitate any normative or universal arguments on its behalf.

In the most general sense, a genre is a conventionalized communicative system, represented by an empirical class of texts and existing in relation to genres within its genre system (sharing with them any number of features). As befits a functional and historical theory of genre,[30] generic transformations are conceptualized on the level of relational genre systems. Given that generic relations are in continual flux, care should be taken to describe not merely the individual genres of a discourse, but the successive genre systems in which it is built up.

In line with the preceding principles, the attribution of particular texts to particular genres ought to follow the historical record closely. Instead of re-christening texts with more 'accurate' or updated formal titles, or attempting to tell obsolete and surviving genres 'as they really were' in the past, I leave them more or less intact. Instead of a hands-on discourse poetics, I seek to lay bare the forms of extant texts and make informed guesses about the anatomies of extinct genre systems.

Facilitating this effort are the following qualitative and quantitative parameters of discursive form:

(1) Mode of enunciation, or propositional strategy – emphasizing the line of argument (rhetoric). Modes include: evaluative (judicial), polemical, monological, dialogical, poetic, narrative, speculative, descriptive (expository, presentational), informative, didactic, normative (regulative, prescriptive), predictive, suasory (persuasive), jussive (imperative), accusative, individual, or comparative, etc.;
(2) Structure: the organization of textual components;[31] vocabulary and specialized terminology; intertexts (direct discussions of other texts, references, citations, or lexical/terminological borrowings); paratexts (titles and headings, dedications, epigraphs, annotation);[32]
(3) Subject or thematic (complex of themes);
(4) Stated purpose (as originally recorded in the text, gleaned by its association with certain discursive domains, or perceived in the audience's reaction to it), e.g., informative, instructive, or promotional;

(5) Addressivity (conception of the audience's 'anticipated responsive reaction');[33]
(6) Length;
(7) Situation: time and medium of (re)publication, e.g., independent text, journal, etc.

Within the above framework, a genre is a relatively stable, codified system of *modal, formal*, and *thematic* categories. The distinction between mode and genre is essentially this: modes transcend genres (historical entities in another epistemic category) but through strong historical associations become erroneously conflated and identified with them.[34] As Genette argues in *The Architext*, their conflation was responsible for several centuries of confusion in the domain of poetics. Modes, in contrast to genres, are mobile and typically cross-historical, their life span independent of any particular genre they may 'inhabit.' 'Genres can cut across modes ..., perhaps the way individual works cut across genres' (*Architext* 71).

In the life of a discourse genres may be binding, but their exact jurisdictions are difficult, if not impossible, to determine. As Derrida argued in 'The Law of Genre,'

> a text would not *belong* to any genre. Every text *participates* in one or several genres, there is no genre-less text, there is always a genre and genres, yet such participation never amounts to belonging. And not because of an abundant overflowing or a free, anarchic and unclassifiable productivity, but because of the *trait* of participation itself, because of the effect of the code and of the generic mark. In marking itself generically, a text unmarks itself [*se démarque*]. If remarks of belonging belong without belonging, participate without belonging, then *genre-designations cannot be simply part of the corpus* ... This axiom of non-closure or non-fulfillment enfolds within itself the condition for the possibility and the impossibility of taxonomy. (230)

In the latter part of the same essay, we read that, 'The genre has always in all genres been able to play the role of order's principle: resemblance, analogy, identity and difference, taxonomic classification, organization and genealogical tree, order of reason, order of reasons, sense of sense, truth of truth, natural light and sense of history' (252). The trouble is not that texts, by virtue of participating without belonging, retain traces of the irreducible disorder of the empirical; rather, their generic mark gestures back and returns them to the general, generative order of naming.

To avoid the pitfalls of ahistorical, a priori, or a posteriori taxonomies of genres, we need not go to the other extreme and, taking extant discourse 'at its word' without imposing current labels on or reading our ideologies into the past, group texts exclusively into generic categories assigned to them by contemporaries (evidence permitting). Something just short of this, however, seems a sensible way to proceed in what is, after all, a historical study. We must be prepared for texts whose genre affiliation cannot be read off their surface or comfortably inferred, or whose stated affiliation is consciously unreliable. Contemporary designations should not absolutely bind cases where later discursive (generic) tendencies and reader responses give good reason to reclassify a text previously assigned to a genre or mix of genres. Absences of or resistances to generic classification – thus, in a certain sense, subversions of generic systematicity – could challenge us to more than a mere chronological inventory and description of a discourse's common forms, and to define the apparently genre-less 'misfits' as a precedent-altering class of their own. The objects in a structural classification, even one that takes into account diachrony, appear at each point or period in the sequence of cross-sections in the longitudinal frame to be locked in precisely the constellation described, more or less as described. At each moment the recognized genres are presented as relating to one another – if they are to relate at all – in specific 'natural,' ideologized ways. This, of course, does not reflect their real dynamics. Less questionable than such a general poetics of discursive genres, and at once more open than a stocktaking of individual kinds or an index of generic variety, is a time-bound repertoire of relations between genres – a historical genre systematics – not limited to a closed system of generic relations, or even to generic relations as such. On the example of literary criticism, it would give us a sense not just of the overlap of critical and literary genres, but also of the relationships between specific genres and ideologies; of the status and profile of the discourse as a kind of knowledge based on evaluation and as a signifier of the state of the public sphere; lastly, of the state of the universe of discourse (*Gegenstandsbereich*), the *genus universum*, the totality of culture in the broadest sense, with the myriad unstable orders of genre it encompasses.

As might be expected, the cross-fertilization and manifest 'hybridization' of genre forms in 'concrete literary organisms' is of crucial importance for a genre history of literary-critical discourse. According to

Ireneusz Opacki, who theorized the distinction between particular genres and multi-generic constructions (compounds), the latter type are affected by, but also affect, their constitutive genres and their status in the genre system.[35] This complex, dynamic relationship, not just one of generation, but of reciprocality among the categories of genres, characterizes for him the phenomenon of literary genre change: 'In the course of evolution, not only does one genre change, but they all do, constituting as they do a context for that genre' (125). Naturally, Opacki stresses the lack of both invariable *and* distinctive features of any given genre; signalling 'shifts in importance of distinguishing individual features of structure, depending on the literary context of the epoch or literary trend,' every new classification is attentive to different features when categorizing textual events into genres. The thesis of Opacki's 'Royal Genres' is that new genres in any literary current 'enter into a very close "blood relationship" with the form of the royal genre that is particular to that current' (121). This, we might add, makes for family resemblances among genres and among their textual participants.[36] 'Royal' genres (synonymous with formalism's 'dominant' genres) become, in a limited sense, the signatures of their times, encapsulating 'the aspirations of the period' (120). Transposed to the discussion of discourse, royal genres are only the most recognizable genres in a discourse's genre canon, managing its course of engagement and operating rules. For literary criticism in Germany and to the east, the 'royal genre' in the latter half of the eighteenth century was the critical review.

Genre's role as a principle of order implies that the cohesion and relative orderliness of a discourse, itself a genre of noesis and praxis, becomes established generically: through the individual genres commandeered by its discipline and through a visible genre system that serves to disseminate its particular kind of knowledge. Significant shifts in genre use mean shifts at every other level of discursive order: fundamental, even paradigmatic, readjustment to other discourses or distributive media, the engendering of new strategies, new themes and thematic combinations. Such shifts are a discourse's vital signs, just as its generic indistinctiveness or the breakdown of the genres employed by it signifies its failure to identify/articulate itself within the contemporary epistemic horizon.

Discourse, for Foucault the 'archaeologist,' was both a class/series of texts ('individualizable group of statements') and a kind of practice ('a regulated practice that accounts for a number of statements') (*AK* 25). Discursive fields become characterized by the 'totality of all effective events (whether spoken or written), in their dispersion as events and in the occurrence that is proper to them,' their 'effectiveness' appertaining to their constitution of a shared object (27). For Foucault the 'genealogist,' a discourse's productivity of power/knowledge enabled it to sustain itself in the discursive network as well as function in opposition to it.[37] Less mechanistically perhaps, Michel Pêcheux (exploring Althusser's interconnections among discourse, ideology, and language) saw discourses come into power through struggles with other discourses, whose language is ruled by competing ideologies. For Pêcheux, 'Possibilities for meaning are pinned down and made into definite meanings through the social and institutional position from which the discourse comes (and not through a structure of positive terms) ...,' notes MacDonell (12).[38] For both theorists, the study of discourse was a way of systematizing the historical dimension of ideological language use and function.

In *Mastering Discourse*, Paul Bové takes a critical look at the uses, limits, and possibilities of this work in the field of discourse analysis, which replaced the old interpretive questions about identity, meaning, and method (legacies of the discourse of meaning and hermeneutics) with questions about the emergence and materiality/form of discursive events, as well as their function.[39] This new set of concerns constitutes the description and practical criticism of discourse as a system of power vested in social relations, institutions, disciplines, and systems of knowledge. Bové thus joins Nietzsche and Foucault in defining the aim of genealogy: to follow 'the surface linkages between power, knowledge, institutions, intellectuals, the control of populations, and the modern state as these intersect in the functions of systems of thought' (6–7). He is careful to accept only superficial connections; they are, after all, an environment in which discursive events can be seen to function, but which does not rob them of their irreducible singularity. Non-essentializing and relational, genealogical history

> describes events as transformations of other events which, from the vantage point of the present and its needs, seem to be related by a family resemblance. It shows how these transformations have no causal or historical necessity; they are not 'natural.' It shows how the adjacency of events, that is, their simultaneity within ostensibly different fields, can transform entire domains of knowledge production ... (13)

In generic terms, each text, as a transformation of other texts, is both an instantiation ('actualization') and a transformation ('deformation') of a particular genre or genres – and, however subtly, of the genre of discourse in which it partakes. In Bové's view, events within each disciplinary cluster are marked by randomness and coherence (so that 'in their randomness events form a coherence' [8]), in addition to contiguity and family resemblances (within 'individual' knowledges and across disciplines). There is also the 'constitutive reciprocity' between the statements and the objects of discourses (9). In the case of criticism, then as well as now, such reciprocity does not exist merely between it and literature (the author, the literary form/genre); given the inner-dialectical textuality (crisicality) of criticism and its generic overlap with literary textuality, the discourse is in a formally constitutive reciprocity with itself – in re-marking itself it de-marcates itself, to use a Derridean idiom. Criticism's 'own' generic classification of its 'own' formulations structures and effectively alters future expressions, which in turn leads to the revision of the classification, etc. The etymological kinship between 'genre' and 'genealogy' comes to the fore when we consider the importance placed by genealogy (in Foucault's sense again) on the scrutiny of knowledges and disciplines less as classes of discursivities than as dynamic systems for their classification in order to expose exclusionary mechanisms at work in them and such textual events as resist classification.

In the same book, Bové also makes a genealogical case for the 'privileged place "lit. crit." has held in the construction of modern subjectivity' (17). In this, he aligns himself with Foucault, who, following Nietzsche, saw criticism as complementary to genealogy: 'The critical task will be to analyse the processes of rarefaction, but also of regrouping and unification of discourses; genealogy will study their [effective] formation, at once dispersed, discontinuous, and regular.'[40] Criticism's strength as a conduit for genealogy is one of the motivations behind its discursive study. Here, texts and authors – its key objects and 'tenets' – undergo by turns both sacralization and profanation. '[I]t is the very utility of the discourse,' adds Bové, 'that must be seen as functional and regulative. It hierarchizes not only poetry and prose but, implicitly, identity and difference, authority and subservience, taste and vulgarity, and continuity as well as discontinuity' (Bové 3). However, highly reciprocal relations with literature, equally its alter ego and its nemesis, lead criticism to take itself intermittently as an object of critique via a kind of literary ventriloquism; its typical self-accusations by means of literature are philistinism and perpetual discontent about method.

Suggesting a route for historical inquiry, Foucault wrote: 'One could also consider the way in which literary criticism and literary history in the eighteenth and nineteenth centuries constituted the person of the author and the figure of the oeuvre, using, modifying, and displacing the procedures of religious exegesis, biblical criticism, hagiography, historical or legendary "lives," autobiography, and memoirs' ('OD' 71). The critical work of de-sacralization, which shares its goals with genealogy,[41] offers a way of analysing how literature emerges during the eighteenth century as a 'discourse[s] said to transcend and subsume all others.'[42] It is, meanwhile, the task of genealogy to investigate 'how sacralization recurs' (xiii). Like literary-historical study, the historical study of literary criticism – a discourse sacralizing and de-sacralizing literary works, minds, and trends – thus becomes crucial to a history of the present. The writing of such a history requires many a shift in epistemic expectations toward both modern literature and criticism, seeing that they operate in conjunction. Their working relationship is perhaps most evident and often most radical in the parallel changes in their genres; fluctuations in the lives of literary forms reverberate in the lives of critical forms. The sacralization of literature (taken in its broad, eighteenth-century sense), established in part through the notion of authorship, certainly extended to the enshrinement of literary kinds as 'natural.' Their de-sacralization would have to involve an appropriately historical theorization and critique of the principle of genre across the apparent divide between literature and criticism. By studying literary-critical genres in this sense, one moves toward de-sacralizing both companion discourses and forming a fuller genealogical picture of ourselves.

Needless to say, genres and their vicissitudes are but one facet of the histories of knowledges. My modest aim here is to make a case for genre as a lens through which to examine discourse. Contrary to Foucault's recommendations, it is not misguided to scan the 'surface of thought' (the formal structures and actual formulations of discourse participants to which his own interests did not extend)[43] for revelations about the architecture and function of discourse, such as its productivity of discursive 'depths.' But one can deflect hermeneutical demands by insisting on this 'surface' of discourse, which in being treated alternately as transparent and as reflective has long been treated lightly.[44]

That particular genres of literary criticism involve particular assumptions about, or conceptions of, literature and codify ways of interpretation (whose reconfigurations are indicated by reconfigurations in the genre system) must therefore be seen within a much larger claim about discursive genre. The main observation behind my proposition was that literary production and literary criticism exist in a relationship of reciprocity, that they do not simply reflect but affect one another on all levels, and that, therefore, the practice of literary criticism and its history are inextricable from contemporaneous literary practice and its history. It is because of this virtually indissoluble bond that literature and criticism, insofar as they co-exist, participate jointly in the greater network of discursivities at any given time – besides imbricating multiple non-discursive spheres of activity.

Writing a history of literary criticism, or for that matter of any discourse, certainly fails in two cases. In the first criticism is regarded as too 'specialized' and its history becomes 'comprehensible only through itself' (Hohendahl, *Institution* 226). It is shorn of literary and socio-cultural connections, steering clear of historicism, and losing all historical relevance. In the second case, criticism is too integrated into socio-cultural contexts, so that its history becomes comprehensible only through them. Entirely contingent on and accountable through external influences, it loses its distinctive qualities, becomes a mere 'effect,' or ceases to exist altogether as an identifiable discourse. According to Hohendahl, it is between this Charybdis and Scylla of historiography that the history of literary criticism must navigate.

Although Hohendahl's own comprehensive, tripartite model of literary-critical history has only marginal use for a genre-based discourse history, the problems raised in his 'Prolegomena to a History of Literary Criticism'[45] with regard to traditional historiographic approaches can serve to differentiate and position more clearly my own line of inquiry. Thus, Hohendahl classifies existing histories of criticism into three main types: 1) positivistic history of taste and judgment; 2) conceptual history or the history of theory; and 3) biographical history of individual accomplished critics (228). The first two types of history are disqualified by him for their specialization and reductiveness, their monocausality and mechanical correlations, while the third type is too naive and narrow in scope. Key to Hohendahl's critique of all three forms is their lack of genuine historicity, particularly in the context of institutional transformation (240–1). He insists that criticism should be studied as an institution, one not merely adjoining but integral to the institution of literature – that 'self-transforming system of literary production, distribution, and consumption together with its subsystems' and itself a 'subsystem of the institution of art' (226, 233).

This relationship, incidentally, seems to be taken for granted in German letters.[46] 'Criticism belongs to these subsystems,' he continues, 'to the extent that it can be classified with the mechanisms that both stabilize and alter the total system' (226). (We might also say that it completes literature as its Derridean supplement.) While his revised socio-historical approach certainly turns the tables on traditional histories, Hohendahl's focus remains on the 'literary' in 'literary criticism' in light of the 'total system' of literature (the latter glossed elsewhere as 'works, norms, values' accorded literary status [*Institution* 234]). This ultimately teleological view of criticism's subjacency to the interests of the literary institution, missing a theory of their generative reciprocity, is bound to result in the historiographic de-emphasis or omission of those functions and formulations of criticism that do not bear greater institutional significance.

Turning briefly to Hohendahl's treatment of the broader context of the literary-critical system (and keeping in mind that in his model the value and historicity of literary criticism is institution-bound), the most context-rich sphere in which criticism operates and should therefore be studied is the *literary public sphere* – 'an essential category of mediation ... between the audience and the system of literature.' The public sphere *tout court* and as a whole – an eighteenth-century development – is indefinable and unexplainable by 'socioempirical data,' but defined basically as a 'construct whose function is to make the dynamic processes between the spheres of society, state, and culture describable' (235). 'Its more specific significance for scholarly literary analysis,' Hohendahl explains,

> is that it brings the relationships between social and literary activity (which for a positivistic sociology of literature can only be considered separately) closer to a nonmechanical interpretation. The structure of the public sphere determines the type of literary discourse, initially influencing its form (means and organization of communication), but also its content, in themes treated or avoided. Since the structure of the public sphere is relatively stable, it reinforces the system of literature. By referring to public opinion (*Räsonnement*), the literary system becomes anchored in the entire societal process. (235)

The question remains whether the structure of the public sphere can really be credited with 'determining' literary form – and, by extension, critical form. Hohendahl's model is more context-specific than he cares to admit: it is not tailored to situations where the literary public sphere comes under systemic strain, dissipated into isolated pockets of uneven activity. Criticism contending with such status quos must do without reference, at least not *expressis verbis*, to public opinion – as when, for instance, the literature it is responsible for mediating is censored or banned by authorities. Its institutional integrity must also come under strain. The Habermasian concept of the public sphere (*Öffentlichkeit*) taken up by Hohendahl has rightly been criticized for its normativity and for leading to a selective, idealized view of how public political opinion was galvanized over the past three centuries. It must be allowed, however, that modern criticism with its institutional framework appears bound to the existence of a public sphere even in the most rudimentary or splintered form (the context for Immanuel Kant's famous words, 'Our age is the genuine age of *criticism* [*Kritik*], to which everything must submit').[47] In the latter, less-than-ideal scenarios we are dealing not with a representative and democratic space accommodating criticism, but with a heterotopic, heteronomous one – a critical, oppositional public sphere (*Gegenöffentlichkeit*) challenging the status quo.[48]

Janusz Maciejewski's sociological study develops another categorization of literary production and discusses literary criticism as an aspect of *literary life*, a more organic and inclusive notion, predicated on the triumvirate of author, mediator, and reader.[49] The following might sound corrective to Hohendahl's institutional integration of criticism:

> Authors and their active, opinion-forming recipients ... constitute the literary public. [The mediatory links between them] became estranged and detached themselves from ... their basis, which is the literary public. Moreover, having detached themselves, not only did they gain the autonomy to pursue their own politics, in accordance with their institutional interests, but they also began to exhibit a tendency to morph into conditions and restrictions on literature, art, cultural activities – as much of creation as of reception. (113)

This, to Maciejewski, is an inevitable development in the institutional milieu. An opinion-based practice whose principal function is adjudication on matters literary, literary criticism is given its due qua discourse 'not only as a kind of writing, but also as a particular, distinct social role' (110), fulfilled by diverse means, of controlling and regulating literary production. Maciejewski describes also the various 'mechanisms of pressure' acting upon the sphere of literature within literary life. In answer to the crucial question, 'So what phenomena, which institutions are the demiurges of literary opinion?' he offers:

> patronage, the literary salon, the literary café, sometimes clubs or various kinds of artistic associations, finally eminent literary individuals or groups endowed with authority (constituting therefore their own kind of one- or several-person institution). Only they represent actual pressures, influence publishers, periodicals, literary criticism, mass media, and these in turn influence scores of readers, modifying their aesthetic experiences, shaping judgment of individual works, authors, currents, and artistic programs. (86)

Thus conceived, literary life is the product of overlapping processes of literary production, mediation, and reception. Literary criticism, though contingent on literature, does not take its orders exclusively from it; it is neither subordinate to its functioning or best interests, nor is it incorporated into its institutional structure or logic. It participates in, and largely subsists on, all of the processes accounting for literary life as a discursive practice with a distinct social role of managing literature, rather than serving it.

There is no question that, as a social practice, criticism consists of discursive acts and makes use of discursive genres which ask to be socially and institutionally situated. In decades past, rhetoric and discourse studies have brought to light some important connections between the historical publication sites for (*inter alia*) literary-critical texts and their genres, notably the letter and the essay. As a case in point, we can now trace the development of the literary and intellectual journals of the eighteenth century (and the popular journals of the nineteenth) to their epistolary sources. As Charles Bazerman observes,

> Letters in the *Philosophical Transactions* increasingly oriented towards the readership of the journal as its primary audience, rather than the nominal recipients of the letters. In this process of reorientation, a tension developed between assertiveness, didacticism, and disputatiousness of public argument and the gentility, politeness, and good-will of personal correspondence among gentlemen ...[50]

The letter form, as it turns out, was 'instrumental in the formation of more specialized and less self-interpreting genres' (27). This genealogy, in evidence throughout the eighteenth century, extends also to literary criticism's generic specialization in the following century.

Clarity about what Bazerman calls the *sociality of texts* is indispensable for a diachronic study of genre systems. 'Because the sociality of texts is often a matter of implicit social understanding embedded in our recognition of genres that shape communicative activity, reading and writing have regularly been mistaken as autonomous processes of pure form and discrete meaning, separate from social circumstances, relationships, and actions' (27). Rectifying this mistake requires relating formulations to socially conditioned generic conventions, which they took part in shaping. To come back to the public sphere and the social-institutional history of discourse it implies, a study focused on formal/generic processes cannot fall back on formalism (which tends to, if not altogether acontextual, then certainly 'asocial' reflection). At the same time, it can avail itself of formalist insight into the structure of these processes.

2 Criticism and the *Genus Universum*

In *The Order of Things*, his archaeology of the human sciences, Foucault makes a number of valuable observations on the epistemological landscape of eighteenth-century Europe. I review them here for they provide a backdrop to the formation of modern critical discourse, and thus of literary criticism. The three main themes of what Foucault classed as the Classical episteme,[51] dating from the beginning of the seventeenth century to the end of the eighteenth, were: 1) *mathesis*, the science of truth, of calculable order, of equalities, of attributions/judgments leading to the quantification of things; 2) *taxinomia*, a qualitative *mathesis*, the knowledge of *beings*, a pre-Kantian ontology, the science of identities and differences, of articulations/classifications enabling *genesis*; and 3) *genesis*, the analysis of the constitution of orders on the basis of empirical series (*OT* 70–5). The advent of discourse in the same period (79), according to Foucault, meant essentially that there could be no 'final word' on reality, due to the infinite accumulation of empirical data, the ongoing need for its ordering and naming, and the inadequacy of language, stripped of its former metaphysical status (as the 'primary Text' of the universe), for that representation. 'Once the existence of language has been eliminated' – its existence, that is, independent of its representational function – 'all that remains is its function in representation: its nature and its virtues as *discourse*. For discourse is merely representation itself represented by verbal signs' (81). Language 'posited and reflected upon as discourse [becomes] the spontaneous analysis of representation,' best positioned to track its movements (232). It is, one might say, this newly degraded status of language that begets the increasingly value-laden and methodical, increasingly scientific scrutiny of its specifically 'literary' (non-propositional) dimension and usage, less and less rooted in the 'definition of *genres* as forms adapted to an order of representations' (300).

As regards the general forms of discourse, 'Since the Classical age, commentary and criticism have been in profound opposition ... And in fact,' Foucault submits, 'every critical language since the nineteenth century has become imbued with exegesis, just as the exegeses of the Classical period were imbued with critical methods' (*OT* 80–1). Elsewhere, Foucault describes commentary as an 'endless' exegetical process, an 'act of "translation"' that could be 'substituted for itself indefinitely in the open series of discursive repetitions.'[52] Criticism's first steps in coming into its own were towards retaining rules of literary form lifted from poetics and rhetoric, which provided a bulwark against the commentarial veneration of content. But this internal othering of criticism led to its simultaneous analysis of language, on the one hand, as 'a pure function,' 'a great autonomous play of signs,' and, on the other, in terms of 'its truth or falsehood, its transparency or opacity, and ... how what it says is present in the words by which it represents it' (*OT* 80). This double interrogation, Foucault maintains, worked to gradually consolidate the opposition between content and form.

Commentary, which sacralized language, sanctioning its unprobed verity, would eventually 'yield' to criticism, which judged and profaned it by analysing language 'only in terms of truth, precision, appropriateness, or expressive value' (80–1). Criticism and ambiguity would become inextricable. With the ascendancy of criticism, definitive knowledge of the text would become not only conceivable but necessary; without it no judgment could stand. Underpinning criticism's autocritique in the nineteenth century (what Foucault calls the modern episteme) is the historical tension between it and commentary: a continued negotiation of its own epistemic limits vis-à-vis the long-standing hermeneutic susceptibility of the text, its privileged object.

Foucault distinguished four types of Classical-age textual criticism: 1) the critique of words (the reflexive order); 2) the analysis of the representative values of syntax, etc. (the grammatical order); 3) the analysis of figures, or types of discourse and their expressive value, as well as analysis of tropes, or relations of different words with the same representative content (the rhetorical order); and 4) the analysis of the relation of existing writing with what it is taken to represent. From the middle of the eighteenth century, other concerns – deriving from fundamental aesthetic questions and a heightened literary-historical consciousness – began to transform this horizon of criticism. Interpretation, unbound from strictly exegetical duties, no longer hovered above the 'precipice of the original text' (*OT* 81) and plunged instead into the verbal universe of an author, discovering in it, variously, the fulfilment of universal aesthetic principles, the signs of the times, ideological concerns and socio-political circumstances, the constitution of a world view or of a world unto itself, or a distinctive use of language in need of decoding, and translating this into the idiom of the reading public – each time attempting to fix what it knew (more than any other knowledge) to be unfixable.

Regardless of the 'profound opposition' between commentary and criticism unearthed by Foucault, we must not forget that commentaries were themselves a legacy of criticism from Classical Antiquity. They gave modern criticism the basic critical nomenclature[53] that by the eighteenth century seemed pervaded by destabilized metaphysical axioms, relics preserving an outdated approach to meaning and texts. Commentary writing had major purchase from Alexandrian scholarship to the Neoplatonists and Christian writers (333). 'Every word' of the commented-upon text was 'significant as part of some greater whole. The neo-Platonists [were] much concerned in introductions to their commentaries with identification of the *skopos* of a dialogue, its over-all theme to which every word must contribute, and in bringing out the unity of the thought' (332). Late Latin secular criticism, practised only in schools of grammar and rhetoric, produced commentaries prescriptive in tone, pragmatic and explanatory in character. Explanation obeyed and relayed the rules of grammar, rhetoric, and prosody (340, 342–3). The writing of commentaries was, moreover, 'a cumulative process, building on but rarely acknowledging the work of previous scholars' (342).

In 'The Order of Discourse,' Foucault himself grouped commentary with two other internal rules for the limitation of discourse, the *author-function* and *discipline* (all three were historically variable). He saw commentary, which preceded disciplines, as a type of discourse concerned with secondary, masked iteration via paraphrase of the original text (59). The opposing principle of the discipline is 'defined by groups of objects, methods, their corpus of propositions considered to be true, the interplay of rules and definitions, or techniques and tools.' In a discipline, Foucault goes on to say, 'what is supposed at the point of departure is not some meaning which must be rediscovered, nor an identity to be reiterated; it is that which is required for the constitution of new statements[:] the possibility of formulating new propositions, ad infinitum.' While Foucault regards disciplines as anonymous and accessible, one must allow for discourses that have all of the characteristics of disciplines save anonymity: those in which the author principle has been retained in keeping with their borderline status between art and science. This was the case with literary criticism for much of its disciplinary existence.[54] At the same time, criticism per se did not enjoy disciplinary status, as it did not match the positivist structure of modern academic discipline. It was not a cumulative body of judgments or a knowledge that explains the mechanisms or nature of culture, but a technology for analysing and estimating individual artefacts.

It would appear that the switch in the author-function between the discourses of the sciences and the arts, as noted by Foucault, correlated with the eclipse of commentary: authorship meant the right to individuality of judgment. Evaluative writing about literature became increasingly motivated by ideological competition, which offset (if not replaced) the selfless scholarly toil of earlier eras. Instead of a 'cumulative' linear activity, criticism became 'episodic,' and the acknowledgment of previous literary scholarship and the critical tradition more common and comprehensive, primarily for purposes of argumentation. The episodic nature of the process also obtained from the sheer volume of discourse being produced.

Commentary could not, of course, become central to literary criticism due simply to its withholding of judgment about the merit of literary work. But as a well-established practice, it nonetheless persisted in enabling 'the (endless) construction of new discourses: the dominance of the primary text, its permanence, its status as a discourse which can always be re-actualised, the multiple or hidden meanings with which it is credited ... [was] an open possibility of speaking' (Foucault, 'OD' 57). Ending the moratorium on systematic critical judgment of literary texts demanded a new form of writing, one that could take advantage of the epistemic power at discourse's disposal. By taking ultimately not language but (literary) discourse as its object (language and textuality remained the domain of philology, 'old' to 'new'), modern criticism could increasingly perceive and analyse its own formative and ideological material. More than any other field, it took seriously to disclosing its internal presuppositions (though their internality was not always beyond doubt) and revolutionizing itself. From the eighteenth century, then, criticism began to function simultaneously as discourse and metadiscourse.

As already mentioned, in the seventeenth century and well into the eighteenth, the three cultural and linguistic spheres I examine equated criticism with the study of literary texts qua objects of philological analysis, along with the historical and cultural contexts (and significant para-/extra-literary works) indispensable to understanding them. Philological study comprised grammar, rhetoric, history, the interpretation of authors (deriving from the medieval school tradition of *accessus ad auctores*),[55] and the corpus of criticism in a given language. The latter encompassed so-called *higher criticism*, the study of the authorship, provenance, and transmission of written texts, as well as *textual criticism*, the reconstruction of an original, authentic text based on extant manuscript variants and historical sources (the philologist then proceeded to work on the grammar of the best version). These practices have given us the *apparatus criticus* in critical and variorum editions. Textual criticism of this sort entailed *iudicum*, or judgment – a function that modern literary criticism would elevate to a principle, asserting it over the commentarial, exegetical mode.

Classical philology only emerged as an autonomous academic endeavour in the late eighteenth century; until then, notes Schlaffer, its presence in the curriculum had been practical, aiding in the study of the canon as model of eloquence and literary style (Schlaffer 172). The first soi-disant *studiosus philologiae* is said to have been Friedrich August Wolf (1759–1824), matriculating in 1777 in *Literaturwissenschaft avant la lettre*. The story captures nicely the expansion of textual criticism in Germany 'to a comprehensive criticism of traditions, which drew their authoritative standing from a corpus of sacrosanct writings' (196). Its critical-historical dimension turned philology into a driving force of the Enlightenment, inflected by the revolutionary tendencies of Jacobinism, Romantic aesthetics, and the critique of Christianity (197). The development of historical consciousness, in other words, deepened the critical distance from authority and one's own culture.

These institutional changes, however, introduced a gap between the academic study of literature and applied criticism, which participated in the literary events of the day. The first half of the nineteenth century saw the establishment of faculties of national philology (such as *Germanistik*) and their progressive scientization (175). Philology had opened up to the contingencies of textual meaning, as traditional hermeneutical reconstruction of pre-given, authorial significances (a model based on correspondence) began to give way to a broader, constructive hermeneutics as the extraction of textual meaning.[56]

The new philology coming out of Germany from the late eighteenth to the early nineteenth century involved an applied historical and comparative grammar – in contrast to the earlier Enlightenment general grammar. It took root at about the time that 'language went public,' as Ian Hacking puts it – when, in other words, it ceased to be thought of as a private (internal) means of representing ideas, mental and physical objects, and became meaningful only in the public domain.[57] Language was thus 'no longer studied primarily as a system of representation,' as it was in Foucault's Classical episteme. Hacking takes issue, however, with the notion of a radical epistemic shift posited by Foucault, arguing instead that 'the new philology has a longer and denser history than that implied by Foucault's proposed decade, between 1808–1818' (146). In his view, it was the 'excessive verbalism' of philosopher-critic J.G. Hamann (1730–88) that had been instrumental in putting an end to the representational theory of language that prevailed in the Enlightenment, making him 'the first unequivocal public linguist' (150–1, 122). Both Foucault and Hacking, however, agree about the transition, around the turn of the nineteenth century, in the conception of language. Only a difference of emphasis accounts for the discrepancy in dating: Foucault's aim was to establish when language became historical and subject to empirical investigation, while Hacking's was to see when it passed from being private (as it was for Descartes, Hume, Locke, Leibniz, or even Kant) to being public (as it was for Hamann, G. Frege, C.S. Peirce, or L. Wittgenstein) – a change that, in his view, 'cannot be structured in terms of ... Foucault's *epistemes*' (125, 121).

Either way, a broad epistemic shift in the meaning and treatment of language underpinned the first hundred or so years of the practice of literary criticism in German as well as, to a lesser degree, in Polish and Russian. The dissociation between textual form and content (which Romantic critics would seek to surpass) no doubt opened the door to greater formal flexibility and generic experimentation in discursive writing. Bookending my present focus on critical discourse of the eighteenth century is the crystallization of hermeneutical criticism, its language 'imbued' with commentary, pursuing more scientific techniques of scholarly textual interpretation.

3 Criteria in Focus: Forms and Transformations

One of my two principal criteria in selecting texts representative of eighteenth-century criticism was their generic spread. The other was that they should be historically unique and seminal.[58] The latter quality might seem on first blush to refer to the ideas found in a given work, which over time has proven seminal on their account. But just as seminality cannot be detached from its medium, so no idea can be considered unique that is not at the same time unique in its formulation, relative to the existing forms of a given discourse. For a unique text to also be seminal it cannot, however, be permanently and holistically unique. This means that its form can no more break with every convention of a discourse's genre system than it can with its entire system of ideas, past and present. It also means that its uniqueness can lie in its radical reconfiguration of even a single aspect of a discursive genre.

Such 'one of a kind' discursive examples, while they clearly cannot be typical of the discourse in question, must in fact share certain features with its typical texts, or the texts that typify it; only possession of such features justifies participation and inclusion in that discourse. Insistence on formal uniqueness as a criterion in a genre genealogy might nonetheless strike many as counterintuitive. It seems prima facie to limit formal generalization and the 'unique' text's genre-potential – its potential, that is, to regenerate a discursive genre or to generate a new and viable generic form, which would later be imitated within that discourse. However, uniqueness in the above sense – the existence of a text sui generis, in a class of its own – depends on the depth of the comparison one is making with other texts and classes in a given discursive field.

Pragmatically, the paradoxical recognition of a discursive 'kind' exemplified in a single text rests on its being *on the whole* and *for the time being* unclassifiable in terms of other formal-ideational categories recognized in the same discursive order – but not at all unclassifiable in its aspects or at a later point in the discourse's history.[59] This historical uniqueness of a textual event lies thus in the temporary impossibility of wholly assimilating it to existing generic categories and series of textual events. Though aspects of it may exhibit strong affinities with members of a known class (or classes) (justifying its participation in a given discourse), these affinities appear not to be enough to classify it fully since they fail to account for certain of its 'properties.' In this way it also contests the genres of its textual relatives. The 'one of a kind' text only becomes fully and generally classifiable – as the founder of a class (genre, kind) – once it begets a formal following. Its 'disciples' modify and expand the genre's definition and conditions for membership in it beyond the properties found in their 'original.'[60] No single text can, strictly speaking, be definitive of a genre, but merely illustrative of it.

I therefore accord the greatest significance to those textual events which either found or contest a genre. As Walter Benjamin notes in his monograph on German Baroque drama, 'It is ... the more significant works, inasmuch as they are not the original and, so to speak, ideal embodiments of the genre, which fall outside the limits of [the] genre. A major work will either establish the genre or abolish it; and the perfect work will do both.'[61] This subversive/generative potential is the meeting point for my criteria: each text selected for analysis is seminal, unique, generically (un)conventional, yet discursively exemplary so as to guarantee generic range. But can one, and should one, write a history of a discourse based solely on atypical examples? Such examples necessarily take precedence in the genealogical model of history. LaCapra speaks to this very point:

> Conventional or stereotypical texts conform most to set discursive and institutional expectations, while the exceptional text has a more problematic relation both to discursive practices it is placing in question and to those it is helping to engender. Indeed one key function of epigones would seem to be to reduce the problematic texts of 'initiators of discursive practices' (in Foucault's phrase) to their generic or paradigmatic level, thereby making them more adaptable to certain institutional uses. The more challenging and, at times, disconcerting text seems to rewrite the genre or to take part in a continual founding and altering of expectations. The apparent paradox is that texts hailed as perfections of a genre or a discursive practice may also test and contest its limits. (*History and Criticism* 140–1)

The endurance – and even the emergence – of a discursivity, to enlarge on a related point made by LaCapra, depends on the recognition of its own limits and 'the fact that those limits must sometimes be exceeded or even radically transformed' (41). The recognition of novel forms resulting in part from the 'interaction of discursive modes' makes for just such 'excesses' and transformations. Before long, some of these limit-forms become institutionalized – generic and paradigmatic – yet the problematic texts in which they were obtained remain historically 'one of a kind.' Their uniqueness notwithstanding, such formally unconventional texts are the dynamo of a discourse.

What is unique about the forms of the selected texts is their untimely ('accidental') departure from the hackneyed 'vehicles' of reflection or their timely arrival from another discursive realm which revitalizes the receiving discourse. To elaborate the unique through such notions as *seminal, precursory, formative, emblematic,* or *canonical* is thus to foreground the historicity of reception: the initially perceived, pathbreaking singularity of certain texts, their subsequent status as models of a set or series, the first of their kind, and their eventual discursive exemplariness (membership in a class of which they are no longer the heartbeat or frontier). By pointing to their powers of dissemination, to their general appeal – as evidenced by discursive production following their appearance and by their very reappearance in references and anthologies – one calls attention to such texts' manifold importance in the 'life' of a discourse.

Is, then, *unique, seminal,* etc. synonymous with *influential*? Does not *influence* imply some form of synthetic continuity between the influencer and the influenced? Is it not often used to pass over intermediate steps which, if taken, would lead nowhere? Is a claim to textual influence, simply left at that, not a lapse into glib obscurantism ('more magical than effective,' as Foucault put it)?[62] The question, 'What is it about this event that has done the influencing?' is seldom granted a satisfying answer (is it not self-explanatory?). When we say, 'This text was influential,' we are in fact imputing agency to it; influence suggests it is a direct extension of the author's voice, meaning, intention. But when one attends to the impersonal aspects of discursive interaction, the category of agency is hardly adequate. Terms like *partial* or *proximate causation, multicausality, causal pattern, contiguity, similarity, regularity, correlation, facilitation, reciprocity, interactivity, interconnection, intertextuality,* and others tending to a descriptive rather than an explanatory framework, seem altogether more appropriate, in that they sidestep any clear-cut attribution of causality. A similar, perhaps more underhand logical shortcut can be made out in the classic recourse to context in historical accounts.[63] 'Context' can vaguely explain just about everything.

What justifies labelling texts as 'unique' is their formal resonance in other texts, regardless of whether these other texts carry more apparent weight ('influence') for their ideational contribution to a discourse. This generic resonance cannot be accounted for by invoking the discursive influence of individuals. Yet Foucault's 'initiator of discursive practice' is, at first glance, just such an invocation, a general theory of individual influence; his examples of writers with discursive industries (Marx or Freud) in their wake are self-evident. LaCapra's above-quoted observation, however, relates this idea to genre in a productive way: the 'initiator's' (or 'founder's') 'problematic' texts, which disrupt existing generic limits, are reduced by epigones 'to their generic or paradigmatic level' and adapted 'to certain institutional uses.'

Let us consider how Foucault handles the notion in relation to modern discourse, which he describes as emerging in German over the eighteenth and nineteenth centuries. He introduces the 'founder of discursivity' in his essay 'Nietzsche, Freud, Marx,' then returns to it in 'What Is an Author?'[64] to outline what led up to and followed the figure's historical emergence. We read here of a development that effectively dispels the myth of 'influence' as a spectre of agency. Around the turn of the eighteenth century, a reversal is said to have occurred in the 'author-function' for the discourses of science and literature: literary discourse had now to conform to the strictures of authorship, while scientific discourse could now stand on its own, 'in the anonymity of an established or always redemonstrable truth' (214–15). The turn of the nineteenth century brought us the system of discourse ownership still in place today (the codification of rules pertaining to authors' rights, author–publisher relations, copyright, etc.); codified, discourse became an 'object of appropriation' (211). Having lost its earlier transgressive edge, it was no longer an act 'in the bipolar field of the sacred and the profane ... the religious and the blasphemous' but a reified product, an article of consumption (212). This fact would be later partly compensated for in literature by the creative imperative of transgression and the rediscovery of the bipolar field of discourse.

Since the eighteenth century, however, the discursive 'author' has functioned as 'the regulator of the fictive'; authorship continues to be a principle of rarefaction:

> the author is not an indefinite source of significations which fill a work; the author does not precede the works; he is a certain functional principle by which, in our culture, one limits, excludes, and chooses ... In fact, if we are accustomed to presenting the author as a genius, as a perpetual surging of invention, it is because, in reality, we make him function in exactly the opposite fashion. The author is therefore the ideological figure by which one marks the manner in which we fear the proliferation of meaning. (221)

Earlier, in 'Nietzsche, Freud, Marx,' Foucault credited the nineteenth century with reviving sixteenth-century techniques of interpretation, dormant or bracketed during the preceding age. These techniques had previously operated within a finite system of succession and analogy and a theory of the sign as a transparent, 'simple and benevolent being' ('NFM' 270, 277). The nineteenth century, by contrast, saw signs as 'linked together in an inexhaustible network, itself also infinite, not because they are based on a resemblance without borders, but because there is irreducible gaping and openness' (274). This (public) conception of language – which Hacking traces back to the latter half of the eighteenth century – gave rise to the essential incompleteness, interminableness of interpretation. If before the 'space' in which signs were homogenously disposed was 'homogeneous in all directions,' it now became 'much more differentiated, according to a dimension that could be called that of depth,' in the sense of a covered-up exteriority, 'an absolutely superficial secret' to be restored by interpretive means (272–3). Whatever the causes of this shift, the loss of innocence opened up language to negative concepts, or post-Kantian critique.

Foucault anchors the modern discourse of hermeneutics in two 'suspicions about language': the distinction between semantic surface and depth, on the one hand, and the existence of extraverbal languages, on the other. To these the nineteenth century added two others. First, there is nothing 'absolutely primary to interpret ... [as] each sign is in itself not the thing that offers itself to interpretation but an interpretation of other signs' ('NFM' 275). Second, interpretation is as much a violent assault on such 'malevolent' signs as it is their elucidation (277). To speak, in this context, of texts (interpretations) 'influencing' other texts is to maintain the illusion of the author being in control over the reality of signs begetting signs, of discourse reproducing itself through writing ad infinitum – the primary trait of modern discursivity. Interpretation became reconceptualized as an endless task which took its authority from criticism and invested it in literature, ensuring the steady proliferation and ideological polarization of literary-critical discourse into the nineteenth century.

The basis of this transformation of the task of interpretation by Foucault's 'initiators of discourse,' whose interpretive techniques necessitated self-interrogation, was critical self-reflexivity ('NFM' 272, 274). But rather than being the 'authors' of their own works, they laid out the possibilities and rules of formation for texts to be written by others. They gave direction to discourse by establishing the 'primary coordinates,' the analogies/resemblances *and* differences/divergences among ideas, that enabled the articulation of heterogeneous (even diametrically opposing) knowledge discourses.

The modern conditions of the 'endless possibility' of discourse thus took shape together with 'the very practices of detachment characteristic of the textual mode.'[65] The development made enormous epistemic waves with the circular message that (infinite) elaboration of fields of learning, or knowledges, is the *raison d'être* and very stuff of knowledge as such. The output of 'founders of discursivity,' with a restricted set of 'founding statements' and theoretical propositions, lent itself most to institutional application as indefinitely expandable, axiomatic, *profoundly* true:

> one does not declare certain propositions in the work of these founders to be false: instead, when trying to seize the act of founding, one sets aside those statements that are not pertinent, either because they are deemed inessential, or because they are considered 'prehistoric' and derived from another type of discursivity. In other words ... the initiation of a discursive practice does not participate in its later transformations ... In this way we can understand the inevitable necessity, within these fields of discursivity, for a 'return to the origin' ... The return is not a historical supplement that would be added to the discursivity, or merely an ornament; on the contrary, it constitutes an effective and necessary task of transforming the discursive practice itself. ('WIA' 219)

Coincidentally or not, the 'founders' named by Foucault all engaged in literary-critical activity, directly and by way of critical inquiries into society, culture, and artistic production. Of course, it would be an overstatement to speak of single-handed 'initiators' of discursivity within (or inclusive of) literary-critical practice prior to the nineteenth century. It is only after we pare down the phenomenon described by Foucault that the idea becomes applicable to an earlier period in discourse history. Criticism, for one thing, had its 'discursivity advocates': individuals or groups whose work sustained its practice or reinvigorated it by polarizing debate or rousing a generation of detractors. Underpinning the apparent continuity between their 'advocacy' and the later forms of discursivity is, again, not influence but an impersonal, disjunctive process of transformation. Good examples of such advocates, working on behalf of the discourse, answerable in varying degrees for such transformative work, can be found much earlier. One of them, Johann Christoph Gottsched (1700–66), will be a pivotal figure in my discussion of German criticism. Maurycy Mochnacki (1804–34) played such a role in the Polish case,[66] Vissarion Belinskii (1811–48) in the Russian.[67]

Between, on the one hand, the view that the propositional values of a discourse can be extracted and kept apart from their 'embodiment,' and, on the other hand, the view of the incommensurability of different texts, Said's 'traveling theory' – endorsed here mutatis mutandis – strikes a compelling theoretical balance. We have, then, the transformation of ideas through their different incarnations, making their way into different genres. While theories consist of paraphrasable arguments, and can to an extent be abstracted from their mode of disclosure, their interpretation and even paraphrase necessarily (by virtue of altered form and genre affiliation) introduces 'errors' which are transformative for the discourse as a whole. This approach draws our attention to the productive dissemination of ideas in discourse, rather than assuming their unity and continuity. Said charges discourse with the following tasks: 1) recording the 'encounter of theory with resistances to it'; 2) measuring the 'distance between theory then and now, there and here'; 3) mapping the 'territory covered by all the techniques of dissemination, communication, and interpretation'; and 4) preserving 'some modest ... belief in noncoercive human community.'[68] These tasks are the imperatives of anti-power, or at least (as in Foucault's project) alternatives to the dominant discourse of truth and the power both sustaining and sustained by it. Indeed, Said concludes the first of his concerted discussions of 'traveling theory' by asking, 'And what is critical consciousness at bottom if not an unstoppable predilection for alternatives?' If we compare this with the final lines of his follow-up essay on the subject, charting theories' 'demographics' proves insufficient. Said stresses the search for the meaning behind theory's 'travels':

> To speak here only of borrowing and adaptation is not adequate. There is in particular an intellectual, and perhaps moral, community of a remarkable kind, *affiliation* in the deepest and most interesting sense of the word. As a way of getting seriously past the weightlessness of one theory after another ... the exercise involved in figuring out where the theory went and how in getting there its fiery core was reignited is invigorating ...[69]

Implicit in this statement is a subtle conceptual shift from the earlier treatment of 'traveling theory' to a conception on which 'individual' theories are divided up amongst theorists to determine not just the system of their dissemination within a given field, but the external bonds that designate the intellectual debt of 'one theory' to 'another.'

A viable theory is without formal or substantial closure: it is a theory out of bounds. 'Theoretical closure, like social convention or cultural dogma, is anathema to critical consciousness, which loses its profession when it loses its active sense of an open world in which its faculties must be exercised' ('TT' 242). This quality, which forms the nucleus of Said's idea, enables a theory to journey and live in so many related, dissembling, chimerical forms and substances. Similarly to a genre, such a theory is modified, to various degrees, through every one of its reformulations, none of which is definitive of it. In terms of the transformation of discursive forms, the life/afterlife of a travelled theory matters insofar as differing historical *formulations* are recognized by their authors or readers as statements supporting 'one theory,' or become part of another recognized theoretical construct that contains the theory's traces. Such a distribution of accents may seem elementary; still, the prevalent assumptions about discursive unities like ideas, theories, and their systems tend to operate within a dichotomy of identity/difference that should be undercut. It is more productive to speak of the relative distinctiveness of texts, and of relative distinctions between theoretical formulations, while grouping them within a single theoretical paradigm[70] – that is, to systematize them with a view to a historical pragmatics of discursive formulation.

To apply this logic to the structure of interpretation is to give *misreading* an active role in a theory's travels, that is to say, in its successive reformulations. Said rehabilitates to a degree the accusatory notion of misreading when he describes it as a natural 'part of a historical transfer of ideas and theories from one setting to another' ('TT' 236). His prefatory statement, 'The idea that all reading is misreading is fundamentally an abrogation of the critic's responsibility,' exposes and subverts the ethical relativism hiding in the conceptual folds. But is all misreading a source or sign of creativity? Said does distinguish between an imprecise or loose reading and a close reading: while misreadings come into play in either situation, the misreading in a close constructive reading has the positive value of a creative departure, while loose constructive readings, in which misreadings can be difficult to spot, are ruled inherently worthless and unjustifiable (still aligned, in other words, with the ordinary, pejorative sense of 'misreading').

It is safe, of course, to say that every creative interpretation, in order to build on its object, must to some extent depart from it – to misinterpret at points what it aims conscientiously to read and transfer. The positive, creative misreading may be significant, so that what was interpreted is not actually conveyed in the interpretation, which nonetheless remains its legitimate kin (it thus differs from the misprision attending the 'anxiety of influence'). However, to fully rehabilitate the concept of misreading as a mechanism in the transmission and transformation of theories (a status it earns once we abandon the notion of a theory as a discursive unity) one would have to recognize the transformative value of even those miscreant misreadings, which misrepresent, misquote, or erroneously recall the 'originals,' illegitimately drawing on them for inspiration.

The relativity of both 'traveling theories' and misreadings is, in Said's view, essential to the practice of criticism. The openness and indeterminacy of theories and systems is part and parcel of modern discourse's hallmark inexhaustibility, the infinity of interpretation:

> unless theory is unanswerable, either through its successes or its failures, to the essential untidiness, the essential unmasterable presence that constitutes a large part of historical and social situations (and this applies equally to theory that derives from somewhere else or theory that is 'original'), then theory becomes an ideological trap. It transfixes both its users and what it is used on. Criticism would no longer be possible. (Said, 'TT' 241)

The intra- and cross-cultural migration of ideas through misreading is, then, vital to the historical transformation of critical dicourse. Insisting on the inextricability of meaning from function, of content from form or structure, we can translate Said's two concepts into generic terms: given that genres limit and orient interpretation, the travel of theories becomes an important aspect of the travel of genres, and significant misreadings become part of generic shifts and transformations. To come back, then, to my selection criteria: texts that are both unique and seminal (form- and content-wise) represent, by the same token, significant transformations of ideas or theoretical models.

4 Looking Ahead

The following parts of this book concentrate on the eighteenth century, an era of so-called 'beginnings' for critical discourse in Central and Eastern Europe. Their pared down comparative frame may disappoint the reader who expects comparisons organized by genre or individual formal values/properties, yielding evidence of influence or uncovering little-known channels of cultural transfer. Instead, I seek to frustrate the presupposition of fixed entities preceding the act of comparison, a premise that obscures textual differences and singularities (tangents, gestures, potentials, silences) that do not fall into line or belong without remainder to the discourse in question, and that ultimately force us to question it. The point is not simply to explode this assumed discursive unity but to worry or tease it at points, in order to draw attention to the atomic and non-cohesive aspect of discursive life. Beyond this, I want to demonstrate, on the neglected level of discursive forms, that what is retrospectively taken for granted as the genetic, monolithic, cross-cultural and -historical unity of a discourse is in fact internally striated, heteroform, asynchronous, divergent, marked by considerable discrepancies of textual practice (such as the misalignment of central concerns and developmental models or unevenness in the rate of production and distribution). These latter disproportions are intensified by inequalities in the spread of literary culture and the development of the public sphere, and turned into historical markers of discursive progress, enabling the comparison of less 'advanced' cultures or modernities with those that 'outstripped' them – while making it vulnerable to scepticism (the incomparability argument) or dismissal ('comparisons are odious'). My goal here is to dismantle precisely this implicit elitism of intellectual history. To acknowledge, quite simply, that the practice of criticism migrated eastward from the West and was late in establishing itself in Russia, and then did not arrive there via the royal road of aesthetics and pedagogical reform, is not simultanesously to claim that by its lateness in those parts it was necessarily inferior to its western cognates and ancestors. (I challenge those tempted to make such a claim to apply the argument to the migration of humanity from its birthplace.) This 'lateness' should be seen instead as an effect of criticism's retrospective specificity. All these qualifications are made, to be sure, in the spirit of comparativity: to compare is after all to match, to bring together as in some sense equal. Yet we must also take care not to overlook inequalities for culture-political ends, *making equal* without regard to differences of standing or organization of the terms compared (and determining historical inequalities that acted as their impetus to struggle for normative recognition) – as though levelling the playing field could level the score. Comparison presupposes even a modicum of inequality as its basis.

Second, the choice of geographical area – none other than the threshold between the West and its other – is intended to add force to this 'intervention' into the practice of comparative historiography. There is a political-historical side to this choice: I confess to personal reasons for setting the historical record straighter. As a subset of the history of critique, the history of literary criticism can cast light on the developmental interrelation of critical discourse and the public sphere, on the one hand, and the political fortunes of a cultural domain, on the other. (Critique, understood as the public use of reason – an extension of Kant's *räsonieren* and Habermas's *öffentliches Räsonieren* – has been fundamental to philosophical reflection since the Enlightenment, or the 'age of the critique,' as defined by Kant, 'when the universal, the free, and the public uses of reason are superimposed on one another.')[71] In the geopolitical case at hand, the eventual target of political aggression by Russia and Prussia was a discursive common ground, of which both sides wanted a piece. (Not even this middle, however, deserves to become the privileged common ground of comparison.) Poland's discursive transitionality suggested it was an (unclaimed) space of cultural overlap, as expressed in the escalation of territorial disputes and proprietary claims, settling a border between the antagonists near the close of the century.

One common feature of criticism in these formative stages was, as I have said, the proliferation of diverse textual forms and generic hybridity. An overview of literary-critical genres then active within the region might seem a feasible task, given the relative paucity of primary material and the relatively stable system of prescriptions for both literary and literary-critical practice at the time. Yet for the same reasons, discussion of the early texts comes up against the need to account for the simultaneous tectonic transformations in criticism's generic macrostructure and profile. Throughout my investigations, two questions added complexity to this inquiry. First, what cultural changes may have offered a motive (and what constants a springboard) for criticism's formal innovation, and how? And second, in what way (if any) did generic change tie into the functions of literary criticism in the public sphere and in academe?

The ensuing historical chapters each open with a discussion of the general organization and formal characteristics of literary-critical discourse in a particular cultural-linguistic space. The second part of each chapter then comprises a cycle of close analyses of critical texts in a range of genres. This manner of analysis is meant to foreground some of the discourse's formal features, as it were, in action. The wider, sometimes uniform generic picture must finally fade before the appreciation of formal detail, diversity, and generic non-conformity on the level of the statement.

In this respect, the choice of German-language sources is the most challenging, owing to the sheer volume of available primary and secondary literature. (Far less has been documented and critically examined in Polish and Russian.) By 1750, German criticism was more widespread a practice than its counterparts in either Poland or Russia – an observation, concealing no judgment of their relative merits, on the comparative intricacy and quantity of discourse. From the plethora of available texts I therefore have selected those that partook in the overarching debate about German literary identity. (As such, they are just one of a number of possible sets that could have served to discuss literary-critical genres in a study like the present one; others might have emphasized alternate formal/generic characteristics, leading to different specific observations and lateral connections, if not ending up with very similar general conclusions.) Nonetheless, wherever the occasion presented itself, I have tried to bring in other, narrower but related concerns.

I have kept to the same principle of selecting texts around major debates in my discussion of Polish and Russian critical discourse. Polish criticism's main concern in the eighteenth century was with the national literature's ascension to the European pantheon, which entailed a modernization of literary standards. Once Poland was stripped of the vestiges of its political independence, this preoccupation was replaced by a nationalist 'survival' criticism – mobilized to sustain the sense of nationhood through the diffusion of Polish letters throughout the annexed territories and to exilic groups abroad. In Russia, by comparison, the question of modernizing Russian literary language overshadowed concerns about a national literary identity. The latter would only dominate the discourse's Golden Age, when, in the first half of the nineteenth century, pro-Western and Slavophile literary movements came to a head over greater socio-political issues and, in the second, literary aesthetics as such came under attack.

The common thematic of the textual analyses does not, however, amount to a historical narrative. The approach chosen for the second part of each chapter – non-narrative but pragmatically synthetic – stems from a basic scepticism regarding the benefits of telling a story or conferring historical unity on a discourse (a unity one must nonetheless allow at least provisionally or nominally if one is to then proceed to deconstruct it or put it 'under erasure'). The presupposition of such unity is always, already, and only a retrospective hypothesis. To counterweigh the unifying, narrative overview in each chapter's first part, the presentation of the analyses forgoes continuity between its segments, freeing each textual study from the demands of storytelling. This mode of presentation permits the formal coordinates of each text to have precedence over the author (who nonetheless clings to it like a burr), allowing them to be named, accommodating the singularity of experimental formulations in the discursive network. These formulations are underscored by their own often polemical, disunifying character and their aggregative, unifying gestures. Only through this suspension or disruption of the larger unities and continuities can disparate formal features and their relations with the generic dominant emerge. A text may traverse or transgress a genre's boundaries, but it does so only by trespassing on another; these generic references to a genre system are binding enough to save our analytical sketches from a fate of *disjecta membra*.

Before rolling out its battery of forms, it is useful to note that literary-critical writing throughout the eighteenth century followed, to a greater or lesser degree, one of two epistemic orders that structured the discourse from the point at which it became self-conscious as an intervention in the (increasingly culturally and historically relative) aesthetics of literature. These orders can be called, loosely, the *interpretive* and the *co-creative*, knowing by turning inside out and knowing from the inside, by affinity or association.[72] If the former was linked to the mastery of literary creations by delimiting, analysing, and explaining their genesis, form, and meaning 'transparently' (e.g., in various styles of review), the latter suggested aspirations to congruity or parity between critical reflection and literature (e.g., through parody). These two tendencies and corresponding types of authority subtended virtually the entire field of criticism, so that all of its observable textual types in this period can be distributed among them – the co-creative manifested in irregular, emphatically literary forms, the interpretive, in straightforward obedience to formal discursive conventions. It is worth adding that an overwhelming portion of European critical writing prior to the eighteenth century fell in the latter category, and that this balance was preserved in areas where modern criticism was only just rising to the surface of discourse.

A brief word also concerning the temporal frame of this study: instead of a period (Classicism, Romanticism), a century seemed the most neutral length of time to submit to analysis. Such apparent neutrality, however, makes sense only relative to more traditional historical accounts and does not imply approximation of some ultimate transparency with respect to my textual evidence. One way of stressing an anti-essentialist comparative stance is, it seems to me, by temporal parallelism (as opposed to the parallelism of traditional literary 'periods'). In other words, by carving out a segment of time, the initial cut is made not with a 'first' but at the point at which texts begin to reflect modern criticism's discursive thickening (around 1700); the second cut, while in a sense more arbitrary, comes after the three discourses can be said to have a certain self-conscious consistency. This arises in part from my reluctance to structure this study as a comparison of levels of advancement and attainment within a given literary-cultural formation, and thus to compare their respective classicisms or romanticisms. My chief interest lies in genres and their manifestations within these formations. I am convinced, however, that we do greater justice to the forms of primary sources by resisting the impulse to group them neatly and apodictically into periods, ages, or epistemes, which would constrain their formal description in ways that are not all foreseeable. From this perspective, 1800 is as good a point to stop as 1805.[73] Continuing to 1805 or even 1815 would entail analysing a few additional works from each tradition – of possible advantage to Polish and Russian criticism insofar as it would portray them as somewhat more 'advanced' relative to German criticism; but doing justice to either would require continuing to the middle of the next century, if not right up to the last. The nineteenth century, during which literary criticism became fully integrated into academe and the public sphere, brought about changes in critical expression – in the relationship between form and genre – too vast to be analysed in the space of this work. The generic scope of the discourse in each context contracted in proportion to the diversification of critical styles. The real justification, then, for stopping short of surveying the modern critical tradition is the investment of the present genealogy in the relation of genre to the emergence of critical discourse and the changes which affected it from the turn of the nineteenth century, the start of its bifurcation and specialization.

There is another reason for the choice of a century: it would be inconsistent to, on the one hand, profess theoretical resistance to habituated and essentialist concepts while, on the other hand, relying on them for my organizational framework. The century-long span helps offset the otherwise common references to well-established literary movements and periods, not to mention the 'modernity' of critical discourse. Unless they are taken monolithically, we should see such categories as effective (that is to say, as having real historical effects). On the other hand, the 'centurial approach' seemed best suited to incorporating and organizing the insights of those who have written on the subject of literature and criticism, but who disagree on the fundamental points of their periodization. In the end, the choice of this study's point of termination was a formal one. While I am reluctant to claim greater transparency for my account than that afforded to more traditional ones, I do see it, and I cannot stress this enough, as an alternative, if not also, in small measure, a corrective.

Chapter One

German Criticism

The self-image of the eighteenth century as an epoch of mythological beginnings was to a certain extent justified in reality, in no small part by the rapid development of literature throughout the century.

(Irina Reyfman)[1]

As much as the authors of journals suppose themselves to be above their readers, they are still twins of one fate … both flee out of revulsion or leisure, over political news and scribble-mania into the lap of the goddess of criticism, here to divert and at the same time to collect themselves, by means of wakeful slumber.

(Johann Gottfried von Herder, 1744–1803)[2]

1 Coming of Age

For much of the eighteenth century, Germany – a loose association of largely independent states in want of a national identity – had no modern, vernacular literary canon of its own. The literary corpus for most educated readers consisted of texts in Latin, French, and English, read in the original or in translation. Reliance on the influx of foreign ideas was widespread in other areas of intellectual culture as well. An institution like the Berlin Academy of Science was run in French, with French faculty members appointed by the king.[3] There was also 'no profession of letters worthy of the name in Germany in the first half of the eighteenth century.'[4] This state of affairs no doubt stemmed from (and, in part, contributed to) the derivative aspect of early German writing on the one hand, and from the literary culture's abiding internationalist character, the linguistic and cultural receptivity of its practitioners, on the other.[5] One result of the dearth of contemporary domestic works was that eighteenth-century discussions of literature consisted predominantly of debates about the ancient literary heritage and modern French and English authors, or was theoretical in nature, forming the backbone of the then-emerging discourse of aesthetics.

Literary reflection during most of the 1700s conformed to various interpretations of classicism. The time frame 1700–1800 encompasses the residually Baroque classicism of *Regelpoetik* (rule-governed poetics),[6] which overlapped with the rationalist, neo-Aristotelian doctrine of *Pseudoklassizismus* (c. 1680 to 1750), imported from the French Enlightenment poetics of the seventeenth century.[7] The older classicisms soon gave way to a more distinctly German, 'Hellenized' form of classicism[8] and to *Wirkungspoetik* (reader-oriented poetics of effect or effective poetics), less normative, more historicist and theoretical in character, linking artistic production with reception.[9] This Neoclassical revival would be undermined in due course by a more formally intuitive, emotion-driven, and individualistic *Geniepoetik* (writer-oriented poetics of genius),[10] which was associated with the revitalizing, class-conscious literary movement of Sturm und Drang in the late 1760s to mid-1780s, known to contemporaries as *Genieperiode* or *Geniezeit*. The last phase of Neoclassical taste, emerging out of (but also in contrast to) Sturm und Drang, was the moderately experimental, relatively apolitical *Weimarer Klassik*[11] (1786 to anywhere between 1805 and 1832), which in the 1790s spurred on and rivalled the radical innovations of Early Romantic theory and criticism, particularly its organicist aesthetics and new, affective-expressive philosophy of literature.[12]

This brisk succession of poetological orientations precipitated a steep decline of interest in foreign literature and theoretical models. The homegrown literary movements Storm and Stress and Weimar Classicism infused a stagnant intellectual culture with fresh ideas and forms, giving shape to the literary-critical idiom. Conversely, a critical genre like the literary review, widely employed by the 'poet-critics' of the day, could inspire new writing by debating questions about artistic beauty, national poetry, drama, folklore, and art.

There was, of course, considerable overlap between each literary and literary-critical period/current, and opinions differ widely on the actual duration of classicism and the de facto beginning of the Romantic breakthrough.[13] Throughout most of the century, however, literature was seen as an orderly domain, amenable to rules or principles wherever they could be devised – until the late 1790s, when many of such self-evidences were swept away. The *Frühromantik*, Jena Romanticism, accommodated not only far greater formal innovation than its predecessors, but signalled a reconfiguration of the relationships between literary author, text, and public. A parallel transformation took place in literary-critical discourse, which saw innovations in the critical idiom and a qualitative change in the relations among critic, critical text, literary text, and public.

German classicism evolved concurrently with the elaboration of aesthetics as a distinct, scientific branch of philosophy and, with Immanuel Kant (1724–1804),[14] as an autonomous theory of art and foundation for critical judgment. Thus, in 1766, Herder maintained: 'language, aesthetics, history, and philosophy are the four provinces of literature, which reinforce each other mutually, and which are all but inseparable' ('FRGL' 95). Developing the aesthetic project, Sturm und Drang anticipated philosophical Idealism through its critical and artistic program, as did later the Weimar Classicists and, especially, the Romantics. A telling feature of Sturm-und-Drang criticism was the 'frequent tendency in these writers to avoid examples – empirical instances that might serve to distract our attention away from the a priori concerns of the transcendental method towards some expectation of a catalogue of good and bad works of art'[15] – the latter deemed one of the vices of normative poetics.

Soon, deep-seated philosophical tensions were becoming explicit within German (and European) classicism. Throughout the 1740s and 1750s, the *Literaturstreit* between the Swiss and the Leipzig critics and their followers – Johann Jakob Bodmer (1698–1783) and Johann Jakob Breitinger (1701–76) contra J. Ch. Gottsched – loosened the hold of Wolffian and Leibnizian rationalism and French Classicist doctrine.[16] One of the consequences of historical study – a vital aspect of classicist systems – was the relativization of a hitherto stable literary canon and poetic rules. Reflective of this marked shift in literary and critical thinking was the adoption of more pliant and direct critical language, and of the review as the primary discursive form. In this way, as Wellek observed, 'The neoclassical scheme was being undermined ... by the success of genres for which its theory made little or no provision,' among them the novel and the periodical essay – the latter, incidentally, introduced by Bodmer (*18C* 20). In contrast to earlier forms with schematic components, the structure of the essay was dictated only insofar as the articulation of argument/opinion was concerned. As well, expanding readership at home and abroad led to a gradual relaxation of formal constraints in criticism: 'The freer form, even in formal treatises, and the less purely learned vocabulary show that the critic came to appeal to an audience wider than that of students in the library or lecture room' (9).

The two strands of critical discourse – the scholarly and the journalistic – grew out of a general evaluative-prescriptive discourse on literature as intensifications of its unreconciled impulses: the pro-ancient and the pro-modern. They differed in evaluative methods and in the weight they gave to ancient and modern literature: scholarly writing channelled antiquarian interests, whereas periodicals gravitated toward contemporary titles. Their dissociation did not arise solely from the transformation and instability of their object (such as the emergence of popular literature and bourgeois theatre at the turn of the eighteenth century); it was buttressed by institutional changes like the flourishing of periodicals and the founding of new universities and academies, which accelerated the process of discursive specialization and standardization. It was further reinforced by inter- and intra-discursive disciplinary shifts and adjustments, including the formation of new objects of inquiry in neighbouring disciplines, most notably the 'beautiful object' in aesthetic philosophy.

The rise of aesthetics was by far the most significant disciplinary reconfiguration. Kai Hammermeister contends that

> the development of this discipline is also a predominantly Germanic affair for two specific reasons. First, the German aesthetic tradition is resistant to outside influences to an unusually high degree. The writers who belong to this tradition respond to one another without introducing ideas adopted from contemporary discussions in other languages, the standard references to antiquity notwithstanding. (x)

In spite of this convergence around aesthetic questions, Herder assessed the state of affairs as follows: 'We are laboring in Germany as in the days of the confusion of Babel; divided by the sects of taste, partisan in poetic art, schools of philosophy contesting one another: and no common interest, no great and universal reformer and lawgiving genius' ('FRGL' 95). Painting a larger picture, Jay Bernstein sees aesthetic philosophy as a response to the conditions of modernity, in particular the threat of relativism and the disenchantment of nature – Kant's project offering the most sustained response to the former menace, the Romantic school to the latter.[17]

The fluctuation of criteria for literary judgment afforded by these discursive changes proved beneficial for literature. W.H. Bruford observes that 'Between 1740 (the year selected by contemporaries as the turning point) and 1800, Germany had changed from a country so unproductive of native literature that every educated man had depended on foreign writings for his culture to a land of "poets and thinkers" ... It had developed a classical literature, and also something very like an intellectual proletariat' (290). While average citizens remained provincial and insular in their interests,[18] major literary figures of the day considered themselves cosmopolitan citizens of an international literary republic. It would be wrong, therefore, to attribute the introspective character of classical German literature to the atmosphere of sectionalism (*Kleinstaaterei*), which bred excessive attachment to local customs. This literature 'was neither national in sentiment nor expressive of the outlook of any particular class of society,' written as it was for a 'heterogeneous public' (Bruford 320–1). In this sense, it did not build on a common foundation but, rather, strove to build the foundation itself. Fritz Strich (who in 1952 substantiated the distinction between imitative German *Klassizismus* and illustrious German *Klassik*) believed that classicism 'has usually been the product of corporate feeling, but German classicism looked upon it as its mission to call this corporate feeling into existence through art.'[19] To the extent that cosmopolitan ideals were realized, the literary-critical apparatus assisting and stimulating literary activity in the closing decades of the century endorsed philosophical *humanitas* (*Humanität*) and universal *Bildung*[20] instead of narrowly nationalist ideals or mere social utility (Bruford 320). The idea of *Bildung* – the education of a new political/cultural public – was as important for Neoclassical thinkers as it was for the Romantics.

If in the seventeenth century literature reflected the 'the absolutist court ideal' – genres like political and heroic novels, opera, and other 'characteristically aristocratic forms' – the growing importance of readership in commercial centres like Freiburg, Hamburg, or Zurich, emancipated from the fashions of the courts, manifested itself in the proliferation of periodicals and bürgerliche literature – with genres like domestic drama and family novel registering a new value system (Bruford 10–11, 315). Gradually, an agglomeration of states without a shared cultural centre and national political identity,[21] with the courts as sources of patronage and dissemination of literary work, was being transformed into a linguistic community with a common infrastructure and in possession of several such centres, most containing universities (e.g., Königsberg, Heidelberg, Riga, Leipzig, Göttingen, Frankfurt, Munich, Würzburg). Francophilic Leipzig and Anglophilic Hamburg, which swelled into economic centres, became the hotbeds of periodical publishing, popular with their middle-class. It might seem that any literature worthy of the name would emerge from these centres. However, much literary initiative, most notably Weimar Classicism, sprang from more obscure settings (297–8). Thanks to its burgeoning network of sites of cultural exchange, Germany grew 'eager for literary prestige, long before it was a nation in any other respect' (296). However, the cultural multicentrism, independently of the lack of political centralization, meant that German-speaking lands could not yet boast of a unified cultural domain.

As already mentioned, literary-critical discussion tended, at this stage, to be highly theoretical. But the impetus for writing critically about literature was the growing linguistic identity of the region and the related notion of creating a literary language to rival and surpass those of other countries. As communication in German increased, so too did the regularization and purification of the spoken and written language (Bruford 294). It became imperative to evaluate and, in the classicist manner, determine the principles of a native German literature from accomplished literary works, and the most engrossing debates revolved around which works were part of this grouping. At the same time, a distinct national character was beginning to emerge and be cultivated by those writers most conscious of linguistic unity, past or present. Needless to say, the uneven state of pre-unification German did not easily translate into a coherent body of literature.[22]

Herder's ideas resonate in all post-1770 discussions of German national identity. Apart from being the first, along with Justus Möser (1720–94), to accuse France of 'superficiality' and 'frivolity,' he championed the hitherto overlooked *Volkskultur* (folk literary culture) as a natural source of national identity ('Genius'). Although directly inspired by similar interest in folk literature in England and France, Herder saw the fates of language and nation as intertwined, the one defining and emancipating the other. The *Volksliteratur* movement proved a vital component of Germany's national consciousness, as did the methodical accumulation of homegrown literary capital by various scholars and writers, which put it distinctly on the map of the supra-national Republic of Letters.[23] Anthologizing – and hence rediscovering – Germany's 'lost' popular tradition, composed of old songs (*Volkslieder*), tales, legends, and myths, enriched the German literary language with idiomatic locutions and enhanced the reputations of emerging writers engaged in promoting folklore (e.g., Gottfried August Bürger [1747–94]). The trend soon gained a vibrant following not restricted to German material: in 1778–79 Herder published his *Stimmen der Völker in Liedern: Volkslieder* [Voices of the People in Songs: Folk Songs], a collection that included songs from other cultures; between 1782 and 1787, Johann Karl August Musäus published his five-volume *Volksmärchen der Deutschen* [German Folk Tales]; and in 1789–93 Christiane Benedikte Naubert followed with *Neuen Volksmärchen der Deutschen* [New German Folk Tales]. Early in the next century, the Romantics would continue their efforts, with compilations by Achim von Arnim and Clemens Brentano and by the brothers Jacob and Wilhelm Grimm.

Through this acknowledgment and exploration of a 'primitive' literary past, classicist literary values were gradually put in perspective. Historicism thus became the groundwork for the increasing relativization and pluralization of critical standards and the proliferation of standpoints proposing to re-evaluate neglected works or authors (e.g., Homer or Shakespeare). While its earlier, more naive form postulated the incommensurability of different ages and was prepared to reject ancient standards for judging modern works, the more mature version of historicism saw the moderns as standing on the shoulders of giants.

As previously noted, the effort to improve the state of German literature began as an imitative dependency on French models, but by the 1790s, owing to critics like Herder who reconceived (ahistorical) imitation as (historical) *emulation*, German literature had shifted gears.[24] Herder's idea of creative emulation offered a superior alternative not only to the derivative classicist model but also to Storm-and-Stress *Geniepoetik*. More importantly, the destabilization of the German Francophilic paradigm did not usher in a new literary-theoretical absolutism. What better proof of this than the 1780 pamphlet by Frederick II of Prussia, *De la littérature allemande, des défauts qu on peut lui reprocher, quelles en sont les causes, et par quels moyens on peut les corriger* [On German Literature, the Defects for Which It May Be Reproached, the Causes of These, and by What Means They May Be Corrected].[25] A Francomaniacal soi-disant philosopher-king who had hopes of becoming a French poet and supplied the Berlin Academy with French faculty, Frederick the Great (reigning between 1740 and 1786) thought it high time to polemicize with the new wave of German writers. Formally resembling an essay – hardly a treatise, though referred to as such – the text lampooned (all but ignoring) the accomplishments of young German literature. A reform of German was proposed; the language was still too 'unrefined,' too 'unpleasing to the ear' to produce a classic work (Casanova 19). Flexing his French Classicist muscles – he was both an admirer and a friend of Voltaire (1694–1778) and d'Alembert (1717–83) – the monarch outlined a plan to refashion the backward and impoverished German letters according to traditional Enlightenment aesthetics, a summons which, for late in the day, seemed doomed to fall on deaf ears.[26]

The paradigmatic ramifications of decades of animated discussion became unmistakable once Romanticism appeared on the horizon: there was to be no be-all and end-all of literary achievement. Progress in the field of literature was still possible within and relative to individual historical formations – and the Romantics were the first to embrace this as central to their credo. If Friedrich Schlegel's (1772–1829) aesthetic theory of *Romantic irony*, the dialectic of self-creation and self-destruction, was inspired by philosophical Idealism, it also manifested itself in the subversion of literary *nomoi* and creation of new forms in a (self-consciously) futile effort to express the inexpressible. In Schlegel's words, 'An idea is a concept perfected to the point of irony, an absolute synthesis of absolute antitheses, the continual self-creating interchange of conflicting thoughts. An ideal is at once idea and fact.'[27]

The Enlightenment notion of historical progress was presentistic and positivistic. At the same time, the artistic perfection that was the ancients' fait accompli was *reproducible* by the moderns as long as one applied art's timeless precepts. Early Romanticism, by contrast, dispensed with such transhistorical 'criteriological thinking.'[28] In perspectival encounters with the text, Romantic critics strove to mediate – on behalf of the individual work and literature considered as a historical series – between the claims of history (the acknowledgment of literature's historicity and historical value) and theory (along with the imperative to evaluate a work by current standards, to determine if it stood 'the test of time'). Looking to the future, they saw perfectibility as an infinite process, and envisioned perfection as attainable only in ideality. The ultimate artistic principle was *progressivity*: universalizing art, thought, life through increasing ironic self-awareness.[29] Thus, *progressive poesy* (*progressive Universalpoesie*) needed a *poetical poetics* (*poetische Poetik*).[30] If in the Enlightenment paradigm the ideal was a complete(d) *being*, in the Romantic it was found in an endless, fragmentary *becoming*. The notion of infinite perfectibility applied equally to literature and to criticism as the indeterminacy of critical standards and inexhaustibility of interpretation, marking the birth of modern hermeneutics.[31]

Thus, Schlegel could celebrate incomprehensibility for 'fuel[ling] discourse, provok[ing] critical exchange and debate, incit[ing] new readings' (Leventhal, *DI* 13).[32]

To establish itself as a recognizable critical practice in the seventeenth and eighteenth centuries, German literary study had to break away from textual (philological) criticism, consisting of the in-depth study, evaluation, and commentary on ancient texts, and draw upon French Classicist debates on literary taste and abiding genre laws. To establish itself as a modern, public discourse, literary criticism had to dismantle this French Classicist scaffolding, unbefitting a German literary edifice, while continuing to engage foreign ideas in addition to native ones. The benefits of this transition were immense: the plurality of literary-critical genres and individual styles, modernity of technical language, and sophistication of original thought – all this raised the stature of German literary criticism in the West above its analogues to the East.

2 Overcoming Dogma: Periodicals and Review Criticism

As a general marker of the status of literary-critical inquiry at this time, let us take the occurrence of the term critical (*kritisch*) in the titles of early eighteenth-century German texts concerned with literature. There are at least six instances of this among the better-known (frequently anthologized) works from the period from 1700 to 1750, but scarcely any between 1750 and 1800. Notable examples include Breitinger's *Critische Dichtkunst* (1740), a polemic against Gottsched's *Versuch einer kritischen Dichtkunst* (discussed below), and Bodmer's *Critische Briefe* (1746), followed by *Neue Critische Briefe* in 1749. The term's frequent use before 1750 suggests that criticism was in its formative stage; titles containing the word announced their works' evaluative quality, identifying themselves intertextually as part of a growing group of texts specifically concerned with the evaluation of literary material. In a larger sense, its use underlined the general questioning of received authority characteristic of the Enlightenment. Accordingly, when criticism (in its enlightened guise) comes into its own as a distinct discourse around 1750, the term's titular use becomes superfluous and falls off. *Kritisch* and *Kritik* (criticism, critique) referred now mostly to erudite texts offering wide-ranging judgment of conceptual foundations in related fields (such as aesthetic philosophy or art history). As Hammermeister points out, Kant's use of the term *Kritik* in his three critiques (1781–90), where it designated inquiry into the conditions and limits of a concept or a field of knowledge, differed from its use in art criticism, where it meant 'the process of the qualitative evaluation of individual works of art ... [as] in Herder's *Kritische Wälder* [Critical Forests, 1769] ... and practised in G.E. Lessing's *Hamburgische Dramaturgie* [1767–69]' (24). (That said, the entwinement of the universal claims of criticism and reason – with *nullius in verba* – was spreading to all domains.) The rare titular appearance of the term metacriticism signalled the self-regarding and self-scrutinizing mode of critical thought. In the first half of the eighteenth century, a more common name used for the part of literary evaluator was, however, not *Critiker* (or *Criticus*) but *Kunstrichter*, 'judge of art.'[33] It was only in the second half that criticism (*Kritik*) became more established and intertwined with reviewing as the daily practice of a *Kritiker*.[34]

From about 1750, many writers who sought to break away from nonmetacritical adherence to classicist French literary models began of necessity – simply by grappling with these distinctive problems in print – to redefine the very shape of literary reflection. Like its French counterpart, earlier German classicism obsessed over maintaining clean generic boundaries, in keeping with the lore of decorum. The body of the text had to be kept within the frames of abstract principles and technical rules, the latter 'rarely defined in general terms but rather specified according to genres.' Typical of neo-Aristotelian approaches to criticism was breaking up the text into rigid 'categories viewed almost in isolation: the fable, the characters, the diction, the thought, and the meter, which in Aristotle's analysis of tragedy had formed a unity, became fragments discussed separately' (Wellek, *18C* 19). The distinctions made in literary classification mirrored those in the natural sciences, and the function of the text as an organic system was secondary to its structure. Before long, however, writers trying to address anew traditional poetological questions began to move away from the schematism of classicist poetics, opting instead for modal, thematic, and stylistic heterogeneity and an increasingly organicist aesthetic. Forms put to use in literary-critical discourse before the middle of the century signalled a move towards a more flexible and personal critical style. They included the *comparison* (*Vergleichung*) (e.g., *Vergleichung Shakespears und Andreas Gryphs* [Comparison of Shakespeare and Andreas Gryphs] from 1741 by Johann Elias Schlegel [1719–49]); *reflections* or *meditations* (*Betrachtungen*) (e.g., Bodmer's *Critische Betrachtungen über die poetischen Gemählde der Dichter* [Critical Reflections on the Poetical Paintings of Poets] from 1741); *treatise, disquisition*, or *essay*[35] (*Abhandlung, Versuch*) (Bodmer's *Critische*

Abhandlung von dem Wunderbaren in der Poesie und dessen Verbindung mit dem Wahrscheinlichen [Critical Treatise on the Marvellous in Poesy and Its Connection with the Probable] from 1740, or J.E. Schlegel's *Abhandlung von der Nachahmung* [Treatise on Imitation] from 1742); and *contribution* or *article* (*Beitrag*) (e.g., the collectively authored *Beiträge zur Historie und Aufnahme des Theaters* [Contributions to the History and Reception of Theatre] from 1749 to 1754, or, to give a much later example, the 1798 'Beiträge zur Kritik der neuesten Literatur' [Contributions to the Critique of the Newest Literature] by August Wilhelm Schlegel [1767–1845]). After 1750, other forms (used earlier in the century mainly for scientific writing) made their presence known: *thoughts* (*Gedanken*) (e.g., Johann Georg Sulzer's [1720–79] 'Gedanken vom dem vorzüglichen Werte der epischen Gedichte des Herrn Bodmers' [Thoughts on the Excellence of Mr Bodmer's Epic Poems] [1754], or Friedrich Müller's [a.k.a. Maler Müller, 1749–1825] 'Gedanken über Errichtung eines deutschen Nationaltheaters' [Thoughts on the Construction of a National Theatre] [1777]) and *notes* or *remarks* (*Anmerkungen, Bemerkungen*) (e.g., Jakob Michael Reinhold Lenz's [1751–92] 'Anmerkungen übers Theaters' [Observations on Theatre] [1774]). The assortment of names is deceptive; without them, the designated forms and approaches would lose much of their distinction. Yet such a variety of generic markers in the titles of works indicates the fledgling discourse's formal flexibility and control of a system of functionally related genres. Command of such a system enabled discursive participants to, on the one hand, clarify and refine existing rules for the treatment of their subject, and, on the other hand, find new techniques of critical appraisal through the friction between genres. Certainly, countless critical works from this period bear content-oriented titles, typically beginning with 'über' ('on' or 'about').[36] Although they do not bear their generic affiliation on their sleeve, their topic usually gives adequate clues.

The first major work of literary theory in German, *Laokoon, oder über die Grenzen der Malerei und Poesie* [Laocoon, or on the Limits of Painting and Poetry] (1766) by Gotthold Ephraim Lessing (1729–81), was a revision of French Classicist assumptions about literature. Suffice it to say at this point that it had roughly the form of a treatise, albeit resisting (self-consciously distancing itself from) the typical scholarly format. Other established genres widely utilized for literary-critical pronouncements were the *poetics* (*Poetik or Dichtkunst*) and the *preface* (*Vorrede*, also the older *Vorbericht*, or *prefatory report*).[37] In this category, one might cite Gottlob Friedrich Wilhelm Juncker's (1702/5–46) 'Untersuchung Herrn

Gottfried Benjamin Hanckens Weltlicher Gedichte' [Investigation of Mr G.B. Hancken's Secular Poems] (1727, as part of the last volume of the *Neukirchschen Sammlung*), Gottsched on his tragedy *Cato* (1732), Bürger's 'Vorrede zu den Gedichten' [Preface to the Poems] (1778), or Christoph Martin Wieland's (1733–1813) 'Allgemeiner Vorbericht zu den "Poetischen Schriften"' [General Preamble to 'Poetic Writings'] from 1761. In a 1798 dialogue addressing the market's glut of new books – a 'book-making epidemic' that more often than not produced a 'load of letters' – Friedrich Leopold von Hardenberg (better known as Novalis) (1772–1801) would make this facetious remark about the evaluative value of a book's preface:

> The mere title is often a pretty readable profile. And the preface too is a subtle measure of the book. Which is why nowadays wiser writers usually omit that treacherous advertisement of its contents ... because a good foreword is more difficult to write than the book itself – for, as Lessing put it in his younger, revolutionary days, the foreword is at the same time the book's root and square. And, I would add, it is also its best review.[38]

As in Poland and in Russia, many of the earliest general periodicals were modelled after the popular English moral weeklies, *The Tatler* (1709–11) and *The Spectator* (1711–12, 1714). In the German case, their value and immense popularity among urban middle-class readership can be understood in the context of *Bildung*, or enculturation. Criticism of literature fell within this territory through its development of sensible *Geschmack* (taste). In the mid to late '20s, Gottsched published two such cultural *Wochenschriften* with literary content: *Die vernünftigen Tadlerinnen* [The Sensible Tatlerines or The Sensible Female Critics] designed for the improvement of women and the more philosophically oriented *Der Biedermann* [The Honest Man]. Apparent from the titles of early literary journals is also their generalist profile. Since their discursive style was predominantly didactic, literary work was evaluated insofar as this served the improvement of public taste – that is, evaluated in its moral and mimetic dimensions. Reviews and literary discussions tended also to be informal and conversational.[39]

But the stirrings of critical consciousness can be traced to the seventeenth-century *gelehrte Zeitungen* or *Zeitschriften*, learned journals with limited readership, containing – aside from erudite book criticism (*Buchkritik*) – abstracts, digests, notes, notices, and advertisements for literary and scholarly works.[40] The first publication to feature critical content pertaining to current German literature was Christian Thomasius's (1655–1728) *Monats-Gespräche* [Monthly Conversations], which appeared between 1688 and 1690.[41] Thomasius was also the first consistent *Rezensent*: his collected 'discourses,' each devoted to a particular book, appeared in 1690 under the colourful title *Freymüthige Jedoch Vernunfft- und Gesetzmäßige Gedancken über allerhand fürnemlich aber Neue Bücher ...* [Forthright yet Reasonable and Legal Thoughts on Sundry but Especially New Books ...]. It would not be long before German literary debates were conducted primarily in the pages of *Rezensionsorgane* (review-organs). These early representatives of the 'Age of the Journal' were dominated by the norms of *doctrine classique*.[42] Later, the bulk of the responsibility for keeping abreast of literary activity was assumed by *literarische Zeitschriften*, literary periodicals with a broader readership and extensive reviewing.[43] Newer literature was also given space in the weeklies, in entertainment magazines (e.g., *Hannoverschen Magazin* or *Historisch-litterarisches Magazin* [1785–6]), and in newspapers (e.g., *Königsberger Zeitung* [Koenigsberg Gazette] or *Allgemeine Literatur Zeitung* [General Literary Gazette]).[44] The *Göttingsche Zeitungen von gelehrten Sachen* [Goettingian Gazettes on Scholarly Matters] was the oldest *Literaturzeitschrift* in German, published from 1739 (its name later changed to *Göttingsche gelehrte Anzeigen* [Goettingian Scholarly Announcements]) under the editorship of Albrecht von Haller (1708–77).[45] Wieland started *Der Teutsche Merkur* [The German Mercury] (1774–89), the first renowned German literary periodical (in 1790 superseded by *Der Neue Teutsche Merkur*, which ceased publication in 1810). An example of a famous late-eighteenth-century literary periodical for connoisseurs was Schiller's *Die Horen* [The Hours], released monthly in 1795–8 and representing the ferment of Goethe and Schiller's artistic friendship.[46] Its 'successor,' Goethe's *Die Propyläen* [The Propylaea], lasted only long enough for six issues to appear in Tübigen between 1798 and 1800. It contained texts by Goethe, W. von Humboldt, and Schiller (among them Goethe's critical essays 'Über Laocoon' [On Laocoon] and 'Über Wahrheit und Wahrscheinlichkeit der Kunstwerke' [On Truth and Probability in Works of Art: A Dialogue], and 'Über den Dilettantismus' [On Dilettantism], co-authored with Schiller).

It is, however, not until the joint initiatives of Christoph Friedrich Nicolai (1733–1811), Moses Mendelssohn (1729–86), and Lessing that one can speak of professional *review criticism*, with its centre in Berlin and the review as its most standardized form (Wellek, *18C* 148). Review journals brought together for critical analysis all types of native and foreign publications, including (but not limited to) *belles lettres*, philosophy, medicine, history, as well as other periodicals. Among the most accomplished and comprehensive of Enlightenment literary-critical journals was Nicolai's *Allgemeine deutsche Bibliothek*[47] [General German Library] (1765–1806), which saw itself as a 'public place where one conducted the affairs of the learned and literary, a kind of forum for open literary discussion' so as to build a new audience (Van Der Laan 97–8). His earlier ambitious review weekly, *Briefe, die neueste Literatur betreffend* [Letters concerning Most Recent Literature; also known as *Literaturbriefe*] (1759–66), with himself, Lessing, Mendelssohn, and Thomas Abbt (1738–66) as its main contributors, set new standards in German criticism and 'did much to end the French domination of German literary culture.'[48] In his rejection of prevailing critical conventions, Nicolai went so far as to identify reviewing with criticism, thereby endowing it with a higher purpose (Van Der Laan 95, 98, 109).[49] In Herder's opinion, the *Briefe* came closest to his blueprint for an ideal literary journal, one that 'contains more than letters, excerpts, and interpretations serving as diversions; a work that draws the outline of a complete and entire portrait of literature,' employing intellectually mature critics who 'judge not books, but the spirit within them …' ('FRGL' 94–5). By the 1760s, a flood of novice reviewers led Herder to complain about the declining number of original works, deterioration of reading habits, intellectual laxness, and shortage of independent thinking – a casualty of unseasoned reviewing in response to the growing demand for literary news. In effect, undiscriminating review journals were cultivating a culture of distraction. The bottom line for Herder was: 'the more journals, the less genuine scholarship' (94).

A prolific reviewer of new literature, Lessing can be regarded as the first great literary critic 'in a narrow sense' (Wellek, *18C* 151). He was also positioned among those who sought to overthrow the ascendancy of French Classicism in German-speaking territories, especially amongst the ruling elites. In T.J. Chamberlain's opinion, the heated polemics against French supremacy in German courts, as well as the 'demonstrative embrace of the English' (advocated first by Bodmer and Breitinger, then by Lessing and Herder), became instrumental 'in establishing a German literature that by the end of the century had essentially freed itself from the imitation of foreign models.'[50] On the other hand, Simpson warns that 'we should resist going so far as … to claim that the entire and extraordinary creation of a German literary and philosophical identity was the result of a massive reaction against a taste and literature imported largely from abroad' ('IOC' 4). For it must be a given that even the generally anti-French critics owed not a little to later French Classicist theorists like Jean-Baptiste Dubos (1670–1742) and Charles Batteux (1713–80) (Chamberlain xii).[51] Breitinger's *Critische Dichtkunst*, for example, is heavily indebted[52] to Dubos's *Réflexions critiques sur la poésie et la peinture* [Critical Reflections on Poesy and Painting] (1719), a work credited with altering the tone of classicist artistic doctrine with the category of taste (*goût*). A German adaptation (with German examples) of Batteux's 1746 poetics appeared in 1762–3 under the title *Poetische Bibliothek, zur Ehre des Deutschen nebst einen kurzen Anweisung zur Kritik nach den Grundsätzen des Herrn Batteux* [Library of Poetry, for the Glory of the Germans, together with a Short Instruction on Criticism based on the Principles of Mister Batteux].

The importance of polemical reviews was matched by *Briefe* (critical or critical/literary letters)[53] and *Briefwechsel* (exchange of correspondence) devoted to literary topics. 'Even criticism not composed in response to actual opposed views,' notes Chamberlain, 'often employed the form of such a response, such as the fictional letters of Herder on folk poetry ...' (x).[54] At the time, of course, *letters* stood for literate writing in general. Through its use in the titles of German periodicals,[55] the word came also to connote 'briefing.' *Letters* on literature (*Literaturbriefe*) in this secondary sense could also be fictional: while the piece of writing had the outer form of a letter – suggested by an implicit or explicit addressee – the addressee was an imaginary stand-in for an intended reader (as in Lessing's contributions to the *Briefe*), one of compatible intelligence or, on the contrary, exemplifying the qualities being criticized. Notable examples of published letters/correspondence, the majority of them first printed in periodicals, include Wieland's *Briefe an einen jungen Dichter* [Letters to a Young Poet] (1782–4); Lessing, Nicolai, and Mendelssohn's *Briefwechsel über das Trauerspiel* [Correspondence on Tragedy] (1756–7); Heinrich Wilhelm von Gerstenberg's (1737–1823) *Briefe über Merkwürdigkeiten der Literatur* [Letters on the Oddities of Literature] (1766–71); A.W. Schlegel's *Briefe über Poesie, Sylbenmass und Sprache* [Letters on Poetry, Metre, and Language] (1775); F. Schlegel's 'Brief über den Roman' [Letter on the Novel] (1800); and Johann Georg Hamann's (1730–88) *Fünf Hirtenbriefe, das Schuldrama betreffend* [Five Pastoral Letters concerning the School Play] (1763).[56]

Review criticism in eighteenth-century Germany was founded on virtually identical conceptual and ideological grounds as *Aufklärungskritik*, whose purpose was to build an intellectual base by educating the German public in the sciences, arts, and literature through the dissemination and specialization of knowledge. Serious literary-critical periodicals – such as the above-mentioned *Allgemeine deutsche Bibliothek* – seized upon the concept of *Aufklärung*, so that the urban scholarly associations and academic milieus ceased to be its sole purveyors. Very soon, the more intellectually formidable of these publications earned sufficient credentials to redefine the rationalist paradigm and shape public taste with a view to advancing general learning.[57] With these goals came the responsibility of making learned literary discussion not only available and accessible to the public, but also open to its contributions. The stage was set for public literary criticism and the formation of public opinion in the arts.

As mentioned earlier, the growing awareness of the historicity of ideas in the last quarter of the eighteenth century impacted the literary critic's function and obligations. In his *Versuch einer kritischen Dichtkunst vor die Deutschen* [Attempt at a Critical German Poetics] (1730), Gottsched assumes the role of a historian of literature concerned with study beyond the disunified, irregular practices of his age: of unified literary and proto-literary cultures and immutable generic laws. He gives *critical* attention to ancient literature and on its basis elaborates a timeless poetics. Other critics, however, did not share this flat view of history. Throughout the eighteenth century, following the rise of the educated bourgeoisie, German academic criticism traded the vestiges of *ars critica* (close philological criticism of older texts and a general philological approach to newer ones)[58] for the close, *practical evaluation* of contemporary literature.[59] Preoccupation with present-day writing and the application of established literary principles to new literature curtailed antiquarian explorations of the past. The mounting historical and literary consciousness among the middle-class public presented an opportunity not only for re-evaluating classicist norms but also for departure from classicist *form* in tone and style when articulating literary-critical opinions (permitting individual styles to emerge, favouring introspection and concrete over representative experience). For one thing, because the criticism of books entailed the criticism of culture (*Kulturkritik*) and of the times (*Zeitkritik*), it also 'motivated the expression of a lighter spirit.'[60] Rather than plodding discourse on literary standards, a freer prose surveyed the cultural sphere and historical moment, more concerned with practical assessments.

The critique of Enlightenment classicism espousing universal 'rational' rules[61] led to a decreasingly normative, objectivist, and systematic view of the history of creativity, poetic process, and product.[62] Over time, interest in general historical tendencies and regularities of literary production, its function in society and the development of human culture, made way for the German Romantic poet – an original creative genius, modern *vates*, seeker of the philosophical 'literary absolute,' keeper of the immaculate dawn and history of humanity. Romanticism's (and, earlier, mannerist Baroque's) cultivation of irrationalism, its belief 'in the identity of all being' (past and present), its vision of a finite (historicized) subjectivity motivated by (and regulated by) the eternal ideal, also led to the decline of commitment 'to any single cultural or stylistic tradition,' to any single literary genre – a kind of 'catholicity of literary taste' subordinated to the creative imagination and dissolution of otherness/foreignness (Atkins 8, 10–11).[63] Romantic metaphysics, endowing history with arcane, larger-than-life significance, soon inspired immense 'substantive' (highly speculative) historical investigation, yet of great factual accuracy, stimulating thereby new areas of knowledge.

The character of eighteenth-century criticism changed in tandem with the period's conception of history. Looking at the general tendency in the philosophical conceptualization of history, Foucault and Gumbrecht note the uncanny presence of temporality in the discourses of scientific and humanistic disciplines during the nineteenth century.[64] This concept of history differed substantially from the *universal history* that preceded it in the eighteenth century. Universal history described a stable diachrony in which the distant past, once rediscovered (through the combined efforts of empirical research and imaginative recreation),[65] is always to hand, literal, transparent. An obvious instillation of this notion in critical discourse was the widespread reliance on ancient aesthetics, and a timeless typology of genres, on the assumption that little of value could have changed in the realm of art. Metaphysical yearning after the inaccessible original and, especially, after the murky ideal of medievalism, had to wait for the Romantics. A fundamental distinction between classicism, including Weimar Classicism, and Romanticism was the more concrete historical sense of the former: 'Antiquity had a real existence for Goethe, and thus can be compared to Columbus's America, whereas the Romanticism of Eichendorff's *Das Marmorbild* presented the ancient world wholly as a creation of poetic imagination' (Purdy 85).

At the same time, the formation of literary classicism dates to the 'critical ferment' of the seventeenth-century *Querelle des anciens et des modernes*, which, as Koselleck notes in *Critique and Crisis*, was articulated in France 'within the republic of scholars by art and literary critics developing an understanding of time that sundered future from past' and electing a future-oriented world view.[66] The German movements of Sturm und Drang and Romanticism grew out of and shared this classicist orientation, which gave rise to a progressive view of literary history and to a literary criticism conscious of its not merely auxiliary but formative role in literature's progress. The historiography of literature ('narrative history ... which had a critical scheme in mind and a critical ambition to re-evaluate the past' [Wellek, *18C* 29]) brought with it a new set of literary-critical terms, signalling a new conception of literature as subject to and developing within history (understood as progress) (26–7). The ritualistic pomp and stuffiness of classicist poetics sat ill with this new breed of criticism and had to be thrown off to complement the creative calling.

The Jena Romantics had a deep sense of their group importance in the history of humanity. Their creativity and philosophy exceeded the narrow frames of the aesthetic and scientific and attempted to fuse knowledge of the arts and sciences based on universal analogies.[67] In practice, on the formal level, this involved the introduction of concepts and analogies from music, medicine, physics, biology, chemistry, and mathematics. 'We are on a *mission*,' wrote Novalis, 'Our vocation is the education of the earth.'[68] The historical dimension of Early Romantic writing clearly attests this belief in a higher purpose and unifying vision. When Novalis speaks of the 'artistic critic' (*artistischer Kritiker*) 'whose labors prepare the history of art,' he sees all of the Romantics' activity as 'qualitatively potentiated' and integrated within a historical dimension.[69] The strength of this conviction had much to do with the collaborative character of the Jena circle. Nurturing their collaboration were the principle of conviviality (*Geselligkeit*), the bonds of intellectual friendship, and personal rapport (Stoljar, *Athenaeum* 33). In other words, while the confrontation of differing opinions was welcome, petty, vindictive polemics had no place in such an atmosphere.[70] Romantic polemics was to administer an 'electric shock' between reason and unreason that sharpened the mind.[71]

The idea of collaboration – and resulting cross-pollination – found a radical, emblematic expression in the '*Athenäums*-Fragmente' [Athenaeum Fragments] (1798). The collection, which appeared in the Romantic periodical *Athenäum*, was authored collectively and therefore retained a level of anonymity. Stoljar contextualizes the Romantics' choice of genres in the concept and practice of *Symphilosophie* (literally, 'philosophizing together') (*Athenaeum* 34). The form of the *dialogue* (different from dialogical rhetoric) was as apposite to the Early Romantics' credo as was the aphoristic *fragment*, if for somewhat different reasons – although Novalis spoke of his *Blütenstaub* [*Pollen*] fragments as 'fragments of my continuing dialogue with myself,' and F. Schlegel described the dialogue as 'a chain or a garland of fragments' (in another translation, 'aphorisms'), subsuming the genre of correspondence, which is 'a dialogue on a larger scale.'[72] While both the fragment and the dialogue, as vehicles of literary-critical opinion, exhibit the openness and open-endedness so valued by the Jena group, the latter's strengths were greater formal capaciousness and structural complexity, which conveniently allowed the 'rapid changes of subject' (a potential explored in the most celebrated of their dialogues, F. Schlegel's 'Gespräch über die Poesie' [Dialogue on Poesy] [1800], discussed below).[73]

In the closing years of the eighteenth century, the Romantics turn to and reconceive not only the fragment, but also the book-length study of literary history (a speculative prototype of comparative literature),[74] and, along with the Weimar *Klassiker*, the personal essay as so many means of critical expression. The genre syncretism characteristic of their texts, however, turns their generic identification into an issue of contention, further compounded by a lack of consensus about even the central tenets of Early Romanticism (Horne 289). In dealing with these texts, one 'takes them at their word' only to consider how they deliberately modify or confound certain generic conventions as part of a philosophical strategy. Thus, with the advent of Romanticism, literary criticism rose to a new discursive register – where it allowed itself to exhibit playfulness toward genres along with a consciousness of that playfulness.

3 Toward a Critical 'Play Drive': Generic Vicissitudes

Of the multitude of forms in pre-1750 German criticism only one reflected both the older and the reconfigured institutional infrastructure, and adapted remarkably well to shifting criteria in the evaluation of literary works. This was the book review. Throughout the century, the review's discursive role was paramount: an overwhelming portion of German literary criticism was this kind of workaday practice. The reason for the review's lability was its utilitarian and largely content-based conception. During this formative phase – before it became absorbed into professional journalism as a reduced, form-based 'discursive type'[75] – the *Rezension* migrated through (in the sense of either drawing on or assimilating) the formal characteristics of a variety of literary forms: the (satiric) treatise, the dialogue, fictional epistles and actual correspondence, the epigram, the poem, and the dramolet (5).[76] These genres, modified for the purpose of reviewing, were employed along with a number of literary devices, such as the frame of a fictitious reviewer (5). Indeed, the adoption/modification of existing forms and their belletristic modulation defined much of pre-1750s book reviewing. Continuing this trend past the mid-century was Matthias Claudius (1740–1815), editor of the popular weekly *Wandsbecker Bote* [Wandsbeck Messenger] (which counted Herder, Bürger, and Goethe among its contributors), who in 1774 could summarize *The Sorrows of Young Werther* and express his appreciation for it in just ten, albeit deeply lyrical sentences, gushing compassion for human frailty (the mode was proof of the power of Goethe's work over the reader's passions and mind, of its ability to move both). Such freedom of style notwithstanding, the descriptive and/or discursive *Rezension* emerged as the dominant review form from the outset, owing to 'the concomitant premium placed on reason as arbiter in questions of aesthetics' (Rowland, 'Physiognomist' 18). During the latter half of the century, the multiplicity of review-printing periodicals reflected 'a growing pluralism of theoretical orientations, as the Enlightenment proceeded through its stages of development and in the process became self-critical and elicited criticism from without' (Rowland, 'Physiognomist' 18). This self-critical and metacritical reorientation evident in review criticism (though not limited to it) was coterminous with a broadening of the literary audience, as the more specialized periodicals sought to make available proficient literary discourse to the general public. Discussions became more self-referential, requiring readers' familiarity with earlier statements, and frequently touched on issues of aesthetics.[77] Review journals maintained the continuity of debates across individual issues by encouraging dialogue among contributors. The more involved these debates were, the more intertextual the individual reviews.

During the Sturm-und-Drang period, however, this notion of discursivity had significantly expanded. While it is true that the *Stürmer und Drängers* themselves 'characteristically refrain[ed] from theoretical-expository treatment of the issues that concern[ed] them, out of a more or less programmatic disposition against theory,'[78] they were also avid periodical readers and contributors (as a means of revolt in lieu of direct political action). One example was Goethe's involvement with the renowned review journal *Frankfurter gelehrte Anzeigen* [Frankfurt Scholarly Notices] (1772–90), which briefly became the *Hausblatt*, the main critical platform, of Sturm und Drang.[79] Review criticism was never more vibrant than it was at that time, and the main, descriptive-discursive mode of the review was not yet the defining one, if one takes into account the number of journals in circulation. Formally, the 'individual, partly emotionalized, therefore little balanced and poignant' method of presentation in reviews distinguished itself from 'the abstract-theoretical tenor of Enlightenment review-organs [*Referateorgane*].'[80]

The earliest *popular* genre of literary criticism in German appeared in the late Baroque. The monthly conversations (*Monatsgespräche*), modelled after Thomasius's periodical by that name, consisted of an extended dialogue relating several fictive speakers of equal rank in a make-believe discussion, its goal being not consensus but productive disagreement ensuring the continuation of edifying discourse (Bogner 19). The idea of putting imaginary voices representative of one's time in conversation on current literature, focused through one topic, was picked up by Wilhelm Ernst Tentzel in his *Monatliche Unterredungen einiger guten Freunde von allerhand Büchern und andern annehmlichen Geschichten* [Monthly Discussions between a Few Good Friends on Sundry Books and Other Agreeable Affairs] (Leipzig, 1689–98). The participants, instead of meeting, would reply to questions allegedly sent them by the periodical's editor. The answers were then printed in a manner simulating an actual colloquy, sometimes with an introduction of the circumstances of the exchange.[81] This dialogical structure was not Socratic, in the sense that the inherent dynamic was not a student–teacher one, and its culmination not an intellectual conversion of one or more of the parties. The composition resembled, rather, late ancient philosophical dialogues: a mutually edifying debate amongst partners, none of whom is an intellectual authority commanding attention, though a dominant position may emerge in the conversation's course. The interlocutors' respective strengths are played off of one another, even as their weaknesses are exposed in the process. Dialogicity is an essential part of the argument, which is carried by no one in particular, emerging instead in the crisscrossed interstices of communication. Readers, to whom this plurivocal interchange was submitted without final verdict, were thus encouraged to form their own opinions.

The dialogical structure, *modal* or *formal*, emerged as one of the most prominent features of German criticism in the eighteenth century. By *modal* I mean that the structure was not represented in dialogue form, but consisted of implicit or explicit dialogical rhetoric, approaching an imaginary conversation (e.g., in Lessing's *Laokoon*). This distinguishes it from the polemical mode, taking the form of direct argumentation against existing opponents, specific individuals whose names, when not given, can be inferred. The dialogical mode consists of discernible, actual or hypothetical, questions posed to the author by, respectively, a real or a fictional figure, or as objections by the author himself to his own ideas, which then assist in refining them further. Such 'exchanges' are to varying degrees contrived by a unifying authorial perspective: the goal is to reinforce the argument and make it less vulnerable to outside criticism. This kind of controlled presentation is, likewise, not modelled on the didascalic relation; the author, although arbiter and inevitably victor in the discussion he orchestrates, is focused not on imparting new knowledge to his opponents/inferiors, but on addressing challenges, and by this exercise of intellect convincing those neither privy to nor participant in the discussion.

The *exterior* dialogical form in criticism pulled ahead during Early Romanticism, when it became more artful, exposing its fictive status and literary ambitions (e.g., F. Schlegel's 'Gespräch über die Poesie'). The interaction presented often took place between the author and would-be interlocutors whom the author deemed most worthy of debate, and often concluded with a collective adjudication or some resolution on a general aesthetic truth. There were no final victors. The epithet 'Socratic' is applied to the Romantic dialogue because it acts as a dialectical platform for collective reflection. This structuration of Romantic criticism had its philosophical underpinnings in the Idealist philosophy of Johann Gottlieb Fichte (1762–1814); as Behler writes, 'German Romantic criticism represents a fundamentally dialectical type of thinking … of thought and counterthought … towards absolute self-consciousness and self-determination' (*GRC* ix). The dialectical movement undergirding the dialogical structure was inherently creative,[82] consciously headed for a higher synthesis, along the Hegelian model. (The rhythm of this creativity also arose from this philosophical order as the pursuit of a receding ideal.)

Meanwhile, the spirit of 'monthly conversations' continued in periodical ventures to the end of the century, particularly among neo-humanist and classicist authors. The following passage from Goethe's 1798 introduction to the *Propyläen* may serve as both proof of this and as an indication of how differently critical discourse (at the peak of Weimar Classicism) comported itself, in the spirit of *discordia concors* and with respect to readership at large:

> Should the title *Propylaea* call to mind the gateway through which one had to pass to reach the Athenian citadel, Minerva's temple, we shall not protest. But we hope we will not be accused of presumptuously attempting to compete in these pages with so magnificent a work of art. What we wish to convey by this title is at most something that might have taken place there: discussions and conversations which perhaps would not have been unworthy of those hallowed halls … We hope the essays we plan to offer will never be contradictory in essential points, even though the authors' ways of thinking may not be identical. No two persons perceive the world exactly alike, and different minds will often apply differently a principle they otherwise agree on … Although the authors ardently desire that harmony prevail among ourselves and with the majority of our public, at the same time we must expect dissonant voices from various quarters, especially since we depart from prevailing opinions in more than one point. We do not at all intend to censure or change anyone's way of thinking, but we will express our opinions firmly and will decline or accept the challenge, whichever we deem appropriate. In general, however, we will adhere firmly to principles and reiterate especially those prerequisite conditions that seem to us indispensable in the development of an artist. If you are serious, you must take a stand, otherwise you do not deserve to play an active role … The format of our journal is such that we will publish individual essays, and most of these in installments. However, we have no desire to fragmentize, but rather ultimately to create a whole from these many parts.[83]

A reconceptualization of criticism was central to Early Romantic critical writing. At bottom, it was a criticism that theorized poetry as the universal, without a direct poetics.[84] This *organicist* approach to literature became manifest in many texts considered as literary criticism and theory; as self-consciously organic compositions (e.g., the dialogue) they did not conform to either the academic or the literary-journalistic types of discourse. The ideology subtending it was of critique as poetic activity. The work was collaborative, formally experimental, and stylized – inviting 'constant mixing and mingling,' evidently reveling in the 'emergence of new literary forms' (Behler, *GRC* vii). To be sure, the *Frühromantik* could also present critical observations in more traditional language and form.[85]

The shift of critical concern to larger problems of aesthetics from the 1760s onward correlated with interest in the socio-psychological spectrum of reception of literary texts. This had to do with the formation of a fairly homogeneous bourgeois public sphere and the valorization of emotion in literature and literary criticism.[86] As Wellek notes, criticism 'shifted attention to the emotional effect of art, and, if pushed to its extreme ... it became destructive of the essential feature of art: its appeal to contemplation. Art became identified with persuasion, rhetoric, and even raw emotion' (*18C* 26). The link between these changes in literature and alteration in the style of critical writing is to be understood not so much literally, as the (retrospective) articulation of emotions experienced by the critic while reading a literary text, but as the relaxation of the hitherto formulaic, prescriptive, and depersonalized character of critical idiom. This is not to say that logical coherence and the tenor of rationalism and objectivity were not previously infringed upon, only that the rules of rhetoric played a significant part in presentation, targeting an academic public, which therefore followed a prescribed order with relatively limited flexibility. The teaching of *ars bene loquendi*, however, disappeared from school curricula in the last quarter of the century (Leventhal, *DI* 66). *Auslegungskunst* (the art of exegesis), the Enlightenment theory of interpretation, had much to do with allegiance to this discursive model.

> As an historical discourse or *language* concerning interpretation which sought to insure the veritable transmission of a set of ideas, it taught the construction of a discourse or text in accordance with established text or discourse type, the formation of the ideas in keeping with the conventional forms of signification, the rules of rhetoric and the teachings of reason: clarity, comprehensibility, perspicacity and a clear use of the standard learned language. (63)

This discipline placed hidden constraints on the polemical mode; instead of being direct, polemics for the most part tended to be allusive and encrypted as satire or parody. But in the second half of the century, in Germany as well as in Poland and in Russia, a tendency toward expressivity and poeticization in the critical idiom on the one hand, and toward subjectivism in judgment on the other, could be discerned. The trend ran parallel to, and counterbalanced, the conservative, 'levelheaded' critical approach of *Aufklärungskritik*, or Enlightenment (self-) critique – now used with the shorter, more open forms of the review and critical essay. Within this framework, Lenz could write an apologia-like 'self-review' of his own play.[87] The most metaphorical, subjective, and emotive theoretical-critical writings, however, belong to the representatives of an anti-Enlightenment, precursors of *Empfindsamkeit* (Sensibility, or Sentimentalism) and *Romantik*: Hamann and Herder.

Bruce Kieffer expressly contrasts Herder's style with that of Enlightenment thought (11). While he concedes that Herder 'also organizes his arguments in a rationalistic framework,' he stresses that his prose 'frequently exhibits the impassioned, subjective interest that is characteristically Sturm-und-Drang.' Thus, Hamann – whose own wild prose is nowadays nearly impenetrable – could reproach Herder's style for being 'hyperbolic-pleonastic' while criticizing his protégé's methods and goals for their conformity with academic standards (14).[88] In his prize-winning work from 1771, *Abhandlung über den Ursprung der Sprache* [Treatise on the Origin of Language], Herder's animated subjective perspective and urgency work to convince the reader of his authority – that he 'really is onto something new, despite his failure to articulate it' (Kieffer 11).

Herder's was an intensification of the essayistic temperament. Post-1750, the essay emerged as the most adaptable form of literary discourse. As Marcel Reich-Ranicki defines it in his canonical anthology of German *Essayistik*, the genre 'criticizes – if not always, then often, if not openly, then in disguise – established views, current opinions, and beliefs. And while the treatise [*Abhandlung*] does not place particular value on aesthetic claims, the essay is attentive to artistic form, to personal and, if possible, lively, memorable formulations' ('Über den Essay'). Already during the Storm and Stress period, thematizing/theorizing language (particularly its mythical origins) in scholarly discourse afforded new discursive registers (metadiscourse, self-reflexivity, self-consciousness) as both an 'important component of Enlightenment philosophy' and an impetus for counter-Enlightenment philosophy (Kieffer 15). The debate about the origins of language, which in Germany took shape in the 1750s, was a nascent form of modern philology and the study of linguistics, which became recognized as academic disciplines in the nineteenth century through the effort of Jacob Grimm (1778–1863).[89]

Schiller's concept of the play-drive (*Spieltrieb*),[90] which appears in the title of this section, pertains of course to artistic production. What relationship can it have to literary criticism? The general trend in critical writing of the eighteenth century was, as we have seen, toward greater creative freedom, hence also towards greater formal diversity in expressing literary judgments and theoretical views. This formally innovative criticism was partly an outcome of the frequent co-existence and cross-pollination of literary and critical pursuits in the most prominent critics. That, along with the far less codified nature of the critical idiom during this time of transition from rule-bound, non-philosophical poetics to aesthetic theory combined with philosophically guided criticism, produced a favourable climate for formal experimentation, modal hybridity (historical/theoretical/applied criticism), and the mixing of philosophical and poetic idioms. Schiller understood the play-drive as engendering a unity of form (*Form*) and substance/matter (*Stoff/Materie*) constitutive of artistic beauty. In the earlier critical texts, we cannot insist on such an aesthetic quality: art was still heteronomous, subject to explicit moral and rational constraints. But the revision of classicism by Winckelmann and Lessing heralded the arrival of a new, historically relative, and autonomous notion of artistic value and, consequently, a new discursive attitude. Another mode to subsequently merge with critical aims was the philosophical-Idealist critique, most evident in Schiller's work. His pivotal *Über die ästhetische Erziehung des Menschen* [On the Aesthetic Education of Man, in a Series of Letters] (1795) opens with the following admission: 'The free mode of procedure you prescribe implies for me no constraint; on the contrary, it answers to a need of my own' (87). Schiller claimed to derive his ideas from the formal procedure of 'constant communing with myself rather than from any rich experience of the world or from reading.' The apogee of these formal developments was the Romantic critical fragment, a generic 'incarnation' of the Romantic philosophical and literary world view (*LA* 39–40). The fragment was, paradoxically, theorized as a form of resistance to form,[91] and to standard systematization generally, envisioning a poetic-philosophic 'system of fragments' that transcended the wor(l)d's fragmentation.[92] Owing to the convergence in it of poetry, philosophy, and criticism, the fragment accommodated the theory of which it was a practice and was its own literary criticism. In this sense its integrity approached that of living form (*lebende Gestalt*) – the object of the play-drive and the fruit of a dialectic between form and content, fulfilling therewith Schiller's requirement for aesthetic experience.

4 Textual Analyses

(a) J.Ch. Gottsched's Versuch einer critischen Dichtkunst vor die Deutschen [*Attempt at a Critical German Poetics*] *(Leipzig, 1730)*[93]

Gottsched was a prolific critic, whose output spanned reviews, prefaces, 'thoughts,' and 'opinions' (*Gutachten*), among other forms. He became, in the 1720s, one of the initiators of German Enlightenment literary reform and, from the 1730s onward, of German literary-historical scholarship and theatre criticism. The main topics of one of his periodicals, *Beyträge zur critischen Historie der deutschen Sprache, Poesie und Beredsamkeit* [Contributions to a Critical History of the German Language, Poetry, and Eloquence] (1732–44), were poetry and literary history; the Leipzig monthly *Belustigungen des Verstandes und Witzes* [Amusements of Intellect and Wit] (1741–5), on which he collaborated with J.J. Schwabe, published texts on literary theory and education. Gottsched's writings on theatre considered dramatic language in relation to *bienséance*, and high and low style – he was, for instance, against diction that was either too refined or too vulgar. 'In advocating French Classicist tragedy as the model for the new German drama, Gottsched called for the reproduction of the idiom developed by Corneille and Racine. His primary aim ... was to introduce a natural manner of speech to the German stage, as an antidote to the bombast of baroque drama' (Kieffer 21). As could be expected, what for Gottsched was natural, for the younger critics was artificial and stilted.

Lessing, building on work by J.E. Schlegel and Christian Fürchtegott Gellert (1715–69),[94] opposed Gottsched on the issues of dramatic theory and practice, particularly dialogue, and redefined tragedy and comedy through his own plays (Kieffer 24). He accused Gottsched of inaccurate translations of Aristotelian terminology and French drama. In the famous 17th *Literaturbrief* in the first volume of a 1759 issue of *Briefe, die neueste Literatur betreffend*, he attacked the notion of Gottsched's undeniably crucial role in the advancement of German theatre: 'I am that no one; I downright deny it ... [I]n short, he did not want to improve our old theatre but to be the creator of an entirely new one. New how? Frenchified [*französisierenden*]; without ascertaining whether or not this Frenchified theatre fits the German mentality.'[95] Provocation of opposition was, in some ways, Gottsched's biggest but involuntary contribution to critical discourse of the eighteenth century. His was an orthodoxy *against* which a new generation of writers and theorists effectively defined themselves. It must be said, however, that Gottsched contributed to the revitalization of German literature in a positive sense, by launching programs to purify the German language and develop literary style. Two works stand out in this respect: the *Ausführliche Redekunst* [Complete Rhetoric] (Leipzig, 1728; expanded version in 1736),[96] a classicist instruction manual in rhetoric drawing heavily on Boileau, and the *Grundlegung der Deutschen Sprachkunst, Nach den Mus-*

tern der Besten Schriftsteller des Vorigen und Jetzigen Jahrhunderts Abgefasset [Of German Oratory, Based on Examples from the Best Writers of the Previous and Current Century] (1748), which served as a textbook on grammar.

Gottsched's most famous work, however, appeared in the guise of a poetics, which was to remedy the lack of a contemporary German poetics. The program outlined therein became the cause célèbre of literary debate in the first half of the eighteenth century. On the whole, it appeared to be a continuation of the cruder, Baroque-era classicism, because of its attention to the traditional genres, the highly specific nature of its rules, and its plentiful use of textual examples from seventeenth-century poets. The most renowned German predecessor of the *Critische Dichtkunst* was the normative Baroque poetics of Opitz.[97] Gottsched, however, reduced both the number and the specificity of rules (which in Opitz were many and more particular), modifying their earlier character as practical instructions by adopting a more rigorously theoretical angle and subordinating them to a moral and educational purpose. He also opposed the fantastical extravagance of literary Baroque, downgrading the role of the creative imagination. Following Aristotle (via Boileau), he regarded sound reason (*gesunde Vernunft*) and unchanging human nature as the basis of all rules and literary-critical evaluation. These aspects, combined with his dependence on established (seventeenth-century) French Classicist theory – most notably, the principles of mimesis (*Nachahmung*), probability (*Wahrscheinlichkeit*), the three dramatic unities (*die drei Einheiten*) – place his text more in the tradition of Enlightenment classicism. In fact, early German classicism, like French Classicism, was forever caught in the Enlightenment antinomy of reason and tradition. That being said, to better understand the uproar around the *Critische Dichtkunst* requires seeing this text as reflective of a *transition* in literary values, instead of deciding which – Baroque or Enlightenment – is the more accurate ideological classification.

On the formal side, his prose has an uncommon stylistic stiffness and tonal monotony, passed down to him perhaps by his teacher, the eminent German rationalist philosopher and mathematician Christian Wolff (1679–1754) (a polymath said to have originated 'a truly philosophical German Style'),[98] himself a prolific manual-writer on topics ranging from aesthetics to physics. Although an unrepentant Francophile, Gottsched sought equality for German literature in relation to other European literatures. He saw language, including literary language, as the instrument promoting Enlightenment values – rational order, above all. Accordingly, he envisioned literature as an orderly and functional system of definable and invariant styles and genres, based on formal and social codes with roots in Antiquity ('So the surest means to preserve good taste is to keep to the rules which have come down to us from the ancient critics and masters').[99] This rationalist-normative view of literary art is reflected directly in the organization and communication style of the *Critische Dichtkunst*, as are his pedagogical pursuits, which in 1756 led him to revise the text for use as a school textbook.

Gottsched discredited the magniloquence of Baroque poetry – echoes of which he discerned in contemporary imaginative writers, such as Friedrich Gottlieb Klopstock (1724–1803) – as a corruption of taste. He favoured German court poets who abandoned or openly criticized Rococo refinement and identification of poetry with wit (*Witz*) and entertainment, among them Friedrich Rudolf von Canitz (1654–99). Gottsched's campaign for a new, *bürgerliche* poetry was founded on rationalist (mainly Wolffian) and Aristotelian literary principles and classicist generic norms. As he gained followers in younger writers and continued his work in periodicals and the university, his detractors became more vocal and acerbic. Bodmer (whose *Critische Abhandlung von dem Wunderbaren in der Poesie* countered Gottsched's inflexible rationalism) and Breitinger (who in 1740 responded with his own *Critische Dichtkunst*) saw Gottsched's combination of rationalist literary theory with the dated *Regelpoetik* of aristocratic circles as ultimately at odds with Enlightenment ideals and the moral edification of the middle-class and thus as an unsuitable foundation for the new literature. The debate over the viability of Gottsched's classicist program and his efforts to implement it lasted until the 1760s. That the *Critische Dichtkunst* saw four editions between 1730 and 1751 is more an index of its controversial status than of widespread assent.

The full title of Gottsched's poetics was originally longer than in later editions: *Versuch einer critischen Dichtkunst vor die Deutschen: darinnen erstlich die allgemeinen Regeln der Poesie, hernach alle besondere Gattungen der Gedichte abgehandelt und mit Exempeln erläutert werden. Anstatt einer Einleitung ist Horatii Dichtkunst in deutsche Versse übersetzt, und mit Anmerckungen erläutert von M. Joh. Christoph Gottsched* [Attempt at a Critical German Poetics: In which are Treated Firstly General Rules of Poesy, Afterward all of the Particular Genres of Poems and Explained with Examples. Instead of an Introduction a German Translation of Horace's Poetics, Explained in Notes by M.J. Christoph Gottsched].[100] Generally speaking, well into the third quarter of the eighteenth century long critical studies tended to bear descriptive titles (another example is Lessing's treatise, discussed below). The title acted not only as a unique identification of a work but as a summary of its parts. One potential reason for this is that the author and/or publisher wanted to reach as broad an audience as possible. Another, related, reason could be that the German critical study was in the early stages of codification and quite simply rare (and therefore not readily identifiable as such). The author/publisher may have felt that the contemporary reader would not approach the work with the right assumptions and needed to be informed in advance. In other words, one should not be quick to ascribe the length of the title to pedantry and rigidity.

The *Critische Dichtkunst* is not only considered Gottsched's main work, but also the first systematic poetics in the German language. That being said, its content is largely borrowed from Boileau's *L'Art poétique* [Poetics] (1674) – rendering it unpopular among emerging literary Germanophiles.[101] It is largely a theoretical text with a practical component, although the positive examples discussed as part of the latter are generally French. Its primary concern is a normative systematic of genres and decorum, but also, by extension, of the qualities required of a poet. A glance at the basics of organization may be helpful here. The text is split into two parts, the first part concerned with the principles underlying literary art, and corresponding to the Enlightenment aspect of Gottsched's project, the second concerned with laying down strict generic laws, the aspect of Baroque *Regelpoetik*. The chapters are organized neatly according to theme, with descriptive titles, such as 'On the Character of a Poet,' 'On the Good Taste of a Poet,' 'On the Three Kinds of Poetic Imitation and Plots in Particular.' Instead of notes, Gottsched places the author and source of quoted passages in the lead-in or directly below the quotation.

Part 1 begins with a chapter on the emergence and development of various literary genres. Chapter 2 moves on to more general precepts, presenting an outline (*Abriß*) of the characteristics of the true poet. Here, for example, Gottsched expounds the interdependence of poetic/artistic and critical ability – quoting Pliny's dictum 'Only an artist can judge another artist' (*CD* 36).[102] He proceeds to discuss national taste, and along the way, puts forth his concept of *bon goût* (*guter Geschmack*) – 'a matter about which everywhere so much today is said and written' (37) – of which every good poet must be possessed. This category does not encompass both sensual and rational criteria for judgment, only the latter. Here he also distinguishes between the character of a poet and that of a philosopher and a critic. Gottsched has in mind the philosopher of literature – not a common *philosophical* topic ('not everyone has time and occasion to turn their philosophical studies to the liberal arts …' [38]). With time and dedication, the literary philosopher earns the special title of *Criticus*, who is 'nothing other than a scholar who can philosophize about the liberal arts.' 'What such critics, such philosophical poets or philosophers knowledgeable about poetry, may well tell us will be doubtless far more thorough and arouse in us a more accurate conception of a true poet, than what the great mass, after the deceived dictate of its fickle taste, cares to praise or censure' (38). With these words Gottsched re-establishes the function of the critic, dating back to Aristotle, as protector of the character of the poet.

The chapters in the second part deal with the main dramatic genres comedy (*Lustspiel*) and tragedy (*Trauerspiel*), respectively. Both are tapestries of prescription, learning (providing historical background of ancient achievements and surveying modern national theatres with a wealth of examples), and evaluation (paying attention to both a work's merits and its flaws, which depend on proximity to or departure from ancient rules). For example, Gottsched's discussion of modern comedy delves into differences between Italian, English, and French comedy. The former is criticized for its fantastical 'nonsense' ('and when one laughs at such comedies, it is not at the foolery of the characters on the stage, but at the harebrained ideas of the author of such a play'). English comedy, meanwhile, is said to be best at ridiculing human follies and the moral edification of the audience. French playwrights are commended for highest comedic achievement, but are not without their mistakes (*CD* 182–3).

In part 1, chapter 3, a historical-relativistic counterargument is voiced only to be disposed of in the space of a paragraph (such rhetorical dialysis will later be utilized by Lessing with far greater dexterity and subtlety): 'Finally it has also been asked whether a writer has not cause to adapt himself to the taste of the times, his place or his court, rather than to the rules of art?' (*CP* 4). This stance is elaborated using the 'editorial we,' qualified by 'it is said.' Gottsched's reply begins: 'The objection appears important, for it flatters our vanity. It would be unanswerable if it were mere willfulness which declared a thing beautiful' (5). He then proceeds to correct this viewpoint by claiming the 'nature of things' – and not 'vain presumption' – as the basis of beauty. The artistic preference of the ancient Greeks for 'imitation of perfect nature' imbued their art with the atemporal (and God-given) natural perfection. Hence, deviating from the Greeks' artistic methods produces only things unnatural and tasteless. In Gottsched's mechanistic system, history can improve neither on imitation in ancient art nor on the principle of mimesis itself. Greek culture earned the right to define taste by its unmatched supremacy. In this sense, although relying on history for providing absolute artistic principles, Gottsched's argument here is entirely ahistorical and circular; he makes no attempt even to justify Greek superiority by its continued and profound historical influence on other cultures, because he never actually questions it as a foundation. When he speaks positively of other cultures (Roman or Italian, for example), it is as perpetuators of Greek taste; the rest is discredited as more or less corrupt. Specifically, the moderns have invented nothing that upstages ancient taste in dramatic art.

The *Critische Dichtkunst* does not offer any original theories or theoretical framework. In a preface to a later edition of the text, Gottsched not only admits but stresses this point; he is satisfied with being indebted to the great theorists of past ages. He compares himself to a resourceful bee, collecting ideas here and there as a bee collects pollen.[103] He is a great apologist of the poetics of imitation.[104] For all its derivativeness from Boileau's poetics (which in turn imitated Horace's poetics), Gottsched's *Critische Dichtkunst* borrows ideas and examples from an array of other sources, which (though he likely viewed them as the collective intellectual property of the scholarly *République des Lettres*)[105] are everywhere properly attributed. Apart from *L'Art poétique*, Gottsched draws, for instance, on the *Réflexions sur la rhétorique et sur la poétique: Dialogues sur l'éloquence* by Messire François de Salignac de la Mothe-Fénelon, which appeared in 1685, a decade after Boileau's text. Neither is the versified Boileau treatise in four *chants* (songs) a formal template. The *Critische Dichtkunst* contains extensive quotations from theoretical works by Horace and Boileau, which, like passages from Homer, are reproduced in the original without translation. In the final paragraph, Gottsched sums up his position on national literature and the means of developing it:

> We Germans must make do with translations from the French until we become poets who can themselves produce something regular. This depends only on whether our great men can finally be taught to develop taste for German spectacles: for as long as they are enamoured only of things foreign, there is not much to hope for. (*CD* 196)

(b) J.G. Hamann's 'Aesthetica in nuce: Eine Rhapsodie in kabbalistischer Prose' [Aesthetics in a Nutshell: A Rhapsody in Cabbalistic Prose] (Königsberg, 1762, as part of Kreuzzüge des Philologen *[Crusades of the Philologist])*[106]

A critic's craft has much in common with the rhapsodist's: both have become professional institutions of literary interpretation – the former primarily in print, the latter in an oral culture. The rhapsodist of pre-Homeric and Homeric times was an *active* interpreter: he expressed through the style, force, and accentuation of his performance – declamation – what the critic formulated conceptually and discussed through words on paper. Quoting Plato's Socrates, Hamann calls rhapsodists the 'interpreters of the interpreters' (the latter being the poets themselves) ('AN' 22, note jjj). Indeed, the rhapsodist's recitatory skill lies, as Plato relays to us in *Ion*, in interpreting and praising what the authors, the epic poets whose work he recited, wished to convey (rhapsodists were seldom authors of their texts). Rhapsodizing was applied to one's literary preferences; in other words, it was uncritical. In calling his work a *rhapsody* and in allowing his ideas to unfold the way they do – *eccentrically* – in the text itself, Hamann not merely deliberately departs from the ancient parameters of this literary genre,[107] but also deconstructs contemporary literary-critical practice and idiom.[108] (One would be hard pressed to find another noteworthy literary-critical rhapsody, be it self-styled or not). However, this rhapsody is not a written interpretation of any particular text whose greatness Hamann wishes to extol; although Biblical poetry and Klopstock do take the place of the ancient rhapsodist's poetic material, they do so only obliquely, *cabbalistically*, through metaphor and simile, and the text is as much rhapsodic as it is meta-rhapsodic and metacritical. But before we look at the fabric of Hamann's 'cabbalistic *prose*' (emphasis mine) let us recall Socrates' parting words to the rhapsode Ion, who has thus far failed to define for Socrates the nature of his art:

> No, you are just like Proteus; you twist and turn, this way and that, assuming every shape, until finally you elude my grasp and reveal yourself as a general. And all in order not to show how skilled you are in the lore concerning Homer! So if you are an artist, and ... if you only promised me a display of Homer in order to deceive me, then you are at fault. But if you are not an artist, if by lot divine you are possessed by Homer, and so, knowing nothing, speak many things and fine about the poet, just as I said

> you did, then you do no wrong. Choose, therefore, how you will be called by us, whether we shall take you for a man unjust, or for a man divine.[109]

Ion chooses the latter vocation as the nobler, and the dialogue ends there. But Socrates' position at the conclusion of *Ion* tends to be interpreted as (unsurprisingly) ironic: he does not truly believe in the rhapsode's (or the poet's) divine afflatus and inspiration (*enthousiasmós*) – Plato after all banished poets from his Republic. Yet in another dialogue, *Phaedrus*, Socrates associates a certain kind of madness with prophecy, allowing for its divine origin, and placing it above sanity, reason, and sound judgment (*sophrosune*). Indeed, Hamann put faith in demonic possession of this sort, in the emotions and the senses, just as he was evidently in favour of an anti-rationalist Socrates (a singular view in those days). It is more likely that his ironic disposition was an homage to the self-affirming sense of humour of Plato's 'muse' than that his exuberant rhapsodic pronouncements were themselves marred by irony – that disenchanted modern sense of the futility of one's quest for meaning.

The main part of the 'Aesthetica in nuce' is framed by long quotations from Horace's *Odes*. The first excerpt, preceded by quotations from the Book of Judges and from Job in Hebrew, is Horace's address to Roman youth and bold proclamation of his poetic superiority and originality.[110] Horace speaks of himself as a *sacerdos* of the Muses – interpreter of the sacred and commentator on the arcane. Hamann begins his own text – a 'philological dispute' – by distancing himself from artistic ambition and asserting his role as philologist-critic: 'Not a lyre! Not a painter's brush! A winnowing-fan for my Muse, to clear the threshing floor of holy literature!' (2). As this pairing of arts and instruments is delivered, so to speak, in one breath, Hamann retains for his task – the winnowing, the judgment, of literature – a trace of higher, artistic consciousness. The second long quotation from the *Odes*, which appears near the work's conclusion, returns to the theme of judgment (here, in a divine sense: the coming of the Day of Judgment) (22n98).

That final quotation from Horace is followed by a brief section titled '*Apostille*' [Apostille, or Gloss]. An *apostille* is defined as a philologist's marginal note or annotation – and originally (as *postille*) an explanatory marginalis in the Bible that followed the text. Hamann's *Apostille* is pro forma true to this original positioning. The title implies there being something in need of authorial explanation and, conversely, a difficulty in understanding on the part of the reader. In this case, of course, the author and the apostille writer are one and the same person; the inclusion of an apostille gives the reader the impression that the ambiguities and obscurities of the main text may have been deliberate, and that the author has left their clarification until the end. A *gloss*, however, is also a sophistical or disingenuous explanation, a potential misrepresentation of another's words. This equivocation in the title of the final section seems intentional considering both its consistency with the paronomastic, disjointed, oracular, and idiosyncratic character of Hamann's pronouncements and his vehemently anti-rationalist poetological stance.[111]

The 'Aesthetica' relies heavily on annotation. This feature conforms to the miscellaneous character of the text. In his footnotes, Hamann enlarges on many of his points, polemicizes them further, includes excerpts of relevant texts, and maintains a first-person authorial presence. Examples include, respectively: addition of multiple references to and mini-discussions with a number of writers; quotations from Greek (e.g., Plato), Latin (e.g., Cicero), French (e.g., Voltaire), English (e.g., Pope's 'Essay on Criticism' [1711]), and German texts (e.g., the *Briefe, die neueste Literatur betreffend* critics Nicolai, Lessing, and Mendelssohn); extensive passages from the works of Francis Bacon or Ovid's *Metamorphoses*; and the many instances of self-reflexivity. These diverse and copious footnotes often enter into a dialogue with the main text – naturally not in the sense of contestation, but of supplementation.

It has been noted that the titular 'nutshell' of the 'Aesthetica in nuce' probably comes from the title of Christoph Otto von Schönaich's (1725–1809) work *Die ganze Ästhetik in einer Nuß* [Complete Aesthetics in a Nutshell] (1754) – a satire on Klopstock's Biblical epic poem *Der Messias* [The Messiah] (1748–73) glorifying *heilige Poesie* (sacred poetry).[112] In this light, Hamann's rhapsody – the centrepiece of his collection *Kreuzzüge des Philologen*, has, then, also a retaliatory, polemical character. Like Schönaich's text, the 'Aesthetica' has a satirical thrust, without, however, overtly satirizing the author of *Ästhetik in einer Nuß*. In fact, the main target of Hamann's satire seems have been one Johann David Michaelis (1717–91), a theologian and philologist whose rationalistic approach to the poetic language of the Hebrew Bible offended Hamann's sensibilities.[113] The question remains whether one can find in the 'Aesthetica' a parodical intent with respect to Schönaich's text.

Hamann's text is, in one important sense, a response to the debate on the origin of language then unfolding in French- and German-speaking intellectual milieus. This debate – in which Michaelis and later Herder also took part (receiving academic prizes, in 1759 and 1772, respectively) – frames Hamann's remarks about language and literature, since literature, or that deserving of the name, was very much implicated in determining the origin (animal/evolutionary or divine?) of human speech. Although for Hamann the original idiom was closest to the divine spirit, it was nonetheless innately human, or as Kieffer succinctly phrases it, 'human language corresponds to the divine language represented in the world' (12). Contrary to the accepted view, Hamann was also convinced of the 'total linguisticality of the world' – that language is anterior to perception and thought, which are bounded by it (12–13).[114] For these reasons, content and form cannot be separated. The verity and the sign embodying it constitute a unity (an idea opposed to the dualistic view of language inherited from Antiquity). Logos *is* Creation, the Word the Deed.

The literary-critical import of 'Aesthetica in nuce' is not direct, argument-driven, and cumulative, which is to say, not rationally structured. Rather, it is episodic, construed from motley provocations, scattered allusions, and asides. The form does not resolve intelligibly, mirroring the thought process of someone who believed that there was no getting at 'the origin of language through eighteenth-century philosophical discourse because such discourse, as an advanced form of language, necessarily points the user away from the original idiom' (Kieffer 15). This is not to say that Hamann's point is obscured or lost in his style:

> When Hamann asserts that 'poetic language is the mother tongue of the human race' ... he also claims that language use reveals the speaker's subjectivity precisely because it is always to some extent poetic. But it is Hamann's own rhapsodic style that, by revealing his subjectivity during the act of writing, supplements his theoretical claims for a new type of interpretive practice.[115]

Hamann's '*newest aesthetic, which is the oldest,*' to which he explicitly refers only in the final lines of the 'Aesthetica' – in the section named 'Gloss' (*Apostille*) – seems, if one attempts to gloss it, a mystical imitation of nature as an emanation of God, replicating nature's dynamics as does the Bible ('AN' 23, my emphasis; Kieffer 15).[116] It resembles somewhat late Neoplatonist conceptions, which had a part in the development of Transcendental Idealism and which were present as a minor strand in classicist aesthetics (Wellek, *18C* 17). The faithful path toward true, creative thought is *cabbalistic* in the lay sense of 'esoteric' and 'occult,' as creativity leads to the sacred heart of genesis. Thus, Hamann writes, 'The thinker who wants to intimate to us the schemes which thoughtful writers in a critical place devise in order to convert their unbelieving brethren must have the keys to heaven and hell' ('AN' 9, note w). Herder noticed this dual function of his writings when he wrote of Hamann: 'he *punishes* or *prophesies* ... in the manner of Juno eavesdropping on adulterers or Pythia murmuring oracles in cabbalistic prose' ('FRGL' 156).

Hamann's text effectively *performs* his aesthetic and philological approach. The 'Aesthetica' describes itself as 'cabbalistic,' and in this sense it represents the aesthetic theory it *contains in a nutshell*. '[S]o do not think ill of me,' writes Hamann self-consciously, 'if I speak to you like the ghost in *Hamlet*, with signs and beckonings, until I have a proper occasion to declare myself in *sermones fideles*'; in other words, I will speak hermetic 'nonsense' until I can find plain and true expressions ('AN' 21).[117] Elsewhere in the text, he muses: 'If some modern Levite were to take passing note of this rhapsody ... "Oh no, thou one possessed, thou Samaritan" – (that is how he will scold the philologist in his heart) – "for readers of orthodox tastes, low expressions and unclean vessels are not proper"' (6).[118] Would it, then, be an exaggeration to suggest that Hamann's quotation from Bacon about the optimal way of reading the Scriptures indirectly pertains to reading his own 'cabbalistic prose'?

> [T]hey are not to be interpreted only according to the latitude and obvious sense of the place; or with respect to the occasion whereon the words were uttered; or in precise context with the words before or after; or in contemplation of the principal scope of the passage; but we must consider them to have in themselves, not only totally or collectively, but distributively also in clauses and words, infinite springs and streams of doctrines, to water every part of the Church and the souls of the faithful. ('AN' 8, note u)

If the above suggestion is an overstatement, it is because of its inconsistency with Hamann's own reading of Scripture, which would not permit the presumption of comparing his cabbalistic prose to the poetry of the Holy Writ. Hamann cites Bacon's advice on avoiding two kinds of 'excesses' when reading Scripture: 'The one presupposes such perfection in Scripture, that all philosophy likewise should be derived from its sources; as if all other philosophy were something profane and heathen ... The other [excessive] method [that] appears at the first glance sober and modest ... [is] when the divinely inspired Scriptures are explained in the same way as human writings.' It is particularly noteworthy that Hamann prefaces the above quotation with the words: 'the following passage [from Bacon] ... may help guard me against the crude and ignorant idea of pronouncing the present imitation of cabbalistic style to be good or bad.' So while, at numerous points in his text, Hamann intimates his valorization and cultivation of something resembling Biblical diction and rhythm (consider, for example, the line: 'Speak that I may see Thee! This wish was answered by the Creation, which is an utterance to created things through created things, for day speaketh unto day, and night proclaimeth unto night' [4]), the profane word remains incommensurate with the divine word – an ideal and the ultimate measure of aesthetic achievement.

Hamann extrapolates from God's Authorship the law of interpretive Authority (whether it is generalizable to human authorship is another matter):

> The author is the best interpreter of his words [he is referring to God and Scripture]. He may speak through created things and through events – or through blood and fire and vapour and smoke, for these constitute the sacramental language ... The unity of the great Author is mirrored even in the dialect of his works – in all of them a tone of immeasurable height and depth! ('AN' 10)

He goes on to refer to Klopstock as 'that great restorer of lyric song' whose writing is a 'happy imitation of the mysterious workings of sacred poetry among the ancient Hebrews' (21).[119] He takes issue ironically with 'delicate' (*feinen*) and 'most thorough' (*gründlichsten*) critics (*Kunstrichter*), whose incompetence leads them to dismiss Klopstock's prosody of *vers libre* as 'artificial prose' (*künstliche Prose*).[120] He phrases his defence conditionally and through litotes: 'Despite the gibberish of my dialect [*kauderwelschen Mundart*], I would willingly acknowledge Herr Klopstock's prosaic manner to be a model of classical perfection.' Hamann's idea of classical perfection, however, differed from the norm: what he admired in Klopstock was his Christian piety and biblical language.[121]

In its stylistic ebullience, metaphoricity, idiosyncracy, and wit, Hamann's writing defies the status quo of Enlightenment classicism. In the 'Aesthetica in nuce,' he identifies himself as a cabbalistic philologist who considers language as a subject of inquiry 'in subjective, aesthetic terms' (Kieffer 15). His preferred method of interpretation was a hermeneutic, textual criticism seeded by biblical exegesis and enabling not merely a better understanding of the *word* (the text), but its rebirth in the *spirit of the letter*.

> Ascribe the fault to the foolishness of my way of writing, which accords so ill with the original mathematical sin of your oldest writing, and still less with the witty rebirth of your most recent works, if I borrow an example from the spelling-book which doubtless may be older than the Bible. Do the elements of the ABC lose their natural meaning, if in their infinite combinations into arbitrary signs they remind us of ideas which dwell, if not in heaven, then in our brains? But if we raise up the whole deserving righteousness of a scribe upon the dead body of the letter, what sayeth the spirit to that? Shall he be but a groom of the chamber to the dead letter, or perhaps a mere esquire to the deadening letter? ('AN' 9)

The procedure Hamann is obliquely critiquing is that of standard biblical exegesis. Here is how Leventhal outlines it: 'the interpreter first sought to explicate the text in terms of the disciplines of grammar, text criticism and the canon of interpretation; only after the explication of the primary meanings was the interpreter in a position to *apply* the text, to make the text have a meaning in terms of the specific context or situation' (*DI* 201).

In the 'Gloss' section, the final part of the 'Aesthetica in nuce,' Hamann turns his critical attention to himself, referring to himself in the third person, and applying the law of interpretive authority:

> As the oldest reader of this Rhapsody ... I feel obliged to bequeath ... one more example of a merciful judgement, as follows: Everything in this aesthetic nutshell tastes of vanity, vanity! The Rhapsodist has read, observed, reflected, sought and found agreeable words, quoted faithfully, gone round about like a merchant ship and brought his far-fetched cargo home. He has calculated sentence for sentence as arrows are counted on a battle-field ... Instead of stakes and arrows he has, with the amateurs and pedants of his time, ... written obelisks and asterisks. ('AN' 22)

The self-deprecating judgment Hamann passes on himself *as rhapsodist* is 'merciful' by the standards of Hamann *the author*, who has given himself full licence as his best *critic*: once again, an ironic position, like Socrates' toward Ion. Hamann's eccentric position in the German Enlightenment, his prioritization of the religious, Judaeo-Christian tradition over the secular legacy of the ancients gives us a sense of what was at stake. If Hamann sees himself as having acted in vain, it is because his text as a whole is an *apostille*: a marginalized discourse, an unauthorized postscript. On the other hand, he has not sufficiently broken with his prosaic contemporaries, the 'amateurs and pedants of his time.' He writes with them, like them (in his own opinion at least), and for them. He thinks and writes in an abstract (mathematical) culture removed from the language of divine revelation. He necessarily writes *prose* because his meaning is not part of nature's poetry; poetic language is inaccessible to him. His prose is rhapsodic in that it pays homage by rendering and delivering what it cannot beget. In this aesthetics, what appears to be the newest (by Enlightenment standards, non-traditional and dubious) is in fact the oldest (by Hamann's standards, the most traditional and foundational).

Another formally interesting feature of Hamann's writing is that he relegates to the footnotes astute critical comments and direct references to various thinkers, often contextualizing them in his reading experiences. 'If he [George Benson (1699–1762)] has tried to convey some earthly propositions about the unity of reading, his thoroughness would strike us more strongly. One cannot leaf through the four volumes of this paraphrastic explanation without a sly smile, nor miss the frequent passages ...' ('AN' 9, note w). Another such comment is made in reference to Luther's 'Preface to the Epistle to the Romans,' 'which I never weary of reading. Just as I never tire of his Preface to the Psalms' (18, note ccc). These *embodied* reading/writing experiences are sometimes more personal and amusing: 'I have, unfortunately, only a defective copy' (of the punning *Ars Punica*) (18, note bbb) or 'The devout reader will be able to complete the hymnic cadence of this section for himself. My memory abandons me out of sheer willfulness,' and he serves us a Horatian excuse: 'Ever hastening to the end ... and what he cannot hope to accomplish ... he omits' (19, note ddd). The role of these rather inconspicuous elements seems to be sabotage of rationalistic abstraction. This is apparent in an instance (this time in the body of the text) of embodied contrariness: 'to place this small detail in the appropriate light ... compare it with several other phenomena, trace their causes and develop their fruitful consequences would take too much time' (22).

(c) G.E. Lessing's Laokoon, oder über die Grenzen der Malerei und Poesie *[Laocoon, or on the Limits of Painting and Poetry] (Part 1, in Berlin, 1766; second, expanded edition including the 'Paralipomena' in 1788)*[122]

The *Laokoon*, part 1, is often referred to as a treatise. It consists of twenty-nine chapters with a preface (*Vorrede*). The text is annotated, the footnotes containing critical and polemical statements, digressive lines of argument, additional textual examples, or citations. Chapters 26–9 are no longer concerned with the main argument, but contain a discussion of Winckelmann's monumental *Geschichte der Kunst des Altertums* [History of the Art of Antiquity], which appeared in 1764, in the interval between when the *Laokoon* was written and when it was published. Lessing's prose style tends to be described as lucid and rigorous, and the *Laokoon* is no exception. It is literary criticism at a considerable remove from the literary object: theoretically grounded, comparative (between two artistic mediums), disciplined, intelligible, un-poetic. We should not, however, infer from the above mundane characteristics that the *Laokoon* is an example of the conventions of scholarly and philosophical form at the time. In fact, it is – in principle and in practice – a significant departure from it, self-consciously informing its reader of its unconventional status in the very first pages.

Lessing was a proponent of classicist aesthetics inspired by Winckelmann's pioneering study of ancient art, which evinced an almost intimate familiarity with sculpture.[123] He was also a fierce opponent of the dated classicism of Gottsched and his followers as a slavish imitation of French models. Instead, he proposed a return to the original Classical sources and reappraised the works of Shakespeare, dismissed by the French as grotesque. The *Laokoon* is one of the best-known works of enlightened *German* classicism, that is to say, a classicism that bypassed the French Classicist doctrine in search of a specifically German link to Antiquity. Its premise is a seemingly minor disagreement with Winckelmann's ethical (as opposed to strictly aesthetic) interpretation of the Laocoon sculpture as the expression of 'noble simplicity and quiet grandeur.' But this point turns on the greater issue of the fundamental distinctions between the visual and the literary art that the Laocoon, among other works, serves to demonstrate. Accordingly, in discussing literature, Lessing draws upon a vast array of Greco-Roman texts, among them Aristotle, Homer, Horace, Longinus, and Virgil, as well as Italian, contemporary French, and English authors (including

Pope and Shakespeare), and his contemporaries Winckelmann, Mendelssohn, and the polymath A. von Haller.

The *Laokoon* owes a part of its renown to a sophisticated polemical and dialogical style.[124] This approach to discursivity allows Lessing, in the process of articulating his own normative position, to not only take issue with divergent views, but also to engage them and extract what is of value for his project (without dismissing them across the board). Another feature of Lessing's style is its essayistic quality. The chapters of the *Laokoon* function as mini-essays, stages in the heuristic of truth (as opposed to its upfront propositional communication), with references to the tentative nature of conclusions, and informal and witty turns of phrase. In effect, the entire work has a less-than-systematic, quasi-episodic structure. That being said, Wellek's observation on Lessing's criticism – that it was 'sometimes marred by the demands of an existence absorbed in literary journalism and thus in the necessity of writing on ephemeral topics of the day and also by the acerbities and brutalities of contemporary polemical manners' (*18C* 152) – does not apply to the *Laokoon*.

The preface to the *Laokoon* opens with a sketch of three discursive domains. In a few precise strokes, Lessing describes three figures through their distinct approaches to art, only later revealing their titles. Thus, he places the literary/art critic (*Kunstrichter*) alongside the amateur (*Liebhaber*) and the philosopher, as one 'who examined the value and distribution of these general rules [of art], [and] observed that some of them are more predominant in painting, others in poetry.'[125] This introduction offers insight into the contemporary discursive situation, as well as into the importance, if not of establishing specializations of inquiry into artistic production, then at least of maintaining discursive rubrics during a time of ferment for German-language reflection about art and literature. But Lessing's systematic does not only stem from a need to organize and formalize emerging discursivities; it is likewise a redrawing of old discursive boundaries. Thanks to the third figure's – the critic's – observation of the differences between painting and poetry, 'poetry can help to explain and illustrate painting, and ... painting can do the same for poetry' ('L' 3). The rhetorical seamlessness of one art form 'explaining' and 'illustrating' the other is predicated upon the critic's literal invisibility: his kind of mediation is so (at once) indispensable and unobtrusive as to be effaced in the process of the arts' mutual illumination.

In contrasting the critic's task with the figures of the amateur and the philosopher, Lessing maintains that 'The first two could not easily misuse their feelings or their conclusions. With the critic, however, the case was different. The principal value of his observations depends on their correct application to the individual case' ('L' 3). For every one 'discerning' (*scharfsinnig*) critic there are scores of 'clever' (*witzige*) ones. This inflated statistic suggests that considerable skill, taste, discipline, and experience are needed to fulfil the proper task of criticism. The critic's task, as Lessing will go on to delineate it, is to discriminate, to compare and contrast, to remark on identities and differences – with 'mere analogies furnishing neither proof nor justification' and, as Foucault put it, silenced to a 'murmur' (*OT* 119). Lessing then targets the (in his day) widely accepted doctrine expressed – by way of Horace's *ut pictura poesis* – in a dictum by Simonides of Ceos: 'Painting is silent poetry; poetry eloquent painting.' Exposing *correspondance des arts* as a flawed way of defining and distinguishing between the two provinces of art, and arguing for their intrinsic dissimilarity, Lessing sets out to rectify and effectively redefine critical standards, which continue to either try to 'force poetry into the narrower limits of painting' or 'allow painting to fill the whole wide space of poetry' ('L' 4–5) – a mutual compromise that homogenizes the two but says nothing about the *limits* of each independently. To this widespread belief Lessing responds with an idea from Plutarch – which is also the motto for the *Laokoon* – that 'the two arts differed … in the objects imitated as well as in the manner of imitation' (4). But he somewhat radicalizes the difference referred to in this proposition into a semiological one – of 'means or signs' (78).

To counteract the 'false taste' (*falsch Geschmack*) that corrupts both forms of artistic production, whose carrier is a 'spurious' or 'pseudo-' criticism (*Aftercritik*) – its 'unfounded judgments' and 'ill-digested conclusions' uttered 'with the greatest self-assurance' – 'is the principal aim of the following chapters' ('L' 4–5). Here, then, Lessing challenges the critical establishment for its reductive approach to different art forms, which by focusing on their common denominator strips these forms of their autonomy. The first announcement of a *redefinition of both art forms by their limitations* comes in the *Laokoon's* title. Lessing commences his work by outlining the formal and semiotic differences between literature ('Poetry') and art ('Painting'), by noting what is *permissible* in one but not in the other. It is the denial of limits – a mistake the ancients resisted by 'restricting Simonides' statement to the effect achieved by the two arts' – that irks him most about the modern theoretical enterprise (4). He sees this as a result of modern arrogance: 'in many respects we moderns have considered ourselves far superior [to the ancients] when we transformed their pleasant little lanes into our highways, even though shorter and safer highways themselves become mere footpaths as they lead through wilderness.'

Lessing goes on to explain the reference to the Laocoon group in his title, while simultaneously preparing his reader for the argument and evidence which lie ahead: 'Since I started, as it were, with the Laocoon and return to it a number of times, I wished to give it a share in the title too. Other short digressions on various points of ancient art history contribute less to my intent and are included only because I can never hope to find a more suitable place for them' ('L' 5–6). With these words Lessing distances himself not only from artistic unity, for which he would strive in his dramatic works, but also from the customary systematic presentation of critical arguments,[126] opting for a less orderly *cluster of ideas*, and a main argument surrounded by a number of divagations. The book stands as a collection of thoughts, not of final pronouncements: his repudiation of one erroneous reading (Winckelmann's) occasions a series of reflections on laws already laid out. He appraises his contribution in this modest comment on methodology (or lack thereof): 'They were written as chance dictated and more in keeping with my reading than through any systematic development of general principles. Hence,' he instructs, 'they are to be regarded more as unordered *collectanea* for a book [*unordentliche Collectanea zu einem Buche*] than as a book itself' (5, modified; 'LGMP' 15).[127]

In other words, the *Laokoon* is not (to be read as) another philosophical treatise, a 'systematic book,' but a text that resists easily identifiable genre designations without ceding its authority, a work without a set aesthetic doctrine, one that is more intuitive, experimental, even essayistic, to the extent that it follows its author's thought process rather than just its results. The text consciously distinguishes itself as falling outside existing genres: it is not to be treated (or used) as a primer, a classicist poetics, a manual of 'rules' for generating poetry. It lowers the reader's expectation, on the one hand, and, on the other, inspires curiosity about how we can be convinced differently and learn from discursive forms/frames not associated with learned investigations. The preface makes also direct reference to two of Lessing's contemporaries: Alexander Gottlieb Baumgarten (1714–62) and the popular classicist poet and painter Salomon Gessner (1730–88). Baumgarten, the father of aesthetic philosophy, used examples from Gessner, and so will Lessing. With this genealogical gesture, Lessing officially establishes his *Laokoon* within the newly emergent German discourse of aesthetics. It is clear which side of history Lessing is on: decidedly the modern.

I now turn to selected passages from the main text of the *Laokoon*, which are at once the culminating parts of Lessing's argument and some of the richest in the above-named formal qualities. Chapters 16 and 17 reveal fully two dominant features of Lessing's work: consciousness of its own discursivity (which may coincide with but is not the method/process of composition), and an internally dialogical structure. Chapter 16 begins with the following 'statement of purpose': 'But I shall attempt now to derive the matter from its first principles. I reason [*schließe*] thus: if it is true ...' ('L' 78; 'LGMP' 116). Here Lessing offers several relevant definitions/propositions and further emphasizes the deductive process by setting them off in short paragraphs. Lower down, he writes: 'I should put little faith in this dry chain of conclusions [*trockene Schlußkette*]' – an auto-critical remark, which ultimately makes the following discovery much more convincing – 'did I not find it completely confirmed by the praxis of Homer, or rather if it had not been just this praxis that led me to my conclusions [the above *Schlußkette*]' ('L' 79, modified; 'LGMP' 117). Through this conditional statement, the author presents himself as someone capable of both dispassionate self-scrutiny and scholarly enthusiasm, and if his chain of reasoning appears dry, it is because one must be mindful of bias when formulating one's opinions. Moreover, the proposition is not a hypothesis later confirmed, but a *conclusion* based on prior research. Lessing moves from elaborating his theory 'to analyz[ing] the style of Homer more closely' ('L' 79). Despite this seeming digression, the discussion of Homer's style is still meant to test Lessing's central point: that Homer depicts progressive actions and avoids description wherever it does not serve the action. As elsewhere in the book, the observation is followed by an abundance of examples (rendered in the original Greek, Latin, English, and French, and in German). The chapter ends rather suddenly – literally cut short by authorial exigency. 'If I were to set down all the examples of this sort, I should never finish the task [*Art*, meaning also 'form' or 'kind']. They will occur in great numbers to everyone who is familiar with his Homer' (84; 'LGMP' 123).[128] Truncating his Homeric examples accomplishes two things: it lets him promptly move on to his next point without much formal ado, and it makes his claim more compelling (by creating the impression that examples in support of his opinion could continue ad infinitum, which in turn projects the author's confidence in the truth of his claim).

Leventhal notes that 'Lessing's insistence on application and his immersion in his examples as a critic are not at all inconsistent with his critique of the instrumentalization of tradition for specific literary-theoretical interests' (*DI* 12). The example of Homer's style supports this; Homer is not treated instrumentally but as a genuine (potential) impediment to the theory's formulation. Chapter 17 begins with a dialogical 'But the objection [*Einwurf*] will be raised ...' This objection is, in the next paragraph, unpacked as a 'twofold [*doppelten*] objection,' to which Lessing says he 'shall reply' ('L' 85). The doubling of the objection (elaborated by Lessing) and the challenge this poses would serve to strengthen the overall argument insofar as both objections are refuted convincingly, with 'a correct deduction [*ein richtiger Schluß*]' valid even 'without examples [*ohne Exempel*]' (85; 'LGMP' 123). But the 'double' of the objection as initially raised appears to be Lessing's bane: it is his own weakness for Homer (as example), as if counter to his theoretical argument, which carries weight with him ('bei mir von Wichtigkeit ist') even when he is unable 'to justify it by means of deduction [*durch keinen Schluß*].'

We soon come across another token of the dialogical set-up – Lessing again raises an objection (which can never be a full opposition), posed by way of prosopopoeia, to something already stated and responds to it. The next paragraph begins with a concession ('It is true that ...') to an imaginary/potential interlocutor who is immediately shown up as missing the semiotic specificity of literature. This structure is repeated throughout the entire text. It reappears, for instance, in the next chapter and is signalled by the interjection 'it will be said' ('L' 94). This is an *engaging* way of writing, in the sense that our objections seem intermittently articulated and addressed, if not resolved. The technique is effective in that the reader feels his concerns, or concerns *like* his, are being taken seriously; in those moments he is placed on an equal footing with the writer. The reader, inasmuch as he identifies his views with the objections, feels himself involved in the process of rectifying errors, of improving the logical progression, of tightening and strengthening the argumentation of the principal author.

Of course, Lessing's dialogizing of his ideas renders his knowledge a product of an internal conversation; the process is meant to represent his own reasoning – and awareness of its critics – as it attempts to refine itself and arrive at a less biased opinion. The technique, whether a genuine personal aid or a rhetorical device, is among the means that allowed the *Laokoon* to provoke *fermenta cogitionis* and fulfil 'the performative function of activating … critical sensibility.'[129] At every point in which this structure is repeated, however, the buoyancy of Lessing's argument seems in momentary jeopardy. This would pose a problem if Lessing were indeed composing a 'philosophical treatise'; but since the text explicitly asks to be read as an assemblage of 'unordered collectanea,' any risk to its order or coherence would be a contradiction in terms. What for another type of text would be deleterious, is for Lessing vital and invigorating. Yet despite the brevity of each chapter, of each miniature *essay*, the periodic interlocking of propositions, objections, and examples, the text's critical construction is a largely seamless weave. The impression of seamlessness arises from the reader quickly becoming used to this internally dialogical pattern.

Lessing ties in his discussion in chapter 17 with his earlier explanation (in chapter 16) of the properties of the 'poetic picture,' and changes his focus to the objects suitable for poetic 'painting.' He is engaging conventional critical terminology – however much such terminology may be in need of revision. In the paragraphs immediately following, he describes his own vision of the sensory-perceptual process for spatial objects. Here (as elsewhere) he encourages the reader to partake in the process of reasoning with phrasing such as 'let us assume' (*gesetzt*), or underscores a point by 'I say' (*sage Ich*) or variations on it ('L' 86, 88). This is as close as one can come to empowering the reader without sounding patronizing (that is, if the reader follows the arguer's logic). Although Lessing is credited with informing, never with fooling, his audience, one cannot help but notice that a susceptible reader, thus encouraged to agree and prodded to 'see for himself,' might become so accustomed to the undeniable soundness of the reasoning, that he is at risk of accepting Lessing's claims without closer examination.

In chapter 18, we find evidence of what was already advertised in the preface as both contrived and spontaneous – the work's digressive, uneven character. 'But I am lingering over trifles,' Lessing owns up, 'and it may appear as if I were going to forget the shield, the shield of Achilles' – the foremost example of ancient 'poetic painting' ('L' 94). We are also reminded of Homer's poetry (and his Greek tongue) as a potential exception to Lessing's rule of poetic language. But exceptionality to the rule is ultimately not granted even to Homeric verse. Homer is shown to be, on the one hand, conforming to and, on the other, codifying and exemplifying the Classical rules of poetry. While Lessing is ostensibly demonstrating the need for distinct standards for ancient and modern art (deducing them from the respective aesthetic and discursive practices), and *not* submitting universal rules for art, but defining only the qualities of its existence by 'a posteriori explanations' (the titular *beiläufige Erläuterungen*), he inevitably ends up in the aprioristic and normative woods of theory. He imposes definitive 'regularities' upon past art and ultimately prescribes some of these 'rules' for the present, however disguised they are in their theoretical generality. They support his invective against so-called 'descriptive' poetry (at least in German or French, where the grammatical rules hinder the immediacy of part following part).

Through Lessing's compelling rhetoric in *Laokoon*, we are constantly made to identify both with the opposing/sceptical stance toward Lessing's reasoning, which the author then addresses in productive dialogue, and with the author himself in his attempts to formulate, refine, and defend his position for 'us moderns' – the locution 'wir Neuern' appears on several crucial occasions, signalling that this is an appeal to a new public. Near the end of chapter 18, a series of sentences utilizes the first-person plural construction to appeal to shared experience in support of the author's claims and include us in the enjoyment of the rewards of diligent reasoning. It features the example of the Achillean shield. Here, with increasing dramatic momentum, Lessing guides us toward the right understanding of the art work and art form ('Homer does not paint the shield as finished and complete, but as a shield that is being made'), grants us an eyewitness's perspective on the artistic process ('We do not see the shield, but the divine master as he is making it ... We do not lose sight of him until all is finished'), and, finally, the end result ('Now the shield is complete, and we marvel at the work. But it is the believing wonder of the eyewitness who has seen it forged') ('L' 95).

The supposed descriptive superiority of Homer is again acknowledged, this time more elaborately. Lessing, however, dismisses the possibility of it being an exception outright: 'My answer to this particular objection is that I have already answered it' ('L' 95). Homer, in fact, is *not* a descriptive poet and no exception; rather, he paints in the true spirit of Poetry – *actions*, not objects, and this distinction Lessing draws with remarkable clarity. This shows another facet of the complicity of readership spoken of earlier; here, however, the reader, no longer an insider asked to corroborate or verify, has become enlisted on the other side, the outside, and treated as opposition – mercilessly, condescendingly, and subtly put to shame.

While in chapters 1–25 Lessing treats of various theoretical issues surrounding the two mediums and analyses in great detail their ancient examples, chapters 26–9 turn specifically to a contemporary work of scholarship – Winckelmann's *Geschichte der Kunst des Altertums*. The main issue for Lessing is no doubt the accuracy of Winckelmann's dating of the Laocoon statue, which links this part to the earlier chapters. The excursus thus takes care of 'unfinished business': Lessing lays out his argument and evidence for a more recent date. It is, however, followed by a chapter-long general review of the *Geschichte*.

In fact, chapters 26–9 assume the shape of one long *Rezension* if one takes note of the announcement opening chapter 26: 'Herr Winckelmann's *History of Art* has appeared, and I shall not venture another step until I have read it' ('L' 138). But its thorough reading is delayed until the last chapter; drawing on shared readerly experience, Lessing admits, 'We usually leaf through an important work before beginning to read it.' The book's appearance allows Lessing, first of all, to learn Winckelmann's thoughts about one pressing and relevant issue, and to contest them. It also presents an occasion for restating his position on such empirical case studies of ancient art as he himself has just engaged in and as he finds in Winckelmann, which 'speculation may boldly follow.' He writes: 'To speculate subtly on art merely on the basis of general ideas might lead us to fanciful conclusions, which sooner or later and to our shame we should find refuted in the works or art.' Not only is ancient art the keeper of its own verities, but the ancients also knew the true 'bonds connecting painting and poetry, and they have not, I believe, drawn them more tightly than was advantageous to both.' In Lessing's view, this justifies the normative interpretation of his ancient findings. 'What their artists did will teach me what artists in general should do' – the ancients teach the truth about beauty through the ages.

The next few pages present the problem of the Laocoon's dating, at once acknowledging and undermining the authority of Winckelmann's estimation. Lessing then marshals evidence for an alternative date based on his close analysis of passages from Pliny. Chapter 28 contests Winckelmann's identification of another ancient statue; again Lessing offers his own idea. In chapter 29, he begins the more general part of his review by stating that, despite the erudition of the work, there are more errors to be found in the *Geschichte*. The value of Winckelmann's work is borne out by the inconsequential nature of these 'minor' inaccuracies (such 'as anyone might have avoided'), which Lessing is quick to ascribe 'simply [to] slips of memory' ('L' 157, 156). Lessing feigns reluctance in naming these apparently numerous mistakes, and stops at correcting a symbolic few. Immediately after doing so, he concludes the

Laokoon. The halting construction should by now seem familiar: 'But I shall refrain from accumulating more such trifles. It could scarcely be taken as censoriousness, but anyone who knows my high regard for Herr Winckelmann might consider it *krokylegmus* [pedantic quibbling]' (157). Lessing's consciousness of the insubstantial nature of the flaws he has pointed out leads him to pre-empt criticism of the insubstantiality of his own judgment. Everything considered, the inclusion of these increasingly digressive discussions in the final four chapters of the *Laokoon* fulfils Lessing's promise of *collectanea* for a book, instead of a book proper. Absent these chapters, the *Laokoon* would be much more systematic.

(d) J.G. von Herder's Über die neuere deutsche Literatur: Erste Sammlung von Fragmenten, als Beilage zu den 'Briefen, die neueste Literatur betreffend' *[On Recent German Literature: First Collection of Fragments, as Supplement to the Letters concerning Most Recent Literature] (Riga, 1766)*[130]

Herder's first collection of fragments, eighteen in all, was (like the second and third collections which appeared shortly afterward) a response to the twenty-four volumes of the *Briefe, die neueste Literatur betreffend* – a periodical Herder held to be of great literary-critical and literary-historical merit. Similarly to the work on which he was commenting, whose five authors concealed their identities under pseudonyms, Herder published all three of his fragment collections anonymously. But the anonymous *fragments*, which are also described in the preface as commentaries (*Beiträge*) and supplements (*Beilagen*),[131] served Herder as an occasion to substantially develop his views on language in relation to national literature and German literary history.[132] They are commonly taken to frame the beginning of Sturm und Drang (Menze and Menges 281n9).

What makes these texts fragmentary? Their presentation forms at least a palpable unity: a 'collection' by the author himself, organized by subject (language as foundation for a national literature and intellectual culture in the first collection) and furnished with a metacritical preface (*Vorrede*), a descriptive table of contents (*Inhalt*), an introduction (*Einleitung*), and a conclusion (*Beschluß*).[133] At first, the fragmentariness of these 'fragments' appears to be more nominal than real. (One would sooner acknowledge the *entire* project – all three collections taken together – as fragmentary, because left incomplete as per its design: of the four collections initially planned only three appeared.) However, the 'fragments' often overlap, obscuring the line of argumentation and hindering a systematic treatment of the issues. Within each fragment, the paragraph format is roughly: *quotation* from *Briefe*, followed by *discussion* – although this does not contribute to thematic systematicity. Therefore, the impression given by many pieces is indeed that of incompleteness. To be sure, Herder's remarks on choosing this form fall short of a theory of the fragment – such as was later to be voiced in the *Athenäum* fragments.[134] At the same time, a passage about his work's formal, fragmentary composition equals – in its subtle self-referentiality and expressivity – the Romantic poetic temperament:

> I collect the notes to the letters and expand their purview, then again I limit it, or digress. I take apart and sew together, perhaps in order to fashion the supple whole of a pantin. As far as I can see, I am free to do so, for if the letters cut paths for themselves across others' fertile soil, I may, to the advantage of the owners, plow them under again. If they have led rivers into some deserts, I may navigate these streams. If they have, here and there, discovered islands in the sea, so I may yet look for the mainland. ('FRGL' 89)

This gives the impression that the fragment was above all a form of modesty, in that Herder could not hope to equal but merely wanted to take advantage of the magnitude of the accomplishment of the *Briefe*.[135]

According to the editors of the English translation, Herder's *fragmentary* method of supplementation makes him a participant 'with Lessing, Nicolai, and others in a new literary discourse that signifies in its formal components a departure from the systematic treatise in the tradition of Cartesian rationalism' (such as that of Wolff or his disciple Baumgarten). 'Basing his approach,' they continue, 'on the open-endedness of the fragment, which precludes the canonization of knowledge, Herder proceeds to "fill the gaps" in the "edifice" of a German literary history ...' (Menze and Menges 281n38). Herder, in fact, draws explicit parallels between the forms used in the novel venture that was the *Briefe* and his fragments: 'they speak only of patchworks and reflections, as I speak of *Fragments*; thus, they do not wish to have their work evaluated as a [doctrinal] system' ('FRGL' 97). He is also grateful to those who 'sometimes resort to their favorite mode of expression in order to speak randomly about a subject: epistles, preludes, and episodes, which are worth more than entire critical essays.' Methodological/ideological fragmentation is thus a form of opposing the stuffiness and, despite their breadth, the narrowness of perspective in longer, more tightly structured works. Briefer and less cohesive forms, not conventionally used for written critical evaluation, offer much more linguistic/stylistic, and thus intellectual,[136] freedom to a writer labouring under the felt constraints of treatise- and essay-writing. Titling his work 'collection of fragments' is strategic: it allows him licence to say many different, loose, and often scattered things, to speak *directly* to specific passages in the *Briefe*. In this sense, the 'choice' of fragmentation may have been equally a matter of expediency, since Herder continued to write non-fragmentary, more conventional prose (for which he incurred Hamann's critique). To make the formal motivation of this text more complex, its self-identification as 'fragments' may have been a rhetorical gambit (understatement), which protects and pre-empts criticism. (Still more complexity is added when we consider that participation with mere 'fragments' is a more unassuming contribution to literary discourse, in accord with Herder's intention of offering 'private' opinions [see below].)

What of 'supplementarity'? Does the supplement-status of the *Fragmente* (implicitly not measuring up to the original) compromise the discursive authority of Herder's project? Recent opinion inverts this hierarchy of discursive status: 'The *Literaturbriefe* represent first and foremost modern literary criticism; the *Fragmente*, on the other hand, are more ambitious, in that they often launch into questions regarding a contemporary theory of aesthetics' (Menze and Menges 270). Herder does not concern himself with individual reviews but with adjudging the whole of German literature, and thus assumes a synoptic historical perspective ('I wish only to instruct myself about the literature of my fatherland and sketch a silhouette [also, 'a portrait'] of that literature over the past six years' ['FRGL' 89]). In fact, he distances himself from criticism as a 'public service' (review criticism): 'I do not appoint myself a judge in the name of the public, an office for which I do not trust myself to have sufficient calling ... That is really a vocation that has become as canonical today in the world of literature as it appears to us *apocryphal* in the Bible' (88). Instead, Herder prefers to pass 'private judgment, to do no more than lend my voice' (the distinction between public and private makes sense if one considers that the *Fragmente* appeared anonymously and independently of periodical venues). His answer to a hypothetical question about the timing of his publication is that the discourse of a 'famous critic' (the *Briefe*) should be uninterrupted until it concludes, that, in other words, one should respectfully await one's turn. 'But *after the work is completed*, one may judge indeed!' (This unwritten critical code of conduct was breached in Herder's case, when the journal *Deutsche Bibliothek der schönen Wissenschaften und der freien Künste*[137] criticized his *Fragmente* before their completion, distracting Herder from finishing his work [Menze and Menges 273].) '[T]hereupon,' Herder continues, 'it is fitting to produce *a few small supplements* to the twenty-four volumes ...' ('FRGL' 88, emphasis mine). If one reads the text's self-humbling 'supplementarity' against the grain – in terms of the anti-binary, 'differantial' logic of the *supplément* (as both addition and substitution)[138] – Herder's 'supplements' are indebted to the *Literaturbriefe* as a pioneering critical project that inspired Herder's own critical stance. They are at the same time 'guided by,' build on, 'pass judgment,' and improve upon (i.e., supplant) the *Briefe* ('FRGL' 89).[139] In 1766, Herder had not yet the aversion to classicist doctrine for which he would eventually become known (the sporadic polemical remarks are reserved for Lessing, the most reverential comments for his teacher Abbt) (Menze and Menges 270). The ambiguity of Herder's text's intent – filling the gaps left for it by the *Briefe* (gaps presupposing it), as well as contesting the *Briefe* – is inherent to the text's self-affirmation as supplement.

At the end of his metacritical introduction – where he indeed *reviews* and compares three journals and acknowledges their 'service to the development of German taste,' Herder re-establishes the *Literaturbriefe* as (with reservations) the most exemplary of the group and the object of his commentary ('FRGL' 99). It it here that, in a separate paragraph, he sketches how he will proceed: he will be commenting, agreeing with, and objecting to passages found in the *Briefe*. After his earlier comments on the implications of *excerpting* (pedantry, indulgence, lack of opinion), he declares that whenever he passes judgment ('objects' or 'agrees'), he will 'merely cite' instead of excerpt. 'Thus I avoid the tone of the faultfinder and the eulogist,' he concludes, 'and enter into a mimelike dialogue with some authors, as it was reported by the Greek oracle; [The Lord ... neither tells nor conceals but indicates]' (99). 'Mimelike dialogue' is here meant as the gesture of sending 'the reader who owns the work to refer to the citations himself' (otherwise the pantomime becomes charade).

Herder's valorization of translations (mainly from Greek, Latin, and English, but also from the French) and the study of historical idioms (e.g., Old Norse) are the constellation around his theory of the essential differences between oral culture ('language of song') and written culture ('book language') and the evolution of language from the sensuous, immediate, and poetic into the abstract and prosaic ('FRGL' 160).[140] The enriching potential of translations is evident when one considers that Herder thought poetry 'almost untranslatable': in the pursuit of equivalence, new 'harmony, rhyme, parts of speech, composition of words, phrasing' (165) must be invented in the target language. These ideas find expression in the theatricality and originality of Herder's style, which, in his 1772 essay on language, culminated in an 'outrageous hodgepodge of idioms and languages'[141] (although Herder championed German above all).

In Fragment 1, Herder appeals to critics in general: 'know you language ... and seek to shape it ... Thereupon, ... provide tools for the [prose] writer; for the poet forge thunderbolts, render resplendent the rhetorician's armor, and sharpen the philosopher's arms' ('FRGL' 101). For Herder, critical judgment is inseparable from critical idiom; when one falters, so does the other. In Fragment 16, he disapproves of the character of 'our critical literature [books]' for inheriting the tendency to be 'explicit to the point of boredom' from the older German weeklies modelled after the British moral weeklies (145). The above-mentioned call to arms for critics highlights the importance given by Herder to critical judgment in shaping 'the literature of a land' as well as the expanded terrain of letters (before literature was 'raised to an art') (101; *LA* 82). At the same time, the *Fragmente* rarely ventures direct commentary on passages outside of the *Literaturbriefe*. In the third fragment, which deals with the divergence of the ideals of poetry and of philosophical discourse (*beauty* and *perfection*, respectively), Herder weaves in a quasi-quotation from Breitinger's *Critische Dichtkunst* – it is actually his summary / interpretation of Breitinger's argument placed in quotation marks – as revelatory of the mistaken notions held by 'so many recent reformers of language' ('FRGL' 107). Also miscited in this fragment is Klopstock's critical essay on poetic language from a 1758 issue of *Der Nordische Aufseher* [The Northern Custodian] (Herder's footnote gives the source as *Briefe*), alluding to the needless doubts of 'a scholar learned in languages.' The allusive nature of these references (both of which are, however, attributed to their authors in the two footnotes) serves the purpose of generalizing both the notions and the doubts referred to as representative of wider tendencies. But the excursion stops there; the legitimacy of the argument is secure; in the final paragraph Herder states that citing 'more authors who ... are not sufficiently prepared to shift from their vantage point back into another age, to pass judgment upon distant ages and departed languages' is, in fact, 'not part of my book' (108).

Noteworthy from a formal point of view is also Fragment 14, which includes a subsection 'On the Hexameter' (a fragment within a fragment?) and makes reference, by quoting a favourable remark from the *Briefe*, to Klopstock's preface-treatise to volume 2 of *Messias* – another 'fragment.' The long 18th fragment concluding the first collection is actually a series of nine (numbered) portraits, in language replete with superlatives and mythological conceits, extolling the talents of 'a *few more recent* original authors … who occupy a place of honor in German literature' ('FRGL' 150) – mainly classicist philosophers and literary theorists, among them Winckelmann, Moser, Abbt, and Lessing. The 'pantheon' focuses on each author's literary prose and poetic styles and has a comparative dimension. The final, signal place in Herder's gallery is reserved for Hamann – if not an undisputed 'star in our literary firmament,' then 'a meteor … a phenomenon at any rate' (156), and, like the other greats, not without his flaws.

While Herder commends Hamann for the profundity of his insights, he acknowledges also that it can be inaccessible. His sketch is, in fact, a drawn-out, uneasy justification of Hamann's notoriously cryptic style: the appeal of his work is not 'the consequence of acquired rules'; he 'abhors the spiderwebs of systems, each thought is a pearl unstrung, each thought is garbed in a word without which he could not think it and say it'; his insights 'a toilsomely woven texture of pungent expressions … and budding words'; his 'mystifications, allusions, and the distribution of light and shadow, occur regularly' (hence, are not accidental errors) ('FRGL' 156). Although Herder's unease stems from his partial agreement with Hamann's many critics, he dissociates himself from one review which calls Hamann 'the offender against style' – choosing, instead, to call Hamann's 'offence' a 'particular way of thinking and seeing [resembling] a certain Socratic ignorance' (the ambiguity of 'particular' and 'certain' is telling) (157).[142] In his acceptance of the inseparability of linguistic form from content, Herder anticipates Romantic aesthetics. The consistency of this view becomes apparent as Herder vents his impatience: 'Reader, you who are able to understand, to make use of, and to complement these scattered observations, you have invented them!' (156). Hamann's portrait, saturated with allusions that mimic his textual gestures, concludes the 18th fragment. The alleged resemblance but, more accurately, diametrical opposition of Hamann's discursive style to Winckelmann's, with whose portrait this fragment began, completes the gallery tour.

The better part of the literary praise in the *Erste Sammlung* is reserved for the 'genius' of Klopstock (Fragments 6, 14, 15). Apart from the above writers, frequently mentioned are 'the Gottschedians,' the 'philological philosopher' Baumgarten, 'the patriotic Bodmer' ('FRGL' 113, 117, 289n82), Opitz and Leibniz, Luther, Ramler, Kant, and scores of other German and non-German writers. The final section of the *Fragmente*, the 'Beschluß' (conclusion, subtitled 'von der Idealschönheit unsrer Sprache' [On the Ideal of Our Language]) completes the self-conscious framing of the fragments. Incorporating (often modified) quotations from the seventeenth volume of the *Briefe*, Herder summarizes which issues he has addressed and commented upon in which fragments. This concluding section follows roughly the pattern: *quotation* (containing points of contention or raising a set of productive questions, upon which his observations are founded), then *summary* (angle taken and points made by Herder in the main text and their exact location). It occasionally reads like a topical checklist, and occasionally like an addendum, containing new material/examples – a supplement to the supplements. It complements in obvious ways the expository table of contents, since it emphasizes different topics and recapitulates Herder's position on the most essential questions. In the final paragraph, Herder recaps, in diction thick with italics, the special qualities of foreign languages that would benefit the German language – but then qualifies this in his last sentence, which ends with a Hamannian accent on genesis (via Genesis 6:1): 'for every proficient author the thoughts are the *sons of heaven*, the *words* are *daughters of the earth*' (165).

(e) G.A. Bürger's 'Herzensausguß über Volkspoesie' [Outpourings from the Heart on Folk Poetry] (Leipzig, 1776)[143]

'Herzenausguß über Volkspoesie' is the second and longest part of Bürger's 'excerpt-text' *Aus Daniel Wunderlichs Buch* [From Daniel Wunderlich's Book]. It stands out as the only self-contained piece. It begins in an unbroken series of image-laden rhetorical questions conjuring Apollo and the Muses. The exclamations that follow (e.g., 'But how little the German muses have done so until now!') suggest that an enumeration of German shortcomings is forthcoming. Instead, however, Bürger proceeds to lament the 'trivial learning' (*Quisquiliengelahrtheit*) of a German clerisy focused on things non-German. The critique of education as attendance to foreign customs and achievements and 'join[ing] the clique' (*zünftig zu sein*) is contrasted with the native wisdom of the 'unlearned' folk.[144] Bridging the subject of literature and the problem of German education is not only their obvious interdependence but also the metaphor of *Kapital* (the word is used by Bürger virtually in our modern sense of 'intellectual capital'). 'For the most part it [trivial learning] remains dead capital; and how can coin that often has no intrinsic value at all, and whose impression has long since gone out of fashion, go into circulation?' Bürger relates the muses' neglect of German poets to the prevalence of this kind of worthless learning among the literati; the latter is antithetical to *German* poetry. 'By rights, the German muse should not go off on learned journeys, but rather stay home and learn its natural catechism by heart.' Conversely, the appreciation of German culture is the way to true German literature, and Bürger uses folk poetry in support of this approach. Ancient folk songs, for instance, 'present to the maturing poet a very important opportunity of studying art that is naturally poetic' ('OHFP' 255). The weaker articulation of German literary character is due, first, to its weaker political cohesion relative to other modern nations with advanced literary cultures, and, second, to a combination of the ignorance of German authors with regard to the richness of contemporary local German life and language as revealed by their aspiration to 'paint not human, but heavenly suns; in the manner [of] ... other ages and climes' (254). These are the lessons of Herder's historical relativism. Let us examine more closely *how* Bürger's argument is put forward.

The text could be fairly categorized as an essay, were it not that it belongs to a larger work that is, moreover, quite self-contained. Complicating its generic classification is its frequent recourse to hyperbole, ridicule, and absurdism to make its points memorably. Consider, for instance, how Bürger describes the German familiarity with foreign cultures: 'We are thoroughly acquainted with their fields and forests, cities and villages, temples and palaces, houses and stables, their kitchens, cellars, attics and rooms, wardrobes, coffers, and heaven knows what else' ('OHFP' 253). The physical objects on this list stand, of course, for specific customs (religious rituals, cuisine, or fashion), which German travellers eagerly adopted. Their infinite extent ('and heaven knows what else') suggests the absurdity of such foreign cultural 'study.' Consider also this portrayal of Germany's 'infant' poets attempting to mime divine inspiration: 'they stand on a precipitous crag, throw their head back in ghastly ecstasy, roll their eyes ...' But Bürger addresses these poets directly when referring to their misguided complaint about the 'sloth of the audience'; he speaks here from the position of an experienced writer who has appealed to this audience (254). The audience, which is potentially 'the whole people,' is the only 'natural' (*natürliche*) source of inspiration. It is that 'Book of Nature' held open for the poet who wants to explore its 'imagination and sensibility.' At this point, Bürger's rhetoric becomes frenzied at the possibilities of such natural education. He vents a long, uninterrupted concatenation of imperatives, emphases ('Truly!'), and promises. 'Let this be the real ultimate height [*non plus ultra*] of poetry!' – poetry of *universal* interest, resonating with 'the refined sage' as much as with 'the rude forest dweller,' and – lest this range seem exclusive – with the 'lady' and the 'daughter of nature.'[145]

The next passage imagines the rather dogmatic reaction of the sceptics among 'the makers of poems and theories,' who smile 'in wise condescension' at Bürger's call to German poetry's universality (he later addresses them, perhaps also condescendingly, as 'My dear people' ['OHFP' 254]). His comments here are cautious, prefaced twice by the phrase 'I have a feeling' (*deucht mir*). The passage also contains an amusing personification of poetry, or rather, of several of its demoted genres (e.g., didactic poem and epigram) as entities 'about to jump up and cause an uproar.' Bürger introduces here the distinction between the art of versifying (*Versmacherkunst*), the realm of wit and understanding (*Witz und Verstand*), and poetry proper (*Poesie*), the realm of imagination and sensibility (*Phantasie und Empfindung*) – even as he stresses that their delimitation is not absolute. At one point, he equalizes the two by insisting they 'dwell side by side as peaceable neighbors' or even 'go hand in hand as friendly neighbors' – in other words, that they are in unison. As if this were not enough, they 'borrow dishes, pots, brooms and yardsticks' (here the metaphor turns absurd), and are allowed to 'speak the same language, distinguished only by dialect, as it were!' Ultimately, however, Bürger is merely proposing that *Versmacherkunst*[146] be given a fairer share of recognition. Again, the 'art of versifying' is personified, but this time as a 'dignified' and 'nice woman.' Along with the preceding paragraph, where, among the imagery already mentioned, we are told to seize the 'magic wand' of poetry and where 'golden arrows' fly before our eyes, this is the most visually rich segment of Bürger's essay.

Next, Bürger distances himself from *Versmacherkunst* since 'It is the weal and woe of poetry [*Poesie*] that are near to my heart' ('OHFP' 255). The rest of the essay is therefore devoted to poetry proper – by which he means particularly lyric and epic genres. He then turns to extolling the poetic qualities of popular songs, and commends those who have already recognized them (an allusion to Herder). *Volkslieder* are said to be 'the true outpourings [*wahre Ausgüsse*] of indigenous nature both in imagination and feeling.' Recall the titular 'outpouring' which becomes, in a sense, the signifier of Bürger's personal take on the essay, underlining its sentimental motivation. Assuming that this wording in relation to 'natural poetry' is not accidental, Bürger analogizes between his heart-felt expression and native poetry. Terms like *Herzensausguß* or *Herzens Ergiessung* were not commonly used to describe the style/form of literary-critical reflections (the only other instance of which I am aware occurs in the title of Ludwig Tieck's [1773–1853] and Wilhelm Heinrich Wackenroder's [1773–98] *Herzensergiessungen eines kunstliebenden Klosterbruders* [Outpourings from the Heart of an Art-loving Friar] from 1797). The use of a term that connotes strong subjectivism and sentimentality in the title conveys the author's passion for his subject. It is a departure even from the discourse of the 'cultivators of sensitivity' (like Lessing, Gellert, or Klopstock), and certainly from the self-identification of standard formal exposition. Bürger's writing is a metaphoric outpouring also because it is involuntary or self-indulgent, and for this reason has to be, as he will say near the end, hemmed in if he is to conclude.

Again, Bürger turns to imagery to express the virtues of folk poetry, without however remaining blind to the deficiencies of the oral tradition in toto. Even when he urges others to invest the time necessary to 'separate the gold from the dross,' he cannot be faulted for selective appreciation. Naturally, not all popular songs can have the universal appeal he envisions for true poetry; not all are thus 'suitable for imitation as a whole, nor for the common reader' ('OHFP' 257) (their selection would clearly involve difficult decisions). Moreover, the dynamics of the oral tradition are such that the ancient gold needs to be not only isolated but also rid of incrustations. Bürger's own formulation is, in fact, less metaphoric, as he makes explicit reference to the 'critical' mind needed to 'restore the ancient reading' obscured by 'heterogeneous incrustations,' a reading potentially lost (255). Popular poetry is in need of discerning critics to make it shine.

Bürger adopts a more personal approach to convince the reader of what his own experiences had imparted to him, namely, the *natural* beauty of *Volkspoesie*. He recalls, somewhat wistfully, listening to it 'beneath linden trees in a village, at the laundry, and in spinning rooms' ('OHFP' 255). Indeed, there the location of his ear relative to the singers is left ambiguous (did Bürger spend time in spinning rooms listening to them?). The metonymic application of the ear and especially the collapsing of that presumed (class) disparity might strike one as lyrical – and quite to be expected from such a popular poet. His feelings for the *Volk* are strong enough to put the notion of poetic distance into question; his ear can perceive and his mind appreciate their songs as if he partook in their culture, accompanying the singing women at their work. The closeness he feels is expressed also in his solicitude: 'Rarely has a ditty, as they call it, been too nonsensical and absurd not to have offered at least something, even if only a brush stroke of magically rusty coloration, which edified me poetically' (255). (A very similar assurance/recommendation recurs at the end of the text: 'Some of those I heard had true poetic merit as a whole, many in individual passages; I am sure the same is true of far more I have not seen' [257].) This vivid foray into oral culture, which Bürger breaks off after identifying lyric and epic poetry with ballads and romances and a remark on the quality of native recitation, resumes two paragraphs later, where *Volkspoesie* functions already as a general term that groups together German folk songs and Homeric epics.

Next to be personified is 'so-called higher lyric poetry' which resists such classification ('OHFP' 255). It is imagined as conceited and recalcitrant. Bürger questions its status by noting that it is not uncommon for such works to appeal to the people, the representatives of the 'earthly race.' This observation strikes at the core of the 'high' versus 'low' literature controversy. 'That which is not for the people may take itself off wherever it wants,' even toward the divine. Its fate is of no interest to Bürger; his love is reserved wholly for the human. He strengthens his resolve – which he calls a judgment (*Urteil*) – by adding, somewhat absurdly, that he would make it 'even if I were such a son of the gods myself, for I am more concerned with my beloved human race than with gods or sons of gods' (256). What follows is a paragraph of humble effusions concerning the glory of the monotheistic God, God's original design for poetry (which poetry can approach by its appeal to the people [*Popularität*]). (Bürger's diction resembles at such points Hamann's.)

At this juncture, Bürger returns to his earlier contention that the muse of *Volkspoesie* is not the 'pseudomuse' (*Aftermuse*) – or, worse still, the maid of the muses – it is taken to be. He considers this degradation of the folk song, ballad, and romance genres abominable considering that 'after all it is she who has sung' the great epics of the past from Ariosto to Homer ('OHFP' 256).[147] 'It's true!' he adds for emphasis, in advance of any scepticism to this claim. Although those individual works are 'no longer in harmony with the *German* people,' the spirit of *Volkspoesie* certainly is. The passage turns into an appeal to national sentiment: 'We are Germans ... who should not make Greek, Roman, cosmopolitan poems in the German tongue ...'[148] (in the span of five lines, 'German' appears six times). Again Bürger taunts the younger generation of poets who do not obey this rule, repeating their injudicious complaints about a lazy audience. Again we hear of their 'cloudy learning' and remoteness from 'the human race in this vale of tears.' Again we hear a challenge and a promise: 'Give us a great national poem of the kind described, and we'll make it our vade mecum [*Taschenbuch*]' – a guide or reference not to foreign cultures, but to the native one. His critique does not end there; the young poets are now targets for ridicule as thoughtless, boring manipulators. His caustic parting words to the 'naive poetic youngsters' end with a patronizing 'from now on don't forget it: folk poetry, just because it is the ultimate height [*non plus ultra*] of art, is the most difficult of all' (256–7). Yet, as we have seen, Bürger's essay is far from containing open aggression; several ideas are repeated in the muted form of a reminder or reassurance. For all its announced emotional verve and stylistic effusiveness, the text's structure turns out quite disciplined. All the points seem to have been made, and the most important, pertinent, and immediate ones, with which the text opens, are repeated toward the end. This recurrence gives the text closure.

I have left the most important matter for the end. Who, indeed, is *Daniel Wunderlich* – the individual from whose book this text claims to derive? No actual person of that name who would warrant this distinction is known to have existed. In that case, 'Daniel the Fantastical' may well be the fictitious saviour of old folk songs, whom Bürger envisions at the end of his essay and whose consequence is implied throughout – an anthologist for whom he has looked 'in vain.' The dream of this 'German Percy'[149] is what finally checks the flow of Bürger's outpouring ('OHFP' 257). He is to be no ordinary collector but 'a man who understands art' and who, 'in the process' of gathering its 'remnants,' is to 'uncover the secrets of this magic art more than has happened until now.'

Within two years' time, Nicolai answered Bürger's call by publishing a travesty of his 'dream' folk-song collection. He entitled it *Eyn feyner kleyner Almanach vol schönerr echterr liblicherr Volckslieder, lustigerr Reyen unndt kleglicherr Mordgeschichte, gesungen von Gabriel Wunderlich weyl. Benkelsengernn zu Dessaw, herausgegeben von Daniel Seuberlich, Schusternn tzu Ritzmück ann der Elbe* [A Fine Little Yearbook Full of Beautiful

Genuine Charming Folk Songs, Merry Rounds, and Lamentable Tales of Murder, Sung by Gabriel Wunderlich ...][150] – the German spelling and punctuation a caricature of sixteenth-century popular idiom.[151] Nicolai's *Vorbericht*, or notice to the reader, is an explicit parody of the 'Herzensausguß,' composed in the same exaggerated diction. The choice of songs in *Eyn feyner kleyner Almanach* is meant to ridicule Bürger's excessive valorization of folk traditions as the measure of poetry by exposing them as grotesquely primitive. Nonetheless, the *Almanach* contributed to preserving artefacts otherwise likely to be lost. More importantly, the project backfired by stirring the literary and philosophical anti-Enlightenment to organize itself (Verweyden).

(f) J.W. von Goethe's 'Literarischer Sansculottismus' [Literary Sansculottism, also known as Response to a Literary Rabble-Rouser] (Tübingen, 1795)[152]

The majority of Goethe's literary-critical works are *occasional* pieces: neither fragments saturated with abstract philosophical ideas, nor treatises espousing a coherent aesthetic program or explicit interpretive framework, but essays filled with theoretical insights rooted in a specific time and place, encapsulating critical judgments of specific literary works.[153] Goethe's literary-critical output, spanning five decades, did not serve, then, to expound a theoretical system (as did much eighteenth-century criticism), but, instead, recorded theoretical-critical positions held by him at one point or another. Reich-Ranicki takes this *occasionality* a step further toward this generalization: 'Goethe came repeatedly to speak of the [genre of] occasional poem, which he held to be, as he put it in *Dichtung und Wahrheit* [Poetry and Truth], the "first and most genuine of all kinds of poetry [*Dichtarten*]."[154] In this sense one can arguably call the essay an occasional pronouncement. As the essay derives from the treatise, so the feuilleton from the essay.'[155] Thanks to Goethe's *occasional* productions, at least in the German essayistic tradition the notion of *occasionality* seems implicit in the essay as a genre written in response to or suggested by a specific event or set of circumstances, in more informal diction, and bringing to bear on its subject the author's personal experience (in the case of critical essayism, it is often the experience of reading/writing), which gives it a distinct monological quality.

In his Postscript to an English edition of Goethe's literary-critical essays, John Gearey makes a case for their being written 'in a style and form commensurate with' Goethe's literary works of the same period (although he admits they do not 'reveal quite the same pattern of growth as the body of his creative work') (229, 232). Such correspondence would confirm that much of the German theoretical criticism of the late 1790s written by poet-critics harmonized with their creative work. This finding should not in itself be surprising, yet it blurs the hitherto sharp divide between literature proper and literary criticism (231).[156] Neither was Goethe's occasional criticism confined to prose: the *Xenien* were rhymed epigram-style couplets composed in retaliation for the bad judgment of contemporary critics (most importantly Nicolai).[157]

Gearey notes also that the impact of Goethe's literary-critical essays was modest compared to that of his *metaliterary* pronouncements.[158] Goethe's literary versatility – his unequalled achievements in poetry, prose, epic, and drama – instilled in him an appreciation of these forms' distinctive capabilities. His criticism is 'classicist' only to the extent that he disapproved of the self-indulgent subjectivity of contemporary Romantic poets (Gearey 231). His style lacks any of the formal pedantry typically associated with classicism (of which even Lessing's preamble on the *Laokoon's* formal unconventionality is an atypical example) – hence being truer to his earlier literary writing and appealing to the emerging Romantic ethos. Like the *Frühromantik* critics, Goethe made use of conceptually more open forms like the conversation/dialogue. No doubt the informality of his tone owes something to Goethe's conception of his readership. As Gearey puts it, 'Goethe in tiny Weimar, despite his worldwide renown, seems generally to have conceived of his audience as a small, interested public rather than a cosmopolitan group well enough versed in particulars to desire and expect generalities and theory' (231).

Goethe's first literary-critical essay, 'Literarischer Sansculottismus,' already contains the seeds of his concept of *Weltliteratur*, an 'extension' of Herder's ideas about national literatures. With *Weltliteratur* Goethe would later advocate (albeit covertly) the facilitation of mutual, international, public understanding and cooperation through literature in the broadest sense of the term, and caution against a narrow outlook on other contexts and indigenous cultures. This view of literature's 'inevitable'[159] universal future informed his choice of literary-critical objects from the start (Greek drama, Dante, Calderon, Sterne, Carlyle, Shakespeare, Byron). By the 1820s, he also counted German literature among the distinguished members of *Weltliteratur*: 'All the nations review our work; they praise, censure, accept and reject, imitate and misrepresent us, open or close their heart to us. All this we must accept with equanimity, since this attitude, taken as a whole, is of great value to us' ('WL' 89).

'Literarischer Sansculottismus,' published anonymously in volume 1 of *Die Horen*, is contemporary with Goethe's richly metaliterary *Wilhelm Meisters Lehrjahre* [Wilhelm Meister's Apprenticeship]. The essay was penned in response to a 1795 essay by Berlin critic (and clergyman) Daniel Jenisch (1762–1804). Complaining as he did of the meagreness of German prose and lack of German classical authors, Jenisch must have been aware of his provocation. Duly provoked, Goethe responded with a succinct and to-the-point counterargument. First, his essay attempts a rebuttal of Jenisch's critique by shifting the responsibility for literary might onto the shoulders of the cultural environment in general. Second, it deflects Jenisch's dissatisfaction by complaining in turn about the poor state of German literary criticism, Jenisch's including (it is thus partly metacritical). Third, it assesses the literary scene in general with the optimism that Goethe argues it deserves, not least for the commendable efforts on the part of writers to overcome the cultural limitations into which they were born. It is, therefore, a defence.

From the first lines, Goethe invests himself explicitly in these three purposes. His polemical thrust is apparent already in the title: the analogy between German critics such as Jenisch and the French Revolution's ultra-democrats, the *sans-culottes*. The label *sans-culotte* can be regarded as doubly derogatory, evoking the image of an ill-equipped popular volunteer to the French Revolutionary Army as well as the Reign of Terror's genteel poseurs, the *citoyens sans culottes*, who adopted the name to win the favour of the populace. Use of the term *sans-culottes* was proscribed in France in 1794, just months before the publication of Goethe's essay. Thus, the essay draws a clever parallel between a doubly detrimental brand of criticism and a dubious contemporary political phenomenon. Jenisch, too, is a poseur seeking to win over the populace – in a word, a 'rabble-rouser'; his own coarse manners enable him to appeal to the lowest popular taste and to stir up trouble. With one well-chosen term, Goethe exposes this strategy, and turns the table on Jenisch for his caricaturing of reputable writers[160] by, in turn, caricaturing him as Thersites. Jenisch is alluded to throughout the essay as a blundering, ill-humoured criticaster (*ungeschickte Tadler* or *Krittler*, literally, 'fault-finder'), proffering uneducated presumption (*ungebildete Anmassung*) and passing it off as literary judgment. This 'half-baked critic' (*Halbkritiker*) is juxtaposed with the *littérateur* (*Literator*), a 'capable, diligent' (*verständiger, fleissiger*) critic, whose place he wants to usurp ('RR' 191; 'LS' 243). The cost of this insidious parasitism – the further debasement of popular taste – gave Goethe cause for concern.

Goethe's excoriating advance to the optimistic core of his own argument is remarkable for its speed and trenchancy. It serves as a kind of rhetorical calibration. In the span of the first four paragraphs, Goethe criticizes the journal that permitted the appearance of Jenisch's polemic, 'Über Prosa und Beredsamkeit der Deutschen' [On the Prose and Eloquence of the Germans] (he does not refer to Jenisch by name, but per *Verfasser* [author], likely in deliberate contradistinction to *Schriftsteller* [writer]). His technique here is sarcasm: a journal which titles itself an 'Archive of the Times and Its Taste' cannot be faulted for preserving a 'representative' impropriety. (By the essay's end, however, Jenisch's text is reduced to an aberration, since 'our critical papers, journals, compendia – furnish [all kinds of proof] of a uniformly good style' ['RR' 192, modified]).

Speaking as a collective, authoritative 'we, the editors of the journal *Die Horen*,' Goethe then gives a laconic summary of Jenisch's argument and his attitude of 'lukewarm praise and sharp criticism' ('RR' 189). He then proceeds to defend the unnamed writers Jenisch had disparaged, claiming they do not pretend to be 'classical' (*klassisch*). After this he appeals to readers as his allies to elicit their sympathy for these writers. The first point on which Jenisch is admonished is not his opinion per se, but his primitive and *destructive* attitude,[161] not merely an 'arbitrative tone and certain mannerisms' (which are 'anything but unusual among our critics') but a lapse 'into more primitive behavior' ('RR' 189, modified). The terminology and implied aesthetic standard is classicist, and while Goethe admits the scarcity of works identifiable as classical, he observes also that 'People who consider it indispensable that their spoken or written words express specific concepts rarely used terms such as "classical work" or "classical writer"' (190). The introductory section, as one is tempted to call it, concludes with another direct dismissal of Jenisch's approach in conjunction with his opinion:

> Far be it from us to comment on the poorly conceived and poorly written text we have before us; after reading through the pages in question, our readers will react with indignation and judge and castigate the rude arrogance with which the author tries to invade the territory of his betters with the intent to usurp their places – this case of veritable sansculottism. (189–90, modified)

In the overall design of Goethe's essay, this rather tenacious rhetoric of the first four paragraphs is, as it turns out, only a way to let off steam. They culminate suddenly in an act of composure (a reaffirmation of superiority, without succumbing to pettiness or condescension) which marks the essay's 'proper' beginning: 'Only a few remarks shall be made in reply to this insolence.'

The brevity, conviction, and multitonality of Goethe's article clearly indicate that its author could expect its sympathetic reception in a domain where exchange of conflicting ideas happens regularly without violating the *sensus communis*.[162] The reading/writing public, however, is presented here as polarized: on the one hand the initiated, productive, and partisan to Goethe's politics (the pervasive, exclusive 'we' of this text, which can be editorial or collective), on the other those who have it wrong, the dilettantes, the second-rate arrogators of public opinion. Goethe's status as not merely part of a generation with artistic (*klassisch*) potential but as its primary exponent raises his apologetics to a (non-agitational) defence.[163] This defence also rapidly burgeons into a social diagnosis: the German public's all-pervasive bad taste is partly to blame for the regrettable state of affairs. Goethe remarks on the value of decorum and 'good taste' – by then a waning, relativized category. Specifically, he mentions the native poet Wieland, also a notable critic of the day, as someone whose oeuvre would be sufficient to derive from it the doctrine of taste ('die ganze Lehre des Geschmacks' ['LS' 242]). 'Literarischer Sansculottismus' ends on a caustically jussive note, its aim clearly being to provoke further discussion on the subject. The tone of the concluding paragraph is reminiscent of the opening part, in that Goethe again becomes specific in his chastisement ('RR' 192).

> It is not proper to vent one's bad humor in good society … The numerous examples of style, the previous labors and endeavors of so many accomplished writers[,] enable the beginner at an earlier stage to present in an appropriate style and with lucidity and grace what he has received from the outside world and developed further within himself. Thus any kindly disposed and fair-minded German will see the writers of his nation at an encouraging stage of development. He is furthermore bound to be convinced that the public will not be misled by an ill-tempered, small-minded critic, who should be excluded from literary society, as should everyone whose destructive [*vernichtende*] efforts only leave active members scowling, supporters listless, and onlookers distrustful and indifferent. (191–2, modified)

In the preceding paragraph, Goethe placed supreme value in literary tradition as an 'invisible school' (*unsichtbare Schule*) of literary greatness. As Gearey observes, Goethe's classicism had a strong historicist dimension – his ideal of beauty was therefore non-absolute (231). Both this 'school' and the 'onlookers' in the above-quoted passage are, of course, the invisible but overseeing institutions of the larger context, in which Germany as a literary nation is to rise. The verdicts of the 'would-be critic' are not merely muddled and pretentious, deliberately controversial, and hurtful; they are also too laboured and belated (he 'would light the way for us with his little lamp' but 'daybreak is here, and we will not close the shutters again' ['RR' 191, 192, modified]). A true critic, by contrast, employs prophetic judgment – an idea the Romantic school will raise to a higher power. Criticism emerges also as an anticipatory sense: part intuition, part observation, but nevertheless standing up to reason. Speaking on behalf of and in solidarity with the discredited writers as a group (they are 'unsre Schriftsteller,' our writers,[164] and 'ehrwürdige Gesellschaft,' venerable company ['LS' 239]), Goethe insists on appreciating their efforts, *avant la lettre*, as proto-classical, whatever their current literary merit. This *proleptic* notion of their achievement is inseparable from *constructive* criticism – if any classical literature is to materialize; it is a discursive cornerstone of the literary edifice being built. The strength of Goethe's conviction is manifested again in his plan for a future issue of *Die Horen* ('a study of the development of our best writers as revealed in their works'), in which he moreover suggests ceding the floor to the writers themselves on their own terms: 'Their personal participation would be invaluable,' he concludes; 'it would add new dimensions to what can be gleaned from their works' ('RR' 191).

Goethe's constructive investment in the future is a sign of temperance, attributable to the historical moment: in the aftermath of the French Revolution he was disinclined to call for upheavals to pave the way for classical works. His anticipatory, seemingly lenient approach was to him in retrospect entirely vindicated. 'I look back as a cooperator in this work over many years,' he wrote in 1827 in relation to *Weltliteratur*,

> and reflect how a German literature has been brought together out of heterogeneous, if not conflicting, elements, – a literature which for that reason is only peculiarly *one* in the sense that it is composed in *one* language, – which, however, out of a variety of wholly different talents and abilities,

minds and actions, criticisms and undertakings, gradually draws out to the light of day the true inner soul of a people. ('WL' 89–90)

(g) F. Schlegel's 'Gespräch über die Poesie' [Dialogue on Poesy] (1799–1800)[165]

The 'Gespräch über die Poesie' was published in the last two issues of the *Athenäum*. A second, revised edition appeared in Schlegel's *Collected Works* in 1822. As Behler points out, however, it is the earlier version that became 'the living force in the literature of the period and a source of great influence of German and other European literatures.'[166] Significantly, the 'Gespräch' was the only text in the *Athenäum* explicitly and at length devoted to the subject of poetry (*LA* 84).

A formal reading of this multiform text could begin with its composite character. Comprised of several pieces of theoretical-critical writing presented before an audience of close friends who then discuss them, the 'Gespräch' is by no means a direct transcription of conversations taking place in Schlegel's company. The dramatic situation of a *symposium* is, however, realistic and the written *dramatis personae* modelled on Schlegel's intimate circle of friends. In formal terms, the 'Gespräch' is actually a combination of several genres: prefatory remarks (untitled), essay (*Versuch*), talk (*Rede*), literary letter (*Brief*), and, of course, dialogue, which is interspersed throughout.[167] These function as digressions designed to feed the discussion. The text is structured so that each generic element diegetically/dialogically introduces the next as the characters take turns reading their manuscripts. 'Afterwards they could talk and argue all the more. Andrea opened the manuscript and read' to those gathered – the *lecture* is the 'Epochen der Dichtkunst' [Epochs of Poetry] essay immediately following.[168] After this is over, we re-enter the narrative frame – now, however, altered to direct dialogue concerning the piece just heard/read. A few pages later, the character Ludoviko makes his offering – the 'Rede über die Mythologie' [Talk on Mythology] – and again amicable intercourse resumes. The 'Brief über den Roman' – introduced as 'lighter fare,' consisting of 'instructions' originally directed by Antonio only to Amalia, but with her permission shared with the others (*DP* 104, 93) – leads into Marcus's 'Versuch über den verschiedenen Styl in Goethe's früheren und späteren Werken' [Essay about the Different Styles in Goethe's Early and Late Works], framed by the final stretch of dialogue. Another kind of formal reading could do justice to the unstable, *mise-en-abyme* character of the

'Gespräch' by parsing the text's *literary* techniques and the function of fictionalized dialogical and narrative frames.

The most compelling line of analysis, however, is reading the entire 'Gespräch' the way it asks to be read: as a *dialogue*, both explicitly and implicitly. Each of the pieces contains a dialogical premise and dialogical markers (some very similar to those found in the other texts already discussed). The concept of dialogue is, therefore, expanded to include correspondence and solitary composition written with a concrete audience in mind. Although the omniscient narrator of the opening section describes a physical meeting, this is first of all a meeting *in language*: 'Without premeditation or rule, it usually happened that poetry was the subject, the occasion, the center of their gathering' (*DP* 56). And, although initially omniscient, he soon gives up his high command, for 'As always in romanticism, no position is provided from which one might enjoy a commanding overview of the ensemble; no fixed point is offered on the basis of which a system might be securely set in place (and thus ordered, if not organized)' (*LA* 87).

The structure of the 'Gespräch' seems to arise from extemporization. It is programmatically undisciplined, while staying within the parameters and structure of such a language-centred gathering. All this *suggests* a bona fide exchange of ideas – complete with ambiguities and conceptual inconsistencies, intellectual tension and show of wit, that 'fragmentary genius.'[169] Indeed, the author's introduction illuminates a personal predilection for the dialogue form: 'For there has always been a great attraction in speaking about poetry with poets and the poetically-minded. Many such conversations I have never forgotten; in the case of others I do not know exactly what belongs to my imagination and what to my memory; much in them is true, other things are invented. So, too, is the present dialogue' (*DP* 55).

By contrast, the fluidity of each integrated segment of the 'Gespräch' suggests that the voices – which give the impression of being both scripted and spontaneous – had been poeticized, reworked to create an organically coherent work mirroring and illustrating Schlegel's aesthetics. Throughout, the characters act as foils to one another, even when, near the end, the conversation touches on the fraught issue of *de gustibus non est disputandum* ('And even when we do not agree,' observes Antonio in response to Marcus's sanguine speech, 'in the end it is a matter of one saying: I love the sweet. No, says the other, quite the contrary, I prefer the bitter') (*DP* 116). In this way, the Socratic dialogue – the archetype for the 'Gespräch' – is brought to fruition. And – like

Socrates' engagements – despite its elaborate construction and fictional embellishment, the text is ultimately monological: 'the dialogue form is the surface and not the essence ... Ultimately nothing but the opinions of Friedrich Schlegel himself are revealed. That is to say, he speaks through the mouth of his puppets' (Behler, 'IDP' 9–10n2). At the opening, however, Schlegel gives credit where credit is due: his intention and motivation is 'to set against one another quite different opinions, each of them capable of shedding new light upon the infinite spirit of poetry from an individual standpoint ... It was my interest in this many-sidedness that made me resolve to communicate publicly things I had observed in a circle of friends and had considered at first only in relation to them ...' (*DP* 55).

The dialogue form is thus the acknowledged *source* of many of Schlegel's ideas. If one is to give credence to the above credits, the critical reflections undertaken in the dialogue are all collaborations. The male voices are the only ones to present and tend to dominate the ensuing discussions, but the dialogical atmosphere is created by the female characters ('The interest grew with the work and preparations, the ladies made a festive occasion of it,' or 'Amalia and Camilla were just getting involved in an increasingly lively discussion about a new play, when two of the expected friends, whom we shall call Marcus and Antonio, joined the company, laughing loudly') (*DP* 55, 57–8).[170] The scene is set for a dialogue among peers. The group implicitly agrees on the benefits of Socratic dialogue, the spirit of which governs this *symposium*, but no one assumes the role of teacher in the style of a Socrates. The floor is levelled as the male characters, potentially 'in charge,' become introduced in the narrative preamble: 'Lothario, who usually said and argued the least and often remained silent for hours, not letting himself be disturbed ... no matter what the others might say and argue ...' (indeed, Lothario never prepares or gives a presentation);[171] 'Antonio, who occasionally liked to introduce polemical ideas into the conversation although he rarely led it ...'; of Ludoviko it is said that 'only in a comic poem could he do properly what he had in mind. He wanted to say more about it, but the ladies interrupted him and asked Andrea to commence; otherwise there would be no end to forewords'; of Marcus not much is divulged (*DP* 56–9).

The by turns expository and elenctic-maieutic mode of presentation in the 'Gespräch' corresponds to its two discursive functions: a critical statement and a Platonic dialogue – in other words, the articulation of an aesthetic project and an instance of its realization. Fundamentally, the text 'pretends to be nothing but a collection of opinions, an imitation of the "play of life"' (Behler, 'IDP' 13); appearances aside, this 'play' is the spirit of all genuine art and philosophy. In this sense also its, so to speak, 'external' form enacts the 'internal' one. At the end, the characters step back from and critically reflect upon the form of their discussions. 'I object in the essay on Goethe only that its judgments are expressed somewhat too dictatorially,' says Antonio (*DP* 115). Marcus's summary speaks directly to the Socratic ethos:

> Be that as it may. A true aesthetic judgment, you will grant me, a formed and thoroughly complete view of a work is always a critical fact, if I may say so. But it is also only a fact and for this very reason it is a futile task to want to motivate it, lest the motive itself contains a new fact or a more accurate definition of the former. Or, too, as for the external effect where nothing else is left but to show that we do have a discipline, without which aesthetic judgment would not be possible; this discipline, however, is so little an aesthetic judgment that we see it all too often only as being most strikingly the absolute opposite of all art and all judgment. Exhibition of skill among friends is out of place; ultimately there can be no other claim in any communication, no matter how artfully prepared, of an aesthetic judgment, but the invitation to everyone to formulate clearly and determine strictly, so that the communicated impression is worth the trouble of his reflecting whether he can agree with it and, in such a case, of his recognizing it voluntarily and readily. (115–16)

Schlegel's 'Gespräch' – like the fragments composed variously (collectively, individually, anonymously) by himself, his brother, Novalis, and Friedrich Schleiermacher (1768–1834) – was a nuanced embodiment of a new aesthetic and critical law – *irony* – inherent in the conflict between the real and the ideal. Romantic irony came in at least three guises: textual/generic, historical, and 'existential.' It described the literary/philosophical work's awareness of the incongruity between its finite physical shape and that which it longed to express, and the modern consciousness of its idealization of ancient Greece. As well, it marked the soul's striving after a total and harmonious representation of the ideal yet finding always only a (higher) fragmentary competency. But, as the path of knowledge, irony was also 'logical beauty.' Schlegel's elaboration is very apropos: 'for wherever philosophy appears in oral or written dialogues – and is not simply confined into rigid systems – there irony should be asked for and provided.'[172] In

Lacoue-Labarthe and Nancy's reading, the 'Gespräch' is 'no stranger to fragmentation,' fully exhibiting 'this earliest exigency of romanticism' (84). Its fragmentariness arises from the plethora of subjects touched upon and dropped, pursued with conviction but not exhaustively. It is at some times a rehearsal, at others an intermission.

In order to fulfil its titular promise of being about poetry, the 'Gespräch' ironizes itself as *poetical dialogue*.[173] Furthermore, in another example of reflexive, ironic logic, it contains a plan (Marcus's) for a genre poetics *in principle*.[174] A view expressed a year or so earlier in the '*Athenäums*-Fragmente' posited literature (Poesy) as the supreme form of critical and philosophical discussion. The language of philosophy was most lucid when aware of its literary character. In their *Literary Absolute*, Lacoue-Labarthe and Nancy tease out the philosophical grounds for this preference.[175] In reply to Kantianism, Romantic philosophy becomes self-critical. The privileged discourse capable of approximating the ideal (remaining for Kant outside representation) was inherently self-transcending, reflectively poetic, and poetically reflective. 'The fusion of poetry and philosophy,' notes Behler, 'also has for Schlegel the meaning of a "poetic reflection," inseparable from the creative process, animating the entire poetic work, and blending the author's artistic creation with his critical, theoretical discourse.'[176] The Romantics' formal choices were thus motivated by the Kantian theory and practice of *Kritik* and tied to the Romantics' theory/practice of criticism. Judgments were to be passed in aesthetic terms – *on art's own terms*. Schlegel held that criticism should be the 'representation of the impression' the work of art makes on the critic – an approach which – being 'divinatory' (*divinatorische*),[177] intuitive, immediate, organic – could not be impressionistic, generalizing, or didactic (Behler, *GRC* ix). Critical sensitivity should be on a par with the poetic.

The dialogue chooses an inconspicuous way of symbolizing and reflecting the ironic logic of fragmentariness that is synonymous with the modern condition in general, and was evocative of the German condition in particular.[178] For, indeed, the text was intended to demonstrate not only the Jena Romantics' engagement in stimulating conversation on the philosophy of art and the task of new poetry, or their superior sensitivity to language and history, but also their seminal role in forging a German national identity – for 'the less finished a nation is, the more it is a subject for criticism.'[179]

Socratic-Platonic irony ('a configurative, indeterminable, self-transcending process of thinking and writing,' originating, for Schlegel, 'in the conjunction of a perfectly instinctive and perfectly conscious philosophy' [Behler, *IDM* 20])[180] was therefore immanent in the modern notion of self-consciousness. Like other *Frühromantik* texts, Schlegel's 'Gespräch' aims to reconcile and fuse the two streams and phenomena of German literary life and cultural consciousness: the *Romantic* and the *Classical* (*DP* 112–14). The path to a national intellectual identity broke with rationalist attitudes but salvaged and treasured the achievements of the true 'Classical' masters. Thus, Behler argues, 'True modernity does not separate itself from true classicism, but maintains a vivid relationship with the ancient world. Bad modernity, one could say, is a mere separation from classicism, a mere progression' (*IDM* 63).

For Schlegel, as for the others in his circle, the 'creative impulse' sprang from the local and historical, which in the subjectivity of creation became a glimpse of the objective universal. Writes Behler:

> If we wanted to determine the special style of the new poetic and critical discourse brought about by the early Romantic authors, we would have to abandon the dominance of one single principle (reason, creative imagination, structure, progress, perfectibility, and so forth) and stress the counteractive movement of several tendencies (affirmation and skepticism, enthusiasm and melancholy) as the characteristic mark of their discourse. (*IDM* 59)

Behler is speaking here from the Romantic standpoint, and sees the compromise clearly on the side of the 'Classical.' His further point, that 'Schlegel's sharpest weapon is not polemics, but, as in the case of French Classicism, omission' (22), provides another ground for, this time, a positive comparison between the two critical denominations. Also, with regard to the question of literary criticism and history, the 'Gespräch' nowhere takes history directly as its theme, but only as a means to historicist musings. Schlegel's historical relativism implies that even the Classical heritage with all its unsurpassed beauty does not hold the key to objectively perfect artistic expression; it is a model and example to be not imitated but emulated.

In *The Order of Things*, Foucault describes 'Classical' discourse as bound for its own limits through the project of *nomination* that would, if pushed to its logical conclusion, put an end to discourse as such. The Jena Romantics' idea of discourse stymied this project of nomination and its utopian expectations of linguistic exactitude and transparency – renouncing with it the classicist notion of an attainable perfectibility of language. Although discourse, in the modern sense, was in principle seen as unlimited and inexhaustible, the dreams of perfection harboured by the rationalists drew a line, however fine, between principle and reality. The Romantics proved them wrong (and put any endist worries to rest); they unsettled the *name*, subjectified discourse, revived its figurativeness, and refashioned it into a mutable, kaleidoscopic image of itself (in contrast to the 'Classical' view of language as identical with itself – based on a stable duplication of representation upon itself). In light of an (unattainable) Absolute, the desire for the ideal was for them at once an incitement to discourse and a guarantee that it will not cease – the ideal's evasiveness, its protean resistance to being pinned down by labels and hypostasized, made sure that the desiring will continue indefinitely. Behler makes this point more concretely when he speaks of the rise of literary modernity as partaking in a shift in epistemic fields; literature finally joins philosophy and is admitted to the party of 'infinite perfectibility.'[181] This, as has been mentioned, had immense consequences for historical scholarship, particularly for the representation of Antiquity; the moderns had at last reached parity with the ancients.

In conclusion, the Romantics' self-referential, self-critical literature saw itself as – and, for all intents and purposes, became – a synthesis of philosophy and poetry, of history and universal values. In Behler's words, Schlegel favoured 'expanding the notions of genius or imagination by including reason, reflection, critique, and self-criticism ...' (*IMD* 67–8). The Romantics' seemingly superficial preoccupation with form masked the profound reconfiguration of thought taking place, a radical displacement of means and ends, an upsurge of hardly restrained desire. The crumbling of *representation's* epistemic edifice – of its power to sustain the nearly monolithic foundation of Western thought (Foucault, *OT* 239) – became the raison d'être and methodological and structural principle for post-Kantian dialogue.

Chapter Two

Criticism in Poland

... of works to come out in print every reader is judge...

(anonymous, 1789)[1]

1 A Discursive Inheritance

Like its German counterpart, eighteenth-century Polish literary-critical writing did not obey a regularized, 'tightly typified' system of genres.[2] This is not only because criticism was (and continues to be) a domain of discursive activity with relatively few 'interrelated genres that interact with each other in specific settings' and with considerable freedom of innovation and diversity (97, 88). Another reason for its low generic systematicity is to be found in its entropic and 'oedipal' generic lineage, viz., its vacillating descent from a long and near-ossified line of ancient, medieval, and Renaissance rhetoric and poetics, which jointly and separately formed systems subordinated to liberal arts education. In other words, to find its own forms of articulation, modern literary criticism had to break away from a discursive tradition, grappling with its strongly codified generic bequest by revising and wedding old generic elements to a new enunciative mode.

Another reason for Polish literary criticism's weak generic profile was that, in its earliest phases, it was still an appendage to the institution of literature whose genres, needless to say, constituted a powerful, overarching system of subsystems, overlapping in some areas with other discursive domains, but otherwise highly integrated (particularly during the reign of classicism). Literary-critical genres were, in one sense, *transformations* of kinds historically coded as 'literary' (i.e., verse, as well as oratorical, epistolary, and historiographic prose, from the mid-eighteenth century jointly known as *belles lettres*). On the other hand, the generic system constituting 'literature' in the narrower sense (i.e., imaginative literature) was undergoing circumscription and sacralization, with the less distinguishably 'literary' (artistic) genres – those 'semi-' or 'paraliterary' kinds falling outside or nearly outside the core, allegedly Aristotelian triad of epic–lyric–drama[3] – simultaneously distancing themselves from it, or pushed toward the non-literary sidelines of 'all other quality writing' (this process inversely correlating with that of literature's sacralization). In due course, criticism went from being generically peripheral to literature to being generically distinct: a visible discursive domain comprised of a more structured genre-system – though far less so than literature. Let us not overlook that the presence, or semblance even, of distinguishable genres, and thus of patterned relations among individual texts, is what regularizes further utterances and stabilizes the apparatus of discursive intelligibility, helping establish a discourse as such (Bazerman, 'Systems' 99).

If the genres in eighteenth-century Polish literary criticism cannot be seen as wholly distinct in a strict formal sense, an incipient discursivity can nonetheless be discerned in the refashioning of authoritative, ultra-conventional kinds, like poetics and rhetoric, with a different dominant *modal* purpose: evaluation.[4] Thus, Wacław Rzewuski's (1706–79) *O nauce wierszopiskiej* [On the Art of Poetry] (1762) is nominally and externally a poem (*poemat*) but, in the main, thematically and modally akin to poetics,[5] crossing philosophical with theoretical reflection, though already with a discernible speculative-evaluative import (Rzewuski spends time discussing potential flaws, instead of providing examples for emulation). By virtue of not being tightly wrought, the forms of literary-critical expression, eclipsed as they were by the literary genre-system, had indeed 'wider ranges of freedom for novelty and multiplicity' (Bazerman, 'Systems' 88). The obverse of criticism's formal freedom was, of course, the search for genres of its own. We may say that the product of Rzewuski's reflection on literature as tradition and as craft – issuing from a sweeping historical-pastoral, humanistic perspective and in high-flown diction – is a *modulation* of genre and mode (that is, a hybridization still unrecognizable in its own right).[6] It does not, therefore, belong to 'literature proper,' although this categorization may not have been as clear-cut to its author. It probably seemed to Rzewuski that, to resonate, his work had, at least in part, to respond on generic and intertextual levels to the literary tradition of which it treated, and not just to the generic repertoire of literary-theoretical writing (Horatian verse epistles, Aristotelian poetics, and the like). The instance of *O nauce wierszopiskiej* illustrates, in fact, that criticism's emergence as a discursive domain was initially a *modal* affair.

One of the main features of rationalistic (Cartesian) literary-critical methodology emergent in France and embraced in Poland was the isolation and treatment of 'clear and distinct' aspects of the literary work (form and style versus content; plot versus moral thrust, etc.), referred to 'universal' aesthetic and ethical standards. On the other hand, British empiricism (Lockean and Humean) found resonance with philosophical debates on the subject of aesthetics, underpinning the belief that standards of beauty and art can, in principle, be derived from experience and, from there, generalized. (In England, the conjunction of elements of rationalism and empiricism was particularly potent.) Polish reflections on literature drew freely, if not heavily, on both French and British sources.

The most popular genres adopted for literary-critical compositions of the European Enlightenment were: the versified poetics, the speculative treatise, and, later on, the review and the feuilleton. In Poland, the gradual adaptation of these genres (particularly the middle two) to suit a new content and audience began with the abandonment of Latin for the vernacular, with the rendition of classicist treatises (mainly French, mostly Boileau's *L'Art poétique*) in more accessible language, with the use of examples from Polish literature, and, from the turn of the nineteenth century, with the adoption of increasingly precise, specialized terminology – after the customary lexicon of ancient provenance and elaboration in moral philosophy and ancient rhetoric/poetics (nature, imitation, etc.), functioning as common currency in established disciplines, became too vague and in need of redefinition.

Eighteenth-century French criticism attempted (more or less successfully) to import methodology from other areas of inquiry, even the hard sciences (e.g., natural sciences and mathematics). Hence, a parallelism can be observed 'between an intensification of Cartesian influence and a rationalist orientation in the theory of literary criticism.'[7] This sent obvious generic ripples: the insistence on analysis (as scientific reasoning) and comparativity as the primary methods of literary study and literary-critical articulation. This trend was very pronounced in Poland in the work of Adam Kazimierz Czartoryski (1734–1823) (discussed below). Within the context of the sciences, the literary work began to be seen as an organic system. The analysis of the work thus became a taking apart of a whole – reducible, in this case, to the sum of its parts – a 'divisible whole' unified by a single purpose. The comparative method was deployed for entire oeuvres, individual works by the same author, or works by different authors. A similarity became manifest 'between comparison as a rhetorical figure or parallel as a literary genre and comparison as a critical procedure' (Ziętarska 108). The *tertium comparationis* varied from work to work. For instance, in Grzegorz Piramowicz's (1735–1801) treatise *Wymowa i poezja dla szkół narodowych*[8] [Elocution and Poetry for National Schools] (1783),[9] the evaluation of a literary work is executed by comparing it with a 'model' (ideal) of its 'kind' (genre) for which the author supposedly strives (even without realizing it) (Ziętarska 109). Nonetheless, literary criticism – in Poland as abroad – tended to be seen not as scientific, but as a sphere of special erudition and eloquence, linking it with art (*ars*) (106).

2 Profiling Polish Criticism

The eighteenth century does not coincide, in its beginning or end, with a Polish Enlightenment, which fell approximately between 1740 and 1830. The first three decades of the nineteenth century are, however, regarded as 'transitional,' based on the co-existence of classicism and pseudoclassicism with the rise of romanticism (the symbolic beginning of Polish romanticism is 1822, the date Adam Mickiewicz published his *Ballady i romanse* [Ballads and Romances]) (Libera, *Problemy* 8, 15). According to Teresa Skibniewska, Polish classicism was initially a progressive, revitalizing force pushing out the residual Baroque elements of literary style, which began to transform into the reactionary pseudoclassicism only in the last decade of the century.[10]

The first stirrings of modern literary criticism in Poland are said to have appeared in the 1740s.[11] It is not that literary-critical opinion did not exist earlier, but that the critical texts found before 1740 were a scattered, 'embryonic,' 'atomistic' lot – alive, but somehow not yet vital as a textual form of intellectual mediation between writers and audiences that impacted literature's reception.[12] The major changes in the institutional and discursive fabric of the country took place in the second half of the century; the first indisputable manifestations of literary-critical activity and initiatives with the most bearing on the development of criticism occurred after 1764, the coronation of Stanislaus II August Poniatowski as King of Poland, and clustered around the year 1772. Most important for the development of literary criticism was the formation of a national capitalist infrastructure that facilitated investment in publishing, journalism, scholarship, and education.

The year 1772, a dramatic turning point for politics in the region, was the date of Poland's first partition by neighbours Austria, Prussia, and Russia. The next year, 1773, marked a major educational reform – the foundation of the Commission of National Education (*Komisja Edukacji Narodowej*, or *KEN*), enjoying full autonomy and the king's patronage, and considered to be de facto the world's first ministry of education. The *KEN* was designed as an alternative to the Jesuit-controlled system of education.[13] It introduced Polish as the language of instruction in its schools and promoted contemporary Polish writing. Although, in *KEN* schools, literature lacked full autonomy as a subject of instruction, it did become a prime subject of critical reflection (Libera, *Wiek Oświecony* 89).

In 1775, the *Towarzystwo do Ksiąg Elementarnych*, Society for Elementary Books – set up by the *KEN* to oversee the preparation of programs and textbooks for the reformed schools, and later the entire school system – announced a contest for a new textbook on rhetoric and poetics to be used in the new school system. The winner was the work of the Society's secretary, Piramowicz's already-mentioned *Wymowa i poezja dla szkół narodowych*; one of the losers was Franciszek Karpiński's (1741–1825) notable *O wymowie w prozie albo wierszu* [On Elocution in Prose or Verse]. Rehashing a traditional formula to serve new aesthetic ideas and a new audience was not necessarily reactionary or generically anachronistic (the blight of literary reformers were the older, primitive technical primers on rhetoric). Just a decade earlier the opening of the public National Theatre in Warsaw created the demand for reviewing theatre productions. The success of a seminal literary journal, the *Monitor*, espousing a new, Enlightenment ideology, galvanized the periodical press. Publishing was supported by the *Towarzystwo Literatów w Polszcze Ustanowione*, Society of Literati in Poland Established, which, with funding from the king, subsidized Polish authors and imported foreign publications. The *Biblioteka Załuskich* (Załuski Library) in Warsaw, which opened in 1747 as one of the first public libraries in the world and one of the largest in Europe, was nationalized in 1774 and entrusted to the *KEN*. The formation of these new institutions of literary life in the republic – a modern patronage system and periodical press, a national public stage and library, a centralized authority on all matters of education, a society to oversee the production and implementation of standard textbooks to streamline educational reforms – became the backdrop for the institutionalization of literary criticism. The cultural and political elites' concerted efforts to educate the population as a whole[14] (instead of catering only to elite tastes) nurtured a public sphere receptive to critical intervention in its thriving relationship with literature.

One of the Polish Enlightenment's 'communicational situations' sketched by Teresa Kostkiewiczowa was the reconceptualization of readership's relationship to writing as a communion with 'autonomous cultural value.'[15] She noticed a sociocultural shift, in the mid-1770s, stemming from increased readership and individualized intellectual needs, and accompanied by new demands on literature: that it function as a diagnostic tool and 'recognize the progressive tendencies of society' (25). The relationship between reader and text was democratized, 'creativity appear[ed] as an offer directed at the reading public' now 'increasingly released from functionalism and utilitarianism,' and regarding the text as the currency of intellectual participation (26). This went hand in hand with (and was a reflection of) the reading public's 'activisation' in the political sphere and its interest in journalism (30). Kostkiewiczowa adds *en passant*:

> It seems that only in the sphere of such a communicational situation could authentic literary polemics be possible [e.g., the polemic about *Podolanka* (discussed below in the section on Dmochowski)] ... The most important issue, however, is the change happening to the status of readerly communion with writing, as if a disinterested recognition of its literariness, freed from narrowly conceived pragmatic functions. (26)

The first aspect of the shift meant that criticism, hitherto concerned with promoting and theorizing literature as such for enlightened connoisseurs, could insinuate itself between literary works and the reading public as a *practical*, interpretive activity focused on day-to-day evaluation of new writing. This more publicly integrated role of literary-critical practice would only become apparent two decades later, after the disintegration of Poland as a political entity – when the nation struggled to keep alive its literature.

A prototype of literary criticism in Poland can be located in the Renaissance practice of philological/textual criticism, involved in the publication and editing of valuable texts. Strong apologetic and laudatory motifs appeared in early-Renaissance humanist writings vigorously arguing for the value of poetry in human life, denouncing critical opinion of poetic works, and paying homage to authors (Sarnowska-Temeriusz,

'Krytyka' 19). These apologias dealt with and judged poetry not in its concrete instances but as an abstract, 'de-individualized' universal. At the time, they formed 'a unique borderland of philosophical and theoretical poetics,' and radiated into the appreciation of ancient literary heritage through the philological study of individual texts (20). Their popularity led to the foregrounding of the role of literature in general, and the popularity of opinion-bearing forms, divested of the rigidity of older genres.

> The norm of 'literariness' operative during the Polish Enlightenment allowed the consideration on one and the same plane works of poetry and elocution, historiography and the novel or scholarly treatise. One may assert that the singularity of this norm is one of the manifestations of a more general cultural situation, in which present-day stratifications – of literature *sensu stricto* and paraliterary writing – did not play as fundamental a role in its recipients' consciousness. (Kostkiewiczowa, 'Rozważania' 11)

Thus, the Polish discourse of literary criticism (as, after 1795, literary criticism *in Polish*), while initially not readily distinguished from other, more 'creative' types of literature, became the 'internal' grounds on which this very distinction was being negotiated (12). At the same time, criticism, by generating its own demand, rapidly formalized itself in the periodical and daily press – generating with its own recognition the demand for a certain kind of imaginative literature that it needed to then credit or criticize, and necessarily popularizing novel aesthetic standards. Although the publication of periodicals that regularly featured literary content had already begun in the 1750s, this content was informative in nature and therefore conceptually limited. It was only with the birth of a Polish periodical press that the hitherto leisurely institutionalization of literary-critical activity in Poland gained momentum.[16] As a result, the 1740s and beyond saw the emergence and diversification of critical expression, marked by a proliferation of new forms, such as the book advertisement or notice (*ogłoszenie*), the informational report (*doniesienie informacyjne*), the review (*recenzja*), the feuilleton (*felieton*), the polemic (*polemika*).[17]

Surveying the signal publications of literary criticism's pioneers – texts consisting, in part, of critical reflection – one is struck by the generic repertoire represented by them. This compels a return to the question of names. In his article 'On Genre Terminology in Polish Literary Studies,'

Henryk Markiewicz considers the genre nomenclature of studies of literature in the eighteenth and nineteenth centuries, many of which, he notes, were adapted from painting.[18] Incidentally, Markiewicz divides literary studies into literary criticism proper, literary history, literary theory, and the theory of literary research – for the most part, managing to keep them separate. The earliest genre designations recorded by him[19] are to be found primarily in titles and subtitles. They were: most in vogue, the *treatise* or *tract* (*rozprawa, traktat*) and its subtypes (e.g., Karpiński's *O wymowie w prozie albo wierszu*); the theory-suited *thoughts* (*myśli*) (e.g., Michał Jerzy Wandalin Mniszech's [1742–1806] 1775 'Myśli o guście,' or A.K. Czartoryski's *Myśli o pismach polskich z uwagami nad sposobem pisania ich w rozmaitych materiach* [Thoughts on Polish Letters with Comments on the Manner of Writing Them in Sundry Matters], published posthumously in 1810); and *critical letters* (*listy krytyczne*)[20] (e.g., the 1779 anthology *Listy krytyczne o różnych literatury rodzajach i dziełach* [Critical Letters on Diverse Literary Kinds and Works]). Sometimes, of course, letters hid under elaborate titles: e.g., 'Wystąpienie sławnego angielskiego autora Johnsona przeciw klasycystycznym rygorom w utworach teatralnych' [Appeal by the Famous English Author Johnson against Classicist Strictures in Theatrical Works] (1766), published in the *Monitor*[21] under the pseudonym 'Theatralski' (now tentatively attributed to Ignacy Krasicki [1735–1801]).[22] Works claiming completeness in a given field often simply bore in their title the name of their objects.

Interestingly, the essay (*esej*) was non-existent in Polish letters before the turn of the nineteenth century – but it was first taken up, opposite the sketch (*szkic*) (the terms were used interchangeably), in literary criticism. The 'most semantically neutral designation' ends up being the article, indicating only a text's placing in a periodical (Markiewicz, *Dopowiedzenia* 108). Understandably, the shifting usage and instability of reference urges Markiewicz to submit a 'modern' systematization to 'establish some order' and 'enable a more rational and consistent economy of the existing names' (109). He turns to an earlier study for its helpful differentiations and groupings of genres, but, while summarizing it, makes further distinctions. The *polemic* is relegated by Markiewicz to 'a discursive reference to earlier texts' (111). The most precise of the literary-critical genres cited appears to be the review.

My own (less restrictive) appellative search yielded further genre designations: *preface* (*przedmowa*) (e.g., Czartoryski's 1779 'Przedmowa do *Kawy*' [Preface to *Coffee*]);[23] *conversation* or *dialogue* (*rozmowa*) (e.g.,

Krasicki's 'Rozmowa między Horacjuszem a Boileau, satyrykiem francuskim' [Conversation between Horace and Boileau, the French Satirist], published posthumously in 1804); *dissertation* (*dysertacja, rozprawa*) (e.g., Czartoryski's 'O wzroście i prawidłach sztuk teatrowych' [On the Growth and Rules of Theatre Plays] from 1780); *poetics* (*poetyka*) (e.g., Józef Nowaczyński's [1748–1801] *O prozodii i harmonii języka polskiego* [On the Prosody and Harmony of the Polish Language] from 1781, or Krasicki's unfinished *O rymotwórstwie i rymotwórcach* [On Rhyming and Rhymists], written 1790–9, published posthumously in 1803); and *doctrine* (*nauka*) (e.g., Józef Aleksander Jabłonowski's [1711–77] *Nauka o wierszach i wierszopiscach polskich wszystkich* [The Doctrine of Polish Poetry and Poets, All-Considered], published in Lvov in 1751). However, what do all these designations tell us? For one thing, that new genres and their modalities were introduced as literary study became more rigorous and institutionalized: the specialization of research created the demand for more specialized forms of its transmission. Also, it is apparent that a good many genres of literary criticism were, nominally at least, different from literary kinds. It is also safe to assume that criticism's genericity was no greater than the genericity of other research fields, at least in Poland; the genres of criticism often coincided with those of history or philosophy, the formal overlap correlating positively with thematic overlap.

Kostkiewiczowa makes a number of contextualizing points about the generic facet of Polish Enlightenment criticism. By far the most viable *new* genre mobilized by literary criticism once it entered on the process of institutionalization – in the second half of the eighteenth century – was the newspaper article (*artykuł prasowy*). The article quickly became the primary means of formulating literary-theoretical views (Kostkiewiczowa, 'Myśl' 9), which in turn nourished the increasingly clipped, lapidary debates about literary (or literary-critical) standards. Discussions about the rejuvenation of national literature and the proper task of the critic became, by the turn of the century, as controversial as they were routine. The pages of *Monitor*, offering tight journalism and discussions of a programmatic and normative nature in a wide range of subjects, already contained the seeds of more liberal fare addressing questions of creativity and standards of evaluation (9).[24] The preface contributed to the discourse's becoming more specialized (though less compartmentalized) as discussions focused on specific theoretical problems of the writer's craft (e.g., genres). Literary polemics – in which Marcin Fijałkowski's 1790 treatise *O geniuszu, guście, wymowie i tłumaczeniu* [On Genius, Taste, Elocution, and Translation] took part[25] – provoked the elucidation of innovative views that broke with classicist doctrine. Kostkiewiczowa summarizes the formal developments in the literary knowledge of the period as follows:

> In the course of several decades, which separate the first publications by Brodziński [1810s] from the writings of Jabłonowski, Rzewuski, or Konarski, the ways of formulating literary knowledge, as well as the aims that the texts consolidating this knowledge were to serve, had altered. At the outset we saw the practical textbook of rules for prose or verse composition, at the conclusion – treatises, articles, sketches undertaking the problematic of artistic disposition, of the specificity of literary expression, its place in the social life of the nation, and its ties to the character, aspirations, and situation of the said nation. ('Myśl' 9)

Elsewhere, Kostkiewiczowa notes that the 1780s were marked by new, official genre laws, laid by the highly selective 'lawgivers of contemporary literary taste' Franciszek Ksawery Dmochowski (1762–1808) and Filip Neriusz Golański (1753–1824) (also discussed below) ('Rozważania' 10). This 'legalistic' approach went hand-in-hand with the ongoing legitimation of literary criticism as a journalistic endeavour. The new generic *nomoi* endowed criticism with more or less typical forms, stylistic and thematic features (including a revised notion of the 'literary'), and, increasingly, a professional code – in other words, with a basic set of discursive parameters. The Polish Enlightenment program – shaped chiefly through struggles against aestheticism, *zoilism*,[26] formalistic and anti-realistic tendencies of courtly rococo, elements of irrationalism, mysticism, faux devotionality, megalomania, conservatism, and the cultivated subjectivism of a revived *sarmacja*[27] – was, in Stanisław Pietraszko's view, 'best served by models with distinct polemical assumptions, not models of speculative, objectified, academic treatises, of which hundreds were published by European aesthetics.'[28]

An authority on the history of Polish literary criticism, Pietraszko examines the rise, in the late 1700s, of a 'new poetics,' still theoretical but far less codifying than the old. The new poetics was conceived in the ideological milieu of the Piarist order following its modernization by Stanisław Konarski (1700–73). While bringing to the surface the seams in the ideological fabric of Enlightenment 'precursors' (Konarski, Krasicki, Adam Stanisław Naruszewicz, and Stanisław Trembecki), Pietraszko reconstructs the then-new ideology and literary know-how.

Thus, he accounts for the divided nature of the new poetics, suggesting that a general revival was sought after, and the illusion of basic methodological-ideological consensus and homogeneity was inevitable thanks to widespread usage of shared terminology (e.g., *nature* and *imitation*).

> The aesthetic terminology of the early Polish Enlightenment was to become solidified and preserved in literary criticism and theory for several decades ... It was to be a unitary 'epoch of pseudoclassicism.' This supposed identity of aesthetic views over seventy years of literature is, however, deceptive ... Even the same aesthetic terms, woven in an allegedly straight hereditary line through successive articles and theoretical treatises of the age of Stanislaus [1764–95], constantly modify their original content. ('ISR' xlix–l)

It was only later, after critical discourse branched out in search of disciplinary support, that novel terminology eventually staked out distinctions in the ideologies and critical methods of the leading critics of the day.

The 'new poetics,' concerned with teaching the essence of literature rather than recipes for its craft ('ISR' xlix–lii), lent a greater sense of mission to Polish literary criticism, binding it discursively. The project entailed filling not a 'blank slate,' but an *erased* one – purged of many of the old elements so as to avoid old mistakes (the old elements being Baroque-style school rhetoric and poetics from the time of August III the Saxon [King of the Polish-Lithuanian Commonwealth from 1734 to 1763]). This 'purified,' salubrious vision of literature – now integrated with, and understood as, literary criticism – went hand in hand with modified ideological standpoints and philosophical positions (mostly rationalist, with their 'cult of theory' (cix), and scaling down the earlier preoccupation with aesthetic form). It was, according to Pietraszko, 'simultaneously a literary criticism and a normative poetics' – a 'symbiosis' stemming from the 'saturation of theoretical works with the current literary problematic and the search by criticism for a basis for its pronouncements' (liii). Criticism was effectively called upon to organize itself into an agency for the systematic control of all literary production, to further the goals of social reform espoused by the court between 1770 and 1777. '[S]cattered across prefaces and digressions of literary works, [criticism] gave birth to the main aesthetic postulate – that of the cognitive and pedagogical value of literature. In this way, the new poetics was discovering its character and role: it was to be the justification of the new literature' (liv). This activity organized and united literary criticism during the Polish Enlightenment.

3 Textual Analyses

(a) J.A. Jabłonowski's 'Opisanie albo dysertacja pierwsza prawie o wierszach i wierszopiscach polskich wszystkich' [Description or Dissertation, Nigh Premier, on Polish Poems and Poets All] (Lvov, 1751)[29]

This 'description or dissertation' is the introduction to Jabłonowski's *Nauka o wierszach i wierszopiscach polskich wszystkich*, composed in verse in the narrative mode of a legend. The aim of that work was to assess the state of Polish literature, past and present – a not uncommon endeavour in the literary criticism of the day. Nonetheless, judging by the compass of Polish literature, such a critical account must have been perceived at the time as a vast undertaking. Jabłonowski, however, makes certain decisions which save him from an encyclopedic approach. He refers the reader, for example, to textbooks on grammar, as sources of further instruction on poetic composition. Indeed, the text is one of the earliest examples in Polish of literary criticism self-circumscribed by references to more or less contemporaneous scholarly expertise without attempting to reproduce its findings.

For all its descriptive-critical edge, the majority of Jabłonowski's text does not stray far from an edifying and educational purpose. One in the series of normative-theoretical remarks warns against foreign linguistic influence eroding Old Polish ('ODW' 57). The author goes on to offer pointers on metre, declaring vigilance about the rules of grammar, syntax, orthography, punctuation, and figurative expression as necessary for the mastery of the poet's craft. Even as Jabłonowski demands of poetry that it avoid the use of foreign-sounding words (only the Greek-derived receive his sanction), his 'dissertation' avails itself of a great many macaronics. The text is interspersed with popular Latin sayings, phrases traced by editors to Horace and Cicero, and terms in the discussion of proper poetic grammar. (According to Kostkiewiczowa, such references and borrowings from Antiquity amounted to a literary-critical convention in their own right, but were very often instrumental ['Myśl' 15].) Its modal unevenness and the decisive formal shift in the rest of the *Nauka o wierszach* mark it as a transitional exercise, notable for its confidence and intertextual richness.

The first Latin adage in the text, which comes from the late ancient poet Terentius Maurus, is 'habent sua fata libelli [books have their fate]' ('ODW' 56). This unfortunate fact puts Jabłonowski on a mission to save at least the knowledge of Polish literature from oblivion. Polish poetry has had many talented poets,

> however little information about like works comes down to us descendants and their imitators ... One cause of it is that the most ancient of them became extinct and this is the common fate of all our books, that have been devoured by Antiquity, consumed by fire, destroyed by careless storage and keeping of them.

The other cause is said to be poor availability of works still in print, as their authors were 'great and fortunate' enough to have escaped the 'malice of all-devouring time.'

(b) A.K. Czartoryski's 'Przedmowa do Panny na wydaniu*' [Preface to* Miss in Her Teens*] (Warsaw, 1771)*[30]

Czartoryski wrote this well-known preface for a 1771 adaptation of British actor David Garrick's comedy *Miss in Her Teens or the Medley of Lovers*. Contemporaries are said to have considered it 'an exemplary theoretical treatise on the theatre.'[31] Irrespective of its input in the diversification of literary-critical genres, the preface – like many of Czartoryski's other critical texts – is not comprised of original historical or critical ideas (nor is it the first critical preface in Polish). It is not a *cultural* adaptation/translation – a common literary endeavour at the time, wherein equivalents are found to foreign literary references, not least because of their obscurity – but it is an adaptation, nonetheless. The text it draws most heavily on is Dubos's *Réflexions*. Dubos's work was highly popular in Poland, where (as a result) the rigorous classicist notion of dramatic probability and a literal understanding of the three unities also did not go unchallenged. Most importantly, however, for the institutional rise of the discourse, Dubos's reputation in Poland signalized the presence of an 'interpretive community' committed to a way of valuing literature that was not, at the same time, considered the only conceivable one. The multiplication of interpretive views began in France more than a century earlier, with the publication, in 1674, of Boileau's *L'Art poétique*, but did not occur in Poland until the middle of the eighteenth century.

On the most superficial level, Czartoryski's preface is noteworthy for its generous signage. By this we mean that it makes an effort to spare the reader confusion, and it does this by referring back to earlier threads and sections, or to a digression immediately following (e.g., 'As I already mentioned ...' [and variations on this], 'I shall deviate here slightly, wanting to explain the signification of this word genius,' 'Let us pause here and, making mention of a translation into our language as equalling the original, let us throw a flower on Kochanowski's grave,' or 'Let us go on now ...' ['PPW' 95, 96, 102, 103, 108]).[32] The text nevertheless unfolds without revealing what lies ahead in the form of a line of argument or a plan, or foreshadowing its destination in the form of a thesis or conclusion stated in advance. Its signage is retrospective and perspectival – offering an awareness of matters discussed as it unfurls – rather than prospective. The transitional sentence – set off as a paragraph – between the first (historical) and second (theoretical-historical-critical) part of the preface reads: 'I here end my historical examination of the basis, varieties, and state of theatre in nations familiar to us' (107).

The first part of the text is a measured lesson in literary history. We learn of the dawn of drama and its development in the ancient and modern world. The signage works in unison with paragraphing, with the average length of paragraphs kept to a minimum (with the effect of a well-paced succession of complete ideas), to render Czartoryski's exposition lucid and digestible to a reader unfamiliar with even the basics of the history of dramatic art. Additional information about literary figures mentioned in the body of the text is provided in footnotes. Explicit critical opinions in this section are kept to a minimum, and seem not to depart from the mainstream – for instance, medieval letters are said to be 'without grace,' and French drama 'the most modest, most honest ... worthy of imitation' ('PPW' 102, 105).

The second part of the preface has a theoretical dimension combined with the normative mode. Czartoryski clearly indicates a change in discursive direction to a discussion of rules: 'Let us now proceed to selecting arguments for tragedy and comedy and listen to what the wise abbé Dubos advises in his *Réflexions ...*' ('PPW' 109). We learn here of the larger benefits of theatre-going (as compared with reading) for the common man and for national taste and morality. Czartoryski argues the need for the choice of subject and setting to be culturally specific to affect a native audience (thus touching on the Enlightenment-era problem of a universal human nature versus local ways of being human). Predictably, we encounter frequent quotations from Horace and Aristotle's definition of comedy. Here, too, we finally obtain insight into the history and state of Polish theatre and the reasons for its relative infancy, or long overdue resurrection. The final part offers applied criticism of Polish playwrights, as well as remarks on acting technique, concluded by a didactic anecdote (*historyjka*, or 'little story') about Garrick (114). Czartoryski then takes the opportunity to encourage Polish dramatists to aim for higher literary standards, and offers some professional advice to translators of foreign plays, suggesting they practice adaptation over translation. By the end, Czartoryski's preface, representing a distinct genre in name only, appears as an eclectic compound, integrated into a coherent whole through its author's generous signage and his intention simply to contextualize the play itself with whatever information is of relevance.[33]

Czartoryski expands references to other critical views and results of historical research to include in the text-body the titles of works being cited (his historical exposition relies on the opinions of older French writers/critics, e.g., Jean de la Bruyère [1645–96], whose sympathies were with the *anciens*). Even this minuscule addition, however, bespeaks the gradual growth in the international self-recognition and practice of literary criticism. That Czartoryski's references are not Polish but French suggests that foreign scholarship was still more highly regarded than homegrown ideas: France was still where theoretical breakthroughs took place. Yet the first reference to Dubos's *Réflexions* (and the sole one – remarkable considering the derivative character of the preface) appears only in the second half of the text. This might perhaps be explained by the fact that most of Czartoryski's readers would have been familiar with Dubos's work (so that the intellectual debt would have gone without saying), and that a distinct concept of plagiarism and crediting rites around intellectual property were still in the making.

The preface contains also one of those 'telling' moments in the history of a then still inchoate Polish criticism. This is a parenthetical expression of humility on the part of the critic, to forestall impressions of him as opinionated and arrogant (the criticism is of none other than Shakespeare): 'The flaw, which they ascribe to him, is that he builds up above common measure things of which he treats, and that he becomes (if I dare say so) gigantic' ('PPW' 106). Of course, out of context, 'if I dare say so' can be interpreted as a critical swipe at the unanimity of opinion about Shakespeare's genius as admitting no disagreement. But, to my mind, it is no such thing; it is genuine hesitation. Another, more excessive feature of Czartoryski's preface is an extensive quotation (over a page long) from Joseph Addison's (1672–1719) essay in *The Spectator* on the subject of humour – which the author then supplements with his own observations) (112).

All of this is crowned by the preface's terminological merit. The last paragraph, quoted here in full, reads:

> My quill carried me beyond intended brevity; perhaps it was overbold of me to have to partake in this writing of new words, but when writing of a new thing, almost unknown in our parts, one needs to create words, or express oneself with ones unused. I expect that this difficulty is capable of excusing me before the gracious reader, and besides, 'hanc veniam damus petimusque vicissim [I ask this privilege for myself and grant it to others].' ('PPW' 114)

Hence, even in its neologistical capacity, the preface is limited to borrowing from another literary culture. The coinage of new words in Polish was, by Czartoryski's own admission, done from necessity – the necessity of participating in a world of discourse from which one has thus far, or in some areas, been removed. Terms like taste, wit, or genius still appear in need of definition (a clarification of the term genius even occasions a detour ['PPW' 102–3]), indicating that only a modest degree of discursive integration had occurred. An introductory note to Czartoryski's preface tells us, however, that the author's copy included multiple handwritten corrections testifying to his particular 'sensitization to historical-literary terminology' (the change from *obiectum* to *przedmiot* [subject] being one example intelligible to a non-Polish speaker) (92).

Czartoryski's preface draws attention to the inseparability of literary-critical judgment and the historical understanding of literature. It was a curious development that, a century or so later, would make the former ostensibly exclusive of the latter. Thus, historians of literature would not patently pass judgment, and journalistic critics, in the growing belief that each new age has its aesthetic standards for what is valued and what is not, would not see the need for extensive historical knowledge in professional practice. This polarization meant that historical study evolved a discriminating set of standards and procedures – it was hard to pursue history as a discipline *in addition* to criticism without seeming a dilettante. It was also quite natural that, in historical writing, shorter forms were supplanted by longer, or that their average length extended to accommodate increasing available source material and reference (based on greater availability and scholarly production). This happened in the case of monographs, which assumed book volume previously associated with histories.

(c) J. Szymanowski's List o guście, czyli smaku *[Letter on Taste] (Warsaw, 1779)*[34]

Józef Szymanowski's (1748–1801) 'letter' in fact comprises two letters, which were sent as personal correspondence and apparently circulated by their addressee in manuscript among those interested in forming a literary-critical periodical.[35] Kostkiewiczowa adjusts its genre to a composition of two essays ('Myśl' 9). Nonetheless, the singular in the title asks – to the best of my knowledge, without generic precedents – that we consider the two letters as two halves of one. The first attends to the tasks and value of literary criticism and revolves around the theme of taste – the faculty uniting writers and critics; the second resumes the discussion where the first left off. The direct, primary addressee of *List o guście* is not named, but is assumed to have been Piramowicz, under whose editorship they were to appear;[36] the secondary audience, however, must have been Czartoryski (who was Szymanowski's close friend), because of this text's correspondence to Czartoryski's preface to his own 1779 comedy *Kawa* [Coffee], which had the form of a letter to Szymanowski, and because of Czartoryski's patronage and directorship of the projected periodical. *List o guście* was included in the first Polish anthology of literary criticism, *Listy krytyczne o różnych literatury rodzajach* [Critical Letters on Various Kinds of Literature] (edited by Piramowicz and published by Warsaw's most renowned publisher Michał Gröll in 1779). The collection was concerned not with individual works but with more general topics (the role of criticism, literary genius, taste, or drama). The project and the resulting publication issued from an autonomous cultural and intellectual milieu in Puławy, formed in contestation of the hegemonic tendencies of classicist theory and literary practice, particularly in Warsaw.[37] Like other texts from this period, this publication testifies to a growing awareness and deliberation of the value of their work in the context of major social and educational reform.

The gist of the first letter (though not its argument) is to be found in a formulation of theoretical questions. It comes in the middle of the letter's second paragraph: 'I enclose the entire fabric of my thoughts in these two points: what is *goût*, or good taste? And in what way is it spoiled or improved?' ('LG' 165). To discuss the category of taste (in rather normative terms), Szymanowski draws on British aesthetics. He borrows the three *necessary* components of taste from the *Essay on Taste* (1756) by British philosopher of aesthetics Alexander Gerard. Mentioned as well is d'Alembert's opinion on the matter from his 1760 *Réflexions sur l'usage et sur l'abus de philosophie dans les matières de goût* [Reflections on the Use and Abuse of Philosophy in Matters of Taste].

Also worth tarrying over are the text's two self-referential moments (the second almost a reprise of the first), wherein Szymanowski underscores the self-applicatory – the only credible? – character of criticism: 'With this thought I am prone to throw in some comments regarding taste, which with respectful delay I submit to the judgment of criticism' ('LG' 165).[38] Szymanowski's frankness of tone dispels the impression of affected, conventionalized posturing. Szymanowski's submission to criticism demonstrates a degree of consistency, an integrity of the critical endeavour properly carried out; it betokens his support for the service critics perform despite differences of opinion. It echoes the attitude of the opening paragraph, where Szymanowski addresses an unnamed literary critic (most probably Piramowicz), using the latter's announcement of a critique of that year's literary yield as a launching pad for vigorous reflection on the benefits of criticism to writers. This paragraph ends: 'Criticism ought itself to be an essential model of excellent writing, otherwise not only does it miss its intended target, but with corrupt example reinforces those faults of poor taste which it was to uproot.' His openness is likewise reflected in his embrace of the term *szydność* – after Czartoryski's rendition of the French *le ridicule* in his 1771 'Przedmowa' ('PPW' 109). The implication of Szymanowski's approach is that a certain responsibility comes with being a critic – a responsibility of supporting the conversation. Czartoryski was very supportive of Szymanowski, whose views were less moderate than his own and perhaps for this reason more appealing. Despite his affiliation with the Puławy centre, which was mounting its own aesthetic program closer to rococo sentimentalism, Czartoryski maintained his association with official, mainstream literature (he exhibited the same two-facedness in his political views) (Pietraszko, 'ISR' lxxix–lxxxiv). Thus, it fell to Szymanowski's lot to articulate as a calm protest what in Czartoryski were growing but unformulated objections to classicism, which saw literature as a unity of aesthetic and ethical principles (lxxxiv).

The second letter opens with another humble appeal for the addressee's 'sagacious' (*roztropny*) criticism ('LG' 168). Editors Kostkiewiczowa and Goliński note that the reference here to a 'close friendship' between the author and the letter's recipient suggests that *List o guście* was, in fact, written to Czartoryski – despite the veiled critique it contains of the latter's new comedy *Kawa* (164n1). The letter then proceeds to its subject matter, describing for instance how the acquisition/refinement of taste – of an individual, as well as an entire culture – is aided by education. Szymanowski refers to comparison with the highest achievements to date as a procedure for creating new works of art. In the next two paragraphs, he becomes more overtly metacritical, cautioning against superficial judgment as 'proof of imperfect taste,' and the pitfalls of critical vanity, such as noticing flaws where there are none, for the sake of 'differentiating one's opinion from all others' (169). One of the three elements of taste, *accuracy*, is acquired only by habituating one's reason to diligent attention to the literary work at hand (169).

Next comes a critique of classicist pedantry. Slavish, over-scrupulous adherence to existing rules (like the common attachment to ancient models) is decried as counterproductive for the steady betterment of taste. The great work comes before the rules, which are then inferred from it. Regardless of the universal currency of the author of the *Poetics*, Szymanowski proposes, criticism might as well have fallen under the normative spell of someone else; Aristotelian standards are, to an extent, random and arbitrary – how else could cultural taste be improved? This historical relativism pulls the rug from under any universalist, legislative status quo, not just entrenched Aristotelianism (academic reforms initiated by the *KEN* in 1777 had already begun the expulsion of Aristotelianism for the sake of rationalism). Fundamentally, however, the above remark can be applied to rule-governed classicist theory.[39] As was customary of classicist poetics, the definitive arbiter here is nonetheless the intellect, which, by means of taste, is qualified to judge when and if literature is justified in taking liberties with accepted norms. At the same time, this decision is based strictly on aesthetic criteria – a definite break with the classicist fusion of aesthetics and ethics.

List o guście includes one long note containing a wealth of literary-critical remarks. It is as though the metacritical observations and theoretical questions seemed to Szymanowski more urgent, overshadowing the criticism, which – in need of an outlet – was consigned to an inconspicuous place and markedly casual in diction. Moreover, the plan laid out seems to be deliberately cut short when Szymanowski declares:

> If I were to want to expound the matter undertaken in one letter only, I would evidently abuse Your patience as well as wear out Your precious time, whose every moment You long to sacrifice to essential public service.

> The further fabric of my thoughts concerning the second point: In what ways is taste improved and spoiled? I will at a freer time for both myself and Yourself have the honour to send. ('LG' 167–8)

Necessitating this abrupt conclusion and the stated intention to defer reflections to another day is presumably Piramowicz's taxing status within the discursive milieu, which would render inappropriate a colleague's excessive demands on his time. Late in the letter, we learn of the value of conferences, whereby learning is displayed and critical opinions exchanged, for the purification of taste. Presumably, such an opportunity presented itself to Szymanowski to enlarge on the ideas in his letters.

In his second letter (written before the publication of the first), Szymanowski takes up, as pledged, the thread of his previous epistle by returning to the discussion of taste. The opening of this letter reveals that the publication of the first part prompted and 'encouraged' its author to finish his reflection ('LG' 168). But to think of this critical, formal yet personal letter as an improvisation that midway runs out of steam – only to be resumed because of external stimuli – as a failed assay at literary-critical reflection would be to miss the point not just about its confirmed intellectual value, but about the dynamic, transformative nature of genre life itself. In its accretion of dimensions (metacritical, theoretical, critical) and generic ambiguity, two characteristics of the emergent discourse can be discerned: its formal 'lawlessness' and, more importantly, its liminal place between 'Literature' and 'all other writing.' *List o guście*, for example, is written in a free and elegant style, aligning itself formally with the literary ideal of imaginative, sensual refinement which it espouses. It concludes with a bold rhetorical question: 'I do not know what rank to give us, but if diligence was always bolstered by just respect, wherefore could we not rise to the radiant South?' (171). Despite, or maybe because of, its idiosyncrasies and its not being explicitly rule-governed, *List o guście* shows off the subtleties of expressing critical judgment on contemporary works perhaps better than any other text analysed here.

(d) F.N. Golański's O wymowie i poezji *[On Elocution and Poetry] (Warsaw, 1786)*[40]

The lengths of this and the final text considered substantially exceed those of the previous three. We will discuss them in broader terms, without the same, perhaps fastidious attention given to the others.

Golański's work has been credited with being 'the first full outline of literary doctrine in the Polish Enlightenment' (this accomplishment was recognized with a *Merentibus* medal by the king).[41] Although it was intended as a textbook for the reformed school system, it clearly had 'higher aspirations' (Pietraszko, *Doktryna* 18). The work is a treatise with a theoretical-critical dimension, generically traditional – combining poetics with rhetoric. It is divided into two main parts – the first being 'On Elocution,' the second 'On Poetry' – and into multiple smaller sections: 'The Origin and Aim of Poetry,' 'Poetic Style,' and 'Division of Poetry' (with further subdivisions named after the genre discussed therein: epigrams, satires, odes, hymns, idylls, dramatic poetry, tragedy, comedy, heroic poem, and didactic poetry). The divisions create the impression of a high level of textual organization and conceptual economy. In the following discussion, we will naturally be focusing on the second part concerned with poetry.

'On Poetry' begins with a motto from Cicero's *De oratore*. This citation is only the first of many dozen, be they excerpts of ancient and contemporary literature[42] or quotations from Golański's Polish contemporaries – Joachim Litawor Chreptowicz, Konarski, Krasicki, Rzewuski, and Szymanowski. As in the other texts, allusions to ancient literary-theoretical works abound (most notably those of Aristotle and Horace). The move to openly valorize the scholarship of Polish authors (and thus build a national network of intellectual reciprocity and collaboration) in addition to that of the French cannot be underestimated. Of the latter, Golański relied on works by French contemporaries Charles Batteux (aesthetic philosopher, author of *Les Beaux-Arts réduits à un même principe* [The Fine Arts Reduced to a Single Principle] [1746]) and Jean François Marmontel (literary critic and writer, at that time notable for the 1763 *Poétique française* [French Poetics]). Apart from the customary normative language, mainstream arguments, and substantiation by historical examples, large parts of Golański's discussion of individual genres are plot-driven (to the point of creating separate subsections to summarize the action in the *Iliad, Odyssey,* and *Aeneid*). A noteworthy element is his inclusion of 'Scholars' Opinion concerning Homer and Virgil,' where he relates the dispute over the merits of the two poets, and takes Homer's side (though he does not identify the sides or figures of the debate, perhaps taking readers' familiarity with it for granted). In the final analysis, however, the merit of Golański's work is not its generic status of an outline, but the degree of clarity, systematization, and sustained erudition (as exemplified by the range of his references) that he brings to the topic of literary genre distinctions.

(e) *F.K. Dmochowski's* Sztuka rymotwórcza. Poema we czterech pieśniach *[The Art of Rhyming: A Poem in Four Cantos] (Warsaw, 1788)*[43]

Dmochowski has been described as the 'patron of pseudoclassicist form-polishing.'[44] It is not surprising, then, that his own writings would evince greater attention to form than those of many of his contemporaries. *Sztuka rymotwórcza* is one of a few works in eighteenth-century Polish literary criticism composed in verse (another is Rzewuski's) – though it was not the first. Its original character 'expressed itself ... in the exchange of foreign literary examples for Polish ones, but above all in the new content of borrowed traditional terms and judgments' (cxvi).[45] Dmochowski's critical debut, however – a text titled *List Sandomierzanki do Podolanki* [Letter from a Female Resident of Sandomierz to One of Podole] (Cracow, 1784) – initiated what was to become the first polemic in the history of Polish literary criticism.[46] As this letter makes plain, Dmochowski would have quarrelled with the metaphysics of Gottsched and other prominent classicists, who credited the ancients with exhausting the truth about human nature and art (xxxiii). Dmochowski's position entailed a disregard for normativity in critical judgment, while his aesthetic theory rested on ethics (xl).

The classicism propounded by Dmochowski belonged to the second phase of Polish classicism (the first being that of the 'precursors'). What prescription rears its head in *Sztuka rymotwórcza* (and the work has been condemned for it by supporters of 'pure,' i.e., speculative literary theory) is the result of Dmochowski's intimate connection to literary practice – a fact to which the work owes its valuable generalizations without straying into speculation via the 'idealist tendencies hidden in its philosophical underpinnings' (Pietraszko, 'ISR' clv). Throughout, Dmochowski addresses his intended reader – a writer and reader of poetry – in the informal second person (the pronoun *ty*) and offers, instead of dry instruction in poetical precepts, consistently amiable, commonsensical, and well-meaning advice for poets aspiring to the heights of Parnassus – on everything from critics and how to appease an audience, through the limits of imitation and fine points of poetic style, to the moral grounding of poetic character (e.g., 'But do not spin thought on rhyme but rhyme on thought. / The matter [*rzecz*] is always prime, all art [*sztuka*] on't. / And who this matter guards does not search for rhymes' [*SR* 13]).[47] Here, like in most other instances, Dmochowski speaks from and to the collectivity of experience that includes critics, poet-critics, and readers (his principle that the poet should be his own honest and stern critic [*krytyk*] is entirely in keeping with this stance [32]). He speaks collectively also when he notes:

> But in the precarious art of casting poems
> Who is not the first must be last;
> No intermediate rung bridges these two ends.
> Never should you resign yourself to mediocrity,
> People will not suffer it, nor gods forgive. (129)

The preface to *Sztuka rymotwórcza* is composed in prose and follows a versified dedicatory letter to the Polish king. The main feature of the dedication and the preface is their articulation of the author's design, couched in praise and gratitude to the monarch and humility toward the general readership. Giving us clues to the generic affiliation of the text – the normative, philosophical-theoretical treatise – are several lines that stand out in the dedication:

> I wanted a picture of their art honest
> To ensue and cast laws all its own.
> Everything must fit in some design,
> What blindly rushes, must be bad.
> Philosophers have their precepts,
> As do orators, as do poets. (*SR* 3)

And, a bit further on: 'I have stayed my course by these masters [Aristotle, Horace, Boileau, Pope], / With nature strictly in sight. / If I have not matched my model / I am not ashamed to fail with good intentions' (6). The rest of this brief text contains what most dedicatory letters then contained: the main point of what is to follow. In the preface, Dmochowski elaborates on his motives and intentions, striking apologetic notes:

> Indeed, I will perhaps appear overbold to some, but no matter, as long as I am so fortunate as to complete my intention … I sought therefore a matter untreated by our native pens … This work is neither solely a translation, nor without claim to originality. Spurred on by reading works on the art of rhyming, particularly Horace and Despréaux [Boileau], I wanted to enrich our tongue with like … I will congratulate myself greatly if I find favour with a sensible reader. (7)

Here again, Dmochowski lists his predecessors in *artes poeticae*, whose works he considers models for the work in progress. This time, each of them is given a sentence explaining which of their qualities he appreciates most.

As will be seen also in the case of the Russian Lomonosov, the inclusion by Dmochowski of a dedication was motivated by contemporary realities of publication and legitimation of learned works. The royal address was, of course, a form of flattery of the monarch, whose literary patronage was known far and wide. The advance (somewhat cheerful) apology to Slanislaus for the failure to execute his design is part affectation, part genuine concern – and part of the writerly rituals to secure approval. The layering of both dedication and preface with names of authorities acts as a kind of buffer against potential criticism – though how genuine a concern the latter was for Dmochowski is difficult to gauge. (Pietraszko tells us that *Sztuka rymotwórcza* ended up with 'the misfortune of having more critics than readers' – critics who accused its author of reinforcing French taste, generic rigidity, compartmentalization, and classicist dogmatism ['ISR' clvi–clvii]. On the other hand, the text had considerable acceptance among educators that lasted well into the nineteenth century and even afterward, when it was disseminated in extracts and used as a textbook on Polish literary history [clviii].)

Once the formalities, or pleasures, of the above are over,[48] the text takes on a much bolder tone, continuing to address the reader. The body of the text consists (as the detailed table of contents, appropriately titled 'Content of the Matter,' indicates) of five cantos. The first is devoted to general introductions of poetic intent, talent, rhyme, the proper limits and excesses of fiction, ornamentation, specificity, variety, stylistic refinement, poetic 'harmony,' word choice, clarity, improvement, but most significantly: a detailed, critical literary history of Poland 'up to our time,' as well as sections on 'The Need for Criticism' and 'The Character of a Favourable and Sensible Critic.' The second and third cantos deal with individual genres (pastoral, elegy, ode, epigram, satire, fable, tragedy, and comedy). The fourth canto contains a collection of thoughts on writing and the value of literature ('Remarks concerning Poetry and Poets'), including advice on competent critical evaluation ('The Art of Judging and Choosing between Older and Later Authors'), and warnings of critical ineptitude ('The Reward Merciless Critics Deserve') directly addressing the critic. The work ends with a section titled 'Closing of the Work.' It seems odd that the headings are only given in the contents pages – making orientation in the main text less than ideal.

The section titles and the overarching themes indicate that *Sztuka rymotwórcza* still largely participates in the modern *artes poeticae* tradition, albeit with some considerable modifications of material and diction. Kostkiewiczowa observes that it 'combined a lecture on literary doctrine ... with a sketch of a program of development for national letters and elements of up-to-date literary criticism' ('Myśl' 8). It inadvertently supports classicist aesthetics and literary realism, but (as Pietraszko points out) the 'metaphysical categories' of the day (concessions made to irrationalism and subjectivism) make it blind to its inner irreconcilables, such as the concrete and the general, or form and content ('ISR' cxx). Indeed, the text gropes for a reconciliation of nature/talent with art and poetic rules – a contradiction just then emerging. As the borrowings from Boileau's system of literary genres suggest, its view of literary conventions is somewhat rigid, relying too frequently on binary oppositions. Its tone, often vibrant, is also often flat, its evaluations panegyrical and, in this sense, bordering on subjectivism and sentimentality. Dmochowski's discussion revolves around Polish literature, assaying it and singling out some authors for their excellence, others for their instructive shortcomings, drawing general conclusions about the state of literature in particular periods, and even theorizing about them. In the process, it mentions a great number of foreign luminaries. The author is disposed to listing and glossing not only for instruction's but also for breadth's sake – expanding the knowledge of indigenous and foreign achievement.

Sztuka rymotwórcza, Pietraszko notes, exhibits a tendency 'to rise to the level of the best literary prose of his day' (the exemplar for which was Krasicki); it is a refined Polish, not the courtly variety, but the disciplined Polish of the Piarist libraries – many archaic words and expressions are said to have been used in the text for the very last time ('ISR' cl–cli). What, however, of the genre of Dmochowski's work? Pietraszko makes a case for *Sztuka rymotwórcza* as a didactic poem – of the descriptive variety, including simultaneous textual application of the principles of poetry being described:

> *Sztuka rymotwórcza* is a poetics, it belongs to the theory of literature, but we should not forget that it itself is a poetic work [obeying principles of lyric poetry]. This freed the author from many responsibilities commonly imposed by the scholarly treatise. Thus, Dmochowski had the right to dodge strict definitions, which he did not like anyway in nonpoetic writing ... Its construction depends on the didactic subject, whose line of reasoning defines the order of the content. This subject's monologue approached in principle the art of oratory, and owed much to rhetoric in

> its means of expression. The artistry ... in essence came down precisely to rhetorical means, to repetitions and metaphors, more than to the vividness of the word. One is struck by the excess of abstraction – and soon reminded that this is a poem professing the principles of classicist aesthetics. (cxlviii–cl)

In his attempt to explain the genesis of *Sztuka rymotwórcza* through a broad set of factors (sociological, political, biographical), Pietraszko identifies the mnemotechnical character of verse – and therefore the superiority of the didactic poem over the prose textbook – as one reason for Dmochowski's choice of form. Dmochowski's prefatory homage to Horace's *Ars poetica* (a work whose authority in Poland was at the time immense) takes the following form: 'Horace, a man of great wit, deliberately seems to feign disorder, and as a poet to poets speaks' (*SR* 6). This is clearly telling of Dmochowski's design – given, too, his own creative aspirations during the writing of *Sztuka rymotwórcza*.

The text moves from subject to subject with exceptional buoyancy and firmness of purpose. Dmochowski makes prolific and clever use of metaphor, stock imagery (mainly mythological), and the narrative mode. In a brief history of dramatic art, the grim lines devoted to the Middle Ages paint a real 'dark night of the soul,' while the Renaissance is, predictably, the coming of dawn (*SR* 77). In an extended metaphoric parallel, the writer's craft is described in terms of the painter's (for example, the colour palette as the tonality of poetic language), though this does not serve to validate the theory of *ut pictura poesis* (15–22). Dmochowski's wit not only conceals the text's normativity but works to downplay the rigidity of norms and plays up Muse-inspired spontaneity:

> No art without nature, work to no avail
> ...
> Albeit do not cling to art as a drunkard to a fence.
> Not every work suffers the same rules.
> Art, taken from examples, limits human works.
> Has it encompassed all in its time? (130)

Canto 4, apart from being the most diverse in subject matter, takes up the question of universal literary merit. Dmochowski argues for the value of studying the ancients. His argument for parity with the ancients is derived from ancient philosophy:

> What does Antiquity write? Can one do greater
> harm to human nature, thinking it so flighty
> That, to others a mother, to us she is less?
> ...
> Let us cast an unprejudiced glance
> At the works of the famous, and we will surely see
> That we have many riches to equal the ancients. (140)

The fourth canto contains also a section extolling the virtues of rural life and nature's bosom, a section on the art of translation (and the scarcity of good translators), a brief history of poetry's origins, and a section instructing and castigating harsh and petty critics. The latter thematic brings the reader back to Dmochowski's remarks in canto 1. While praise is easy, critical praise requires skill. Every work deserves to be evaluated with the benefit of the doubt, as negative criticism – indolent and destructive – should be the critic's last resort. 'It is easiest, putting on a pair of spectacles, / ... / To remain blind to beauties, and mark only flaws' (142). Dmochowski tells a cautionary tale about a *zoil* who received his just deserts (143). 'You laugh?' he continues, addressing *zoils* directly, 'You yourself deserve such reward. / The critic's stern office is not for everyone: / Let him judge others who does something himself.' The final lines of *Sztuka rymotwórcza* underscore their author's modest literary-critical objectives: 'May the benefit of this writing be at least / That it to others become a whetstone, / Which, though it alone cannot cut in two, / Makes sharper knives which can' (150).

Although over twenty-five years apart, Dmochowski's statements have their analogues in Rzewuski's text. They have frequently been paired on the generic level, with Dmochowski's text remaining the better known. Horace and Boileau figure prominently as sources of ideas in both works. Both texts rarely depart from normativity in their view of literature. Rzewuski's criticism is oriented toward a popular view of literature (poems should be short, so as not to tire the reader, and *dulce*, in keeping with the placid economy of poetic art; drama is well-written when it jerks tears from the audience). A classicist conceit such as the grandiose invocation of the Muses, present in Rzewuski's work, is absent from Dmochowski's. Compared to the elevated style of *O nauce wierszopiskiej*, the verse of *Sztuka rymotwórcza* may seem rough-hewn at times; its unquestionably greater merit can be found in its comprehensive historical survey of native literature and its high readability.

4 Excursus

In a comparative study of this sort, one naturally seeks not only common conceptual and practical ground but also concrete threads interlacing two or more of the phenomena being compared. Such a thread exists most often in the form of a text (in the original or in translations), but much less so in the form of an individual. Wawrzyniec Mitzler de Kolof (1711–78) was just such a transnational mediatory figure. He became involved in Polish culture while studying in Leipzig, when he was asked by the Załuscy brothers to help organize their library. The rest, one is tempted to say, is history. Stationed in Warsaw from 1749, Mitzler became an avid publisher, publicist, and printer, as well as an intermediary between the Polish- and the German-speaking Polish civic population (which in Warsaw constituted about fifty per cent).[49] Mitzler's strength as a publisher lay in literary, scholarly, and popular-scientific journals – *Monitor* being the highlight of his periodical-publishing career.[50] His chief literary-theoretical contribution was the *Brief eines Gelehrten aus Wilna die polnische Schaubühne betreffend* [Letter by a Scholar from Vilnius concerning the Polish Stage] (Warsaw, 1775). Mitzler's pseudo-letters (the title, as in Szymanowski's case, is misleading), of which only five are known to be extant, are addressed to a certain charactonymous Lorenz von Lehrlieben from 'M' (Kaleta 284). The form of correspondence on a topic of literary interest was familiar to the readers of *Monitor*: in this way, Mitzler facilitated the establishment of a form through his publishing ventures and by practising it himself (284).

Chapter Three

Criticism in Russia

Used to singing the praises of famous works,
I fear becoming a satirist, mean and careless.

(Mikhail M. Kheraskov, 1760)[1]

1 The Emperor's Tongue: Russian Literary Language

To embark on its own Enlightenment, Russia needed to enlarge the discursive purview of Western Europe. Its ambition to 'join the conversation' – and cultural, political, and economic life in general – not merely by parroting foreign discourses, but through original contributions, necessitated the invention and refinement of Russian technical, professional, and literary languages. Unlike Germany and Poland in the eighteenth century, the Russian empire could not boast of a fully-fledged secular literary tradition, as Russian letters were still firmly rooted in Russian Orthodox theological writing. Nonetheless, the emergence of modern Russian literature roughly coincided with the emergence of Russia as a European power. The imperialist ideological underpinnings of the growth of Russian literature permeated also matters of literary genre and style.[2] Imperial ambition drove the emulation of Western literary models to take on a form of appropriation and transmutation into something distinctly Russian. Classicism, which reached its apogee in the seventeenth century, was compressed in Russia into a short period of time in an attempt to bridge the cultural gap. The main representatives of Russian classicism were Mikhail V. Lomonosov (1711–65), Aleksandr P. Sumarokov (1717–77), and Vasilii K. Trediakovskii (1703–68).[3] Other proponents of classicism were writers: M.M.

Kheraskov (1733–1807) (whose work fell on the cusp of late classicism and new trends),[4] Vladimir I. Lukin (1737–94), Gavrila R. Derzhavin (1743–1816) (who increasingly turned away from classicist formalism), and dramaturge Piotr A. Plavilshchikov (1760–1812). In the 1780s, classicism was already giving way to sentimentalism, with Nikolai M. Karamzin (1766–1826) and Ivan I. Dmitriev (1760–1837) as its leading exponents. V.I. Kuleshov – in what is one of the three histories of Russian literary criticism with claims to comprehensiveness – notes that, like literature, 'eighteenth-century literary criticism, its methods and modes of analysis of literary works, its genres, styles, concepts, and terms were also still in an embryonic form.'[5] As in the Polish case, Russia's eighteenth-century literary theory was by and large an imitation of 'originals' travelling from the West, with adjustments made for the characteristics of Russian language. Although intellectual opposition to Westernizing reforms on the level of spoken and literary language could be heard in the latter half of the century, it was only in the 1800s that literary-critical discourse assumed a distinctly non-westerly, even anti-westerly, orientation, fully asserting the cultural distinctiveness of the native heritage.[6]

Russian literary language developed differently from those of Western Europe, first, because of the much later separation of church and state and, second, because of Russia's proximity and access not to Latin but to Greek and Byzantine culture. Viktor Vinogradov described the processes and projects of linguistic synthesis that began in the 1600s, following the influx and fetishization of Western European lexical, phraseological, and semantic forms. The wide-ranging and forcible modernization instigated by Peter the Great (who ruled between 1682 and 1725, from 1721 as *Imperator i Samoderzhets Vserossiiskii*, Emperor and Autocrat of All of Russia), enabled the emergence of an educated elite, immersed in contemporary European discourses and literary life. The Europeanization of secular written language in Russia during this period 'clearly bore the stamp of government' and 'was reflected in [the language's] polytechnicalization' (Vinogradov 32–3). This meant that literary language did not develop apace with technical-scientific language. A national literary language was taken for granted as developing out of the interaction of Church Slavonic (the language of professional, polemical, or dogmatic church literature, which had already been nationalized) with Russian (57).[7] Paraphrasing Lomonosov, Vinogradov observed 'that the forms of national speech were an essential, organic part of the literary language and that the composition and relationship of various literary genres were conditioned by the methods and principles of the mixing and interaction of Church Slavonicisms and Russianisms' (56).

The asymmetry in the development of technical and literary languages became apparent with the increasing secularization of literature throughout the eighteenth century, as the *literary* function of Church Slavonic was limited (notably, by Lomonosov) to its 'living structural elements' found in the Bible and popular religious and common liturgical writing, as well as to its transmission of Classical and Christian Byzantine culture (Vinogradov 56–7). In its stead, theorists looked to the colloquial speech of the lower class or the West-infused speech of the upper class (alternately, their democratic synthesis) as models for a national literary language.

Peter's initiatives in the arts and sciences yielded a variety of translations that introduced new Western terminology, concepts, and genres. The 'barbaric' mechanical borrowings, calques (loan translations), and replacements with foreign equivalents were mainly derived from Polish, German, Latin, and French (however, the 1700s saw a decline in translations from Polish) (Vinogradov 30).

> [A]lthough Poland remained an intermediary of West European concepts ... growing knowledge of Latin and other Western languages permitted [its] by-passing ... Polish influence gave way to German. But the Polish and Latin influences, which had penetrated the written language and the speech of the upper classes quite deeply, provided a background for continued Europeanization of the literary language, particularly in the development of abstract concepts. (30)

The evolving norms attached to these conceptual renditions were to act as foundation for a standard, stylistically stratified, nationalized literary language – an autonomous 'Slavono-Russian' – that had certainly arrived by the end of Catherine's reign in 1796. However, before the 1740s, the '[d]emocratization and Europeanization of the language could not regulate the different stylistic varieties of the literary language. No firm system of literary styles and genres had been worked out, despite the fact that new forms of literary expression had appeared in the Petrine era' (Vinogradov 55).

At this point in time, the linguistic stratification of the nobility was immense. In the latter half of the century, it was the aristocratic literary salon (modelled on the French pre-revolutionary salon) that gained purchase on literary stylistics and overthrew the tyranny of church tradition.[8] In this highly Europeanized environment, French was the most fashionable currency. Vinogradov asserts that, 'the Russo-French salon style must have been close to the literary language which was just being formed' (87). At the same time, opposition to the mechanical borrowing of foreign words to express foreign concepts in translation work exposed the 'unstable and undeveloped … means of expressing abstract ideas in the Russian literary language' (88–9) – ideas central to the French discourses on art that were then being translated, absorbed, and imitated. The influx of Gallicisms in the transmission of Western concepts can account for the obsolescence, by the end of the century, of Lomonosov's main principle of linguistic formation – the mixing of Slavonic and folk elements – among writers associated with Russian nobility. Karamzin arrived on the scene with a call to create 'a new literary language which would satisfy a developed linguistic taste and would correspond to the spirit and style of European civilization' (92). This entailed valorizing the speech of refined society, with its liberal admixture of French, but, above all, being creative with inherited lexis and syntax, with little sympathy for the everyday speech of lower social strata (92, 100).

Despite the precursory *Grundriss* laid by Peter and the major sociocultural changes taking place from the middle of the century, it was 1762 – the year of Catherine's coronation – or, in any case, the early years of her reign, that came to signify the commencement of the Russian Enlightenment. Catherine built on the Westernizing achievements of her predecessor, and, like Peter, was recognized internationally as a great patron of learning and the arts. Her rule was characterized by relative internal and external political stability, given Russia's policy of expansionism (by 1795, for instance, the empire annexed a large part of what was then Polish territory). Although Catherine harboured consummate ambitions for enlightened reform and, through correspondence, gained approval and respect from *philosophes* Voltaire and Diderot, her efforts remained, at the core, conservative. The French Revolution – as well as the passing of the May 3rd Constitution in Poland – became a source of disenchantment and occasion for redoubled repression, aiming to stifle progressive, libertarian ideas in Russia. However, Catherine's grip on dissidence did not prevent a profound intellectual transformation from taking place, as the last decades of the eighteenth century ushered in an educated elite separate from the court and 'something like an independent public opinion that differed from the views in enlightened court circles.'[9] This intellectual elite, though far from homogeneous, was united through critical, anti-reactionary sentiments.

Throughout most of the century, Russia possessed two thriving cultural centres. In 1712, just nine years after its founding, St Petersburg – hailed as Russia's 'window to Europe' – became the imperial capital. It soon shared the empire's cultural responsibilities with the much older Moscow, and contended for primacy in many spheres of intellectual and aristocratic life (their dynamic bears similarity to that between Warsaw and Cracow during the same period). The two cities became home to the empire's growing journalistic, literary, and artistic enterprise, and rapidly accumulated internationally recognized cultural capital. Their development ran more or less parallel: for example, Russia's first academy of sciences opened in St Petersburg in 1724, while the first university was founded in Moscow in 1755 (largely through Lomonosov's lobbying) – although in the eighteenth century the school was still predominantly run by German academics, much like the Berlin Academy was by the French. It was in these rival cities, too, that the ideological reorganization of Russian society after 1750, as a result of its exposure to European sociopolitical and revolutionary currents, became most pronounced.

2 Criticism's 'Generic Unconscious'

My reason for focusing on Russia's linguistic concerns is this: the language agenda strongly conditioned the beginnings of its literary criticism.[10] In this respect, literary-critical reflection develops in Russia as a response to the need to normalize a national literary language and to come abreast of the literary developments of France, England, and Germany (at that time, all were variations on classicism). The main concern for literary innovators such as the early Trediakovskii, Sumarokov, and Karamzin was to bring the written literary language closer to the spoken language of the upper classes (i.e., court nobility and educated bourgeoisie), instead of reorienting it toward Church Slavonic, as was advocated by Trediakovskii later in his career (1750s and 1760s). As a corollary of this literary formation-consciousness, the mode of emerging criticism was 'overwhelmingly normative.'[11] By contrast, Poland and Germany had by this time established their national literary languages and, in systematizing their literary-critical/theoretical vocabularies, had been moving away from predominantly prescriptive argumentation toward an appreciation of individual artistic systems. Newer literary-critical genres, like the *letter* (*pis'mo*), the *essay* (*sochinenie*), and the *review* (*retsenziia*), placed significantly more emphasis on actual evaluation and description, with a tendency to explore the scope of the literary at the risk of digression. But while in mid- to late-eighteenth-century Germany the French doctrine was as embraced as it was reviled, French Classicism travelled as dogma to both Poland and Russia.

Along with derivative literary theory came the translated and adapted Classical and European literary heritage – the effect of this cultural inundation was telescopic. The influx of both French and German ideas in forms such as poetics and rhetoric can be traced to their popularizations in the work of two key figures: Trediakovskii (who in 1727–30 studied at the Sorbonne) and Lomonosov (who, like Gottsched, was in the 1730s a student of Wolff at the University of Marburg) (Reyfman 50, 52).[12] Nonetheless, the Russian reception and interpretation of foreign literary norms and forms were bound up with each individual's linguistic politics. Their different assessments of the state of the Russian language and their literary-linguistic programs shaped their representation and imitation of foreign literary models.[13] The 'generic drift' is particularly evident in the work of Trediakovskii, who, in the mid-'40s, modified his conception of the literary language. Thus, he moved away from stressing the analogy between Russia's literary culture and the literary cultures of Western nations (which called for basing the literary language on the spoken) and toward emphasizing Russia's linguistic, stylistic, literary-historical distinctiveness (which entailed postulating the 'intrinsic unity' of secular Russian and Church Slavonic, based on common syntactical, lexical, and morphological features – a view also held by Sumarokov) (62–3, 88). While his earlier literary works invoked spoken language and were composed in the genres of European classicism, the later one hearkened back to the church book tradition, laden with archaisms, didacticism, and spiritual meaning. Also worth mentioning is the fact that the theoretical discourse of the trinity Lomonosov–Sumarokov–Trediakovskii – most of it patterned on the same Western literary-theoretical sources – could be quite divorced from their own literary practice (62).

The preoccupation with language in the Russian case, although it addressed generic concerns and spurred innovation, did not require the invention of a generic repertoire: linguistic, lexical, semantic, and structural concerns were mainly expressed in treatises on rhetoric and versification, genres assimilated from the classicist West. These forms also – as in other countries – accommodated literary-critical material to the extent that it proceeded from reflection on literary language, and not, for instance, on literary aesthetics. Like literature, criticism too was in the process of formal installation; pronouncements and debates on the correspondence of language, style, and genre became, as it were, the fibres of nascent literary criticism. To come into its own, the discursivity just then being spun needed self-consciousness and *literary* specificity. It would be only at the turn of the nineteenth century that criticism disengaged itself from linguistic concerns as such and concentrated on contemporary literature and individual literary systems – judged as, or relative to, current standards of social and political commentary. Thus, disengagement in one area, an area whose main task was the enthusiastic standardization of writing, brought with it new, *critical* responsibilities for writers, and, in the latter half of the nineteenth century, a radical ideological ferment that led to a clash between two literary-critical/theoretical camps: the 'aesthetic' and the 'civic' (or, in Wellek's politicized terms, the 'conservative' and the 'radical').[14]

In his short history of Russian literary criticism, Robert H. Stacy classifies Lomonosov, Trediakovskii, and Sumarokov as pre-professional, academic critics. On the other hand, Irina Reyfman recognizes Trediakovskii as 'the only professional literary scholar among the three,' by virtue of his better philological training, first-hand knowledge of contemporary European writing, and contacts with literary figures in France (Reyfman 50). Both Lomonosov and Sumarokov reproduced many elements of Classical and Neoclassical forms in their literary work, tailoring them to the Russian context; but because these standards were never agreed upon or threshed out, there ensued between them a protracted and bitter infighting. Lomonosov polemicized with Trediakovskii on versification, and with Sumarokov on poetic style, while the latter two disputed these matters vehemently between themselves.[15] As Grigorii Gukovskii painted them: 'Literary disputes inevitably spilled over into the moral arena and resulted in personal abuse. Obscene epigrams were directed against one's literary enemies; highly immoderate language was poured into their polemic by Trediakovsky, Lomonosov, and their contemporaries; there was a tendency to accuse opponents of excessive drunkenness …'[16] The vitality and sobriety of each depended on it.

Lomonosov's literary-critical output fits squarely into the venerable generic tradition of rhetoric and poetics. His 1748 *Kratkoe rukovodstvo k krasnoriechiiu* [Brief Guide to Eloquence] (discussed below) borrows from Gottsched's classicist *Ausführliche Redekunst* [Complete Rhetoric].[17] Sumarokov's *Dve epistoly* [Two Epistles] draws its generic debt directly from Horace's *Ars poetica*, known in medieval manuscripts as *Epistula ad Pisones* [Epistle to the Pisos]. At the same time, the complex linguistic mutability and mixing of styles and genres in Russian literary culture led to the appearance of hybrid, *improvised* forms for literary-critical expression, particularly in the last quarter of the eighteenth century. (This contrasts with literary practice, which strove to apply to the Russian situation the genre system of Western classicism.)

The emergence of literary periodicals in Russia had much to do with the promotion of these newer, and frequently shorter, forms. As in Poland, the primary function of periodicals until the mid-1750s or so was advertising and abstracting new and mainly scholarly publications. The number of periodicals did not experience steady growth due to the ebb and flow of state censorship; before 1760, they were very few and most of them short-lived. All three writers, 'heroic isolated founders of Russian literature,'[18] contributed to a number of periodicals in the course of their careers. The first periodical-hosted literary polemic – between Lomonosov and Trediakovskii – took place in *Ezhemesiachnye sochineniia, k pol'ze i uveseleniiu sluzhashchie* [Monthly Essays to Benefit and Amuse], published by the *Imperatorskaia Akademiia Nauk* (St Petersburg Academy of Sciences) from 1755 to 1764.[19] Another famous periodical polemic of the latter part of the century transpired between writer-publisher Nikolai Ivanovich Novikov (1744–1818) and the empress herself. Catherine was the only monarch of the three regions under study to launch (albeit covertly) her own periodical, modelling it on the British journals *The Tatler* and *The Spectator* (Segel 255). Her satirical weekly *Vsiakaia vsiachina* [All Sorts and Sundries][20] and Novikov's own *Truten'* [The Drone] (1769–70) hosted their disagreement about the object and purpose of satire.[21] Both journals began publication in 1769 and both ceased just over a year later. In no time, the polemic as structure of discursive interaction became the modus vivendi of Russian criticism, as literary discussion drew in further participants.

This overt alliance between the imperial sovereign and literary/literary-critical publishing was intended not to further Catherine's own literary ambitions but to cull political dissent by supposedly fostering genuine critical dialogue within a controlled forum. Suffice it to say, the political climate that welcomed the proliferation of satirical journals was short-lived, since the criticism of ossified or unrefined customs quickly became rampant. (This alliance, as well as encroaching upon censorship, became the foundation for the lasting association between literary criticism and veiled social and political criticism in the following century.)[22] Contributing to the popularity of satirical periodicals, Sumarokov himself published the literary journal *Trudoliubivaia pchela* [The Busy Bee] (1759), as one of the two first Russian private periodicals (to whose title *Truten'* paid parodic homage) (Reyfman 56). This publication consisted largely of translations of Classical and French authors. Karamzin's editorship of the monthly *Moskovskii zhurnal* [Moscow Journal] (1791–92)[23] opened new vistas for periodical publishing, since part of its mandate was to stimulate a national culture to rival that of other European countries at the time. *Moskovskii zhurnal*, considered the first modern Russian literary journal – instead of classicist idolatry it promoted contemporary Russian writing – was also a prototype of nineteenth-century *tolstye zhurnali*,[24] of which Karamzin's own *Vestnik Evropii* [The Herald of Europe, or Messenger of Europe], a monthly published in St Petersburg between 1802 and 1830, was probably the original. Despite the rapid development of journalism (as of most other aspects of Russia's high culture), 'The literary-critical journal, like the informational newspaper, lagged in development behind western Europe ... [and] as an instrument of intellectual connection assumed importance only after the accession of Catherine II in 1762' and the ensuing 'governmental permissiveness.'[25] Catherine's leniency was, however, the opening act of a rather 'spasmodic' development of Russian journalism (Ambler 15). Lomonosov and Novikov, who wrote for the semi-weekly *Sankt-Peterburgskie Vedomosti* [St Petersburg Notices] (active from 1728 – currently Russia's oldest newspaper)[26] and *Moskovskoe obiavlenie* [Moscow Notices] (founded by Moscow University in 1756),

> did much to ... establish certain enduring characteristics of Russian journalism: its strongly literary nature; its comparatively great importance to national cultural life; its strong sense of mission to enlighten and elevate; its preference for analysis and interpretation rather than for 'news' properly speaking; and its close, informed attention to political, social, and cultural developments in western European countries. (13–14)

3 Parody and Polemics

In the rapid rise and demise of satirical journals, humour as a mode of (increasingly surreptitious) criticism rose to prominence. Parody soon became a frequent, if not the main, implement in literary-critical writing. Reyfman names four critical methods developing in Russia in mid-eighteenth century. The first is literary parody, represented in polemic-borne genres – mainly epigrams and comedies – which would qualify the result as metaliterature. Literary parody is generally achieved by distorting 'what is of normative status in the original to a convention or a mere device' through the ostensibly unrecognized imposition by the parodist of his own artistic system.[27] The second critical method is generating a parodical effect in genres such as the critical letter, treatise, or essay. This tends to turn on points like flaws in logic or common sense, innovative usage, idiosyncratic spelling, grammatical inaccuracies in the targeted work or author, printing errors, and other even pettier features. Mockery – making absurd or grotesque – was attained by 'laying bare the devices' of an author's style, by dissecting the text and making the figural literal, or by uncharitably paraphrasing to expose the text's semantic absurdity. The third and more sophisticated critical technique – the logical demonstration of a work's/author's defects – was analogous to parody in its lack of 'respect for authorial individuality' and exposition of the work's 'incongruity in comparison with its implied abstract ideal' (Reyfman 73). In other words, the essential distinction between metaliterary parody (parody enlisted for literary-critical goals) and literary criticism is that the first shows what are seen as flaws by way of hyperbolized reproduction while the second describes a work's features and argues why they should be viewed as flaws – a distinction between, to use an analogy from narratology, *showing* and *telling*.[28] The last critical method employed around this time is the correction of perceived flaws by way of their repetition with variation: by rewriting the criticized text or parts of it with a view of having improved it. Even though all four approaches qualify for Reyfman as *critical* methods and clearly belong to one extended family, she distinguishes parody and rewriting from 'criticism proper,' i.e., logical argumentation (77).

As Reyfman's analysis makes clear, the early days of Russian criticism did not shy away from aspersion to humiliate its targets. Criticism was conducted as a series of more or less inimical acts of provocation. Examples of parody or its logical counterpart – *reductio ad absurdum* – can be found in the exchanges between Trediakovskii and Sumarokov (their texts are discussed below). Eighteenth-century critics' disregard for authorial individuality (leading Gukovskii to speak of the 'essential anonymity' of literary works in that period) meant applying poetic norms 'as they understood them' and to the exclusion of other norms, 'no matter how appropriate it might be within the artistic system under analysis' (Gukovskii 13; Reyfman 73–4). A similar tendency toward disparagement can be observed in criticism with respect to imagery in literary texts. Lack of logic and literacy became stock accusations levelled at even seasoned writers, and 'migrated from one critical essay to another.'

> As with infractions of poetic rules, the critics saw individual variations in imagery as blunders, grave mistakes, or ill will ... This notion of personal responsibility and the habit of harsh castigation for seemingly minor mistakes ... coupled with the firm belief in the correctness of their own views of language and nature, produced the painfully personal tone in the polemics between Trediakovskii, Lomonosov, and Sumarokov, which was responsible for the abuses of civility. This feature was not an accidental and superficial detail of the polemics but a fundamental trait of eighteenth-century literary life in Russia. (68–9)

The lengths of this homegrown ridicule, a mode of judgment which savoured of superficiality and pedantry but which also produced some of the most enduring texts still enjoyed for their diacritical wit, is what distinguishes Russian criticism from the Polish and the German. A general impression after reading through the major works of Russian literary criticism and commentary is one of internal discord, of barely suppressed odium and desire for elimination of the opposing side in a game with very high stakes – national literature, no less. But there is also a case to be made for the under-enlightened absolutism and religious orthodoxy of critical polemics, snuffing real dialogue between warring parties. The temperature of Russian literary discussions contrasts with the overt homogeneity of literary-critical opinion in the Polish case – conditioned by the preservative, unifying pull of nationalism in the face of external threats – and with the civil individualism in the German situation, affected by the political disunity of German-speaking areas and the aspiration to overcome this state. As Simpson notes, German aesthetic and literary criticism of the day evinced a longing for unity as an ideal 'achieved at the level of an individual mind' ('IOC' 7).

The parody-inflected mode of articulating negative opinions finds its realization in larger generic patterns organizing Russian criticism at this time. The most obvious characteristic of the two texts discussed below which utilize it is their high degree of a certain type of intertextuality: they are, after all, caught in a discursive web – that of the polemic – which the sides must 'harmonize' to cast. Of course, the 'parties' (and even 'camps,' since we should not neglect those who aligned themselves with one or the other side as they followed and abetted their polemic) must be seen as discursive through and through – they are only 'parties' in a manner of speaking; as the accumulation of attitudes and arguments channelled by this sample of critical discourse, they comprise (at the very least) all previous polemical words passed between the authors in question, not all of them conflicting. At this point, literary criticism is not yet a discourse heavily conditioned by the writers' relationship to their institution, binding them to a certain formal code of writerly conduct – although this relationship gradually becomes a variable with the forays of literary criticism into journalistic publishing.

Karamzin's piece (analysed below) testifies to this to some extent: he is writing for a foreign journal, and his mode of analysis is tailored to the estimated interests and expectations of the target audience. When writing for a Russian audience he, again, is compelled to place emphasis on edifying his reader above venting personal disagreements. Throughout the 1780s and 1790s, the polemic ceased to be as prominent a form of discursive engagement, losing out to publicistic pieces like the personal essay (which evaluated contemporary literature) and the feuilleton (which often contained literary satire and theatre reviews), but by the 1830s it had manifestly made a comeback. To return to Lomonosov and Trediakovskii, however, their work is undeniably framed by the formalities of dedication and tone by virtue of their addressees (members of the Academy of Sciences); these frames are, however, a very superficial imposition on the content of their texts as such. The formal framework and the values of academics were dictated in part by the writers themselves; literary-critical/theoretical polemics played out as a necessary component of the development of ideas about literature – most significantly, ideas about the future course of Russian literature.

While recognizably literary-critical pronouncements had various formal precursors (that is, were conditioned by their generic and broadly discursive associations – such as parody and Classical and post-Renaissance rhetoric, poetic, and grammar – and by concrete textual sources), the discursivity – thus also the genericity – of literary criticism was not a matter for serious, conscious consideration. This explains the rather derivative, repetitive, and sparse nature of much of the criticism produced during the eighteenth century; it is not yet a criticism that is aware and reflective of itself as a discourse, a criticism cordoned off through discursive rules of exclusion and inclusion – but, rather, one that is nameless, without a 'fixed address' that facilitated focused discussion about literature. The existing generic repertoire delineated, to a great extent, the scope and depth of literary-critical discourse, determining not merely how something could be said but *what* could be said in the first place. It was only when the discursive distinctiveness of literary criticism began to be recognized that its generic innovation really took off. Already with Karamzin we see a departure from many of the earlier concerns, most importantly from the resolute casting of absolute principles which all writers should follow. On the other hand, part of the legitimacy of the discourse from its very inception was owing to the academy – and this kept in check generic expansion and, especially, generic experimentation. A key role in the integration of literary criticism into the public discursive domain was played by polemics. It was, in many ways, a transitional form that, in the explicitly agonistic deployment of the initial, or 'founding,' texts, greatly facilitated criticism's discursive coherence. It was, however, a form to be transcended as more convergent attitudes became articulated.

One final question is how to account for the individualism in and the divergence of still technically classicist theories. The easiest answer is that Russia's literature was only then coming into being, and the competition for the title of 'founding father' mattered fiercely. Another explanation is that classicism came late and necessitated a crash course in ancient Greco-Roman and modern literature alike. This accelerated introduction rendered the gradual diachronic changes in Western thought as synchronic discrepancies in Russian, and, as a result, the elements of different periods co-existed in Russia to a much greater degree than they did in the West. Their co-existence meant that participants in this discussion disagreed on the most fundamental literary principles.

4 Textual Analyses

(a) M.V. Lomonosov's Kratkoe rukovodstvo k krasnoriechiiu. Kniga pervaia, v kotoroi soderzhitsia ritorika, pokazuiushchaia obshchie pravila oboevo krasnoriechiia, to est' oratorii i poezii, sochinennaia v pol'zu liubiashchikh slovesnye nauki *[Brief Guide to Eloquence. Book One, Which Contains Rhetoric, Showing General Rules of Both Kinds of Eloquence, That Is, Oratory and Poetry, Composed for the Benefit of Those with Love for Oral Learning] (St Petersburg, 1748; reprinted four times by 1800)*[29]

Kratkoe rukovodstvo k krasnoriechiiu is the first Russian rhetoric. It is an expanded version of a 1744 text (titled 'Kratkoe rukovodstvo k ritorike na pol'zu liubitelei sladkorechiia' [Brief Guide to Rhetoric for the Benefit of Lovers of Eloquence] and published only in 1895). The 1744 version is much shorter, consisting of a page-long introduction and 140 sections, divided into four parts, each subdivided into several chapters. It deals with the customary topics of invention and composition of ideas, ornamentation, arrangement, and delivery, with examples from both prose and verse – including excerpts from Lomonosov's odes. The 1748 version differs from the former in fundamental ways. First, it is more than twice the length (consisting of 326 sections). Second, it does not have the internal fragmentariness of the earlier text. One way to look at the difference is to see the 1744 text as a draft.

Kratkoe rukovodstvo is supplied with a substantial introduction, which takes as its object the definition of eloquence (*krasnorieche*), its study, and its scope – listing the two modal types as prose and poetry and their generic parameters as 'sermons, histories, books of instruction, hymns, odes, comedies, satires, and other kinds of verses.'[30] Strictly speaking, however, the text opens with a lengthy dedication to Peter Fiodorovich, grand duke and eventual successor to empress Elizaveta Petrovna (grandson of Peter I, he became Peter III, but ruled for just six months in 1762). In this dedicatory passage, Lomonosov presents his text as a contribution to knowledge encouraged by the growth of Russian learning and, with an ingratiating show of gratitude, submits himself to the prince's attention. The text provides evidence of the seminal importance attached by Lomonosov to his own work. Proficiency in rhetoric in the public use of language is described by him not only as a medium of learned discourse, but also as a tool of empire, shaping hegemonic relations and binding the people to their religion and history. 'Nowadays,' he writes,

> there is not as great a need for verbal ornamentation, especially in judicial matters, as there was among the ancient Greeks and Romans; nevertheless the condition of those nations in which the verbal arts (*slovesnye nauki*) are flourishing clearly demonstrates how useful it is in preaching God's word, in correcting human manners, in describing the glorious deeds of great heroes, and on many occasions in political conduct. The language by which the Russian power rules a large part of the world has by right of its might a natural abundance, beauty, and force, in which it yields to no European language. (92)

Subsequent sentences largely echo Sumarokov's contemporaneous opinions (discussed below): the Russian language has the potential to attain the perfection granted to other languages, and this belief reassures Lomonosov of the value of his present undertaking.

The term used by Lomonosov to refer to his subject matter, *krasnorieche* (previously *sladkoreche*),[31] a compound noun, qualifies speech as 'beautiful' or 'sweet' – corresponding to dulce in dulce et utile. In the literary dimension of speech, 'beauty' and 'sweetness' combine and, in keeping with the Horatian doctrine, form part of literature's dual purpose. In his *Kratkoe rukovodstvo k krasnoriechiiu*, Lomonosov expounds the practical aspect of literary production, focusing on technical instruction. When laying out the principles of eloquence (or rhetoric – though *sladkoreche* and *ritorika* appear side by side in the 1744 title, *ritorika* was later dropped), he names first natural ability (intellectual and physical) that cannot be taught, and its lack should dissuade one from pursuing a literary career. At the same time, however, Lomonosov subordinates the meaning of *krasnorieche* – of speaking beautifully (*krasno govorit'*) – to speaking *effectively*. His opening proposition contains this definition: 'Eloquence is the art of speaking beautifully about any given subject and persuading others of one's opinion' ('KRK' 91). Thus, the beauty/sweetness of language attends its effectiveness, or, rather, its beauty is an indispensable part of its effect (persuasion) – making *krasnorieche* not a poetics (which did not establish itself formally in Russian literary culture) but the aesthetic dimension of rhetoric.[32] Thus, Lomonosov's 'rhetoric' differs from medieval rhetorics, which not infrequently approached poetics. By the same token, his express concern with 'oral learning' also distances Lomonosov from poetics, traditionally associated with written discourse. Removing him specifically from the rationalist poetics of classicism (which de-emphasized emotion) is his emphasis on stimulating the passions even at the expense of reason (in section 100 we read: 'profound reasoning and arguments are not so moving …; for this, reason must be brought down from its high seat to the senses and must be united with them so that it may be set aflame with passion').[33] This feature, along with the theoretical preference for ornamentation and experimental phraseology, leads critics to call the treatise 'Baroque.'[34]

Throughout Lomonosov's treatise, the systematization of ideas is brought out by the lucid categorical layout, which gives the impression of a methodical and exhaustive treatment of its subject. The tripartite exposition announced in section 10 of the introduction is said to proceed from the 'natural order' (*po natural'nomu poriadku*) of the material:

first, a study of eloquence in general, of its relevance to prose and verse, along with examples measured against the rules of eloquence ('KRK' 97). This is to be followed by a study of the specific nature of prose and another of poetry, with respective examples from eminent authors. The tripartite division corresponds, Lomonosov explains in the final sentence of his introduction, to 'three books of this guide: Rhetoric, Oratory, and Poesy.' This projected format is a modification of a plan from 1747, in which rhetoric, oratory, and poesy were the three main parts of one book.[35] Lomonosov never published the latter two books, and book 1, claiming comprehensiveness on the level of rhetorical principles (as 'a study of eloquence generally,' 'showing general rules of both kinds of eloquence, that is, oratory and poetry' [99]),[36] is forever expecting the unborn. From the generic point of view, *Kratkoe rukovodstvo* is not only paradoxically long, but also terminally unfinished. It ends even more abruptly than it begins – in anticipation, no doubt, of its sequels.

Under the auspices of instruction in rhetoric, *Kratkoe rukovodstvo* includes multiple evaluations of literary texts under the pretext of justifying its selection of exempla. The discussion of rhetorical rules is threefold, composed of *izobretenie* (invention, or the Latin *inventio*), *ukrashenie* (ornamentation/style, or *ornatio*), and *raspolozhenie* (arrangement, or *dispositio*). By ignoring memory (*memoria*) and delivery (*pronuntiatio/actio*), Lomonosov's 'rhetoric' inherits the post-Renaissance bias – the two 'canons' were often excluded from rhetorical pedagogy. This tendency is also exhibited in his valorization of ornamentation, which effectively reduces an elaborate art of rhetoric to a how-to manual. At the same time, it is at odds with the contemporary Western tendency to circumscribe rhetoric by poetry and reduce it to the study of the poetic function of language.

For the reasons above, let us comment mainly on those parts relevant to poetry. In part 1, this would be chapter 8, which deals with fictions (*o vymyslakh*) as products of an active imagination, which can be either pure or mixed depending on the proportions in them of reality and fantasy ('KRK' 220). The examples Lomonosov gives of both kinds of fictional representation are taken largely from the ancients: Homer, Aesop, Apuleius, Lucian, Petronius, Virgil, Ovid, etc. Although his primary concern is the use of *vymysly* for effective communication (he suggests that the 'elevation of speech' depends as much on adornment as on fictions), he notes early on that they 'can be fairly called the soul of high poetry' (221). The rest of part 1 is consumed with distinguishing between pure and mixed, as well as direct and indirect, fictions. The order of presentation is invariant: definition followed by examples – citations or excerpts – followed by techniques followed by more examples. In the case of pure fictions, Lomonosov gives several modern examples: Erasmus's dialogues, Swift's *Gulliver's Travels*, Fénelon's *Télémaque*, French stories – 'which they call novels' (223). The latter are deemed not to contain any morals whatsoever and to be no different from Russian fairytales, save for their ornate style. It is such remarks that ultimately justify the choice of Lomonosov's *Kratkoe rukovodstvo* as a literary-critical text. While its subject is not literature per se or its purpose the judgment thereof, it does aim to impart to the reader the methods of elegant writing, including the literary variety. Needless to say, one is also led to make concessions when dealing, as in the Russian case, with the very germination of a discourse.

The first law for creating pure fictions (section 155) is that of unity and harmony ('KRK' 225). Here, the *Aeneid* serves as an example. The second principle or technique is illustrated by two examples from the *Metamorphoses*. The fourth (addressing amplification and diminishment) draws again on quotations from Virgil, as does the fifth, multiplication. The sixth method (metamorphosis) again summons Ovid, the seventh (displacement and anachronism), excerpts of Seneca's verses. Besides the examples named, Lomonosov frequently uses examples from his own oeuvre. Section 162 summarizes the poetic devices just discussed by repeating almost word for word the introduction to the list in section 150; it culminates the series of demonstrations from poetry and commences with examples from oratory, which takes us through the sections on indirect fictions.

By analysing this pattern of exposition – which admittedly soon becomes monotonous – one can appreciate the methodical nature of Lomonosov's endeavour. The point of this is pedagogical: to lay out the material, much of it rudimentary, as cogently as possible, in the manner of school textbooks, which instil information via repetition. *Kratkoe rukovodstvo k krasnoriechiiu* is method- and formula-driven: its main goal is to provide practical instruction to writers and speakers. The choice of examples establishes which texts Lomonosov holds in high esteem, although it never cohesively argues this esteem. As Stacy puts it, 'It is a work of criticism ... only in the sense that its rather frigid precepts *imply* the proper criteria for literary judgment' (15).

With a great deal of space devoted to *strasti*, or passions,[37] Lomonosov sees rhetoric's persuasiveness primarily as redounding not to logic but to affect. Tynianov attributes this to the influence of Longinus's

On the Sublime.[38] More generally, however, Lomonosov's treatise on rhetoric is regarded as a liberal adaptation of *Ausführliche Redekunst*, Gottsched's textbook on rhetoric, which also foregrounds the affective (Stacy 15).[39] Key to Gottsched's rigorous study are the principles of clarity, directness, veracity, and naturalness; they are the means that justify the final result – persuasion. To Lomonosov, on the other hand, it was the end that justified the means – the excitation of passions being one of the main ones. (This shift of accents suggests that Lomonosov may not merely be adapting Gottsched's work but revising it in a crucial sense.) It is in this emphasis on emotions that Lomonosov's 'rhetoric' actually imbricates poetics. As Tynianov observes, Lomonosov 'rejected logically persuasive oratory in favor of the emotionally affective' (567) (of course, Lomonosov is wary of facile affective effects). At the same time, 'Elements of poetic discourse in the ode are used, constructed as if it were an act of oratory.' And this, as mentioned earlier, differed from the then-standard treatment of rhetoric in the West.

One might add here that, although kindred in spirit – that is, both rhetorics, Gottsched's and Lomonosov's, are, broadly speaking, cornerstones of their respective literary languages – in letter they can be quite dissimilar.[40] For our purposes, it is sufficient to say that they are distinct structurally, from their format right through to their conceptual organization. If, as its title (particularly the adjective *ausführliche*) indicates, Gottsched's work aims at comprehensiveness regarding its subject matter and in complexity trumps many a rhetoric handbook, the first part of Lomonosov's title makes one expect a concise treatment, and reads almost as a disclaimer: an exhaustive treatment of rhetoric will not be found here. Indeed, relative to Gottsched's tome of over 700 pages, *Kratkoe rukovodstvo*, at some 290, is just that: brief. It may be that Lomonosov claims to say as much in fewer words, in which case the adjective *kratkoe* could be understood more as *compact*. (A 'genetic' investigation of their generic similarities could begin with Wolff – who, incidentally, taught both Gottsched and Lomonosov – whose philosophy pervaded the German-speaking world and beyond, but whose style of written communication was singularly rigid and uniform even to his disciples.)

Most important from the generic point of view is that Lomonosov barely applies in the treatise the principles of *krasnorieche* that he so scrupulously lays out. The text's lack of self-consciousness may be related to the clear genre distinctions Lomonosov made during his academic career and his instrumental role in institutionalizing further generic restrictions. His literary corpus contains an array of forms (among them odes, hymns, heroic poems, satires, idylls, sonnets, epitaphs, epigrams, tragedies, dialogues, letters – these, as others, versified). Known for his metaphoric flair, which to many seemed high-flown and euphuistic, Lomonosov did not oppose innovation within the sphere of poetic language – as long as it conformed to decorum – or the introduction of new literary genres, as long as these novelties did not offend reason and had proven tasteful in the West. 'Typical for Lomonosov was his "systemic," functional attitude to each element in the work of art and his drive to fix a precise formal element to each function' (Tynianov 574). During this period in Russian literary history, absolute convictions about how literature should be written went hand in hand with polemical non-convergence in aesthetic principles and *against* literary and literary-theoretical originality (Reyfman 70–1). A simultaneous display of one's artistic individuality could dampen the impact of advocating artistic universals.

(b) A.P. Sumarokov's Dve epistoly. V pervoi predlagaetsia o russkom iazyke, a vo vtoroi o stikhotvorstve *[Two Epistles, the First Treating of the Russian Language, the Second of Poetry] (St Petersburg, 1748; second rev. and consolidated edition 1774)*[41]

Sumarokov's *Dve epistoly* was published first as a brochure in 1748, then, in 1774, revised, shortened, and combined into the quasi-treatise *Nastavlenie khotiashchim biiti pisatel'iami* [Instruction to Those Wishing To Be Writers]. Although striving for conceptual analogy with Boileau's classicist versified treatise, *L'Art poétique*,[42] the second epistle bears more generic resemblance to its other intertextual source, Horace's *Ars poetica*.[43] Both works – Horace's and Sumarokov's – are generic hybrids – perhaps it is better to say mélanges, since it is not easy to discern distinct genres that compose them. Dve epistoly was written – as was Boileau's work – in verse form (specifically, iambic hexameter with rhyming couplets).[44] Sumarokov's epistles are 566 lines long, compared to Horace's 476 or Boileau's 1100.[45]

The generic membership of the text is given in its title, as was common at a time when academic genres were still being defined, still elaborating their conventions, shaping readers' expectations and their interpretive techniques. The term *pis'mo* (letter) was in everyday use; although in sophistication the text may have not been any different from a letter, giving it the Latinate name *epistol* was enough to bestow on it a more formal air and place it in the tradition of literary-critical epistles (such as Horace's). It could be that the titular distinction is a mark of feigned vanity; it stands for a claim to stylistic superiority over the regular pis'mo. Sumarokov puts an end to such speculation in the following passage: 'A letter [*pis'mo*], which the folk call 'scrawling,' conducts ordinary discourse with those absent and should be without artifice and briefly composed, or in other words, as simple as we speak.'[46] So defined, the letter cannot accommodate Sumarokov's intention, his audience, or his elevated style. This points to the generic paradoxicality of the letter form as 'written speech,' noted by Stefania Skwarczyńska ('Paradoksy' 178). The paradox stems from the letter's dual status as, on the one hand, utilitarian and, on the other, literary (with an aesthetic intent), as well as from its 'oscillation between dialogue and monologue' (178). In another place in his letter – where he addresses the issue of genre codes – Sumarokov makes this observation, which sums up his didactic letter's literary ambition: 'In epistles, artists choose those phrases that are appropriate to what they compose, and the greatest beauty of such verses is the orderliness in them and the purity of style' ('TE' 236). In her monograph on the letter genre, Skwarczyńska addressed the fineness of the distinction and, consequently, the formal gradations, between the *literary* and the *ordinary* letter (when the latter exhibits literary ambition) (*Teoria* 320–2). Sumarokov's insistence on his text's highbrow, *epistolary* nature, as it were, proves this. Its practical purpose makes it conscious of its intermediateness. Its non-situational and public character and versified form alone seem insufficient to secure a place in the literary treasury. Skwarczyńska sees the literary letter as a derivative form, exploiting the fundamental form of the letter for features such as the immediacy of the private addresser–addressee relationship (324–5). Sumarokov's epistle utilizes such informal dialogical rhetoric to varied literary effect.

Although the second epistle ('Epistola o stikhotvorstve,' or 'On Versification') bears closer resemblance to 'literary criticism proper' by dealing systematically with poetry and genre, it is language, and specifically *literary* language, that receives attention in Sumarokov's text. Lest there be any doubt as to the author's critical interest, the title of the first epistle announces it as a treatment of Russian language. The opening lines clearly establish matters linguistic and stylistic as the focus. The subject is expressed in comparative terms – human discourse is contrasted with animal communication, the Russian tongue with obscure languages – and in imperatives: 'We must have the kind of language the ancient Greeks had, the kind the Romans had, and, following them in this, the kind now spoken in Italy and Rome, the kind as beautiful as French became in the past century or, finally, the kind Russian is capable of being!' ('TE' 224). Sumarokov's diagnosis of the current state of affairs: too few writers writing in Russian reinforcing and refining the language. This judgment is immediately followed by satire on writers who either export their talents or import foreign linguistic culture (though some scholars believe this alludes to Lomonosov and Trediakovskii, Lomonosov himself apparently did not take it personally). Sumarokov then proceeds to ridicule arrogant literary amateurism in a mock monologue by a generically incompetent writer, to which he subsequently replies with bemusement. The segment ends on a signature note of exasperation: 'It is impossible even to think that I could recount all the stupidities of scribblers' (225). This part of the first epistle exemplifies the kind of humour that was to become emblematic of criticism in the eighteenth century.

The next few paragraphs address all aspects of literary production – from conceptual problems, which, in Sumarokov's opinion, underlie problems of literary expression, through letter writing (the most common quasi-literary genre among literate strata of society), to the art/craft of translation. This series of reflections is formulated in normative, even openly prohibitive, terms: 'Whoever writes should first refine his thought ...'; 'Words that are in use in society, whether expressed by pen or tongue, should be more elegantly composed'; or, finally, 'If you wish to translate faultlessly, do not proceed that way ...' ('TE' 225, 226). Sumarokov speaks authoritatively, as a representative of the reading public and of the writing community alike, yet the former group can be presented in rather condescending language: 'Uncomprehending readers ... read in darkness and accept the writer's indistinct composition as something beautiful' (225). Just as there are writers and writers, so there are readers and readers; to make literary harmony both need to be tuned. The epistle is an attempt to survey and raise awareness of the regrettable status quo in a general – hence, too, more derogative – manner. Individual accomplishments are not named, as this would be dissonant with the epistle's purpose to communicate his observations forcefully.

Thereupon, Sumarokov launches into a discourse on translation. In this section he resumes addressing the reader qua translator, and the exposition of his ideas on the relative status of translator, author, and work continues in this dialogic fashion until the end of the letter. For example: 'Why follow him step by step? ... But catch up to him and you will be equal to him' (Sumarokov defended a liberal approach to translation, favouring poetic licence to 'improve' the original – a view for which he was rebuked) (Rosenberg 54–5). He switches also between the first-person singular pronoun and nosism, or more inclusive plural forms: 'Lest we be disgraced for not knowing it, we must improve our whole style even a little'; 'all should know how to write correctly' ('TE' 226) – to the overall effect of sounding paternalistic.

Some of the most remarkable formulations in the 'Epistola o russkom iazyke' are also the most theoretical: 'by dint of our voice we divide our thoughts into small parts'; 'Art means being able to compose one's style correctly, in the artist's expressing his thoughts clearly, in one's words flowing freely and harmoniously'; and 'reading opens the door to art' ('TE' 224, 225, 226). Perhaps the most pedantic point in the first epistle is Sumarokov's straightforward remark about the importance of handwriting, discrediting an earlier suggestion (by a fictitious 'clerk') that penmanship can be acquired by good reading alone: 'But my opinion is that although you may be someone, you will never be truly literate that way. Even in the best handwriting, with the clerk's advice, weave four letters into the word "year" and learn to write "the end" fancifully – believe me, you will never be a writer.' The image conjured by dialogism – these ceaseless engagements with imaginary speakers, appeals to imaginary listeners, or pseudo-quotations of invented characters – is that of an interior debate between Sumarokov and a group of wayward colleagues, novices, and confirmed incompetents, as observed by a passive, befuddled audience.

The climax of Sumarokov's discourse comes in the penultimate paragraph in a form that equals the homily, quite in keeping with Sumarokov's linguistic credo: 'Be angry that we have few books, and lament, "Since there are no Russian books, who is there to imitate?" However, be angrier at yourself or at your father for his not having taught you. For if you had not passed your youth frivolously, you might have been sufficiently skilled in writing' ('TE' 227). The concern with language terminates the first epistle. A definite development has occurred since the initial thread: the tone here is not one of enthusiasm and hope, but of stern censure of linguistic heresy – forgetting about the church-book heritage. The closing sentence is rhetorically weak and tangential to the foregoing series of remarks. Only in it, however, does one discern a more personal, permissive tone, as if the letter was indeed addressed to someone in Sumarokov's care, but over whom, for one reason or another, he has trouble exercising control. In the last line,

Sumarokov deflates his own inflated expectations: 'Do not learn sciences, if you never have any liking for them, but of course it is necessary to know how to express one's thoughts.'

Epistle II opens with an apostrophe to would-be poets requesting them to 'desist from singing.' The entire formulation, at once lyrical and disciplinary, contains the core of the criticism that follows it: 'O you who strive – desist!' 'Your song is not attractive when music itself is unfamiliar to you' ('TE' 227). The protective tone resonating through this injunction may have its source in Sumarokov's own, recognized abilities as a poet. It is important to note as well that Sumarokov reminds us he is addressing not only his compatriots, but the entire race of poetasters and criticasters of their own work ('they have no artistic talent and their judgment [*rassudok*] is bad'). Mediocrity is breaking out everywhere, and it is one's duty, as an experienced poet and critic (doubling one's attack), to bring it to light. As in the first epistle, the root of poor writing is located by Sumarokov in improper use of language: improper in the most basic sense of bad grammar, of slapping words together 'for rhymes' but clearly without reason, of 'weav[ing the text] awkwardly' (*sopletiot neskladno*) into 'plaited nonsense' (*sopletenny vzdor*) (228). This extended textual metaphor of weaving is interesting from an etymological perspective: it makes use of the Latin derivation of *text* (*textus*, from the past participle of *textere*, 'to weave'). What is woven is a text, but as the weaving is done without skill, the product does not deserve to be called poetry or writing (*pis'mo*), and is here referred to as 'that' (*to, chto*).

After naming foreign (French) authors of little and of great importance, Sumarokov turns to Russian examples of great intellect coupled with artistic mediocrity: Antiokh D. Kantemir (1708–44; precursor of Russian classicism and early linguistic reformer) and Feofan Prokopovich (1681–1736; author of *De arte poetica libri tres* [1705; first published 1786]). A clear line is drawn between these authors' achievements as prose writers and thinkers and their artistic ineptitude. This idea flows again into the proscriptive and normative discourse of earlier passages. Good writers need skill and inspiration, not rhymes and perspiration. Sumarokov never mocks the poetaster; he maintains his position of unequivocal authority through a serious, even concerned tone. He also allows his poetry to seep into his prose, most notably in the following line: 'He who never strolled through a garden of pleasant fruits eats cranberries for cherries, ashberries for grapes, and, possessed of a coarse taste, presents his empty labors to society like the fruits of a sweet harvest' ('TE' 229) (his point being that many a mediocre versifier is unaware of his mediocrity). It is the critic's duty, it would seem, to 'weed out' unpleasant fruits, thereby removing the illusion-giving sustenance of untalented would-be poets.

After this series of observations, Sumarokov leads us ('let us ascend,' he urges ['TE' 229]) to the heights of literary talent. What follows is a paragraph's worth of famous names (a list of about thirty) which concludes with 'Let us follow such great writers.' Is this a consciousness-raising exercise, suggested reading for aspiring writers? Indeed, the movement of Sumarokov's argument is at its most erratic here. The next paragraph begins with another direct address: 'But you, uncomprehending, sing in a savage voice.' All of a sudden, the above list appears in sacred relief – the hermetic domain of a loner surrounded by literary heathens. One cannot ignore the zeal with which the sermon is spoken: the writer who fails is a 'boor' who 'insolently transforms his labors into shame.' There is, in Sumarokov's critique, no encouragement, no redemption, only censure and contempt.

One prominent formal feature of the second epistle is its alternating address of the untalented and the gifted. The gulf between the two is unbridgeable; those without talent will never become poets, and, curiously, only where there is talent is there still room for improvement. Training enhances innate ability – an opinion voiced by Horace. We enter the realm of rigorous instruction and propriety typical of classicist poetics. 'In verse, know the difference in genres and look for the appropriate words for whatever you begin lest you bring offence to the Muses …' ('TE' 229). An extended poetic allegory on pastoral poetry (passages which closely resemble those of Boileau), into which Sumarokov lucidly incorporates the principles of the idyll, is followed by images germane for the genre. Sumarokov's speech shifts from the abstract and prescriptive to the invitingly self-referential ('sing to me of …' [230]), where the as yet unshaken authorial perspective morphs into that of a potential reader: 'Let me know what it is to feel the pastoral simplicity and, when reading your verses, to put vanity from my mind.' The discourse on 'rules of the wise Muses' again rises to the allegorical-mythological register, and we find ourselves reading of 'the voice of the plaintive Muse [that] penetrates more swiftly when she tears out her hair from love' (236, 230). However, at the end of this passage, Sumarokov avers that true poetry comes from spontaneous, authentic feeling (231). (Far from noncommittal in its classicism, however, his poetic practice gave precedence to artistic form. Feeling and subject matter became abstract, conceptual, moderated by and subject to the rules of style and genre.)[47]

Subsequent genres – ode, satire in verse, madrigal, fable, drama, mock-epic poem, epistle, sonnet, ballad, rondeau, song – are all treated in a highly metaphoric fashion. The tools necessary to produce them are always: apposite and genuine affects or mode of perception (expressed for the ode as a kind of spiritual/psychic itinerary – 'The creator of such poetry casts his glance everywhere, flies up to the heavens, descends into hell, and rushing in haste to all lands of the universe, always has an open road and open gates before him'); and knowledge of the forms' essential qualities ('The sound roaring in an ode like a whirlwind pierces the hearing … The lightning in it divides the horizon in half,' or, 'This verse is full of metamorphoses') ('TE' 231). The most evocative passage is one that establishes a distinction between the lyric and the epic forms: 'In epic poetry tumult is orderly. The lyric voice, like a whirlwind, pulls by gusts, but the epic voice … breaks just like the wind that storms for many days after rising from the bosom of the earth.' As in other instances, mythological and historic events and figures file past our eyes, demonstrating their literary affiliation to each of the genres.

As the discussion moves to the dramatic form, Sumarokov aligns himself again with a potential audience of 'Townsman, nobleman, marquis, count, prince, ruler,' telling the writer what these stations dispose him to want from a play, what to do to obtain the desired effects (pity and passion, tears and laughter), and what the duration of the play ought to be ('TE' 232). In this interlude, Sumarokov gives guidelines about the classicist unities of action, time, and place. Several summaries of tragic plots from French drama give way to examples from French comedy. However, Sumarokov's chief focus – and mode used in the epistles – is satire, reflecting the increasingly satire-friendly climate in Russia at the time. In this context comes the one major reference to Boileau, an exhortation really, which credits him with authority superior to Sumarokov's (in contributions theoretical, critical, and creative). 'O secretary of the Muses! Giver of their statutes! Connoisseur of poetry and meticulous writer who revealed to France the altar of the Muses and served it himself by his own example in pure style. Tell me, Boileau, your laws of satire by which you cleansed in verse coarse manners!' (234). Sumarokov briskly enumerates the many virtues of satire executed according to the rules, using the first-person plural pronoun, as if to signify his subjection to Boileau's satiric law (to which, he says, the master also subjected himself). The subsequent list of specific plots given to satire ends with the appeal: 'Satirist, it is such things you should present us' (235). Here the referent of the first-person plural form has shifted from the potential writers of satire to its audience.

The treatment of genres (their source, content, style) continues in this normative mode until the final spirited directive: 'O marvelous creators, stop spinning [*spletat'*] nonsense! There is no glory in senseless writing' ('TE' 237). At this moment in the second epistle, the fluid structure seems to solidify. We are given the conventional lead-ins: 'Let us now examine [*Rassmotrim*] ...' followed, again, by normative pronouncements, and 'In conclusion [*Vo okonchanii*] ...' – the latter, Sumarokov explains, involving a repetition of his summons to the would-be poet for a judgment call ('first think, creator, what your head is best fitted for'; 'do not persist, once your reason shows you your limitations, in trying to overcome them'; 'allow your nature to take you where it wants to go'). With facile matter-of-factness Sumarokov spends two long paragraphs advising what places in the hierarchy of literary forms are best matched to what temperaments (and, for the second time, to the use of Russian themes). Significantly, in these concluding passages, Boileau and Horace appear not as sources of Sumarokov's reflections, but in their guise of poets as models for aspiring writers. Also mentioned and praised in the same creative regard (and compared with Pindar and Malherbe) is Lomonosov. Two lines down, Sumarokov addresses a certain Shtivelius ('And you, Shtivelius, you are capable only of talking nonsense').[48] This happens to be the first instance of (and variation on) the parodical image of Trediakovskii amongst his contemporaries.[49] The final line brings us full circle, as Sumarokov suddenly returns to the value of cultivating a modern Russian literary language, the theme of the first epistle: 'Writer, just give enlightenment to the mind; our beautiful language is capable of anything' ('TE' 238).

The striking feature of many of Sumarokov's figurative depictions is how much they leave open to interpretation. This form puts Sumarokov's criticism on the threshold of poetry: the goal was to simultaneously define and demonstrate: the critic's eloquence reflects the criticism's concurrent concern with language. The directions presented within such imagery-flooded discourse do not much resemble the generic directions laid down in German or Polish classicist poetics of the same period, which are, on the whole, descriptive. The combined verse and epistolary models may be partly responsible for the hyperfigural mode of Sumarokov's text, but Boileau's, Dmochowski's, and Rzewuski's (whose theoretical ideas and the versified form also came from Boileau) are considerably more prosaic treatments of the topic. There are also few analogical passages of poetic elevation in Horace's work, where diction is generally humorous and informal.[50] When it comes to the laws and rules of poetic composition, however, all these conceptually and formally kindred texts are explicit in offering practical instruction (metre, structure, number of acts in a play, characterization, and much else besides concerning decorum). In addition, Horace's epistle has an explicit group addressee – Piso and his two sons (who are referred to by name at different points in the text) – while Sumarokov's has multiple intended recipients – addressed not by name but in shifters (words like 'creator' and 'writer'), and through first- and second-person imperative constructions – depending on the topic being discussed. This may account for some of the stylistic unevenness, the lyrical flourishes and stark satire, the passionate extremes of censure and elation that characterize Sumarokov's text. Nonetheless, when compared to Lomonosov's 'overly figurative style,' his diction – though his notions of creativity be couched in Classical metaphor (toward which no less than 'The maidens of Parnassus guided his pen ...') – is indeed clear ('TE' 235; Reyfman 57). When compared to Trediakovskii's critical writings,[51] however, the ideas in Sumarokov's two epistles, devoid for the most part of common methods of structuration (such as an 'exoskeletal' argumentational scheme), come across as convulsive, meandering, and fragmentary, if not cobbled together.

(c) V.K. Trediakovskii's 'Pis'mo v kotorom soderzhitsia rassuzhdenie o stikhotvorenii, ponyne v svet izdannom ot avtora dvukh od, dvukh tragedii i dvukh epistol, pisannoe ot priiatelia k priiateliu' [Letter Containing a Discussion of Poems Just Published by the Author of Two Odes, Two Tragedies, and Two Epistles, Written From a Friend to a Friend] (written in St Petersburg in 1750, not published until 1865)[52]

Trediakovskii's 'Pis'mo ot priiatelia k priiateliu' (as it is often abbreviated) is recognized as the first proper work of Russian literary criticism (Grinberg and Uspenskii 6). As an 1865 introduction to the first publication of the text tells us, its status notwithstanding, it was hitherto known only through allusions made by Sumarokov in his response to it and Trediakovskii's own report to the St Petersburg Academy's president, K. Razumovskii (1728–1803).[53] The text was the high point in Trediakovskii's notorious literary disputes with Sumarokov, which began in the 1740s. In the context of this polemic, it is a lengthy riposte with a vengeance to Sumarokov's *Dve epistoly* and his comedy *Tresotinius*,[54] which parodied Trediakovskii's poetry and his scholarly prose as archaic, stilted, pedantic, and undereducated. Trediakovskii's letter, in turn, elicited from Sumarokov another comedy, *Chudovischi* [Monsters], again featuring a Trediakovskii parody, along with the rejoinder 'Otvet na kritiku' (written in 1750, published in 1782 by Novikov).

The plan to lampoon his adversary's artistic output with poignant rhetoric could not have been more expedient: it was devised during a lull in Trediakovskii's literary career yet with the encouragement of Academy 'assessor' G.N. Teplov (1717–79) (Grinberg and Uspenskii 44). The text was unpublished but, despite being a piece of academic correspondence and a declaration released into closed-circuit politics, it almost instantly reached Sumarokov. It would, indeed, be a mistake to suppose that this polemic was meant to remain confined to the academic milieu and did not, in its design, overstep institutional bounds (the fact that it bears a title at all and is not precisely dated is some indication of its intended audience).[55] In much the same way, one cannot infer that the pointed polemical edge of Sumarokov's comedies parodying Trediakovskii – comedies that were produced at court – was lost beyond the cognizance of a high-society audience, including the imperial family. Trediakovskii himself occasionally sat in the audience – in fact, he began the 'Pis'mo' after attending a performance of *Tresotinius* in February 1750 (44). The subtleties of Sumarokov's parody-wielding polemic were inconsequential to its general effect, and Trediakovskii's reputation suffered enormously.

In the 'Pi'smo,' Trediakovskii is building on previous works, including among others the treatise *Novyi i kratkii sposob k slozheniiu rossiiskikh stikhov* [A New and Concise Method for the Composition of Russian Verses], published in 1735 and soon rousing the young Lomonosov's critical faculty (as testified by marginalia in his own copy of the book). The 'Pis'mo' is a more explicitly critical work, as its focus is a specific writer and contemporary and his apparent lack of poetic talent. With the purpose of exposing his opponent as a sham, Trediakovskii finds flaws in almost every aspect of Sumarokov's literary language, style, and forms of versification.

The letter consists of two parts, each with a number of subsections. The lengths of the latter vary, and their numbering gives only a rough orientation in the text, creating the impression of a loose constellation of points rather than of a coherent argument. The work also includes a postscript reproducing a scene from a new manuscript of *Tresotinius*.

Trediakovskii's letter is an extensive dissection of Sumarokov's works published up to that point. It fits squarely into the category of normative aesthetics: his works are held up to the measure of Trediakovskii's principles, while the principles proper to Sumarokov as they are put into artistic practice go unacknowledged. Its title already establishes a subtle irony by its identification of the target as 'the author of two odes, two tragedies, and two epistles.' By enumerating the works as instances of genres without giving their titles, the literary output of Sumarokov is minorised. He appears as somewhat of a newcomer and novice. The latter part of the title – 'From a Friend to a Friend' – stands as witness to the amity between addresser and addressee – not Sumarokov but a 'third party' to the polemic, a liaison of sorts – from which the author being judged is excluded. This dispassionate reduction and de facto exclusion of Sumarokov from a critique of himself prefigures the eviscerating hostility with which he is treated in the body of this text. What recommended to its author this rather unusual title? Through it, Trediakovskii was both underscoring his own friendship and signalling his enmity toward the definitive 'other.' Could the inclusion of the phrase 'friend to friend' be merely an index of the formality and courtesy observed by academicians, or are we to read into it a veiled reference to the inverse relationship – 'foe to foe' – between Trediakovskii and Sumarokov? Authorities on their relationship tell us they were once friends who little by little grew to hate each other, and that their conflict turned particularly acrimonious in 1750.

In the opening passage Trediakovskii addresses Teplov as follows: 'Many times have I written you of various matters; but never could it enter my mind that I should have written you an apologetic and critical letter, such as the present one' ('PPP' 437). The letter proves true to this self-categorization as *criticism* and *apologia,* in that it indeed personally accounts for his strong dislike of Sumarokov's art. The two terms in this generic combination balance out the work's means and ends: on the one hand, Trediakovskii feels compelled to discredit his literary enemy (whom in the opening lines he, with politesse or largesse, calls 'friend'), on the other, to defend his position in advance, knowing it will be perceived by Teplov as severe. There is a hint of self-righteousness in all of this – evident in the next lines, in which Trediakovskii elaborates on his reasons for writing: 'It is now impossible to resist it; in which I humbly ask you to excuse me on account of our friendship.'

On the face of it, Sumarokov's recent personal affronts against Trediakovskii present an occasion to take the higher ground: in his critique, he pledges to refrain from attacking ad hominem, concentrating instead on the evaluation of Sumarokov's work alone (Grinberg and Uspenskii 45). In fact, the critique is still largely reliant on the flaws of the reviled author rather than of the works themselves. Trediakovskii's formal stance, then, is one of objectivity – or at least attempted objectivity – in his intention to not mix feelings and sober judgments. At this point in his literary career, Trediakovskii bore an immense grudge against Sumarokov, and in 'Pis'mo' and his earlier responses to *Dve epistoly* (academic reports which forced Sumarokov to tone down his overtly satirical text) blamed the latter for violating the unwritten 'code of literary polemics' – the prohibition against maliciously targeting the person of one's rival (Grinberg and Uspenskii 58–9). Yet despite condemning Sumarokov and professing fairness, Sumarokov's diatribes against him gave Trediakovskii licence for the same kind of conduct, as he felt his retaliation was more than justified. While part of the polemical structure was already in place, Trediakovskii's conduct, at odds with his official stance, was not a mere *result* of an existing polemic, since it presented the possibility of dialectic as advancement toward impersonality and truth. In other words, it expressed the desire to transcend the personal dimension so prevalent in previous exchanges. On the most basic level, this discursive choice is also, and equally, the sign of the polemic as a law of discursive interaction and formation, since it signals a continuity within which the present text plays a defining role. It does not represent a concessional or conciliatory gesture, but a combative one. Under this equivocal guise, Trediakovskii is neither admitting to having himself stooped to Sumarokov's level in the past, nor is he proposing a more detached approach in order to mitigate any prior malice (to be sure, the apologia is not directed at Sumarokov!).

It could be, then, that Trediakovskii is announcing a shift to a more refined and destructive critique, unmuddled by emotionalism – which lends his diction gravitas. In reality, however, Trediakovskii has donned the mask of the noble, impartial critic so as to dispense with its main duties to more sinister effect. (Either this or, as he plunged into his topic and the former polemical pattern reasserted itself, his genuine goal of re-patterning further interchange with his adversary faded from sight.) Regardless, however, of whether we see the inconsistency between Trediakovskii's theory and practice as devious deception or as self-delusion, the arguments in his letter, even if marred by multiplying vituperation, have sprung from careful execution.

Although much is said in the letter about all of Sumarokov's work to date, Trediakovskii dismisses the offending comedy right at the start (in his second paragraph): 'I do not mention the carelessness of its composition and multiple so-called Solecisms: it is entirely unworthy of criticism' ('PPP' 238). We easily discern the notes of disdain in a customary use of ventriloquism, a common parodic technique; Trediakovskii caricatures Sumarokov by attributing to the latter bombastic lines, following with an absurd rewrite of them, and the sardonic exclamation 'Some philologist!' Other features of Trediakovskii's text are the recurrent references to the poetics of Boileau and Nicolas Chamfort (1741–94).

(d) N.M. Karamzin's 'Un Mot sur la littérature russe' [A Few Words about Russian Literature] (Hamburg, 1797)[56]

Although Stacy groups Karamzin with Pushkin (1799–1837) as one of the key non-professional critics of the early nineteenth century (25), some of Karamzin's notable literary criticism appeared before the end of the century: he wrote reviews from the early 1790s,[57] and it is one of these we shall presently discuss. In 1802–3, Karamzin refined his journalistic style by editing and writing for *Vestnik Evropii*,[58] which was 'the first literary journal seriously and consistently to discuss socio-political questions of current interest' (Ambler 14).[59] Karamzin was, therefore, a transitional figure with respect to the institutionalization of criticism in Russia. At the turn of the nineteenth century, his work began to appear in newly established literary periodicals and journals, making him a precursor of the journalistic critics of the next century.

'Un mot sur la littérature russe,' commissioned by a French-language journal, *Le Spectateur du Nord* [The Northern Spectator] in 1797, had a unique intended audience: the lionized French. The article was not translated into Russian until the twentieth century – as 'Neskol'ko slov o russkoi literature' – given the earlier extent of Russian Francophilia. What is revealed when a Russian writer/critic is asked to assess the history and state of his national literature for a culture deemed superior? How does this task affect presentation, let alone the author's opinions? Is judgment offered or withheld? Is the presentation mode of choice purely expository, leaving explicit judgment to potential readers of Russian in France, or does it steer them (however subtly) toward certain conclusions? Karamzin himself stated, in a letter to Dmitriev, that he 'thought it necessary to write about Russian literature for foreigners lightly, without rarefied details, with a turn *à la française*,'[60] and his essay offered a number of gratifying answers to these and related questions.

Karamzin's aim in 'Un mot sur la littérature russe' is clear from the outset: to bring out a vivid, dynamic picture, the strengths as well as the weaknesses, of Russian literature, and thereby raise its stature abroad and stimulate foreign interest. (His tone is courteous, if not overly so – here and there, there are hints of obsequiousness.) He does the former by invoking evidence of Russian literature's newly discovered seniority: a purportedly medieval poem of the order of Macpherson's Ossian. Curiously, as if to further secure his credibility as a *source* – in the sense both of authority and of wellspring – Karamzin incorporates a lengthy excerpt from his own *Pis'ma russkovo puteshestvennika* [Letters of a Russian Traveller] (published in full in 1797 and already popular with the Russian public) which would 'permit you to judge how we view things, how we write, and how we study the creations of literature.'[61] This, incidentally, is the only selection from Russian literature that Karamzin includes – implying that he himself is (or regards himself as) a representative of, at once, Russian intellectualism, Russian literature, and Russian literary criticism.

While, in the main, Karamzin maintains a descriptive mode, reserving explicit judgment and avoiding effusions or pretence, the relative weight given to Russia's remarkable progress in literature affords a natural bias. At the same time, Karamzin does put relatively young Russian letters in their 'proper place,' and ideas expressed in *Pis'ma* further raise concerns about the value of a literary culture that has advanced with seemingly *unnatural* momentum – without experiencing all of the European cultural periods (Russia having had no Renaissance):

> Comparing its [France's] slow pace with the headlong movement of our nation toward the selfsame goal, one begins to believe in miracles; one marvels at the power of the creative genius that has torn the Russian nation out of the lethargic sleep in which it had long been immersed, and that has moved it along the road of enlightenment with such force that, within a very few years, we have taken our place along with the nations that began their enlightenment many centuries before us. But here other thoughts, other aspects come to mind: Are buildings that have been raised with excessive haste sturdy enough? Indeed, movement is always slow

and measured in nature. Can shining exceptions to the rule be firm and durable? ('FWRL' 436)

These same (feigned?) doubts are already voiced in the first paragraph, where Karamzin writes: 'even in Russia there are gifted people who are modest enough not to dispute the palm of priority of the French, German, and other men of letters, but who can say for themselves while reading their immortal creations, "We too are artists"' ('FWRL' 430). The third paragraph begins with a perpetuation of Peter the Great's mythic proportions, described as '[tearing] away the curtain that hid from our gaze the life of the civilized nations of Europe and their achievements in the arts' (432). Following this is one of the most humorous and telling passages in the essay. First, Karamzin undermines the emancipation of 'Russian man' by recalling his humiliation at his own backwardness; a moment later, he recuperates Russian dignity by mentioning confidence in Russian 'ability to learn, want[ing] to imitate the foreigners in everything.' Then, without mincing words, he continues: 'He [Russian man] even refashioned his language with the mannerisms of French and German. And our poetry and literature were turned into an echo and reflection of foreign poetry and literature' – a notion hardly reconcilable with claims to Russian uniqueness. A still more unflattering portrait comes a few sentences down, beginning with 'but the temple of taste and the sanctuary of art seldom disclose themselves before our authors because we write under the influence of sudden whim ...' And yet, despite its understated title and the profession of objectivity (acquired through the experience of travel itself),[62] Karamzin's 'Un mot' does leave the impression of veiled encomium, directed at the only 'judiciously' deserving subjects: French, German, and less so English letters.[63]

This impression (Karamzin's intent?) is brought out in the narration of the European journey, a *Bildungsreise*, as it were – during which Karamzin doubtless saw himself as a citizen of the *République des Lettres*. The 'Russian traveller' (recognizable via the sentimentalist convention as a younger Karamzin, referred to throughout in the third person by the older) first pays his respects to Germany's famous authors, visiting 'Kant, Nikolai, Ramler, Moritz, and Herder,' before paying his respects to Wieland (whose reception he initially finds impersonal) ('FWRL' 434). Even though heading first to Germany, then Switzerland, then France, then England makes geographic sense, and it is in this order that the traveller organizes his tour, the narrative itself returns to France – in a comparative commentary stressing the greater enjoyment of the French stay – which is an indication of its author's allegiance.[64] After these observations, the journey appears in a different light – as a trajectory of increasing exemplariness and civilization ('The history of Paris … is the history of France and of civilization,' the country that has 'always been … the most amiable of all nations' [436, 439]). The motherland, with the homecoming described in brief yet tender terms, is in complete harmony with the impressed traveller's favourite (foreign) country. Both excel in sensitivity, elegance, and politesse; both are inconstant, subject to (but also memorable for) violent emotions, frivolity, and exuberance, in contrast to Germany or England (438–9). They are each other's next of kin, grown close in the traveller's impressionable mind, or else like two lovers, the one wooing the other: 'I do love my own nation; but permit me also to love these people and their captivating manners …' (438).

Most importantly, 'Un mot sur la littérature russe' makes explicit the central place of 'poetry and literature,' broadly speaking, to Russian society and its critics – for here Karamzin distinguishes between the two, as if *literature* stood not for *belles lettres* (then the common general usage) but for prose, especially novelistic prose. (The essay winds down with a wistful pledge: 'I should like to merit the attention of my fatherland and be worthy of the respect of my people; and if *amour-propre* does not deceive me, I can attain this respect by cultivating the most beautiful of all the arts, the art of writing' ['FWRL' 440]). Illiteracy in Russia was at the time at staggering levels compared to Europe, and the campaign for reading the dailies and book culture was well underway (its greatest advocates were Karamzin and Novikov). The article can be viewed as a bridge between Enlightenment classicist values (e.g., Karamzin's insistence on the cultivation of 'taste') and Romantic ideals (which Karamzin very soon embraced), the two poles never to be fully reconciled in Russian literature. Karamzin defines Russian literature within Montesquieu's framework of a 'democracy' of distinct national literatures, whose character is determined by the climate and geography of the individual nations.[65] (In a later piece, 'Why There Are So Few Talented Authors in Russia?' Karamzin discards the 'climate theory' of art as outlandish).[66]

The self-critical fragment cited above contains a circumstantial excuse. It runs thus:

> but the temple of taste and the sanctuary of art seldom disclose themselves before our authors because we write under the influence of sudden

> whim; because feeble encouragement does not stimulate us to assiduous labor; because, perforce for the very same reasons, just critics are rare in Russia; because in a country where everything is defined by ranks glory has little attraction. Generally speaking, in Russia we write more in verse than in prose; the fact of the matter is that under the cover of rhyme carelessness is more permissible ... ('FWRL' 432–3)

For all its sounding like an advertisement, Karamzin's approach was probably necessary: Russian literature, most of it untranslated until the mid-nineteenth century, was virtually a *terra incognita* for French readers. It is for this reason that the essay assumes a quasi-inventorial structure, along with the rhetoric of a salesman peddling his wares: 'We have songs and romances' (first paragraph, where plots mentioned are abstracted from the works themselves); 'We also have ancient chivalric novels ... and fantastic fairytales – some of which deserve to be called poems' (start of second paragraph); and 'we have successfully tried out ... almost all genres of literature,' 'We have tragedies' and 'There are novels ... witty fairytales ... and so on, and so on' (all in fourth paragraph) ('FWRL' 431). But this economic mode reveals also a sense of genuine pride and belief, on Karamzin's part, in homegrown literature and the potential of emancipated Russian taste.[67] The article, written according to the principles of Karamzin's 'new stylistics' – which was 'supposed to organically unite national Russian and general European forms of expression and break decisively with the Church Slavonic tradition' (Vinogradov 102) – abounds in sentimental phraseology and the occasional elevated note, a moderate display of formal etiquette in exchange for pseudo-colloquial formality. It is, in Vinogradov's words, 'somewhat mincing and mannered, and excessively elegant' (103). Only later on does his language live up to 'elegant simplicity' (104). In Karamzin's journalistic efforts and the results they enjoyed lies the bedrock of the multiplicity of styles and genres that appeared in popular literary-critical discourse during the next century.

Throughout the above discussion, I referred to Karamzin's piece as an *essay* or an *article*.[68] An article it is, insofar as it was first published in a periodical. An essay it may be (if we take the term in its most general sense – as a personal text with an exploratory structure), but only in the first part. The first section of 'Un mot sur la littérature russe' gives an addressee, the 'dear sir' not referred to by name, but we can infer him being the editor of the French journal. Quite apart from its essayistic aspects, this first part is also an *abstract/ed introduction, overview,* or *review* of recent and current Russian writing. Oddly, it lists precious few names of Russian authors (and none contemporary to Karamzin), turning instead to the themes and genres shared by literary texts grouped according to them. As for the fragment of Karamzin's *Pis'ma russkovo puteshestvennika,* its relationship to the first part is, as suggested, somewhat ambiguous. It poses as an excerpt from the actual *Pis'ma,* through the inclusion of the book's title and its place and date of publication (the letters appeared in the *Moskovskii zhurnal* between 1791 and 1792).

What we are given, however, is a kind of *digest* of the original – an author-translated write-up of Karamzin's Russian text (a French translation appeared as late as 1815, and only in 1866 did the full text become available). In the fragment, although the themes of writing and literature are served – aside from sketches of meetings with other famous authors and encounters with special books, Karamzin the narrator quotes from Karamzin the traveller's letters – and although there is continuous talk of high culture, foreign literature is placed above Russian literature. Moreover, the *Pis'ma* digest is not bracketed by a continuation of the essay. The uniqueness and undefinability of Karamzin's chosen form are overcome only to the extent that one calls it a mixture of genres (perhaps Karamzin's own reference to the piece in a letter as a 'something' requested by the French publisher ['treboval' ot menia chto-nibud''] is telling in this regard).[69] Such overt non-correspondence of texts to rough generic distinctions is a feature more common in eighteenth-century Russian criticism than in the Polish or German, by dint of the literary language being much less codified and formalized.[70]

Like his contemporaries, Karamzin wrote in a variety of critical, literary, and historical genres. Another survey-type piece by Karamzin, 'Panteon rossiiskikh avtorov' [Pantheon of Russian Authors], is an annotated, alphabetically organized list of authors, past and present, providing the basic biographic and bibliographic information – he himself described it as 'notes to portraits.'[71] Apart from popularizing the review, although not primarily of Russian texts, Karamzin's *Moskovskii zhurnal* is also credited with promoting a new variety of literary criticism: reviews of translations, which 'educated taste and taught stylistics.'[72] P. Berkov and G. Makogonenko's opinion – namely, that 'It is typical that, judging the works of his own time, Karamzin above all recorded how their essential imperfection is the lack of fidelity, of accuracy in the portrayal of heroes' conduct and the circumstances of their lives' (16) – reminds us that the main measure of a work's success was, at this time, its truth to the original – to life and, in the case of translations, to the meaning of the translated text.

Conclusion

1 Generic Migrants

In my introductory chapter, I proposed that the formal correlations between literature and criticism (insofar as both domains co-exist) develop within the greater epistemic matrix and ideological network. Over the last three centuries, both activities – the literary and the literary-critical – and the writing they left behind interacted not just within national boundaries but within a competitive *international literary space.*[1] The purpose of Pascale Casanova's 2004 publication on the politics of the literary republic – to 'rediscover a lost transnational dimension' of literature that 'has been reduced to the political and linguistic boundaries of nations' (xi) – also animated my comparative approach to critical discourse. Based on their interaction alone, literary criticism of the eighteenth century shared the fate of literature in that it too became nationalized. It is not that criticism followed suit; rather, like other discourses of knowledge, it underwent a gradual formal and procedural regulation. Similarly, it would be misleading to say that modern literary criticism succumbed to the imposition of linguistic and cultural borders, drawn or redrawn at the time. Above all, it hardly existed outside of such divisions, and – through its promotion of *national* literature, of writers' national morale, loyalty, and reputation – was even constitutive of them. But criticism's complicity with the 'powers that be' in the nationalization of literature did not outweigh literature's complicity in nationalizing criticism. Its tendency to spur nationalization did not automatically lead to isolation and xenophobia; on the contrary, discriminating appreciation of foreign works was necessary to maintain the international competitiveness of national writers.

Unlike Hohendahl, for whom criticism is an integral yet subordinate element of the social institution of literature, and for whom the public sphere in which criticism functions is a homogenous, stable construct, Casanova envisions criticism as central to her 'spatialized history' of the 'literary international' (4–5). Her perspective is guided by the Foucauldian notion of the reciprocity of knowledge and power. 'The world of letters,' she contends, 'is in fact something quite different from the received view of literature as a peaceful domain. Its history is one of incessant struggle and competition over the very nature of literature itself – an endless succession of literary manifestos, movements, assaults, and revolutions' (13). The history of literature is inherently critical.

In keeping with Casanova's model, international genre rivalries constituted an important aspect of the competition for literary dominance and authority that makes up literary history. Like literary kinds, forms of critical writing were not only allowed to migrate, but were strategically adopted from reputed literary(-critical) traditions by fledgling literary cultures seeking to join the critical conversation and gain recognition abroad. The reasons for the international normalization and ossification of a genre like the classicist poetics – in economic terms, a discursive monopoly by scholarly form – should therefore be sought in the absence of substantial international competition in the sphere of critical writing. This type of poetics (which in Latin travelled from Italy throughout Western Europe and established its regime in French and in France) governed critical expression in Germany until German letters began to assert, mainly in formally and modally reconceived poetics and in book reviews, its independence from foreign templates. Conversion of the poetics in the service of a new or revived national literature was successful provided the rationalistic and technical paradigm for literary production was in place. Once the classicist model of literary creativity came under scrutiny – the necessary critical distance manifesting itself in conscious expansion and modification of the poetics – critical discourse inevitably welcomed direct formal alternatives. The influx of modern literary works that increasingly undermined the old system's authority sealed the fate of classicist poetics as a genre incompatible with new theories of the literary (including new conceptions of the Neoclassical). As has been shown, this scenario unfolded in eighteenth-century German, Polish, and Russian letters, albeit to different degrees.

If there was one genre that focalized and epitomized eighteenth-century literary-critical discourse, it was the review. It merited this status by virtue of its principally and expressly evaluative purpose and its openness to stylistic variance. At its centre lay the concern with the literary canon. Due to its relative informality, casualness, and brevity, the review also enabled the rehearsal and development of critical ideas for larger, more theoretical or historical projects. This was especially true in the German context, of critics as diverse in orientation as Lessing, Herder, and A.W. Schlegel. While some reviewing was done for earlier learned journals, the review flourished in review periodicals (where it eclipsed other critical forms) committed to the advancement of public education and interested in more recent literary content. That development coincided with the liberation of literary value: although various 'external' criteria were still applied to literature – especially moral and utilitarian demands – reviewing allowed them to be debated with increasing specialization and intricacy, in a less abstract and timelier fashion, within a medium designed for the purpose. Both the poetics and the review were mobilized for the transnational dimension of literary-critical culture: they ensured the commensurability and relative consistency of critical language, principles, and discussions.

2 Time Travellers

Foremost and most durable among the prototypical 'vessels' for theoretical-critical reflection was, of course, the poetological treatise (although the term is no longer interchangeable with poetics). The most pronounced change in its execution in the eighteenth century was the incorporation of a philosophical dimension. This transformation occurred, however, only in German criticism, where longer literary-aesthetic contributions typically identified themselves through reference to Baumgarten's philosophical treatise on aesthetics. In the prologue to his genre study, Benjamin mentions the following defining features of the treatise as a philosophical form:

> Treatises may be didactic in tone, but essentially they lack the conclusiveness of an instruction which could be asserted, like doctrine, by virtue of its own authority ... In the canonic form of the treatise the only element of an intention – and it is an educative rather than a didactic intention – is the authoritative quotation ... [Representation] as digression – such is the methodological nature of the treatise. The absence of an uninterrupted purposeful structure is its primary characteristic. Tirelessly the process of thinking makes new beginnings, returning in a roundabout way to its

> original object. This continual pausing for breath is the mode most proper to the process of contemplation. (Benjamin 28)

The critically oriented treatises that participated in the emergent discourse of aesthetics (Lessing's *Laokoon* may serve as an early example) conform to Benjamin's sketch. Critical treatises of earlier date (like Gottsched's poetics) were too regulated by practical rules mandating clear exposition to allow the contemplative and speculative distance to develop. They spoke with the borrowed authority of *doctrine classique*, and were markedly didactic and less digressive (more assertive) in structure.

Inspiring my study of a period in the life of critical genres was an attraction to literary criticism as a weak spot in the discourses of knowledge, even when, in formulating judgments, it claims to discern truth from mere opinion and falsity. The reasons for this relative weakness must be sought in the fact that criticism was one of the first knowledge discourses explicitly concerned with another written discourse, which at that point was still not entirely separate from it. Paradoxically, criticism's truth claims aspire to objectivity about (and, thus, mastery of) a textual object which defies reduction by such claims and itself, on principle, resists the banality of objectivity. But criticism's epistemic 'weakness' could at times be its strength; a notable feature of eighteenth-century criticism in the three areas was its formal consanguinity with literature through acts of hybridization (although only in German Romanticism did this become programmatic and intimate). The poetics, the critical letter, and the review all manifested such more or less conscious hybridity, which placed criticism within the sphere of literature as opposed to outside it. A general trend in the formation of critical writing in the eighteenth century was away from a small number of codified forms, through a greater *modal* variety of forms that occasionally flirted with literary techniques, and, again, toward fewer but less conceptually homogeneous ones (the real conceptual differences began to be felt on the level of individual style). In the 1800s, after the experiments with literary form of the preceding century, and as the modus operandi, purpose, and social function of criticism became better established professionally (specialized) and institutionally (disciplined), the dynamism of discursive form declined: the academic and journalistic types of criticism settled into a narrower range of genres of greater uniformity: the review, the critical essay, the characterization, the monograph, the published lecture, and the expanded literary history.[2] This formal convergence and resulting simplification of generic choices might go some way towards explaining the neglect of genre scholarship. Jonathan Lavery brings the terms of this lack of interest up to date: 'Matters of exposition, literary form, and presentation are presumed to have more to do with the packaging, marketing, and advertising ...' (Lavery 180). Streamlining form via standardized textual organization, schematic style, and uniform terminology for the sake of efficient transmission of information takes the place of a considered, expansive choice of genre and formal experimentation. In the first case attention to form is secondary (form becomes an appurtenance, derivative of content), while in the second it is primary (form is treated as integral – organizing, expressive, formative of content). Both cases involve generic consciousness – the difference between them lies, rather, in whether the choice is made freely or automatically and whether the law of genre is honoured more in the breach or in the observance.

The Enlightenment self-myth of origins encompassed the birth of literary criticism from the spirit of literature and philosophy. My intention was not so much to demythologize the history of ideas (a task long accomplished without my aid) but, rather, to shed light on the formative ideas' figures of existence or use – that is, on criticism's co-extensive birth from the *letter* of literature and philosophy. One of the guiding questions for my research into the genres of emerging literary-critical discourses was inspired by the persistence in the twentieth century of genres and modes of critical writing minted in the eighteenth. It was not a question of causes but of a trajectory; not a matter of explaining continuity or recurrence but, instead, given the parallel between the two epochs, of unearthing the first signs of formal regularities which still govern the institution of criticism. Like the eighteenth, the twentieth century has also seen its systematizing, quasi-scientific approaches to the text – Formalism, New Criticism, Archetypal Criticism, Structuralism, Genetic Criticism – and its individualist, subjectivist, and 'suspicious' approaches – Hermeneutics, Psychoanalytic Criticism, Reader-Response Theory and Reception Aesthetics, Post-structuralism, Deconstruction, New Historicism, New Rhetoric. This panoply of self-legitimizing critical responses and their formal diversity in the span of the last century represented an intensification and pluralization of those observable in the eighteenth. If most of the nineteenth and the mid- to late twentieth century were periods of the discourse's systemic stabilization and ideological polarization (in all three cases, criticism became overtly political), work done in both the early and late twentieth century began to worry and contest established boundaries, restoring spontaneity to critical expression – and at the same time also generic instability.[3] To read critically today is to read the signs of the fusion of criticism, literature, and philosophy.

3 Looking Back

The above comparison, while beyond the scope of this study, gestures toward the sprawling, international and transnational, genealogy of critical discourse one envisions but cannot hope to complete. In these final paragraphs, I outline two case studies suggested to me by material within the perimeter of the present work (though not in its scope), as well as the most potentially valuable lines of inquiry extending from it.

As the texts analysed demonstrate, the poetics of Horace and Boileau saw their adaptations in all three cultures. The marked differences in their adaptation (and its comparative chronologies) merit their own comparison and contextualization in intellectual and genre history – especially considering that Boileau's text was itself an adaptation of Horace's. Thus: To what extent have the original texts been reworked, extended, or systematized in their adaptations? What discursive factors (e.g., the degree of the critical discourse's establishment in a culture, or the proportion of theoretical to transitive critical interest) could have motivated the formal choices when converting these works? Did the choice of prose over verse typically reflect, for instance, a modernizing theoretical intent and a modernized terminology and content? Did a new selection of examples accompany noteworthy conceptual and theoretical shifts with respect to the original?

Continuing in a similar vein, one could undertake in-depth comparisons with contemporary French criticism. A more systematic juxtaposition of the three traditions with a discourse in many ways their model would further illuminate the role played by French literary-critical forms in the early formative stages of German, Polish, and Russian critical discourses. The importation of critical thought and the naturalization of French poetological debates in these cultures were ensured by the ubiquity of French as the lingua franca of court aristocratic circles and among the nobility, as well as by the largely unreflective acceptance of French intellectual fashions among educated elites, criticized first in Germany, then in Russia. (Exceptions to this rule, such as the 'dialogue' between Batteux and his first German translator, Johann Adolf Schlegel – whose heavily annotated 1751 edition of the poetics provoked the

French author to respond with revisions, and vice versa, in subsequent issues of translation and original – also merit a separate study.) However, as the Boileau example indicates, differences in the naturalization of foreign critical expression point to pre-existing differences in discursive structure and the local stock of discursive forms, which in each case affected the cultural transfer. These features reasserted themselves still in the eighteenth century, once universal French authority had dimmed. Ultimately, I was drawn more strongly to these formal emancipations than to apprenticeship under foreign masters.

Another worthwhile analysis might concern the self-referential occurrence in literary-critical texts of this period of the terms critique and critical (and, somewhat later, metacriticism and metacritical). Such designations sometimes signalized a text's confrontation or struggle with existing discursive boundaries, and served therefore as *crisical* markers – marking the discourse's consciousness of its own epistemic conditions and limits. An investigation along these lines would no doubt benefit from a broader geographic compass (including France and England, for example). The task would be to establish the formal correlates of that self-identification specifically in the early texts. A substantial comparison could then be undertaken between these self-consciously critical works and those that lacked such overt indices of self-consciousness. Here again, teasing out the implications of their chronology would be profitable.

The current historical account is limited by its exclusion of more metacritical or metaliterary texts. Secular metaliterature was the embryonic form of literary-critical discourse that, in the Polish and German cases, dates back more than three hundred years and, furthermore, did not disappear once criticism became established as a discourse external (if contiguous) to the literary domain. As I have found many examples, in the period and the areas chosen, of the thematization, critique, or theorization of critical method and writing, and some examples of metaliterature, I decided, rather than giving them cursory treatment, to omit these entirely for the sake of analytic coherence. There can be no doubt that granting sole attention to these categories of texts would not merely supplement but graduate the accuracy of the picture of literary-critical discourse emerging from this study.

Notes

Introduction

1 René Wellek, *A History of Modern Criticism, 1750–1950*, vol. 1, *The Later Eighteenth Century* (New Haven: Yale University Press, 1955), v. Hereafter cited as *18C*.

2 During the eighteenth century, all three regions saw the publication of their first modern literary-critical texts. For a Germanocentric argument concerning modern European criticism's emergence in the eighteenth century, see Peter Uwe Hohendahl, *The Institution of Criticism* (Ithaca: Cornell University Press, 1982), 47 ff. Hohendahl acknowledges that 'it is difficult to draw a sharp line between the seventeenth and eighteenth centuries in the history of literary theory' (47), although in the German case the line between the Baroque and the Enlightenment is easier to draw. However, the 'modern notion of criticism,' which placed the literary-theoretical postulates of the previous century 'in a new context of legitimation' and had a distinctly public function, is an eighteenth century invention.

3 It is true that two monumental (multinational, multivolume) studies – Wellek's *History of Modern Criticism* and the multi-author *Cambridge History of Literary Criticism* – offer a thorough, chronological survey of the critical tradition. These magisterial, broadly comparative works, however, do not concertedly address the formal and stylistic side of ideas and rarely touch on the generic features of critical writing. To the best of my knowledge, to date there have not been any wide-ranging, comparative-historical, book-length studies of the gamut of critical genres in English. My decision to pursue one was also spurred on by a relative lack of competing research in the three literary cultures in which I was working. Besides several more or less traditional, single- and multi-author histories of

German and Russian criticism, sparse monographs with a formal interest, and analyses of individual critical genre(s) over short time spans, I have found illuminating historical discussions organized by literary period on the pages of 'Literaturkritik im Deutschland' (an online resource run by Thomas Anz of the Institut für neuere deutsche Literatur und Medien at the University of Marburg); also in print under the title *Literaturkritik: Geschichte – Theorie – Praxis* (Munich: Beck, 2004), as well as in several German, Polish, and Russian critical anthologies – only one of them devoted explicitly to representing criticism's generic range, albeit in the twentieth century (V.V. Perkhin's *'To Discover the beauties and imperfections ...': Literary Criticism from Review to Obituary: The Silver Age* [St Petersburg: Litsei, 2001]).

4 The presence of distinguishable genres and thus of patterned relations among individual texts is what regularizes further utterances and stabilizes the apparatus of discursive intelligibility, helping establish a discourse as such (Charles Bazerman, 'Systems of Genres and the Enactment of Social Intentions,' in *Genre and the New Rhetoric*, ed. A. Freedman and P. Medway [London: Taylor & Francis, 1994], 99).

5 Jurij Tynjanov and Roman Jakobson, 'Problems in the Study of Literature and Language' [1928], trans. Herbert Eagle, in *Readings in Russian Poetics*, ed. Ladislav Matejka and Krystyna Pomorska (Cambridge, MA: MIT Press, 1971), 79–81. As Igor Shaitanov has shown, Aleksandr Veselovskii's 'historical poetics,' or 'historical-genetic' view of literary evolution, deserves no small credit for preparing this theoretical shift in genre theory ('Aleksandr Veselovskii's Historical Poetics: Genre in Historical Poetics,' *New Literary History* 32 [2001]: 429–43).

6 Thomas O. Beebee, *The Ideology of Genre: A Comparative Study of Generic Instability* (University Park: The Pennsylvania University Press, 1994), 3n5.

7 The term is taken from Hans Robert Jauss's *Toward an Aesthetic of Reception*, trans. Timothy Bahti (Minneapolis: University of Minnesota Press, 1982). As part of his project to renew literary history, Jauss recognized the 'possibility of a historical systematics' of genres that would account for the sequence of such genre systems, by showing 'the diachronic and synchronic interrelations between the literary genres of a period' (105). Genre is to be grasped *in re* (historically), rather than *ante* or *post rem* (in explicit, normative or descriptive, logical orderings). Jauss, then, saw genres not as self-enclosed, timeless entities but as dynamic social phenomena, such that 'the function of a genre depends not only on its relation to a real, lived procedure, but also on its position within a comprehensive symbolic system familiar to contemporaries' (103).

8 Mikhail Bakhtin, 'The Problem of Speech Genres,' in his *Speech Genres and Other Late Essays*, ed. Caryl Emerson and Michael Holquist, trans. Vern W. McGee (Austin: University of Texas Press, 1986), 60. In Bakhtin's classification, literary-critical utterances would classify as 'complex' and 'ideological' *secondary speech genres* (62).

9 If, for instance, we speak of Russian criticism of the eighteenth century as being highly normative, we are identifying that discourse's modal phase.

10 Jonathan Lavery, 'Philosophical Genres and Literary Forms: A Mildly Polemical Introduction,' *Poetics Today* 28.2 (2007): 181.

11 Working towards a poetics of philosophical discourse, Berel Lang proposes a fourfold generic schema structuring written philosophy and reflecting the different relations between its forms and functions. The main philosophical genres he identifies are *dialogue* (lacking a dominant authorial point of view), *meditation/essay* (featuring a dominant and personal point of view), *commentary* (point of view subordinated to the primary text and its referent), and *treatise* (dominant yet impersonal point of view) (Berel Lang, *Philosophy and the Art of Writing: Studies in Philosophical and Literary Style* [Lewisburg, PA: Bucknell University Press, 1983], 29). In *The Anatomy of Philosophical Style: Literary Philosophy and the Philosophy of Literature* (Oxford: Blackwell, 1990), Lang refines his generic classification by positing two *meta-genres* (which I would rename *modes*): the *expositional* (including such genres as treatise, critique, discourse, and commentary) and the *performative* (e.g., personal essay, dialogue, aphorism, meditation).

12 One is aided in matters of canonicity in the German case by the existence of such collections as *Meisterwerke deutscher Literaturkritik* [Masterpieces of German Literary Criticism] in two volumes, with the first spanning 'series of essential texts from Gottsched up to Goethe's death ... the period 1730 to 1830' (Hans Mayer, Introduction to *Meisterwerke deutscher Literaturkritik*, ed. Mayer [Berlin: Rütten & Loening, 1954–56], 9). It is an open question whether Polish and Russian scholars conceive of a number of literary-critical texts from this period as a *canon*; it seems to me, rather, that while many such texts are acknowledged as significant for their generic originality, enduring message, historical impact (for example, on the Neoclassical literary canon), they do not constitute an identifiable textual canon in the same way as the German one established by the efforts of historians in the last century. This in itself may be a good thing. The reasons may be as simple as the relative scarcity of scholarly treatment of Polish (less so Russian) criticism as a textual domain in its own right – scholars have been at pains to discriminate between literary criticism, literary theory, and (historical)

literary scholarship, or where such discursive distinctions had not customarily been made.

13 Dominick LaCapra, *History and Criticism* [Ithaca: Cornell University Press, 1985], 112–13.

14 In conceptualizing such a genealogy I defer to Michel Foucault's use of the term. In a nutshell, genealogy takes up and makes known what has been subjugated – masked, disqualified, or filtered out – by a discourse, particularly the lowly, awkward, dispersed, and dramatic beginnings of knowledges claiming democratic unity and pure origins, but which were in fact the products of local struggles. Genealogy is interested in the *emergence* of the objects of knowledges through institutionalized discursive and nondiscursive practices. It is seen by Foucault as a complement to archaeology, the structural method used to yield knowledge of *historical* a prioris, the conditions of possibility of individual knowledges, which also does away with a discourse's unbroken continuity and its 'origin that eludes all historical determinations' (Michel Foucault, *The Archaeology of Knowledge and the Discourse on Language*, trans. A.M. Sheridan Smith [New York: Pantheon, 1972], 25; further citations as *AK*). While archaeology seeks to reveal the epistemic grounds for empirical knowledge buried beneath the sedimented ash of discourse in a given period, genealogy studies its eruptions as a dynamic series of events.

15 Foucault defined the 'history of the present' in opposition to a presentistic or teleological 'history of the past in terms of the present,' or to a historicist history of the past in terms of the past. The term appears in his genealogical *Discipline and Punish: The Birth of the Prison*, trans. Alan Sheridan (New York: Vintage, 1979), 31.

16 The death throes can be obvious, or they can take on the form of frantic trendism in today's market-driven academia. For a contribution to the decades-long debate on the internal undoing of academic critical authority/expertise (most recently, the takeover of Literature programs by Cultural Studies which radically relativizes and voids aesthetic value in favour of a pernicious egalitarianism) and the demise of the arbiter of literary value cum tutor of public taste, see Rónán McDonald, *The Death of the Critic* (London: Continuum, 2007).

17 For a discussion of this topic in German, see *Kaufen! Statt Lesen! Literaturkritik in der Krise?* ed. Gunther Nickel (Göttingen: Wallstein, 2005), which includes proceedings from the 2004 conference, 'Literaturkritik. Zukunftsaussichten eines alten Gewerbes,' and which traces professional criticism's decline to the spread of online consumer reviewing. Another assessment from around this time came from a poll of Polish artists under-

taken by *Tygodnik Powszechny*: 'We are living through the crisis of criticism (art, literary, music, film) ... Old authorities have vanished, and new ones have not yet appeared ... It all amounts to the thesis of the death of criticism' – even if its stated source is only the factionalism of national media, rather than the more general and serious problem of *Bildung* or the new mediasphere ('Notatki,' *Tygodnik Powszechny* 18 (2808), 4 May 2003, http://www2.tygodnik.com.pl/tp/2808/notatki.php). Admittedly, these pronouncements on the state of criticism focus on its higher journalistic variety, primarily evaluative and focused on contemporary production, setting aside (explicitly and rather shortsightedly) academic literary-theoretical and literary-historical practices – which, as we know, are next in line for the axe.

18 William E. Cain, 'Notes toward a History of Anti-Criticism,' *New Literary History* 20.1 (1988): 47.

19 'This (especially in the German context) crucial distinction,' writes Hohendahl, 'concerns the specific mode of the search for truth as well as the question of social practice. Given the rapidly increasing professionalization of the social sciences and the humanities during the nineteenth century, the concept of science [*Wissenschaft*] emphasizes strict boundaries which are determined in terms of methodological rigor. This search for strict demarcations also pertains to academic literary criticism [part of *Literaturwissenschaft*]' (Peter Uwe Hohendahl, 'The Scholar, the Intellectual, and the Essay: Weber, Lukács, Adorno, and Postwar Germany,' *The German Quarterly* 70 [Summer 1997]: 218). The endurance of this common modus operandi, a legitimizing rigour, has helped contain the crisical outbreak in academic criticism. Another mitigating factor was the general *positive* need for the crisical in all areas of critical inquiry in the aftermath of the Second World War. Hohendahl's claim in *The Institution of Criticism* is that the crisis of criticism's legitimacy was more fundamental in West Germany than in the U.S. anxiously exaggerates the dependency of critical practice on the 'critical tradition' and, especially, on the 'literary tradition' (38–9). Criticism's fundamental questions and disagreements about its methods, function, and tasks were provoked and mediated by literature's loss of its traditional social function and its institutional deterioration – not, in other words, by criticism's irrelevance vis-à-vis literature or society.

20 Jacques Derrida, *Of Grammatology*, trans. and introd. G.C. Spivak [Baltimore: Johns Hopkins University Press, 1998], 158.

21 Book reviewing and discussion in scholarly publications aside, one can reasonably expect the ascendancy of scaled-down, abbreviated, and fluid critical forms, for example the *reader review*, a potent popular form of con-

sumer feedback and a far cry from the journalistic standard currently on the way out. What some might decry as a decline of journalistic criticism, as it has been practised professionally since roughly the end of the eighteenth century, others might hail as a discursive adaptation to the evolving patterns of digital literacy. The proliferation and growing critical appeal of 'mobile, various, and fluctuating' writing leads Bernard Cerquiglini to ask, 'Does that mean that the written work is itself at stake?' (*In Praise of the Variant: A Critical History of Philology*, trans. Betsy Wing [Baltimore: Johns Hopkins University Press, 1999], xiii). A good question for critics of the new literature, which will no doubt plunge them back into a conceptual and functional crisis. Theoretically, the acceptable unities of today (*text*, *work*) are liable to turn suspect tomorrow.

22 Peter Gebhardt proclaims as much in his introduction to *Literaturkritik und Literarische Wertung*, ed. P. Gebhardt (Darmstadt: Wissenschaftliche Buchgesellschaft, 1980), 1. Reinhart Koselleck's study of these questions in *Critique and Crisis: Enlightenment and the Pathogenesis of Modern Society* (Oxford: Berg, 1988) shows the formative role of the antagonism between intellectuals and political power in the development of critique in the eighteenth century.

23 This is Foucault's term for clusters of discourses that resemble each other in content or function (Sara Mills, *Discourse*, 2nd ed. [London: Routledge, 2004], 145). '[F]or the sake of convenience,' Foucault calls them 'systems of dispersion' of a group of objects, concepts, types of enunciation, and thematic choices (*AK* 37). The concept of a discursive formation is the subject of chapter 2 of *AK*.

24 Diane MacDonell, *Theories of Discourse: An Introduction* (Oxford: Basil Blackwell, 1986), 3.

25 *Style* is taken here in Bakhtin's sense of 'the selection of the lexical, phraseological, and grammatical resources of the language' (Bakhtin 60). In the case of many extraliterary speech genres, individual style (that is, reflective of the individuality of the speaker) 'does not enter into the intent of the utterance ... but is ... an epiphenomenon of the utterance, one of its by-products' (63). When applicable, however, style is bound to genre by an 'organic, inseparable link' (64). Although style is, for Bakhtin, by definition *individual*, he does refer to *functional styles*, which 'are nothing other than generic styles for certain spheres of human activity and communication.' This, indeed, is the only kind of style that can meaningfully be factored into historical descriptions of genre.

26 Elżbieta Sarnowska-Temeriusz, 'Krytyka literacka w Polsce w XVI i XVII wieku,' in E. Sarnowska-Temeriusz and Teresa Kostkiewiczowa, *Krytyka*

literacka w Polsce w XVI i XVII wieku oraz w epoce Oświecenia (Wrocław: Zakład Narodowy im. Ossolińskich, 1990), 12, translation mine.

27 René Wellek, 'Literary Theory, Criticism, and History,' in his *Concepts of Criticism*, ed. Stephen G. Nichols, Jr (New Haven: Yale University Press, 1963), 3.

28 See Henryk Markiewicz, *Główne problemy wiedzy o literaturze* (Cracow: WL, 1965).

29 Gérard Genette, *The Architext: An Introduction*, trans. Jane E. Lewin (Berkeley: University of California Press, 1992), 69. We need not languish in a false dilemma to assess the value of biological analogies for theorizing genre. Bernard E. Rollin ('Nature, Convention, and Genre Theory,' *Poetics* 10 [1981]: 127–43) sees genres and their systematics on the non-essentialist model of natural kinds emergent in evolutionary-biological classification (unstable, reality-based, theory-committed), no longer embroiled in the dichotomy of convention (nominalism or constructionism) and nature (realism). Similarly, Ian Hacking proposes to move beyond this age-old dualism, given the existence of 'social properties' in classification and preference for family resemblance. He argues for a modest version of natural classes, which sees biological differences as independent and natural but the recognition and classification of them as social and non-exhaustive ('A Tradition of Natural Kinds,' *Philosophical Studies* 61 [1991]: 109–26). Where he diverges from Rollin is in restricting the category of natural kinds (species in evolutionary biology are no longer exemplary of it) and in drawing a distinction between natural and *social* kinds (i.e., interactive, self-authenticating, formed on family resemblances of various types). Genre would in fact fall in the latter category.

30 On the distinction between theoretical and historical conceptions of genre, I recommend Tzvetan Todorov's *Genres in Discourse*, trans. Catherine Porter (Cambridge: Cambridge University Press, 1990).

31 This encompasses what is sometimes referred to as 'external form': prose, versification (metrical form/structure), presence of rhyme, alternation of speakers, etc.

32 Intertexts are understood in Genette's 'soft' sense: as instances of quotation, plagiarism, allusion that may or may not have been intentional (see his *Palimpsests: Literature in the Second Degree*, trans. Claude Daubinsky and Channa Newman [Lincoln: University of Nebraska Press, 1998]). The term paratext is also Genette's (see *Paratexts: Thresholds of Interpretation*, trans. Jane E. Lewin [Cambridge: Cambridge University Press, 1997]).

33 Bakhtin 96–9. Bakhtin regards addressivity as a constitutive and definitive feature of many speech genres. He notes that 'the so-called neutral or ob-

jective styles of exposition that concentrate maximally on the subject matter' nonetheless involve a conception of the addressee, his/her 'presumed apperceptive background,' even if 'generalized' and 'abstracted from the expressive aspect ... (minimal in the objective style)' (98). Such objective styles 'presuppose,' in Bakhtin's view, 'something like an identity of the addressee and the speaker, a unity of their viewpoints' at great expense of expressive import. The character of addressivity (and expressivity) varies in literary-critical genres: in this respect, the treatise with a formal dedication and the semi- or informal, personal published letter lie at the opposite ends of the spectrum. Like the remaining parameters, addressivity figures into the overall plan of the utterance: it, too, affects the process of selection and combination of textual units. It can be very legible or hardly at all, depending on one's knowledge of the situation of an utterance.

34 The distinction between genre and mode is addressed, for example, by Genette in *The Architext* 66 ff. Genette's theory is cited by Derrida in 'The Law of Genre,' in his *Acts of Literature*, ed. Derek Attridge, trans. Avital Ronell (London: Routledge, 1992), 228. The distinction is *au fond* between form-bound and content-bound categories. It is echoed by Hayden White, who differentiates between *formal* and *practical* genres – the latter characterized by thematic content ('Commentary,' *New Literary History* 34.2 [2003]: 367–76). But this conception leaves the problem of 'material form' versus 'semantic content' analytically intact. The 'law of genre,' as explained by Derrida, allows not merely for a reconciliation or accord between, even the empirical inseparability of, form and content, but for their absolute inseparability – a view harder to put to work but ultimately more productive. As Derrida put it: 'The question of the literary genre is not a formal one ...' ('The Law of Genre' 243). A more up-to-date discussion of mode with respect to genre can be found in John Frow, *Genre* (London: Routledge), an introductory text to a new generation of genre theory with which my own theoretical soundings have much in common (for a sense of the commonality, see his overview in 'Reproducibles, Rubrics, and Everything You Need: Genre Theory Today,' *PMLA* 122.5 [2007]: 1626–34).

35 Ireneusz Opacki, 'Royal Genres,' trans. David Malcolm, *Modern Genre Theory*, ed. D. Duff (Essex: Pearson Education, 2000), 124.

36 The analogy of family resemblance serves to fine-tune the concept of genre: members of a genre need not all share even a single trait, since, as Ralph Cohen points out, 'to do so would presuppose that the trait has the same function for each of the member texts' ('History and Genre,' *New Literary History* 17:2 [1986]: 210). (For the term's application in genre theory, see for example Alastair Fowler, *Kinds of Literature: An Introduction to the*

Theory of Genres and Modes (Cambridge, MA: Harvard University Press, 1982); and David Fishelov, *Metaphors of Genre: The Role of Analogies in Genre Theory* [University Park: Pennsylvania State University Press, 1993].) The formulation of family resemblances in Wittgenstein's *Philosophical Investigations* can be extrapolated as follows: no single definitional condition is necessary or sufficient; or, in terms of classes of existing things, there are neither necessary nor sufficient conditions for inclusion in a given empirical class. Even so, we have designated *literary evaluation* (mode) as a 'necessary' condition for inclusion in the category literary-*critical discourse*. This is a pragmatic historical decision, not immune to charges of essentialism. It remains vague without further delineations: What exactly does evaluation involve? How is it manifested (e.g., in qualitative language, in audience's impression, in an author's paratextual claims)? Can we define evaluation as a single function or, again, as a historicizeable family of functions, and so on?

37 See, for instance, Michel Foucault, *The History of Sexuality: An Introduction*, trans. R. Hurley (New York: Vintage, 1990), 101.

38 One could also conceptualize genre in discourse on the analogy of the 'ritual' from Althusser's theory of ideology. Utilizing his framework, genre can be thought of as an ideologically bound ritual embedded and performed in institutional settings by texts qua inscriptions in the material existence of ideology (in terms of its reception, a text is a material artefact which occasions a process of interpretation and ideologization, and only in this sense is a text 'constructed'); every text, in other words, is a stem cell in a discourse's ideological tissue. Thus, for example, each literary-critical genre would be a prescribed procedure for producing evaluations of literature. It would be recognized, shared, contested, or rejected by regional or class ideologies that exist below or within the dominant ideology – which they potentially undermine (Louis Althusser, 'Ideology and Ideological State Apparatuses [Notes towards an Investigation],' in *Lenin and Philosophy and Other Essays*, trans. Ben Brewster [London: New Left, 1971], 168). This would make genres the symbolic instruments of ideological struggle within and against a repressive-ideological apparatus like the literary establishment, 'not only the *stake*, but also the *site*' of this struggle. The material instruments of this struggle are the texts themselves, as events partially governed by generic rituals. The effect of the multilevel cohesion of 'discursivity' (used here to mean 'discursive practice' in all its aspects rather than 'the way of being of discourse') is that each system of genres, the complex functioning of these genres in a discourse, is symbolic and in the service of ideology (hence, generic hierarchies). In short, 'Because

people in groups develop genres, genres reflect what the group believes and how it views the world' (Amy J. Devitt, *Writing Genres* [Carbondale: Southern Illinois University Press, 2004], 59).

39 Paul A. Bové, *Mastering Discourse: The Politics of Intellectual Culture* (Durham: Duke University Press, 1992), 4–5, 15.

40 Michel Foucault, 'The Order of Discourse,' trans. Ian McLeod, in *Untying the Text: A Poststructuralist Reader*, ed. R. Young (Boston: Routledge & Kegan Paul, 1981), 71; see also p. 73. All further citations of this source are abbreviated as 'OD.' There is a growing body of scholarship in German treating genealogy as a specific brand of critique (see, e.g., Rudi Visker, *Michel Foucault: Genealogie als Kritik* [Munich: Fink, 1991]; and Martin Saar, 'Genealogische Kritik,' in *Was Ist Kritik?* ed. Rahel Jaeggi and Tilo Wesche [Frankfurt: Suhrkamp, 2009], 247–65).

41 Both make 'tactical use of knowledge,' challenging 'regimes of truth' and critiquing ideology, and both are ongoing tasks (Lee Quinby, Introduction to *Genealogy and Literature*, ed. Quinby [Minneapolis: University of Minnesota Press, 1995], xii).

42 Quinby xii–xiii.

43 Michel Foucault, *The Order of Things: An Archaeology of the Human Sciences* (New York: Vintage, 1994), 16, xiv. All further citations are abbreviated as *OT*. Indeed, Foucault's historiographic approach(es), while stressing 'real historical difference' over continuity, proves limited by design in being 'unable to deal with both real discursive alterity and its logical consequences for understanding the interaction and succession of different discursive forms' (Paul Allen Miller, 'Toward a Post-Foucauldian History of Discursive Practices,' *Configurations* 7.2 [1999]: 211–12).

44 The above foray into theories of genre and discourse has shown where this approach is most aligned with work already done. Of those still unmentioned, Bazerman's incisive historical analyses of discursive genres are particularly valuable, as are the methodological statements by Vijay K. Bhatia and Carol Berkenkotter on the value of critical and historical genre analysis for discourse studies. See, for example: Charles Bazerman, 'Letters and Social Grounding of Differentiated Genres,' in *Letter Writing as a Social Practice*, ed. D. Barton and N. Hall (Amsterdam: John Benjamins, 2000), 15–30; Carol Berkenkotter, 'Genre Evolution?: A Case for a Diachronic Perspective,' in *Advances in Discourse Studies*, ed. V.K. Bhatia et al. (London: Routledge, 2008), 178–91; Vijay K. Bhatia, 'Towards Critical Genre Analysis,' in *Advances in Discourse Studies*, 166–77, and *Worlds of Written Discourse: A Genre-Based View* (London: Continuum, 2004). Berkenkotter cites Peter Dear's article in his 1991 collection *The Literary Structure of Scientific*

Argument: Historical Studies as articulating the centrality of textual and contextual (socio-historical) study of genre and generic change for charting conceptual and cognitive change in scientific discourses. It is to Bazerman's great credit that as a critical rhetorician he did not sidestep genre as a unit of analysis. His landmark study in this regard is *Shaping Written Knowledge: The Genre and Activity of the Experimental Article in Science* (1988).

45 The essay is reprinted in Hohendahl's *Institution of Criticism*, pp. 224–41. His model is anchored in the dialectic of Constance School reception theory and consists of three layers: 1) the study of 'time-bound concretizations' of literary works in their interpretations; 2) 'the poetological and aesthetic norms which entered the text of criticism ... reconstructed in the sense of Jaussian horizon of expectation'; and 3) the analysis of the concepts of literature on which critical texts are based (227).

46 One may cite Heinz Schlaffer's *Poesie und Wissen: Die Entstehung des ästhetischen Bewußtseins und der philologischen Erkenntnis* (Frankfurt: Suhrkamp, 1990), which maintains an institutional focus in tracing the development of a closely allied endeavour – philology – from the festival through the library to the university. Another is the incomplete seven-volume *Literaturkritik: Eine Textdokumentation zur Geschichte einer literarischen Gattung*, ed. Alfred Estermann (Vaduz: Topos, 1984).

47 This is Hohendahl's contention in another essay in *The Institution of Criticism*, pp. 44–82. The Kant quotation is from the Preface of the *Critique of Pure Reason*, ed. and trans. Paul Guyer and Allen W. Wood (Cambridge: Cambridge University Press, 1999), 100–1.

48 The term, also translated as 'counterpublic sphere' or 'counter-publicity,' comes from Oskar Negt and Alexander Kluge's critique of Jürgen Habermas in their *The Public Sphere and Experience: Toward an Analysis of the Bourgeois and Proletarian Public Sphere*, trans. Peter Labanyi et al. (Minneapolis: University of Minnesota Press, 1993). For further clarification vis-à-vis *Öffentlichkeit*, see note 1 to Foreword by Miriam Hansen.

49 Janusz Maciejewski, *Obszary i konteksty literatury* (Warsaw: DiG, 1998), 103–31.

50 Charles Bazerman, 'Letters and Social Grounding of Differentiated Genres,' in *Letter Writing as a Social Practice*, 24.

51 *Episteme* (literally, 'knowledge') refers to the epistemic grid or configuration determining/defining the emergence and formation of empirical knowledges within any given cultural period and organizing their coherence. In another gloss, it is 'a set of discursive structures within which a culture thinks about itself and formulates new ideas'; also, the tools used to think rather than ideas as such (Mills 145).

52 Michel Foucault, Introduction to *The Birth of the Clinic*, trans. A.M. Sheridan (London: Routledge, 1989), xviii–xix.
53 George A. Kennedy, 'Christianity and Criticism,' in *The Cambridge History of Literary Criticism*, vol. 1, *Classical Criticism*, ed. Kennedy (Cambridge: Cambridge University Press, 1990), 346.
54 Wellek takes up the issue polemically in his *Concepts of Criticism*. He sees literary criticism as closer to science than to art in the modern sense of the word. Bound up with its goal of value judgment is a conceptual knowledge of the work of art, which acts as the unavoidable stepping stone to a systematic, scientific knowledge about literature. He does remark, however, that critical insights have been 'conveyed in the most different art-forms' (4). Georg Lukács leaned towards assigning artistic status to critical writing ('On the Nature and Form of the Essay,' in his *Soul and Form*, trans. Anna Bostock [Cambridge, MA: MIT Press, 1974], 1). At the same time, he attempted to define the critical essay (its subject not limited to literature) as 'a form which separates it, with the rigour of a law, from all other art forms,' including literary works of the imagination (2). The essence of this form, representing criticism at its purest, is precisely its multiformity and independence from any specific subject matter; in other words, its status as art does not result from its identity with or mediation of art. The critical essay 'stands too high, it sees and connects too many things to be the simple exposition or explanation of a work; the title of every essay is preceded in invisible letters, by the words "Thoughts occasioned by …"' (15). To take a retrospective look at modern European criticism as a whole, it was in Germany that the argument for criticism (*Literaturkritik*) as a literary art, or its parity with art, first emerged and periodically resurfaced, in reaction to its scientific strain (*Literaturwissenschaft*). In France and England, Wellek tells us, 'criticism' was often self-identified as a 'science of literature' (*science de la littérature, science littéraire*) founded on a combination of biological and psychological principles, before '"science" became so much identified with natural science' that this denotation could not survive (René Wellek, 'The Term and Concept of Literary Criticism,' in his *Concepts of Criticism*, ed. Stephen G. Nichols, Jr [New Haven: Yale University Press, 1963], 32–3).
55 The term designated a 'school prolegomena to the prescribed trivium texts wherein major critical issues are raised' (Alastair Minnis and Ian Johnson, Introduction to *The Cambridge History of Literary Criticism*, vol. 2, *The Middle Ages*, ed. Minnis and Johnson [Cambridge: Cambridge University Press, 2005], 2). It was an introductory commentary, giving 'access' to (predominantly ancient) authors and their texts, containing biographical data,

information about a work's generic membership, structure, style, content, and purpose, addressing questions of its composition and authenticity, and presenting the benefits of studying it.

56 See Klaus Weimar, 'Zu neuen Hermeneutik um 1800,' in *Wissenschaft und Nation: Studien zur Entstehungsgeschichte der deutschen Literaturwissenschaft*, ed. Jürgen Fohrmann and Wilhelm Voßkamp (Munich: Fink, 1991), 195–204.

57 Ian Hacking, *Historical Ontology* (Cambridge, MA: Harvard University Press, 2002), 122, 140, 147.

58 'Uniqueness' is not understood here in its literal, radical sense – in which case one could call every text unique, whether as an event or as an object, in its mental or material inscription. Uniqueness in the extended sense of 'uncommon' and 'remarkable,' as a matter of cultural significance, when it does *not* stem from the uniqueness of idea/form, is also beside the point.

59 Cf. note 29, above, on family resemblance.

60 Cohen's notion of genre as, essentially, a *process* is helpful here: 'since each genre is composed of texts that accrue, the grouping is a process, not a determinate category. Genres are open categories. Each member alters the genre by adding, contradicting, or changing constituents, especially those of members most closely related to it. The process by which genres are established always involves the human need for distinction and interrelation. Since the purposes of critics who establish genres vary, it is self-evident that the same texts can belong to different groupings or genres and serve different generic purposes' (Cohen, 204).

61 Walter Benjamin, 'Epistemo-Critical Prologue,' in his *The Origin of German Tragic Drama*, trans. John Osborne (New York: New Left, 1977), 44.

62 *OT* xiii. See also Michel Foucault, 'The Discourse of History,' interview by Raymond Bellour, in *Foucault Live: Interviews, 1961–1984*, ed. Sylvère Lotringer, trans. Lysa Hochroth and John Johnston (New York: Semiotext[e], 1996), 22.

63 For a discussion of the convenience of 'context' and attendant 'symptomatism,' see LaCapra's introduction to *Rethinking Intellectual History: Texts, Contexts, Language* (Ithaca: Cornell University Press, 1983), 14–15.

64 Michel Foucault, 'Nietzsche, Freud, Marx,' in *Essential Works of Foucault, 1954–84*, vol. 2, *Aesthetics, Method, and Epistemology*, ed. J.D. Faubion, trans. R. Hurley et al. (New York: New, 1998), 269–78 (henceforth cited as 'NFM'); Michel Foucault, 'What Is an Author?' in *Aesthetics, Method, and Epistemology*, 205–22. All further citations of this source are abbreviated as 'WIA.'

65 Dorothy E. Smith, 'Textually Mediated Social Organization,' in her *Texts, Facts, and Femininity: Exploring the Relations of Ruling* (London: Routledge, 1990), 221.

66 Mochnacki's single most renowned theoretical-critical work is the Romantic treatise *O literaturze polskiej w wieku dziewiętnastym* [On Polish Literature in the Nineteenth Century] (1830), inspired by political events and finished on the eve of the soon-to-be-crushed November Uprising against Russian rule.

67 Belinskii is regarded as 'the first professional Russian literary critic' (Robert H. Stacy, *Russian Literary Criticism: A Short History* [Syracuse, NY: Syracuse University Press, 1974], 41), with whom, at different points, both aesthetic idealists and realists, as well as critics on the liberal-socialist or radical and the religious-nationalist sides of the ideological spectrum, claimed continuity.

68 Edward Said, 'Traveling Theory,' in his *The World, the Text, and the Critic* (Cambridge, MA: Harvard University Press, 1983), 247. All further citations are abbreviated as 'TT.'

69 Edward Said, 'Traveling Theory Reconsidered,' in his *Reflections on Exile and Other Essays* (Cambridge: Harvard University Press, 2000), 452.

70 Otherwise, we have absolute, essentialized difference or identity, which leaves no room for gradation and lies concealed by its diffusion into micro-differences, paired with micro-identities enabling comparisons.

71 Michel Foucault, 'What Is Enlightenment?' in *The Foucault Reader*, ed. and introd. Paul Rabinow, trans. C. Porter (New York: Pantheon, 1984), 38, 37.

72 The distinction was mirrored in the twentieth century: on the one hand, traditional evaluative-interpretive approaches to primary texts, on the other, postmodern inventive-interpretive styles of processing them (e.g., *paracriticism*, with its liminal status between literature and criticism).

73 It would be easy to find justifications for this cutoff point in more recent historiography which seeks to correct for the blind spots of past scholars. Thus, for example, Fohrmann and Voßkamp, observing the failure of German literary studies to historicize itself, reach as far as possible into its modern past to the period around 1800: 'Whether one speaks of the change from a society differentiated by strata to that differentiated by function in Niklas Luhmann's sense, or sees the unfolding of diverse forms of reason as a condition of modernity in Jürgen Habermas's sense, or, again, stresses the temporalization-effect of the "*Sattelzeit*" [premodern–modern transition, 1750–1850] in Reinhart Koselleck's sense: the period will always be understood as a phase of that fundamental turn [*Wende*], to which the development of the *modern* sciences is also indebted.' The precipitate bifur-

cation of criticism into the academic (*wissenschaftlich*) and the journalistic, as we have seen, introduces a redirection of energies, and takes us beyond the discourse's emergence (separation from inert literary and scholarly traditions) to its attenuation in the public sphere in an era of crossdisciplinary historicization. The editors' research questions are close to mine, insofar as they start from the possible disunity of the discourse's scientificity (*Wissenschaftlichkeit*), understood differently during the process of historicization, as well as the exposure of whatever happened to go against the synchronic–diachronic identity of *Literaturwissenschaft* (Jürgen Fohrmann and Wilhelm Voßkamp, eds., *Wissenschaft und Nation: Studien zur Entstehungsgeschichte der deutschen Literaturwissenschaft* [Munich: Fink, 1991], 9). This new-generation *Entstehungsgeschichte* comprehends emergence in dispersion, rather than as a single, distinct origin or clear-eyed invention.

Chapter One: German Criticism

1 Irina Reyfman, *Vasilii Trediakovsky: The Fool of the 'New' Russian Literature* (Stanford: Stanford University Press, 1990), 49.
2 Johann Gottfried Herder, 'On Recent German Literature: First Collection of Fragments,' in his *Selected Early Works, 1764–1767: Addresses, Essays, and Drafts; Fragments on Recent German Literature*, ed. Ernest A. Menze and Karl Menges, trans. Menze and M. Palma (University Park: Pennsylvania State University Press, 1992), 93. All further citations of this translation are abbreviated as 'FRGL.'
3 The Berlin Academy was established in 1700 by Frederick I. Initially known as *Societät der Wissenschaften* (Society of Sciences), it was renamed in 1744 as the *Königliche Akademie der Wissenschaften* (Royal Academy of Sciences).
4 Walter Horace Bruford, *Germany in the Eighteenth Century: The Social Background of the Literary Revival* (Cambridge: Cambridge University Press, 1952), 274.
5 As Bruford succinctly puts it, 'This open-mindedness was the obverse of the lack of a national style' (304).
6 The model for it was Martin Opitz's versified rule-poetics of 1624, *Buch von der Deutschen Poeterey*, which based itself on ancient and Renaissance poetics. It proposed a program for the renewal of German poetry, now to be written in a standardized German and subordinated to a moral function. Opitz's efforts, directed at emancipating German from foreign linguistic influences (mainly Latin), would be furthered by Herder (among others) in the next century.

7 The 1730 poetics of Gottsched represented an amalgam of the two positions. Another term for this formation, *classical doctrine* (*doctrine classique*), coined by René Bray in *La Formation de la doctrine classique en France* (Paris: Hachette, 1927) is misleading, considering that the ancients did not debate the minutiae of the rules laid out by Aristotle in his *Peri poietikes* [Poetics] the way the moderns did.
8 The founder of this German Classical revival was Johann Joachim Winckelmann (1717–68).
9 J.J. Breitinger's *Critische Dichtkunst* of 1740 may serve as an early example.
10 Kai Hammermeister, *The German Aesthetic Tradition* (Cambridge: Cambridge University Press, 2002), 12.
11 In referring to *Klassizismus* and *Klassik* as different stages of classicism, I depart from custom in the German literary-historical tradition. While the first term acquired the negative connotations of derivativeness from French Classicism and the mere imitation of Antiquity, *Klassik* retained the positive connotation of literary greatness and originality. When I do use the term classical, it is to mean 'expressive of national unity.' For an analysis of usage in German literary scholarship, see René Wellek, 'The Term and Concept of Classicism in Literary History,' in his *Discriminations: Further Concepts of Criticism* (New Haven: Yale University Press, 1970), 55–89.
12 See M.H. Abrams, *The Mirror and the Lamp: Romantic Theory and the Critical Tradition* (New York: Norton, 1958).
13 According to Wellek, the disintegration of European classicism occurred between 1750 and the 1830s (*18C* 1). Isaiah Berlin placed German Romanticism somewhere between 1760 and 1830 (see his *The Roots of Romanticism*, ed. Henry Hardy [London: Chatto & Windus, 1999]). Later scholarship tends to see the Storm and Stress movement not as part of Romanticism (as pre-Romanticism or its early phase), but as a critical discourse and revolutionary literary movement within the Enlightenment literary canon, which it attempted to re-energize. Its young poets and dramatists came from a bourgeois background and opposed repressive despotism, without however calling for an overhaul of the entire system. Perception of continuity between the two revolutionary currents arose from the fact that the nationalist ideals of Sturm und Drang were taken up again by the Romantics. Retrospectively, Romantic themes appear in the critical and theoretical works of Hamann and Herder. Although the first example of Romantic criticism can be found in the writings of Friedrich Schlegel, Herder's critical pronouncements already evince the polarity – between, on the one hand, formal and thematic classicist orthodoxy and, on the other hand, conceptual revisionism and innovation – so characteristic of

Romanticism. In this sense, the first signs of proto-Romantic thinking did, in fact, appear during Sturm und Drang, reaching their full articulation with Romanticism proper. Despite these affinities, Storm and Stress not only retained continuity with classicism (Herder oscillated between rejecting and embracing it) but, as an outlook shaped by the dynamic between rationalism and late-Enlightenment modernization, it also paved the way for the mature classicism of its one-time participants, Johann Wolfgang von Goethe (1749–1832) and Friedrich Schiller (1759–1805).

14 'Science of sensuous cognition' (of *aesthesis*) was A.G. Baumgarten's inaugural definition of aesthetics in the *Aesthetica*, a treatise in Latin published in 1750–58. Baumgarten's ideas ran counter to the general 'devaluation of sensuality,' even as his aesthetic principles were modelled on those of rhetoric: complexity of content, magnitude of imagination, clarity of presentation (Hammermeister 4, 7, 10–11). (Albert Ward notes that the spread of Pietism during the first half of the century turned individual interest inward, and this 'unsound worship of feeling' was soon embraced in the secular field [Albert Ward, *Book Production, Fiction, and the German Reading Public, 1740–1800* (Oxford: Clarendon, 1974), 10].) Baumgarten's concept of aesthetics differs substantially from our current usage, which we owe largely to Kant's emancipation of the concept of beauty from its subservience to rationality (Hammermeister 23). Wellek gives Kant greater credit in this regard: 'in Kant the argument was stated for the first time systematically in a defense of the aesthetic realm against all sides: against sensualism and its reduction of art to pleasure, against emotionalism and its view of art as stimulus or emotion, against age-old moralism, which reduces art to a form of the useful, and against intellectualism, which sees in art only an inferior, more popular way of knowing, a kind of second-rate (because less systematic) philosophy' (René Wellek, 'Immanuel Kant's Aesthetics and Criticism,' in his *Discriminations: Further Concepts of Criticism* [New Haven: Yale University Press, 1970], 125). Some have noted with disapproval that Kant seldom uses concrete examples from art and literature in laying out his aesthetics; Wellek defends Kant by noting he was neither a practical critic of the arts, nor a philosopher of art, but of aesthetics. The faculty of judgment (*Urteilskraft*), including aesthetic judgment, was for Kant independent from reason (*Vernunft*) and understanding (*Verstand*). Beauty was not an attribute of objects themselves but of the *subjectively universal* judgment regarding these objects (different from the merely subjective judgment of taste). It was also not limited to artistic objects but encompassed all of nature – an emphasis absent from later categories of the beautiful (Hammermeister 25).

15 David Simpson, Introduction to *The Origins of Modern Critical Thought: German Aesthetic and Literary Criticism from Lessing to Hegel*, ed. Simpson (Cambridge: Cambridge University Press, 1988), 17. Further citations are abbreviated as 'IOC.'

16 This does not mean that Breitinger's work was free of rationalistic assumptions, but he was critical of French Classicism and, suffice it to say, admired by Herder.

Hammermeister observes that 'Baumgarten's attempt to consolidate rationalism [Leibniz and Wolff] turned, under his hands, into a critical endeavour. Aesthetics, intended as an extension of a rationalist world-view, became more and more independent, until finally the rationalist metaphysics were discredited and aesthetics remained behind as a survivor' 'productively opposed to rationality' (4, 13). While Baumgarten understood aesthetic perception rather as ancillary to intellection (though he reunited to some extent the sensual/emotional with the cognitive in his notion of 'aesthetic enthusiasm'), Moses Mendelssohn (1729–86) was determined to explore the *sensual* experience of the aesthetic object (12–13). It is only with Kant's third critique (1790) that one can speak of (critical) aesthetic judgment as a faculty for the most part distinct from cognition, that is, from epistemic and moral judgment.

17 J.M. Bernstein, Introduction to *Classic and Romantic German Aesthetics*, ed. Bernstein (Cambridge: Cambridge University Press, 2002), ix.

18 Before 1740, religious books were the most widespread reading matter of the German middle and lower classes, in both town and country. Interest in secular imaginative literature was slow to develop (Ward 4–11).

19 Fritz Strich, qtd. in Bruford 324. Wellek comments that, with Goethe and Schiller, '*Klassik* resumes the old meaning of standard or model, while the stylistic association with the ancients almost ceases to be felt ... [It] pries the German classics loose from international classicism' and separates them from its contemporary, *Romantik* (Wellek, 'Classicism' 78). Nonetheless, Herder saw reason to attack Goethe and Schiller for betraying his teachings in favour of classicism (79) – which makes the conceptual continuity between *Klassizismus* and *Klassik* hard to deny.

20 The narrow sense of this term is 'literacy' or 'education'; more generally, it signified 'broad intellectual culture,' and was akin to the ancient concept of *paideia*.

21 Bruford notes we should not mistake class feeling for national unity (298, 317).

22 David Simpson, Introduction to *German Aesthetic and Literary Criticism: Kant, Fichte, Schelling, Schopenhauer, Hegel*, ed. Simpson (Cambridge:

Cambridge University Press, 1984), 4. Further citations are abbreviated as 'IGA.'

23 Pascale Casanova, *The World Republic of Letters*, trans. M.B. DeBevoise (Cambridge, MA: Harvard University Press, 2004), 77. (The phrase Republic of Letters is used here in Casanova's updated sense, as inclusive of writers of imaginative literature.)

24 The emergence of a new German philology around this time was inseparable from the freeing of cultural understanding from the goal of imitation (which collapses historical distance) to grasp the historical specificity of the literary past and its inimitability (Schlaffer 169–70).

25 For a critical bilingual edition, see Friedrich der Grosse, *De la littérature allemande*, ed. Christoph Gutknecht and Peter Kerner (Hamburg: Buske, 1969). The work was originally published in French. The German translation appeared the same year, also in Berlin and also anonymously.

26 In fairness, its publication did provoke not only polemical but also positive responses. Of the former, one of the best known is Möser's 'Über die deutsche Sprache und Literatur: Schreiben an einen Freund' [On German Language and Literature: Letter to a Friend], which appeared in 1781 in the *Westphälische Beytrage zum Nutzen und Vergnügen* [Westphalian Contributions to Utility and Pleasure] and was reprinted shortly afterward. The letter, addressing an unnamed friend, comes straight to the point: 'Dear, noble friend! It lay fully within the great purview of Your King to have now also cast his glance upon our German literature … Only this does not appear to me to lie in his purview: that we trade with the Greeks, the Latins and the French, and should borrow or buy from foreigners that which we can procure ourselves at home.' The closing lines of this spirited refutation of the old system testify to the newfound German literary identity: 'Finally I must tell You, dearest friend, how it displeases me in many of our German writers that they allow themselves too little justness toward foreigners … [A]ll nations can attain greatness in the character of their literature, without needing to despise their competitors' (Justus Möser, 'Über die deutsche Sprache und Literatur: Schreiben an einen Freund,'in Friedrich der Grosse, *De la littérature allemande*, ed. Christoph Gutknecht and Peter Kerner [Hamburg: Buske, 1969], 121, 140). A representative collection of contemporary replies to *De la littérature allemande* can be found in Erich Kästner's *Friedrich der Grosse und die deutsche Literatur: Die Erwiderungen auf seine Schrift 'De la littérature allemande'* (Stuttgart: Kohlhammer, 1972).

27 Friedrich Schlegel, *Philosophical Fragments*, trans. Peter Firchow (Minneapolis: University of Minnesota Press, 1991), 33 ('*Athenaeum* Fragment' 121).

28 Robert S. Leventhal, *The Disciplines of Interpretation: Lessing, Herder, Schlegel and Hermeneutics in Germany, 1750–1800*, ed. Walter Pape (Berlin: deGruyter, 1994), 13. All further citations of this source are abbreviated as *DI*.

29 See F. Schlegel's '*Athenaeum* Fragment' 116, in Schlegel, *Philosophical Fragments* 31–2, and Novalis's 'Logological Fragment [I]' 66, in Novalis, *Philosophical Writings*, ed. and trans. Margaret Mahony Stoljar (Albany: SUNY Press, 1997), 60. Stoljar's explanatory notes were very helpful in recognizing these conceptual connections.

30 See F. Schlegel's '*Athenaeum* Fragments' 28 and 116, in *Philosophical Fragments* 22, 31. Here and elsewhere I translate *Poesie* as 'poesy' to distinguish it from poetry. Haynes Horne's argument for this choice is convincing (Haynes Horne, 'Introductory Essay: The Early Romantic Fragment and Incompleteness,' in *Theory as Practice: A Critical Anthology of Early German Romantic Writings*, ed. Jochen Schulte-Sasse et al. [Minneapolis: University of Minnesota Press, 1997], 311–12n3).

31 Ernst Behler, Foreword to *German Romantic Criticism*, ed. A. Leslie Willson (New York: Continuum, 1982), xi–xii. (Further citations of this source are abbreviated as *GRC*.) In *Disciplines of Interpretation*, Leventhal dates the explicit emergence of modern hermeneutics as falling between 1770 and 1800.

32 Reference is to F. Schlegel's 1800 essay 'Über die Unverständlichkeit' [On Incomprehensibility].

33 In *Critische Dichtkunst*, Gottsched used the Latin form *Criticus* in the applied sense of day-to-day evaluation of new books, as opposed to the grander ability, on a level with art itself, of the *Kunstrichter* to synthesize and judge an entire period/culture, to prognosticate the future and educate the reader, or, for that matter, to settle disputes about the meaning of the text – as he/she would in the twentieth century. Herder makes a similar distinction in his *Fragmente* (discussed below).

34 Nicolai used the terms *Critiker*, *Kunstrichter*, *Rezensent*, and *Journalist* 'interchangeably and indiscriminately for someone engaged in the review process ... [R]eview and literary criticism were indivisible and indistinguishable' (James Van Der Laan, 'Nicolai's Concept of the Review Journal,' in *The Eighteenth-Century German Book Review*, ed. Herbert Rowland and Karl J. Fink [Heidelberg: Winter, 1995], 95).

35 These first two categories are difficult to distinguish and appear to be interchangeable, with a treatise being generally longer than a tract, say, and a disquisition stressing the analytical formality of a text. I distinguish the early, book-length *essay*, such as Gottsched's *Critische Dichtkunst* (a long and still tightly structured work, although the breadth of its subject matter

was not matched by depth of treatment, so that *Versuch* can be here translated simply as 'attempt'), from its later naturalization as the *review essay*, which was considerably shorter (though longer than the *review*), informal, quasi-conversational, and, most importantly, thoroughly *critical*. The latter was, moreover, published not as a separate work but in periodicals addressing cultural and literary topics. By contrast, the earlier incarnation of essayism in Gottsched needed to be qualified as 'critical' – a practice that continued with other genres, but became superfluous for essays published in literary periodicals when these became virtually synonymous with evaluation. To this latter generation of essays belong the compositions of Winckelmann, Lessing, Wieland, and Herder (Marcel Reich-Ranicki, 'Über den Essay und das Feuilleton,' *Der Kanon. Die Deutsche Literatur: Essays* (Frankfurt: Suhrkamp Insel, 2001).

36 Such titles are common as well to Polish and Russian criticism, where they begin with 'O.'

37 See Peter Küpper's 'Author ad Lectorem. Vorreden im 18. Jahrhundert. Ein Forschungsvorschlag,' in *Festschrift für Rainer Gruenter*, ed. Bernhard Fabian (Heidelberg: Winter, 1978), 86–95.

38 Novalis, 'Dialogues,' trans. Joyce P. Crick, in *Classic and Romantic German Aesthetics*, ed. J.M. Bernstein (Cambridge: Cambridge University Press, 2002), 216–18. B, who is the speaker here, defends the status quo: there is now something to read for everyone, and prefaces help in discarding the bad apples. After B makes his speech about the relationship between a preface and a book's quality, A, instead of contesting the point or building in any way on B's observations, pulls the rug from under B's optimism: 'But I don't know. As far as I am concerned, there are even too many *good* books' (219).

39 Herbert Rowland, 'The Physiognomist Physiognomized: Matthias Claudius's Review of Lavater's *Physiognomische Fragmente*,' in *The Eighteenth-Century German Book Review*, ed. Rowland and K.J. Fink (Heidelberg: Winter, 1995), 18.

40 Among them were a small number of Latinate (in part or in whole) attempts at specialization in German letters: *Nova literaria germaniae collecta Hamburgi* (1703–6) and *Nova literaria germaniae alliorumque europae regnorum collecta Hamburgi* (1707–9).

41 Ralf Georg Bogner, 'Die Formationsphase der deutschsprachigen Literaturkritik,' *Projekt Literaturkritik*, ed. Rainer Baasner, Universität Rostock, *1 May 2006*, http://www.phf.uni-rostock.de/institut/igerman/forschung/litkritik/litkritik/start.htm?/institut/igerman/forschung/litkritik/litkritik/Epochen/ea.htm. The dialogue form and periodicity of the

publication, keeping abreast of new titles, became a model for the future of periodical publishing (Ralf Georg Bogner, 'Die Formationsphase der deutschsprachigen Literaturkritik,' in *Literaturkritik: Geschichte – Theorie – Praxis*, ed. Th. Anz and Rainer Baasner [Munich: Beck, 2004], 18–19).

42 Klaus Berghahn, 'From Classicist to Classical Literary Theory (1730–1806),' in *A History of German Literary Criticism, 1730–1980*, ed. P.U. Hohendahl, trans. Franz Blaha (Lincoln: University of Nebraska Press, 1988), 21; Hohendahl, *Institution of Criticism* 15.

43 Some of these publications 'served collectively as a substitute for the rare public libraries and the rarely extensive private libraries of the time, as indicated by the presence of the word *Bibliothek* in many of the titles' (Rowland, 'Physiognomist' 17). This concept may have been introduced in Poland by Mitzler (Ger. Mützler) de Kolof (1711–78), the prolific publisher of Polish- and German-language periodicals. In the same conceptual fraternity is the Schlegels' famed periodical *Athenäum* (1798–1800) – meaning a building or room in which books, periodicals, and newspapers are kept for use; a reading room or library. 'Athenaeum' became the title of choice for literary periodicals in various countries during the nineteenth century. For instance, the Polish *Athenaeum* appeared on a bi-monthly basis in Vilnius in 1842–51, and in Warsaw (as *Ateneum*) in the years 1876–1901, 1903–5, and 1939.

44 This enormously popular publication from Jena insisted on authorial anonymity (among its review critics was A.W. Schlegel) (Curt Grützmacher, 'Zur Geschichte des "Athenaeum,"'in A.W. Schlegel and F. Schlegel, *Athenaeum*, ed. C. Grützmacher [Munich: Rowohlt, 1969], 250). An excellent discussion of its critical praxis can be found in *Organisation der Kritik: Die 'Allgemeine Literatur-Zeitung' in Jena, 1785–1803*, ed. Stefan Matuschek (Heidelberg: Winter, 2004).

45 International in scope, it reported consistently on Russian literary and general events.

46 James J. Wald, 'The "Small Club of Connoisseurs" and the "Broad Public": Schiller's *Horen* and Posselt's *Europäische Annalen*,' in *The Eighteenth-Century German Book Review*, ed. H. Rowland and K.J. Fink (Heidelberg: Winter, 1995), 113–36.

47 The journal was edited and published by Nicolai in the years 1765–92 and 1800–6. In the interim, he was prevented from publishing by censors. (Censorship, however, did not play a significant role, as it did in Russia for example, in shaping literary-critical discourse.) While its old version continued until 1796, from 1793 on the journal was revamped as *Neue allgemeine deutsche Bibliothek*, with the supplement *Intelligenzblatt der Neuen*

Allgemeinen Deutschen Bibliothek [Intellectual Gazette of the New General German Library] (1797–1800). Its appearance in 1765 signalled the revival of intellectual discourse following the ravages of the Seven Years' War (1756–63). Its publishing location had to change several times to avoid censorship. The periodical pledged to print lists (*Verzeichnisse*) and abstracts of important books published in German in every branch of learning. It was comprised almost exclusively of scholarly reviews by the era's leading minds, with representatives of the various German-speaking regions. One of its ambitions was to integrate the provinces through critical discourse. Although it claimed to write for everybody and about everything, the reality was that the periodical soon devolved into a mouthpiece for the Berlin Enlightenment. Its increasingly conservative bias – while of no hindrance to keeping apace with scientific and technical topics – caused it to fall behind in other intellectual discussions; so much so, that the periodical came to be discredited within Sturm und Drang for feigning an interest in literature ('Friedrich Nicolai [Hg.] – Allgemeine deutsche Bibliothek (1765–1806),' *Projekt Literaturkritik*, ed. R. Baasner, 11 May 2005, Universität Rostock, 1 May 2006, http://www.phf.uni-rostock.de/institut/igerman/forschung/litkritik/litkritik/start.htm?/institut/igerman/forschung/litkritik/litkritik/Medien/MbADB.htm). Herder criticized the journal for its generality in literary judgments and over-reliance on excerpts at the expense of genuine criticism: reviews, but also 'comparisons and viewpoints, commentaries upon flaws and virtues' ('FRGL' 96). According to Herder, merely excerpting literary texts evaded criticism's main responsibilities; it was based 'upon formal criteria, not upon the genius of the author and the significance of the subject,' and limited critical opinion to 'hasty comment[s] on single sentences' (97).

48 H.B. Nisbet, ed., *German Aesthetic and Literary Criticism: Winckelmann, Lessing, Hamann, Herder, Schiller, Goethe* (Cambridge: Cambridge University Press, 1985), 57.

49 'Criticism is therefore the sole means of enlightening our taste ...' (Nicolai, qtd. in Van Der Laan 109).

50 Timothy J. Chamberlain, Introduction to *Eighteenth-Century German Criticism*, ed. and trans. Chamberlain (New York: Continuum, 1992), xii.

51 Dubos elevated the role of emotion in aesthetic judgment and quarrelled with an overly literal application of Aristotle's dramatic rules.

52 For a precise discussion of this debt, see Jill Anne Kowalik, *The Poetics of Historical Perspectivism: Breitinger's 'Critische Dichtkunst' and the Neoclassic Tradition* (Chapel Hill: University of North Carolina Press, 1992), 73–86. Although more rampant than has previously been acknowledged (extending

to verbatim borrowings, adaptations, and summaries only occasionally acknowledged), Dubos's ideas are often generalized, amplified, radicalized, and at times considerably modified by Breitinger's return to Aristotle. Interestingly, Breitinger's poetics was recommended by *Reformpädagogen* and used in schools until the 1770s (132n6).

53 A *literary letter* has one addressee but takes into consideration a larger audience (Stefania Skwarczyńska, 'Wokół teorii listu [Paradoksy],' in *Pomiędzy historią a teorią literatury* [Warsaw: Pax, 1975], 184 (this text is a short supplement to Skwarczyńska's earlier theoretical work on the letter, *Teoria listu*). Most German *critical letters* – that is, letters with a literary-critical function – were written for a wider readership (this is not the case in her Poland or Russia, where they were usually also *literary* letters). To the long and paradoxical history of epistolography, the eighteenth century contributed the theory and practice of the 'letter-conversation' (179), which could carry critical import.

54 The letters by Lenz referred to here are *Briefe über die Moralität der Leiden des jungen Werthers* [Letters on the Morality of *The Sorrows of Young Werther*].

55 The *Literaturbriefe* were ostensibly written for Nicolai's friend Ewald von Kleist, so that he would stay informed about the literary scene while he was convalescing from battle wounds.

56 Also worth mentioning is Herder's *Auszug aus einem Briefwechsel über Ossian und die Lieder alter Völker* [Excerpt from a Correspondence on Ossian and the Songs of Ancient Peoples] (Hamburg, 1773) – a fictitious excerpt from a non-existent correspondence (ironically enough, Macpherson's Ossian cycle was a literary fraud). It first appeared in *Von deutscher Art und Kunst: Einige fliegende Blätter* [On German Character and Art: A Collection of Broadsheets] alongside Herder's essay on Shakespeare and essays by Goethe, Möser, and Frisi, which became the manifesto of Sturm und Drang.

57 'Friedrich Nicolai (Hg.) – Allgemeine deutsche Bibliothek (1765–1806).'

58 The generally negative view of academic philology was reflected in Novalis's comments: 'the older philologists' manner of filling their works with quotations and commentaries – what was it but a child of poverty? Born of lack of books and abundance of literary spirit' ('Dialogues' 219).

59 This transformation is traced by Berghahn (with reference to Koselleck and Habermas) in his history of 'classical' German literary criticism.

60 Steven D. Martinson, 'Comedy and Criticism: Lessing's Contributions to the *Briefe Die Neueste Literatur Betreffend*,' in *The Eighteenth-Century German Book Review*, ed. H. Rowland and K.J. Fink (Heidelberg: Winter, 1995), 76.

61 One of the most vocal critics was Herder, who is said to have 'reconceptualized the relationship between the general rule and the individual literary phenomenon' (Bianca Theisen, 'Drama in Rags: Shakespeare Reception in Eighteenth-Century Germany,' *Modern Language Notes* (*MLN*) 121.3 [2006]: 506).

62 Stuart Atkins, Introduction to *The Age of Goethe: An Anthology of German Literature*, ed. Atkins (Boston: Houghton Mifflin, 1969), 4.

63 The last element references Novalis: 'Poetry dissolves the being of others in its own,' Novalis, *Philosophical Writings* 56 ('Logological Fragment [I]' 40).

64 Hans Ulrich Gumbrecht, in *Making Sense in Life and Literature*, trans. Glen Burns (Minneapolis: University of Minnesota Press, 1992), xii.

65 I owe this emphasis to Daniel Purdy's explanation of the rhetoric of discovery in the classicist discourse on art history (Daniel Purdy, 'The Whiteness of Beauty: Weimar Neo-Classicism and the Sculptural Transcendence of Color,' in *Colors 1800/1900/2000: Signs of Ethnic Difference*, ed. Birgit Tautz [Amsterdam: Rodopi, 2004], 83–99).

66 Koselleck 10.

67 Margaret Stoljar, *Athenaeum: A Critical Commentary* (Bern: Herbert Lang, 1973), 33; Grützmacher 250.

68 Novalis, *Philosophical Writings* 28 ('Miscellaneous Observation' 32).

69 Novalis, 'Kritik und Lesen,' in *Theorie der Romantik*, ed. H. Uerlings (Stuttgart: Reclam, 2000), 192. Reference is also to 'qualitative Potenzierung' from Novalis's 66th 'Logological Fragment [I]': 'The world must be Romanticized. In that way one can find original meaning again. To make Romantic is nothing but a qualitative raising [of the finite, the commonplace] to a higher power … The operation for the … infinite is the converse … it takes on an ordinary form of expression' (*Philosophical Writings* 60, translation modified).

70 Cf. F. Schlegel's observations on polemics in 'Critical Fragment' 81, in *Philosophical Fragments* 10.

71 Schlegel, *Philosophical Fragments* 59, 102 ('*Athenaeum* Fragment' 300, 'Idea' 93).

72 Novalis, qtd. in Margaret Mahony Stoljar, Introduction to Novalis, *Philosophical Writings* (Albany: SUNY Press, 1997), 168, editor's note 1; Schlegel, *Philosophical Fragments* 27 ('*Athenaeum* Fragment' 77). Both the aphorism and the dialogue were Neoclassical forms. The aphorism's authority is undercut by its essential fragmentariness; likewise, the dialogue is subjected to the negative dialectic of Socratic irony.

The relation between fragments and aphorisms in these writings is by no means straightforward. Although Schlegel used the terms interchangeably in his first collection, *Kritische Fragmente,* which appeared in the *Lyceum der schönen Künste* in 1797 (modelled in part on the aphorisms of Nicolas Chamfort [1741–94]), the *fragment* soon underwent philosophical abstraction. No longer merely aphoristic and kin to other minor forms (like the *maxim* or *sentence*), it could be recognized in a spontaneous *note* (fruit of the moment), an *essay,* or a *mini-treatise,* reflecting the multiformity of the world and tending to non-generic form. With the elimination of obvious rhetoricity (of the kind evinced by Herder in his appropriation of fragmentariness), fragmentariness ceased for Schlegel to be a matter of overt form (in fact it was prickly and self-contained like a hedgehog [see notes 92 and 134, below]). Instead, it became a matter of content, of thought, whose programmatic incompleteness registered a longing for cosmic unity and pointed to the ineffable absolute (Anna Kurska, *Fragment Romantyczny* [Wrocław: Zakład Narodowy im. Ossolińskich, 1989], 10–11).

73 Philippe Lacoue-Labarthe and Jean-Luc Nancy, *The Literary Absolute: The Theory of Literature in German Romanticism,* trans. Philip Barnard and Cheryl Smith (New York: SUNY Press, 1988), 86–7 (hereafter cited as *LA*). Another dialogue published in the *Athenäum* was the meta-dialogical 'Ein Gespräch über Klopstocks grammatische Gespräche' [A Dialogue about Klopstock's Grammatical Dialogues]. Its participants are Poesy and Grammar, then a German, a Frenchman, an Italian, a Greek, a Roman, an Englishman, and, toward the end, Whimsy.

74 For a study of A.W. Schlegel's involvement in historico-critical *vergleichende Literaturwissenschaft,* particularly in the sphere of drama, see Hilde Marianne Paulini, *August Wilhelm Schlegel und die Vergleichende Literaturwissenschaft* (Frankfurt: Peter Lang, 1985).

75 H. Rowland, Preface to *The Eighteenth-Century German Book Review,* ed. Rowland and K.J. Fink (Heidelberg: Winter, 1995), 5.

76 A *dramolet* was a short but generically variegated work for the stage.

77 This, however, does not necessarily place their contribution in the category of aesthetics, if we adopt Hammermeister's inclusion criterion. Hammermeister does not include in his roster of aestheticians the likes of Goethe, because theirs was an 'artists' aesthetics' which did not respond to the main questions raised in the discourse of aesthetics, i.e., it did not explicitly join the conversation, and had thus been subsequently excluded by historians of aesthetics. He defines aesthetics as one would any coherent discourse in general, as a body of texts responding to the same, 'previously unsolved or inadequately solved' problems, 'by referring to writings by other[s] ... and continuing or challenging a certain vocabulary' (xiv). Certainly one advantage of early aesthetics was its *explicit* self-definition in terms of general

theoretical aims, questions, and object, so that there can be little confusion as to which earlier writings belonged to this new discourse.

78 Bruce Kieffer, *The Storm and Stress of Language: Linguistic Catastrophe in the Early Works of Goethe, Lenz, Klinger, and Schiller* (University Park: Pennsylvania State University Press, 1986), 16.

79 From the 396 unsigned texts published in 1772 (considered the journal's most fecund Sturm-und-Drang year), between 30 and 60 reviews can be attributed to Goethe – when not as their sole author, then as collaborator. Apart from Goethe, the journal's new reviewing team included editor-in-chief Johann Heinrich Merck (1741–91), J.G. Schlosser, J. Petersen, and Herder. Among the German authors whose works it reviewed were Lessing, Wieland, Klopstock, and J.G. Jacobi (Ariane Neuhaus-Koch, 'Frankfurter gelehrte Anzeigen auf das Jahr 1772,' 2005, Universität Düsseldorf, 1 May 2006 http://www.phil-fak.uni-duesseldorf.de/germ2/neuhaus-koch/drang/pdf/FrankfurterAnzeigen.pdf).

Although traditionally of an Enlightenment profile, in 1772 the periodical served to articulate diverse aesthetic views and formulate the broader aims of the Sturm-und-Drang movement – which, insofar as it was a movement of reform within the Enlightenment paradigm, entailed also some counter-Enlightenment critique. The year 1772 was something of a temporal threshold in German literary culture, in that many talents came together to create a new perspective on literary life. That they afterward dispersed, no longer able to agree on principles and concepts they once held in common, does not change the fact that each came away with a radically altered sense of purpose, which Goethe would later consider revolutionary (Hans-Dietrich Dahnke, 'Intentionen und Resultate des Jahrgangs 1772 der *Frankfurter Gelehrten Anzeigen*,' in *Sturm und Drang: Geistiger Aufbruch 1770–1790 im Spiegel der Literatur*, ed. Bodo Plachta and Winfried Woesler [Tübingen: Niemeyer, 1997], 245–7).

The many subjects (theology, law, history, philosophy) discussed in *Frankfurter gelehrte Anzeigen* in book-review form bespoke the growth of patriotism, interest in emotions and interiority, and the emergence of a proto-Romantic apotheosis of indifferent, 'inhuman nature' (in contrast to the classicist notion of 'general nature,' a human or non-human reality 'free from purely local and accidental conditions,' typical, universal, and too readily idealized as orderly [Wellek, *18C* 14–17]). The freely ranging interests and non-traditional style of the *Frankfurter gelehrte Anzeigen* aroused hostilities from other review periodicals that accused it of scholarly 'heresy' – which eventually led the editors to all but abandon reviewing and shift their focus to more essayistic writing (Neuhaus-Koch).

80 Neuhaus-Koch.

81 Tentzel's journal was revived in 1704 as the *Curieuse Bibliothec, oder Fortsetzung der Monatlichen Unterredungen* [Curious Library, or the Continuation of the Monthly Conversations] (Frankfurt, 1704–6), which forewent fictional dialogues for conversations with its recipients, which, instead of presenting new works without the complex mediation of diverse perspectives, submitted to readers a single opinion (Bogner 20).

82 Behler disagrees with seeing it as 'oppositional' and 'hostile,' as in his view this would preclude the bountiful co-existence of opposites so characteristic of Romantic thought. He, too, stresses the difference between the *Querelle*-type polarization and the dialectic of Romanticism's self-elaboration, which 'rather attempted to mediate between the two worlds by bringing the moderns into a competitive relationship with the ancients' (*GRC* xi). Another perspective on this, as noted by Berghahn, is that the German *Querelle* only resolved itself at the end of the century.

83 J.W. von Goethe, 'Introduction to the Propylaea,' in his *Essays on Art and Literature*, ed. John Gearey, trans. Ellen von Nardroff and Ernest H. von Nardroff (New York: Suhrkamp, 1986), 79, 80–1, 83.

84 See Schlegel's '*Athenaeum* Fragment' 114, in *Philosophical Fragments* 31.

85 For example, Schlegel's *Athenäum* review 'Über Goethes Meister' [On Goethe's *Meister*] (1798) consisted of a straightforward plot summary and an analysis of the components of Goethe's Bildungsroman.

86 This trend reaches its peak with the psychological aesthetics of Karl Philipp Moritz (1756–93) (Hammermeister 18). Moritz was a versatile, cross-generational writer, participating first in Sturm und Drang, then in *Weimarer Klassik*, and even in *Frühromantik*.

87 'Rezension des Neuen Menoza, von dem Verfasser selbst ausgesetzt' [Review of *The New Menoza*, Composed by the Author Himself] (Frankfurt, 1775). Not avowedly and self-confidently experimental, Lenz's piece seems to quietly flaunt its formal transgression of the contemporary etiquette of reviewing. 'It is an awkward thing to speak about oneself[;] when however it cannot be otherwise, and one would not be able, for the present and for posterity, to renounce through silence the suspicion of immaturity, one is sure enough forced into the sad necessity of striking up with the other cuckoos' (Jakob Michael Lenz, 'Rezension des Neuen Menoza, von dem Verfasser selbst ausgesetzt,' in his *Werke und Briefe*, vol. 2, ed. Sigrid Damm [Munich: Hanser, 1987], 699). Despite the text's awkward self-consciousness, this opening note of defiance is unmistakable. Incidentally, Lenz was prepared to defend not only himself, but other works which he valued and others undervalued. He was one of the most zealous defenders

of Shakespeare against classicist quibbling, and in the same year wrote his well-known *Briefe über die Moralität der Leiden des jungen Werthers* to counter Nicolai's *Die Freuden des Jungen Werthers* [The Joys of Young Werther] which travestied Goethe's epistolary novel.

88 Hamann, qtd. in Kieffer 14. Hamann saw the academy as the source of philosophical dogmatism (in his 'Aesthetica in nuce,' he makes an oblique reference to academic degrees as numbers of the 'academic beast' (J.G. Hamann, 'Aesthetica in nuce: A Rhapsody in Cabbalistic Prose,' trans. J.P. Crick, in *Classic and Romantic German Aesthetics*, ed. J.M. Bernstein [Cambridge: Cambridge University Press, 2002], 11; English translations of and editorial comments on the 'Aesthetica' are from this edition. All further citations of this translation are abbreviated as 'AN.')

89 Hamann calls himself a philologist in his *Kreuzzüge des Philologen* [Crusades of the Philologist]. One might guess and say that he meant it also in the original sense of 'lover of learning, dialectic, or language.'

90 Passim from letter 14 onward in Schiller's 'Letters on the Aesthetic Education of Man,' in his *Essays*, ed. Walter Hinderer and Daniel O. Dahlstrom, trans. Elizabeth M. Wilkinson and L.A. Willoughby (New York: Continuum, 2001).

91 Cf. '*Athenaeum* Fragment' 259 ('The form is irrelevant'), in Schlegel, *Philosophical Fragments* 54–5).

92 F. Schlegel, letter to A.W. Schlegel, qtd. in Thomas H. Curran, *Doctrine and Speculation in Schleiermacher's Glaubenslehre* (Berlin: de Gruyter, 1994), 137, 148n44. For an illuminating discussion of Schlegel's position on the fragment–system relationship, see Rodolphe Gasché, Foreword to F. Schlegel, *Philosophical Fragments*, trans. P. Firchow (Minneapolis: University of Minnesota Press, 1991), particularly pp. xi–xiv. Briefly, Schlegel's notion of fragmentation did not exclude systematicity (in the sense of theoretical totality and coherence of exposition). Indeed, to avoid extremes (especially the system's dogmatism and rationalistic abstraction) one must combine fragment and system (xii). A 'system of fragments' is a system humbled by its fundamental openness and incompleteness, even if 'all fragments are systems *in nuce*' (xii). The Romantic system does not transcend the sum of its parts; individual parts do, however, transcend this *expanded* system. The fragment's attraction (as a form) lies in its embryonic suggestiveness of the system, without which thought cannot 'live up to its concept and remains stuck with the manifold' (xi). This implicit, potential totality of a system in the fragment is the ideal counterpart to the progressive and universal character of *Poesie*. For Novalis, however, a fragment had to be 'finished off,' like a stage of thought organizing itself as a part of a pro-

jected totality (14–15). Related to this is the notion of *cyclicality*, to which Novalis's greatest project, the *Romantic Encyclopedia*, was to give fullest expression: rather than a string of stand-alone finished pieces, a centripetal arrangement of parts tending to completeness in the universal unity of all knowledge. Novalis's death cut short his work on the collection, leaving it unintentionally unfinished; its contents survive only as 'notes' in Novalis's *allgemeine Brouillon* (general notebooks) (see Novalis, *Novalis: Notes for a Romantic Encyclopaedia [Das Allgemeine Brouillon]*, ed. and trans. David W. Wood [SUNY Press, 2007]). The crisis of form so fertile for Romanticism is perhaps nowhere better manifested than in this tension of the fragment–system polarity and its theorization in *fragmentariness*.

93 Johann Christoph Gottsched, 'Versuch einer critischen Dichtkunst vor die Deutschen,' in his *Schriften zur Literatur*, ed. Horst Steinmetz (Stuttgart: Reclam, 1982), 12–196. Hereafter cited as *CD*.

94 Gellert, a university professor and a celebrated poet in his own right, argued for a middle ground between rule-based and free readings of literature, in an attempt to evaluate the unique creative work on its own merits and, more generally, to 'liberate literature from lecture halls' (Rainer Baasner, 'Einleitung – Literaturkritik in Aufklärung und Empfindsamkeit – Maßstäbe der ästhetischen Bewertung, Begriff der 'Schönen Literatur',' *Projekt Literaturkritik*, ed. R. Baasner, 11 May 2005, Universität Rostock, *1 May 2006* https://www.phf.uni-rostock.de/institut/igerman/forschung/litkritik/litkritik/start.htm).

95 Gotthold Ephraim Lessing, 'Siebzehnter Brief,' in his *Werke und Briefe: 1758–1760*, ed. Wilfried Barner (Frankfurt: Deutscher Klassiker, 1989), 499.

96 The full title of this first rhetorical manual written in German is *Ausführliche Redekunst, Nach Anleitung der alten Griechen und Römer, wie auch der neuern Ausländer, in zweenen Theilen verfasset und itzo den Zeugnissen der Alten und Exempeln der größten deutschen Redner erläutert. Statt einer Einleitung ist das alte Gespräch, von den Ursachen der verfallenen Beredsamkeit vorgesetzet* [The Complete Rhetoric, According to the Instruction of the Ancient Greeks and Romans, as Well as Modern Foreigners, Composed in Twelve Parts and Now Elucidated through Reference to the Ancients and Examples from the Greatest German Orators. Instead of an Introduction, an Ancient Dialogue Put Forward by the Causes of Lapsed Eloquence] (title of fifth edition, 1759).

97 Opitz's work was itself closely based on the Latin poetics of Julius Caesar Scaliger (1484–1558), *Poetices libri septem* (1561), a text that formulated Classical (Aristotelianist) poetic principles nearly a century before Boileau, with greater erudition but also dogmatism to match it. Another important

German Baroque poetics typifying the *Regelpoetik* category was Birken's 1679 *Teutsche Rede-bind- und Dicht-kunst* [German Rhetoric and Art of Poetry], a summation of the major literary debates of its time.

98 Simpson, 'IGA' 5.

99 Johann Christoph Gottsched, 'Critical Poetics (excerpt),' in *Eighteenth-Century German Criticism*, ed. Chamberlain, 4. This translation is hereafter cited as *CP*.

100 The 1751 edition's title qualified the 'examples' with 'our best poets' (*unserer besten Dichter*).

101 Boileau was originally on the traditionalist side of the *Querelle des anciens et des modernes*.

102 This age-old idea was echoed also by the Romantics: 'Poesy can only be criticized by way of poesy. A critical judgement of an artistic production has no civil rights in the realm of art if it isn't itself a work of art ...' (Schlegel, *Philosophical Fragments* 14, modified) ('Critical Fragment' 117). Novalis's take on the inseparability of poetic and critical labours was this: 'Whoever cannot make poems will also only be able to judge them negatively. To true criticism belongs the ability to create oneself the product being criticized. Taste alone only judges negatively' (*Philosophical Writings* 55, modified) ('Logological Fragment [I]' 31).

103 G.L. Jones, 'Gottsched and the German Poets of the Seventeenth Century,' *Forum for Modern Language Studies* 7.3 (1971): 282–93. The activity of the bee as a metaphor for the industrious compilation of literary opinion surfaces also in Russian criticism. By contrast, Novalis's metaphor of *pollen* recasts the work of criticism as the fertilizing (fecund) element of literature, rather than as the secondary work of (cross-)pollination. This is also the 'mission' for Schlegel's 'prophetic' criticism.

104 As Kowalik points out, use of quotations and borrowings 'appeared not because it added to the sense of the work, but because it added to its legitimacy' (3).

105 At the turn of the eighteenth century, sociopolitical changes ran the humanistic, Latin-based *respublica litteraria* into a crisis of identity and legitimacy. As a result of the French role in preserving the community and the currency of French within it, it 'renamed' itself *République des Lettres*. In the first decades of the eighteenth century in Germany, the Republic came increasingly under attack from secular thought – its elitist, competitive, and politicized organization was perceived as an ideological obstacle to Enlightenment intellectual freedom and individualism. By 1750, the metaphor of an ideal, pan-European scholarly 'unity in multiplicity' was virtually obsolete, giving way to national allegiance (Kasper Risbjerg Es-

kildsen, 'How Germany Left the Republic of Letters,' *Journal of the History of Ideas* 65.3 [2004]: 421–31).

106 Johann Georg Hamann, 'Aesthetica in nuce: Eine Rhapsodie in Kabbalistischer Prose,' in *Sturm und Drang: Kritische Schriften*, ed. Erich Loewenthal (Heidelberg: Schneider, 1972), 119–43.

107 The parameters of this genre are opaque, to say the least. Apart from its ancient sense ('an epic poem, or part of one, of a suitable length for recitation at one time' [*OED*]), a *rhapsody* could also be defined as a written composition or literary work consisting of miscellaneous or disconnected pieces (words, poems, ideas, narratives, etc.), without a fixed plan – a meaning now obsolete. The word is still used to refer to 'an exaggeratedly enthusiastic or ecstatic expression of feeling; an effusive utterance or written work, often disconnected or lacking sound argument' (*OED*). The former meaning seems to be an exponentiation of the latter.

108 The qualifier *rhapsodisch* was seldom used in titles of critical texts. I have found only one other instance of *Rhapsodie*: 'Ueber deutsche Poeterey, eine Rhapsodie an Hrn. Kanonikus Wallref in Kölln' (from 1792, in *Allgemeine deutsche Bibliothek*).

109 Plato, 'Ion,' trans. Lane Cooper, in *The Critical Tradition: Classic Texts and Contemporary Trends*, ed. David Richter (New York: St Martin's, 1989), 37.

110 'The uninitiate crowd I ban and spurn! / Come ye, but guard your tongues! A song that's new / I, priest of the Muses, sing for you / Fair maids and youths to learn!' (Hamann, 'AN' 2).

111 In one note, Hamann tellingly endorses the following statement by Cicero about punning (from *De Oratore*): 'Bons mots prompted by an equivocation are deemed the very wittiest, though not always concerned with jesting, but very often even with what is important ... [F]or the power to divert the force of a word into a sense quite different from that in which other folk understand it seems to indicate a man of talent' ('AN' 18, note bbb).

112 Hamann, 'AN' 1, editor's note 1 (Hamann's notes are alphabetical.) Hamann is referencing here Klopstock's preface to his work, titled 'Von der heiligen Poesie' [On Sacred Poetry].

113 Hamann, 'AN' 2, editor's note 4.

114 This is the Western prototype of the twentieth-century Sapir-Whorf hypothesis – though credit for it is generally given to Herder and W. von Humboldt.

115 Steven Gillies, 'German Theory and Criticism 1: Sturm und Drang – Weimar Classicism,' in *The Johns Hopkins Guide to Literary Theory and Criticism*, 2nd ed., ed. Michael Groden et al. (Baltimore: Johns Hopkins University Press, 2005), 1 October 2005 http://litguide.press.jhu.edu/index.html.

116 In this text of Hamann's, references to the Old Testament take precedence over all others.
117 Hamann, 'AN' 8, editor's note 40.
118 This passage is said to satirize Mendelssohn's ideas on literary decorum (Hamann throws in references to excrement in the same paragraph).
119 Klopstock was then enjoying immense popularity.
120 Hamann is referring to a comment made in the *Briefe, die neueste Literatur betreffend,* to which Herder also responds in the first collection of his *Fragmente.*
121 Hamann, 'AN' 21, editor's note 92.
122 Gotthold Ephraim Lessing, 'Laokoon: oder über die Grenzen der Malerei und Poesie,' in his *Werke und Briefe: 1766–1769,* ed. Wilfried Barner (Frankfurt: Deutscher Klassiker, 1990), 11–318. (Citations of the German original are abbreviated as 'LGMP.') I will not be dealing with the part titled *Paralipomena* but only with part 1, the full original title of which is: *Laokoon: oder über die Grenzen der Malereyn und Poesie, mit beyläufigen Erläuterungen verschiedener Punkte der alten Kunstgeschichte. Erster Teil* [Laocoon, or on the Limits of Painting and Poetry, with Casual Explanations on Various Points of the History of Ancient Art].
123 This was Winckelmann's *Gedanken über die Nachahmung der griechischen Werke der Malerei und Bildhauerkunst* [Thoughts on the Imitation of Greek Works in Painting and Sculpture] from 1755.
124 Incidentally, Lessing's preference as a literary author was for drama. He was also the greatest assailant of Gottsched's generic regime in the area of dramatic dialogue (specifically, the latter's restrictive notion of linguistic realism) (Kieffer 25).
125 Gotthold Ephraim Lessing, *Laocoön: An Essay on the Limits of Painting and Poetry,* ed. and trans. Edward Allen McCormick (Indianapolis: Bobbs-Merrill, 1962), 3. Hereafter cited as 'L.'
126 Lessing is distancing himself from an already *German* custom: 'We Germans suffer from no lack of systematic [*systematischen*] books. We know better than any other nation in the world how to deduce anything we want in the most beautiful order from a few postulated definitions' ('L' 5).
127 *Collectanea* are passages, remarks, etc. collected from various sources. If used in the singular, the term is synonymous with *miscellany* (*OED*).
128 These concluding sentences immediately follow a long quotation.
129 Robert Leventhal, 'Lessing, G.E.,' in *The Johns Hopkins Guide to Literary Theory and Criticism,* 2nd ed., ed. Michael Groden et al. (Baltimore: Johns Hopkins University Press, 2005), 1 October 2005 http://litguide.press.jhu.edu/index.html.

130 Johann Gottfried Herder, 'Über die neuere deutsche Literatur: Erste bis dritte Sammlung von Fragmenten (Auszug),' in *Sturm und Drang: Kritische Schriften*, ed. E. Loewenthal (Heidelberg: Schneider, 1972), 185–287 (hereafter, German original cited as 'Fragmente'). I focus on the first collection because its impact is judged to have been the greatest of the three (Ernest A. Menze and Karl Menges, 'Commentary to the Translations,' in J.G. Herder, *Selected Early Works, 1764–1767: Addresses, Essays, and Drafts; Fragments on Recent German Literature*, ed. Menze and Menges, trans. Menze with Michael Palma [University Park: Pennsylvania State University Press, 1992], 273–4). However, the second collection, which has a more developed comparative literary dimension and concerns itself with the history of literary criticism (opening section), is no less important than the first as a marker of the status and character of critical discourse at the time.

131 Herder, 'Fragmente' 187.

132 Gerstenberg also published a commentary on the *Briefe*, with a tentative title not unlike Herder's: 'Einige unzusammenhängende Bemerkungen über die *Briefe die neueste Literatur betreffend*' [Some Disjointed Remarks on the *Letters concerning Most Recent Literature*], as the 12th letter in his *Briefe über Merkwürdigkeiten der Literatur* (1766–71).

133 The second and the third collections do not exactly reproduce this composition. In the second, a metacritical *vorläufiger Diskurs* (preliminary discourse) precedes an introduction (*Einleitung*), and a postscript (*Nachschrift*) takes the place of the *Beschluß*. The third collection contains no introduction and also ends with a postscript. The fragments in each collection are divided into three or four sections.

134 Indeed, only with the Romantics does the *fragment* acquire theoretical and generic autonomy. Its poetics is defined not merely by opposition to ossified genres of Classical harmony, narrative continuity, and wholeness, but by its conscious resistance to generic definition as such. The Herderian *Fragmente* lack such poetological motivation and evince a straightforward distrust and qualified rejection of systematicity (circumscribed by the task at hand), rather than a thoroughgoing *ambivalence* toward it characteristic of Romantic fragmentariness and registered in its textual forms (Horne 290) (see also notes 73 and 93, above). For a brief analysis of Herder's philosophical style and a more nuanced interpretation of his attitude to systematicity, see Michael Forster, 'Johann Gottfried von Herder,' *The Stanford Encyclopedia of Philosophy (Winter 2001 Edition)*, ed. Edward N. Zalta, 1 May 2006. http://plato.stanford.edu/archives/win2001/entries/herder/. Forster's main point is Herder's apparent anti-systematicity:

'unlike Hamann, Herder is in *favor* of "systematicity" in a more modest sense: the ideal of a theory which is self-consistent and maximally supported by argument. He by no means always achieves this ideal ... But his failures to do so are often more apparent than real: First, often when he may seem to be guilty of inconsistency he really is not. For he is often developing [implicit] philosophical dialogues between two or more opposing viewpoints, in which cases it would clearly be a mistake to accuse him of inconsistency in any usual or pejorative sense; and (less obviously) in many other cases he is in effect still working in this dialogue-mode, only without bothering to distribute the positions among different interlocutors explicitly, and so is again really innocent of inconsistency.'

135 A similar titular use of the term occurs in Herder's 'Fragmente einer Abhandlung über die Ode' [Fragments of a Treatise on the Ode], a much shorter text from 1765, containing an introduction and chapter titles for a planned treatise, and part of a constellation of fragments and outlines written by Herder in 1764–5 (Menze and Menges 252). The use of *fragment* in this case is merely reflective of the exigencies of composition.

136 Cf. '*Words* and *ideas* are exactly related in the realm of philosophy; so much depends on the *form of expression* in the criticism of arts and letters ...' ('FRGL' 101–2).

137 This successful Leipzig journal was founded by Nicolai, Lessing, and Mendelssohn and appeared between 1757 and 1759 (later continued by C.F. Weisse) (Menze and Menges 278).

138 See Derrida, *Of Grammatology* 141–64.

139 For the most part, Herder agreed with the *Briefe* authors' assessment of German literature. As mentioned previously, Hamann (who was in many ways an Oedipal figure to Herder) also availed himself of *supplementary* logic.

140 The theory is later recapitulated in Schiller's categories of naive and sentimental phases of poetry in his 'Über naive und sentimentalische Dichtung.'

141 Kieffer sees it as reflective of the essay's content: 'By fractionalizing his discourse on language, he dramatizes his object's tendency to elude systematic definition' (15).

142 The likening of Hamann's stance to Socratic irony is formally a part of his justification of Hamann, but also of himself – as a reminder, this type of irony involves 'a pose of ignorance, and eagerness to be instructed, and a modest readiness to entertain adverse opinions proposed by others; although these ... always turn out to be ill-grounded' or lead their holders to aporia (M.H. Abrams, *A Glossary of Literary Terms* [Fort Worth: Harcourt

Brace, 1993], 99). Cf. Schlegel's 'Critical Fragment' 108 for an appreciation of this mischievous mode: 'In this sort of irony, everything should be playful and serious, guilelessly open and deeply hidden' (*Philosophical Fragments* 13).

143 Gottfried August Bürger, 'Herzensausguß über Volkspoesie,' in *Sturm und Drang: Kritische Schriften*, ed. E. Loewenthal (Heidelberg: Schneider, 1972), 805–11. The other parts of *Aus Daniel Wunderlichs Buch*, from which the piece is excerpted, are an untitled preface and a section 'Von Einteilung des Schauspiels' [On the Arrangement of a Play]. This pseudo-excerpt (not quite a fragment) was itself the second part of the *Sprache, Literatur, Poesie und Kunst*, which appeared in the pro-Enlightenment monthly *Deutsches Museum* (Leipzig, 1776–88), a publication with a national literary-cultural-historical-political profile, stronger on literary theory than practical criticism (it did not print reviews), and with literary preferences similar to those of Sturm und Drang and advocates of *Empfindsamkeit* ('Deutsches Museum,' *Projekt Literaturkritik*, ed. R. Baasner, 11 May 2005, Universität Rostock, *1 May 2006* http://www.phf.uni-rostock.de/institut/igerman/forschung/litkritik/litkritik/start.htm?/institut/igerman/forschung/litkritik/litkritik/Medien/MeDeutschesMuseum.htm).

144 Gottfried August Bürger, 'Outpourings from the Heart on Folk Poetry,' in *Eighteenth-Century German Criticism*, ed. Chamberlain, 253. All further citations of this translation are abbreviated as 'OHFP.'

145 Bürger's orientation toward pleasing the popular audience was seen as vulnerable to a vulgarization – not an edification – of taste and a lowering of literary standards. In a 1791 review, 'Über Bürgers Gedichte' [On Bürger's Poems]), Schiller accused Bürger of 'unevenness of taste,' and his poetic muse of being 'too sensual, often vulgarly sensual,' and of 'mingl[ing] with the people' (Friedrich Schiller, 'On Bürger's Poems,' in *Eighteenth-Century German Criticism*, ed. Chamberlain, 267–8).

146 Note Bürger's preference of this term over *Dichtung* (poetry) or *Dichtkunst* (poetic art). The neologism, whose literal translation is 'the art of making verse,' emphasizes the strictly technical aptitude in poetic composition over imaginative investment and spontaneous creativity. Another transparent instance of terminological considerations occurs in his 'On Popularity in Poetry' (c. 1784). After rejecting German *Dichtkunst* and Greek *Poesie* as inadequate, Bürger invents *Nachbildnerei* (the forming of replicas) as the best expression for his concept of poetry: *popular* and mimetic, rooted in imagination and feeling ('On Popularity in Poetry [excerpt],' in *Eighteenth-Century German Criticism*, ed. Chamberlain, 258).

147 Herder will voice a similar idea in a preface to his second collection of the *Volkslieder*, where he speaks of Homer as the supreme popular poet and sees these genres as the ancestors of 'high' literary forms.

148 This rejection of cosmopolitanism is consonant with the program of the Sturm und Drang, although some of its writers later reconsidered this position, most notably Goethe.

149 Reference is to Thomas Percy, editor of *Reliques of Ancient English Poetry* (1765), a popular three-volume collection of old English ballads and popular songs. Ironically, Percy incurred criticism for emendations and elisions that rendered the text more readable and not merely of scholarly interest.

150 The *Bänkelsänger* was a balladeer (and pejoratively, a ballad-monger) whose performances used visual accompaniment (*Schilder*).

151 Theodor Verweyden, 'Theorie und Geschichte der Parodie, Teil 3,' 20 September 1997, *Erlanger Digitale Edition: Beiträge zur Literatur- und Sprachwissenschaft*, 1 May 2006 http://www.erlangerliste.de/vorlesung/parodieIII.html. To achieve this effect, Nicolai exaggerated the peculiarities and irregularities of the old idiom, and elevated them to rules.

152 J.W. von Goethe, 'Literarischer Sansculottismus,' in *Goethes Werke*, vol. 12, ed. Erich Trunz (Munich: Beck, 1981), 239–44. Further citations to the German edition are abbreviated as 'LS.'

153 John Gearey, Postscript to J.W. von Goethe, *Essays on Art and Literature*, ed. Gearey, trans. E. von Nardroff and E.H. von Nardroff (New York: Suhrkamp, 1986), 231.

154 The famous distinction between *Dichtung* (whose forms are limited to three) and *Dichtarten* (whose forms are potentially unlimited) received its formulation in Goethe's 1819 'Noten und Abhandlungen zum besseren Verständnis des West-östlichen Divans,' in his *Gedenkausgabe der Werke, Briefe und Gespräche*, vol. 3, 3rd ed. (Zürich: Artemis, 1966), 413–566.

155 Reich-Ranicki, 'Über den Essay.'

156 That this blurring was conceived by late-eighteenth-century German writers in their campaign against tired classicist formulae is added proof of the ingrained nature of the division. The deliberate character of such blurring, however, is absorbed by and validates literary organicism: it is elaborated within the critical discourse qua literary discourse, not an abstract, theoretical metadiscourse. What for the Romantics was a matter of an aesthetic of metaphysical, impersonal, self-created subjectivity, for Goethe stemmed from an understanding of writing – including poetry – as occasional, and authentic only through this occasionality.

157 Co-written with Schiller in 1795–96 and published in his *Musen-Alma-*

nach (1796–1800), the verse cycle 'became the focal point and exemplar of an invidiously polemical strategy of demarcation, emblematic of the militant impetus' present in both writers (Rainer Baasner, 'Einleitung in die Epoche der Klassik – Gattungen der Artikulation von Kritik,' *Projekt Literaturkritik*, ed. R. Baasner, 11 May 2005, Universität Rostock, *1 May 2006* https://www.phf.uni-rostock.de/institut/igerman/forschung/litkritik/litkritik/start.htm*)*.

158 Metaliterature – criticism ensconced in literary texts – functions as an integral part of the literary text, even if an extensive critical discussion seems to be pulling the literary text asunder.

159 J.W. von Goethe, 'Goethe's Theory of a World Literature,' in his *Literary Essays: A Selection in English*, ed. J.E. Spingarn (New York: Harcourt Brace Jovanovich, 1921), 93. Henceforth citations abbreviated as 'WL.'

160 He claims Jenisch portrayed them in such a way 'that, to be sure, one can hardly recognize them in his caricatures' (J.W. von Goethe, 'Response to a Literary Rabble-Rouser,' in his *Essays on Art and Literature*, ed. J. Gearey, trans. E. von Nardroff and E.H. von Nardroff [New York: Suhrkamp, 1986], 239; all further citations of the English translation are abbreviated as 'RR').

161 Cf. J.W. von Goethe, 'On Criticism,' in his *Literary Essays: A Selection in English*, ed. J.E. Spingarn (New York: Harcourt Brace Jovanovich, 1921), 140–2. Goethe saw a point only in constructive criticism (which is harder to provide).

162 Cf. his introduction to the *Propyläen* quoted above, p. 70.

163 This begs the question: Did Goethe become a national classical author in the sense he maintained – as expressive of a nation's unity (Wellek, 'Classicism' 79)? Maximilian Nutz, for example, does not think so (see his 'Das Beispiel Goethe: Zur Konstituierung eines nationalen Klassikers,' in *Wissenschaftsgeschichte der Germanistik im 19. Jahrhundert*, ed. Jürgen Fohrmann and Wilhelm Voßkamp [Stuttgart: Metzler, 1994], 605–37).

164 In another possibly conscious terminological choice, Goethe may be using *Schriftsteller* instead of *Dichter*, as he does later the terms *Poet* and *Prosaisten*, to distinguish more seasoned writers from their less accomplished colleagues (Gearey 258n4).

165 Friedrich Schlegel, 'Gespräch über die Poesie,' in *Früher Idealismus und Frühromantik: Der Streit um die Grundlagen der Ästhetik (1795–1805)*, ed. Walter Jaeschke and Helmut Holzey (Hamburg: Meiner, 1990), 99–211.

166 Ernst Behler, Introduction to F. Schlegel, *Dialogue on Poetry and Literary Aphorisms*, ed. and trans. Behler and R. Struč (University Park: Pennsylva-

nia State University Press, 1968), 49. All further citations are abbreviated as 'IDP.'

167 For a more complex reading of this feature, see *LA* 87. This mixture is, according to them, a 'confusion of all the genres arbitrarily delimited by ancient poetics, the interpenetration of the ancient and the modern' (91).

168 Friedrich Schlegel, *Dialogue on Poetry and Literary Aphorisms*, ed. and trans. E. Behler and R. Struč (University Park: Pennsylvania State University Press, 1968), 59. All further citations of this translation are abbreviated as *DP*.

169 Schlegel, *Philosophical Fragments* 2 ('Critical Fragment' 9).

170 At the same time, Lacoue-Labarthe and Nancy rightly observe the 'feminine injunction' – the female's requests and promptings for the readings (85). It should perhaps be clarified that the opening narration renders the preliminary (more informal) conversation as indirect speech. The mediating narrative voice is, moreover, a heterodiegetic one. It is also the voice of the prefatory remarks – i.e., Schlegel as himself.

171 Lacoue-Labarthe and Nancy mention this absence as central to decentring of the dialogue (90).

172 Schlegel, *Philosophical Fragments* 5 ('Critical Fragment' 42).

173 The irony is lifted from Plato – following from his own 'general indictment of *mimesis*' (*LA* 87). The dialogue was seen as a purely mimetic (dramatic) genre; but parts of the 'Gespräch' involve diegetic narration.

174 In Lacoue-Labarthe and Nancy's reading of the text, this is 'the classic division of the genres … which need not be respected as such … but whose principle must be maintained …' (95).

175 Briefly, the idea of the aesthetic presentation of philosophy was formulated in response to Kant's dilemma of the philosophical self-presentation of the impossibility of an adequate symbolic-sensible presentation of ideas.

176 Ernst Behler, *Irony and the Discourse of Modernity* (Seattle: University of Washington Press, 1990), 60. All further citations are abbreviated as *IDM*.

177 See Schlegel's '*Athenaeum* Fragment' 116 (*Philosophical Fragments* 32).

178 Novalis proposed his theory of *magical idealism* as an artistic and philosophical principle of overcoming conflict, contradiction, and fragmentation (Stoljar, Introduction to Novalis, *Philosophical Writings*, 20, 177n8).

179 Schlegel, *Philosophical Fragments* 21 ('*Athenaeum* Fragment' 26).

180 Schlegel, *Philosophical Fragments* 13 ('Critical Fragment' 108).

181 See the first chapter of *IDM*.

Chapter Two: Criticism in Poland

1 Anonymous, 'Uwagi z przyczyny "Zakusu,"' in *Ludzie Oświecenia o języku i stylu*, vol. 1, ed. Maria Renata Mayenowa, Zofia Florczak, and Lucylla Pszczołowska (Warsaw: PIW, 1958), 679.
2 Charles Bazerman, 'Systems of Genres and the Enactment of Social Intentions,' in *Genre and the New Rhetoric*, ed. Aviva Freedman and Peter Medway (London: Taylor & Francis, 1994), 88, 96.
3 For an orthodox critique and undoing of this attribution, see Genette's *Architext*.
4 Such transformative power not only inheres in located discursive practice (that is, in the enactment of a discourse in local circumstances), but also in the dynamic interaction between environments of discursive and quasi- or non-discursive activity.
5 That he was still working within the older model finds supports in Rzewuski's simultaneous publication of *O nauce krasomówskiej* [On Rhetoric]. The normative character of *O nauce wierszopiskiej* is easily gleaned from the syntax, like the frequency of imperative forms, e.g., the anaphoric occurrence of *niech* (let) (Wacław Rzewuski, 'O nauce wierszopiskiej,' in *Oświeceni o literaturze: Wypowiedzi pisarzy polskich, 1740–1800*, ed. Teresa Kostkiewiczowa and Zbigniew Goliński [Warsaw: PWN, 1993], 59–67).
6 I am drawing on Fowler's concept of *generic modulation*: a generic mixture that is not yet a hybrid, where one of the genres is 'only a modal abstraction with a token repertoire' (Fowler 191). The phenomenon of modulation is, in Fowler's opinion, more common than hybridization proper. He observes: 'Modulation is so frequent that we might expect it progressively to loosen the genres altogether, mingling them into a single literary amalgam'; in reality, however, the generic components remain 'somewhat discrete' and distinguishable.
7 Jadwiga Ziętarska, *O metodzie krytyki literackiej w dobie Oświecenia* (Warsaw: WUW, 1981), 107.
8 *Wymowa* concerned not just oratory but prose generally (Zdzisław Libera, *Problemy polskiego Oświecenia: Kultura i styl* [Warsaw: PWN, 1969], 100).
9 The text was written in 1783 for a national textbook competition. The first part (on elocution) was eventually published in 1792, the second, on poetry, not until 1815. Thus, the circulation of Piramowicz's text in the *KEN* (Commission of National Education) school system was limited (Zdzisław Libera, *Wiek Oświecony: Studia i szkice z dziejów literatury i kultury polskiej XVIII i początków XIX wieku* [Warsaw: PIW, 1986], 98).

10 Cited in Stanisław Pietraszko, *Doktryna literacka polskiego klasycyzmu* (Wrocław: Zakład Narodowy im. Ossolińskich, 1966), 28.

11 Teresa Kostkiewiczowa, 'Myśl literacka polskiego Oświecenia,' in *Oświeceni o literaturze*, ed. Kostkiewiczowa and Goliński, 7.

12 Sarnowska-Temeriusz, 'Krytyka' 16. For a discussion of these earlier expressions of opinion about literature and literary life in Polish in the sixteenth and seventeenth centuries, see Piotr Chmielowski, *Dzieje krytyki literackiej w Polsce* (Warsaw: Gebethner i Wolff, 1902), 16–70. The most one can do to avoid blatant anachronism in deciding what counts as literary criticism is to determine ad hoc inclusion criteria at various stages of discursive formation – for instance, I designated the *literary thematic* and *evaluative function* as 'necessary conditions' for inclusion. In what follows I, for the most part, accept the scope of Polish anthologies and studies of literary criticism, on which I draw throughout the next section.

13 The Jesuit order, since the 1750s persecuted throughout most of the European continent, was officially dissolved in 1773 by Pope Clement XIV.

14 This occurred in combination with the economic and political enfranchisement of cities.

15 Teresa Kostkiewiczowa, 'Rozważania o kulturze literackiej czasów stanisławowskich,' in *Problemy kultury literackiej polskiego Oświecenia: Studia*, ed. Kostkiewiczowa (Wrocław: Ossolineum, 1978), 16.

16 To take one manifestation of this process (though not an exemplary one), a project of a literary-critical periodical toward the end of the 1770s, conceived by those grouped around Czartoryski, involved an institutional backdrop in the form of the *Towarzystwo Krytyczne* [Critical Society]. Its program was: providing critical opinion about authors, in order to 'educate its readers, so that they could make the appropriate choice of readings' (Danuta Hombek, *Prasa i czasopisma polskie w XVIII wieku w perspektywie bibliologicznej* [Cracow: Universitas, 2001], 291).

17 Sarnowska-Temeriusz, 'Krytyka' 16. The feuilleton established itself as a genre on the pages of the *Monitor*.

18 Henryk Markiewicz, *Dopowiedzenia: Rozprawy i szkice z wiedzy o literaturze* (Cracow: WL, 2000), 103.

19 Markiewicz chooses to omit unconventional descriptors, which he apparently regards as devoid of generic characteristics (*Dopowiedzenia* 109).

20 According to Wilhelm Bruchnalski's study of Polish epistolography, critical letters were already common in the second half of the seventeenth

century (cited in Stefania Skwarczyńska, *Teoria listu* [Lvov: Towarzystwo Naukowe we Lwowie, 1937], 336n).

21 This Warsaw-based periodical imitated the British *Spectator*. The *Monitor*, one of many ventures by publishing mogul Mitzler de Kolof, became the most successful periodical of the Polish eighteenth century, surviving for nearly twenty-one years (1765–85) (Hombek 145). It was founded at the king's behest and included Krasicki and Mitzler (1773–6) among its editors. Apart from translations of Classical and Enlightenment authors, the periodical published works penned by literati with access to the court and by reform-minded correspondents. Contributions ranged from literary texts, sketches, short essays, feuilletons, to critical letters. It began as the organ of reformist propaganda: classicism and Wolffian rationalism, a political ideology of pre-Jacobin, Masonic origin, and a mixture of mercantilism and Physiocratic economics (Hombek 146; A. Wertz, 'Regenerating the Republic: The *Monitor* and Economic Reform in the Polish Enlightenment,' *CSEES Newsletter* 17.2 [2000]: 15). However, as Anna Wertz notes, citing a study by Elżbieta Aleksandrowska, 'The *Monitor* remained in reformist hands for only its first three years and metamorphosed many times over the course of publication. After 1767, under the editorship of Franciszek Bohomolec, the journal was made to conform more closely to the generic form of a satirical journal, focusing almost exclusively on customs and culture' (14). Mitzler revived the journal's former radicalism.

22 The use of such imaginative, often humorous pseudonyms (composed of a descriptive base with the suffix -ski or -cki, both characteristic of Polish surnames) became a trend of sorts among contributors to the *Monitor*. Krasicki, if he was indeed the author of the piece, published there also under his real name. 'Theatralski's' text is a letter to the editorial board – 'Mr. *Monitor*' – referring to a discussion printed therein concerning dramatic rules. The epigraph is a quotation from Horace's poetics, giving poets creative freedom, and – in keeping with it and with Samuel Johnson's *The Preface to Shakespeare* (1765) (itself based on Dubos's *Réflexions*), which he read in a French translation – Theatralski exposes the absurdity of the principle of the three unities. The letter's tone is one of courtesy and humility: 'You will allow me to contradict your opinion a little, and I understand that you will not call sagacious audacity impudence, as what I have decided to translate I rest not only on testimony, but also on the words of the famous English author Johnson, who in a preface to the Works of Shakespeare thus announced his thoughts in this respect' (Theatralski, 'Wystąpienie sławnego angielskiego autora Johnsona przeciw klasycystycznym rygorom w utworach teatralnych,' in *'Monitor,' 1765–1785: Wybór*, ed. E.

Aleksandrowska [Wrocław: Zakład Narodowy im. Ossolińskich, 1976], 119–20). The rest of the text is a long excerpt from Johnson, followed only by the valediction and signature: 'I am with the utmost respect, Theatralski' (123). One critic notes that Johnson's name was for Krasicki a pretext for presenting his views on theatrical illusion (Janina Pawłowiczowa, qtd. in *Oświeceni o literaturze*, ed. Kostkiewiczowa and Goliński, 76).

23 It is called by Kostkiewiczowa and Goliński a *rozprawka* (mini-treatise) (in *Oświeceni o literaturze*, ed. Kostkiewiczowa and Goliński, 114). To make formal matters even more confusing, it is written as a dedicatory letter.

24 However, the 'journal was faulted for rarely publishing critical letters that were not of its own invention' (Wertz 14).

25 The treatise was Fijałkowski's (d. 1820) response to an attack on Cracow's literary and scientific academic community (himself included), published anonymously in 1788 by the Warsaw Piarists (its co-authors were F.K. Dmochowski, Onufry Kopczyński, and Franciszek Siarczyński). A second polemical brochure, written by Dmochowski, appeared in 1789. Fijałkowski's reply followed that of fellow academic J.I. Przybylski (1756–1819), whose 1788 *Dysertacja o kunszcie pisania u starożytnych* [Dissertation on the Writing Craft of the Ancients] became a target on account of its obscure and unscholarly style in Latin (both men were academic critics who shortly afterward advanced to the ranks of professors of literature). In his dismissal of the attack as 'duplicitous' in representing itself as a 'critique,' Fijałkowski conscientiously cites Marmontel's definition of critique in the *Encyclopédie* (1751–72). Others echo his concern: criticism is not personal obloquy, such abuse is below the spirit of collegial critique. The polemic is collected in *Bicz na akademików krakowskich: Antologia* [A Scourge on Cracow Academicians: An Anthology], ed. Roman Dąbrowski (Cracow: Universitas, 2003). For more on this and other Enlightenment-era polemics, see also Agnieszka Kwiatkowska, *Piórowe wojny: Polemiki literackie polskiego oświecenia* (Poznań: Wydawnictwo *Poznańskich Studiów Polonistycznych*, 2001).

26 Zoilus was an ancient Greek rhetorician and philologist famous for his petty and acerbic criticism of, most famously, Homer and Plato (for which he earned the moniker *Homeromastiks*, for having 'whipped' Homer). In Poland, as in Russia and elsewhere, he became the eponym of a pejorative critical stance. *Zoil* designated any carping, destructive critic for whom any pretext was sufficient grounds for condemning the fruits of creativity. The existence of such criticism was an established fact of the literary establishment. The equivalent of zoilism on the reception end (in the

reader–critic–work–writer network) is, of course, philistinism, notorious a century later and evocative of the anti-intellectualism typical of bourgeois audience.

27 *Sarmatism* was the exuberant culture-ideology of the Polish nobility (*sarmacja*) in the seventeenth and the first half of the eighteenth century. The negative tendencies associated with the nobility's sociopolitical stagnation persisted well into the 1770s, when strong reform initiatives began to take shape.

28 Stanisław Pietraszko, introduction to F.K. Dmochowski, *Sztuka rymotwórcza* (Wrocław: Zakład Narodowy im. Ossolińskich, 1956), cx–cxi. Hereafter abbreviated in citations as 'ISR.'

29 J.A. Jabłonowski, 'Opisanie albo dysertacja pierwsza prawie o wierszach i wierszopiscach polskich wszystkich,' in *Oświeceni o literaturze*, ed. Kostkiewiczowa and Goliński, 56–8. All further citations of this source are abbreviated as 'ODW.'

30 A.K. Czartoryski, 'Przedmowa do *Panny na wydaniu*,' in *Oświeceni o literaturze*, ed. Kostkiewiczowa and Goliński, 92–114. All further citations of this source are abbreviated as 'PPW.'

31 Kostkiewiczowa and Goliński, *Oświeceni o literaturze* 123.

32 Jan Kochanowski was Poland's foremost Renaissance humanist poet.

33 A look at Czartoryski's other critical writings gives the impression that he liked to experiment with different forms. His 'Przedmowa do *Kawy*' – *Kawa* [Coffee] being self-penned comedy – assumes the external form of a letter dedicated to his friend Józef Szymanowski. It opens with the salutation 'Beloved Friend' and continues throughout to address him in the informal second person.

34 J. Szymanowski, 'List o guście, czyli smaku,' in *Oświeceni o literaturze*, ed. Kostkiewiczowa and Goliński, 164–71. All further citations of this source are abbreviated as 'LG.'

35 Szymanowski, 'LG' 168, editor's note 6.

36 Szymanowski, 'LG' 164, editor's note 1; Pietraszko, 'ISR' lxxxiii.

37 This centre established itself in the 1780s.

38 The other instance concludes the body of the text ('LG' 168).

39 This is also how Pietraszko interprets it ('ISR' lxxxv).

40 F.N. Golański, 'O wymowie i poezji,' in *Oświeceni o literaturze*, ed. Kostkiewiczowa and Goliński, 221–355. I am working with the second, 1788 edition, published in Vilnius. The first edition was published in Warsaw only two years earlier. Due to a delay in the publication of Piramowicz's winning textbook, *KEN* schools relied on Golański's treatment of the topic.

41 See the introduction to Golański's text in *Oświeceni o literaturze*, ed. Kostkiewiczowa and Goliński, 220.

42 Of Polish authors, he cites or alludes to Maciej Kazimierz Sarbiewski (1595–1640), Jesuit poet and literary theorist credited with devising the literary program of the Baroque, and a great admirer of J.C. Scaliger. He was the author of normative poetics in Latin – the *De Perfecta poesi sive Vergilius et Homerus* and the *Praecepta poetica* – in which he granted the poet unfettered *creative* powers. Also mentioned by Golański are Kochanowski, contemporary dramatist Józef Wybicki, poets Marcin Eysymont and Naruszewicz, and Franciszek Karpiński (in his capacity as literary writer). He also exhibits knowledge of contemporary French, English, and Spanish writers.

43 F.K. Dmochowski, *Sztuka rymotwórcza* (Wrocław: Zakład Narodowy im. Ossolińskich, 1956). The text saw two editions in its first year of publication alone. Hereafter cited as *SR*.

44 Pietraszko, 'ISR' xxiv. *Pseudoclassicism* is another term for the formation of Polish classicism in the post-Stanislaus period.

45 Some examples are: *geniusz* (genius, innovative spirit); when applied to nations (*geniusz narodów*), *dowcip* (talent, wit), *imaginacja, malownia* (imagination), *natura* (nature, inspiration).

46 Pietraszko, 'ISR' xxiv. Dmochowski's authorship of this piece is not unequivocal (see Maria Renata Mayenowa, Zofia Florczak, and Lucylla Pszczołowska, eds., *Ludzie Oświecenia o języku i stylu*, vol. 2 [Warsaw: PIW, 1958], 44n1). At least four other brochures addressing questions of literary originality, language, and style appeared in response to the publication by M.D. Krajewski (1746–1817) of *Podolanka* [the title refers to an anonymous female resident of Podolia, a region of Poland until the partitions] (Lvov, 1784). The heroine of this provocatively metaliterary novel, itself a loose adaptation of the French novel *Imirce, ou la Fille de la nature* (Paris, 1760; Berlin, 1765), is raised on the model of Rousseau's Émile and socialized only as an adult. The titles of the polemical texts make explicit and humorous reference to the original, by assuming the voices of fictional characters from the book: F. Siarczyński's 'List Paryżanki do Podolanki, czyli Oryginał do kopii' [Letter from a Parisian to Podolanka, or from the Original to the Copy], the anonymous 'Dyjalog, czyli Rozmowa Podolanki z mężem' [Dialogue, or a Conversation between Podolanka and Her Husband], and, the most amusingly titled, 'Odpis męża Podolanki na list Sandomierzanki' [Reply from Podolanka's Husband to a Letter from a Woman of Sandomierz] by Krajewski himself. These replies were, moreover, written 'in character.'

47 A more obvious example of this less speculative and more intuitive normativity is an anaphoric garland of *niech*'s and *niechaj*'s (let), advising the writer on the treatment of thoughts, tonality, syllables, and words in verse (*SR* 21).
48 However, allusions to the king's magnanimity do recur in the main text (e.g., 'Stanislaus's wise sceptre' [*SR* 27]).
49 Roman Kaleta, *Prekursorzy Oświecenia: 'Monitor' z roku 1763 na tle swoich czasów; Mitzler de Kolof: Redaktor i wydawca* (Wrocław: Zakład Narodowy im. Ossolińskich, 1953), 282.
50 In the 1998 study *Polsko-niemieckie pogranicza literackie w XVIII wieku: Problemy uczestnictwa w dwu kulturach*, Mieczysław Klimowicz unravels the plots of Mitzler's 'double life.' Similarly, D. Hombek speaks of Mitzler as a cross-national figure, retaining professional ties with Germany. Mitzler was the first editor of the *Warschauer Bibliothek* (published 1753–55) and of *Acta Litteraria* (1756–9, 1763) – the former an *ephemerida litteraria* advertising Polish scholarship and literature (written in German, with Jabłonowski's support), the latter as its conceptual sequel with expanded readership (it was written in Latin). *Warschauer Bibliothek oder gründliche Nachrichten von verschiedenen Büchern und Schriften, sowohl alten als neuen, so in Pohlen herausgekommen* [The Warsaw Library, or Complete News about Diverse Books and Writings, Old and New Alike, Published in Poland] – as the full title read – was intended primarily for a German audience and printed in Warsaw and Leipzig. It was, however, poorly advertised, foregoing subscriptions and relying too heavily on the patronage of Józef Andrzej Załuski (1702–74), on whose funds it subsisted as the organ of the Załuski Library. The *Acta Litteraria Regni Poloniae et Magni Ducatus Lithuaniae* was a continuation of the *Warschauer Bibliothek*, similar in its selection and organization of subject matter, and presenting Polish literature under the same heading: *Nova litteraria Polonica*. Marketing-wise, the publication was an improvement on its predecessor, but the irregularity of its appearance did not win for it a stable readership (Hombek 58–63).

Chapter Three: Criticism in Russia

1 Mikhail M. Kheraskov, 'K satiricheskoi muze,' in his *Izbrannye proizvedeniia*, ed. A.V. Zapadov (Leningrad: Sovetskii Pisatel', 1961), 103.
2 See Harsha Ram, *The Imperial Sublime: A Russian Poetics of Empire* (Madison: University of Wisconsin Press, 2003).
3 All three figures were practitioners of literature who generally put their theories into practice: Trediakovskii, author of the popular *Novyi i kratkii*

sposob k slozheniiu rossiiskikh stikhov [A New and Concise Method for the Composition of Russian Verses] (St Petersburg, 1735), wrote poetry on a par with Western European poets, Lomonosov became the mythic father of Russian poetry, and Sumarokov, a dramaturge, was effectively the founder of Russian drama and theatre (he was made the director of the Russian stage upon its inception in 1756), as well as the first nobleman to become a professional writer (Harold B. Segel, introductory note to *The Literature of Eighteenth-Century Russia*, vol. 1, ed. Segel [New York: Dutton, 1967], 252, 56–7).

4 Like Sumarokov, Kheraskov also wrote (versified) critical *epistoly*, among them 'Pis'mo' (1760), 'K satiricheskoi muze' [To the Satirical Muse] (1760) and 'K klevetnike' [To the Slanderer] (1760).

5 V.I. Kuleshov, *Istoriia russkoi kritiki XVIII–nachala XX vekov* (Moscow: 'Prozveshchenie,' 1984), 9.

6 V.V. Vinogradov, *The History of the Russian Literary Language from the Seventeenth Century to the Nineteenth*, trans. Lawrence L. Thomas (Madison: University of Wisconsin Press, 1969), 93.

7 Church Slavonic was fundamentally a written language and, until the end of the seventeenth century, Russia's official language. Once the language of (religious) literature, by the eighteenth century it was reduced to liturgical use and replaced by the Russian vernacular as the modern secular literary language. Written Russian owed much of its lexical and phonetic richness to Church Slavonic.

8 In the second half of the century, Church Slavonic was systematically decontextualized, subjected to selection, prohibition, adaptation, and redefinition by its creative reformers (headed by Karamzin), thus purifying it of 'church ideology' (Vinogradov 86, 101–2).

9 Andrzej Walicki, *A History of Russian Thought from Enlightenment to Marxism*, trans. Hilda Andrews-Rusiecka (Stanford, CA: Stanford University Press, 1979), xvi, 1.

10 In Poland, the *querelle* over the Polish language (chiefly between Cracow and Warsaw academics) also became, at points, intertwined with discussions on literature. The debates reflected a new attitude toward linguistic culture, with emphasis on its crucial role in preserving national traditions and disseminating new knowledge. Arguments for the cultivation of language consciousness involved improving style by reading Polish Renaissance authors, eradicating the accretion of foreign idioms, especially French and Latin (with disagreement about the degree of this purification), as well as specifying scholarly terminology (Libera, *Wiek* 83–9). A superb anthology of source texts dedicated to questions of language and style is

the second volume of *Ludzie Oświecenia o języku i stylu*, ed. Mayenowa et al.

11 Stacy's typology: see his *Russian Literary Criticism: A Short History* 8.

12 Incidentally, as a science adviser to Peter the Great, Wolff had been involved in founding the St Petersburg Academy of Sciences.

13 M.S. Grinberg and B.A. Uspenskii, *Literaturnaia voina Trediakovskovo i Sumarokova v 1740-kh–nachale 1750-kh godov* [The Literary War of Trediakovskii and Sumarokov in the 1740s–early 1750s] (Moscow: RGGU, 2001), 61–2.

14 René Wellek, *A History of Modern Criticism, 1750–1950*, vol. 4, *The Later Nineteenth Century* (New Haven: Yale University Press, 1965), 238–91. The former set of terms is from Stacy.

15 Lomonosov's dispute with Trediakovskii began in 1739 with the brief 'Pis'mo o pravilakh rossiiskovo stikhotvorstva' [Letter on the Rules of Russian Versification], which put forth the following idea: '... Russian verse should be composed according to the natural characteristics of our language; and that which is uncharacteristic of it should not be imported from other languages' (*Polnoe sobranie sochinenii; Trudi po filologii, 1739–1758* [Moscow: Izdatel'stvo Akademii Nauk SSSR, 1952], 9–10). They continued arguing for another two decades – until Lomonosov's death. In 1743, both Lomonosov and Sumarokov attacked Trediakovskii's proclivity for iambs and trochees and, some years later, for hexameters (Reyfman 83). The polemics between Sumarokov and Trediakovskii were particularly venomous and spanned nearly four decades. As late as 1773, in his 'On Orthography,' Sumarokov faulted Trediakovskii for his atrocious linguistic habits: first those picked up from common diction, then from Church Slavonic (80). The beginning of Lomonosov's dispute with Sumarokov came in the 1750s, with Lomonosov's parody 'From Russian Theatre,' and lasted into the 1760s (e.g., Sumarokov's *Odi bzdornye* [Nonsense Odes] [1759]). A high point in these disputes was the 1757 'Predislovie o pol'ze knig tserkovnikh v rossiiskom iaziike' [Preface on the Use of Church Books in the Russian Language] (opening the first volume of his works published by Moscow University), in which Lomonosov advanced the theory of the three styles and their generic and thematic correlatives in relation to Russian linguistic history, and stressed the importance of Church Slavonic for accessing the ancient Greek literary-cultural heritage. This text was a response to the mixing of styles he perceived in his contemporaries – most notably in Trediakovskii.

16 G. Gukovskii, 'From "On Russian Classicism,"' *Russian Literature Triquarterly* 21 (1988): 10–11, modified.

17 Both texts – Gottsched's and Lomonosov's – are commonly referred to as *Rhetoric*.

18 Gukovskii 19.

19 Kevin J. McKenna, 'Ezhemesiachnye sochineniia,' in *Modern Encyclopedia of Russian and Soviet Literature*, vol. 7, ed. H.B. Weber (Gulf Breeze, FL: Academic International, 1984), 125–6. See also P.N. Berkov, *Istoriia russkoi zhurnalistiki XVIII veka* (Moscow: Izdatel'stvo Akademii Nauk SSSR, 1952), 77–107. The academy 'held a virtual monopoly over the publication of *belles lettres* in the empire until the late 1790s' (Karen Rosenberg, 'Trediakovsky on Sumarokov: The Critical Issues,' *Russian Literature Triquarterly* 21 [1988]: 49). This explains why the rivals were subject to one another's scrutiny as internal referees (50).

20 Catherine's involvement in the production of the literary discourse of her political dominion was, on the whole, no more intensive than that of Stanislaus II or Frederick II because of her dictatorial inclination.

21 Novikov's notorious exchange with Catherine fleshed out boundaries that could not be crossed for satire to remain 'useful' (Catherine was manoeuvred to reveal her theoretical position in the disagreement). The flip side of the polemic was that the definition (or, rather, competing definitions) of satire popularized the genre in journalistic discourse.

22 Throughout the nineteenth century, the 'thick journals' (*tolstye zhurnaly*) printing literary criticism hosted many a social commentary and ideological critique without waking the censor, composed in allusive 'Aesopic language' that required reading between the lines. While – in periods when political public discourse was suppressed or prohibited (particularly the *mrachnoe semiletie*, the 'seven-year darkness' of 1848–55, under the reign of Nicholas I) – the 'essential bookishness' of a Russian society 'penetrated by literate values' was a good measure of the success of crafty communication via literature as a whole, the forum of literary criticism enabled more candid and sophisticated discussion of incendiary ideas to take place under the many guises of aesthetic debate (with little or no penal repercussions) (George Steiner, 'Text and Context,' in his *On Difficulty and Other Essays* [Oxford: Oxford University Press, 1978], 6–7). It is a given that the concealed purpose of these polemics, owing their existence to a conducive intellectual climate, shaped the form of contemporary critical writing, as transmitting opinion between the lines. Therefore, many nineteenth-century critical texts must be granted the strategic self-consciousness that accompanies writing craftily under duress.

23 For more on all three journals, see Berkov, *Istoriia* 117–23, 252–7, 497–520.

24 These so-called 'thick journals' had a broadly cultural profile and modern international content.
25 Effie Ambler, Introduction to her *Russian Journalism and Politics, 1861–1881 (The Career of Aleksei S. Suvorin)* (Detroit: Wayne State University Press, 1972), 14.
26 Dostoevskii and Turgenev wrote for it a century later (see Berkov, *Istoriia* 56–63).
27 Tuvia Shlonsky, qtd. in Reyfman 77.
28 By *showing* is meant depicting events through someone's point of view, while *telling* consists of a narrator's (often omniscient) observations.
29 Lomonosov's refusal to publish a Latin edition of the text was a political statement, reflecting his conflict with foreign academics running the Academy.
30 M.V. Lomonosov, 'Kratkoe rukovodstvo k krasnoriechiiu. Kniga pervaia, v kotoroi soderzhitsia ritorika, pokazuiushchaia obshchie pravila oboevo krasnoriechiia, to est' oratorii i poezii, sochinennaia v pol'zu liubiashchikh slovesnye nauki,' in his *Polnoe sobranie sochinienii: Trudi po filologii, 1739–1758*, vol. 7 (Moscow: Izdatel'stvo Akademii Nauk SSSR, 1952), 96. All further citations of this source are abbreviated as 'KRK.'
31 Lomonosov seems to have replaced all occurrences of *sladkoreche* with *krasnorieche* in the manuscript of the 1748 text.
32 A.A. Morozov is of a different opinion: 'To a certain extent, it was his "Poetics"' (Introduction to M.V. Lomonosov, *Izbrannye proizvedeniia*, vol. 1 [Leningrad: Sovetskii Pisatel', 1986], 31). The unfinished status of this otherwise self-contained work is, in part, owing to its prefiguration of the expected continuation. What I see as prefiguration, Morozov likely saw as adumbration.
33 Lomonosov, 'KRK' 169, trans. and qtd. in Stacy 18.
34 Wellek notes and explains the existence, in the mid to late eighteenth century, of this rhetoric-based theory of the effect of literature alongside the neo-Aristotelian one of catharsis, which was interpreted as the ultimate purgation of emotion induced by the literary work: 'simultaneously the view that poetry is persuasion, communication, and even incitement of feeling has its ancient history' and owes part of its success 'to the general rise of sentimentalism. But its theoretical justification was largely drawn from the arsenal of rhetorical theory. Poetry is to move the affections as rhetoric does' (*18C* 22).
35 Lomonosov 97, editor's note 6.
36 The latter quotation is part of the work's long title.
37 Chapter 6 of part 1, 'O izobretenii' [On Invention], treats of their 'excitation, satisfaction, and expression' ('KRK' 166–204).

38 Yuri Tynianov, 'The Ode as an Oratorical Genre,' trans. Ann Shukman, *New Literary History* 34.3 (2003): 567.

39 Stacy mentions the existence and circulation of other precursory rhetorics (many were versions of Greek, not Roman, originals), particularly from the Russian Baroque period (c. 1640–1740), but he claims that 'it was especially Latin school rhetoric, emanating chiefly from the Kiev Academy [anti-Jesuitic in its mission, Jesuitic in pedagogical practice] that, along with German and French pseudoclassical doctrine, reached Lomonosov' (9). He categorically rejects any Greek influence on Russian literary criticism (10). The 'stylistic legislation' proposed by Lomonosov in 'Predislovie o pol'ze knig tserkovnikh v rossiiskom iaziike' was, like Lomonosov's rhetoric, 'also of Roman origin' (16).

40 For an attempt at a close comparison of both texts, see H. Grasshoff, 'Lomonosov und Gottsched: Gottscheds *Ausführliche Redekunst* und Lomonosovs *Ritorika,' Zeitschrift für Slawistik* 6 (1961): 498–507. Grasshoff concludes that, despite numerous points of similarity (and often literal borrowings), Lomonosov's text is hardly a copy of Gottsched's. One important difference lies in its systematization of what in Gottsched appears as 'loosely strung together instructions for the excitement of different passions' (506). However, the text's conceptual merit stems from its author's ability to select and expand on what is useful for remodelling Russian language. So, for example, Lomonosov frequently chose examples more suited to the Russian national literary heritage or to the literary imagination (e.g., where Gottsched used Cicero, Fléchier, Demosthenes, or Mosheim, Lomonosov preferred St Chrysostomus-Zlatoust', Tacitus, Curtius Rufius, Virgil, or Horace – or chose a different oration from Cicero).

41 A.P. Sumarokov, 'Dve epistoly. V pervoi predlagaetsia o russkom iazyke, a vo vtoroi o stikhotvorstve,' in his *Izbrannye proizvedeniia*, ed. P.N. Berkov (Leningrad: Biblioteka Poeta, 1957), 112–25.

42 In regards to their conceptual similarity, Segel is of the opinion that 'while Sumarokov was inspired by and indebted to Boileau it would be incorrect to accept his second epistle as no more than a Russian imitation' (223). Pietraszko's remarks on *L'Art poétique* are pertinent to a comparison of Sumarokov's epistles: 'This code, hailed for its purported dogmatism, is not a scholarly dissertation, not a somber combination of dry regulations, but a lively and witty poetic work. It is a didactic poem, though its generic character explodes with satirical and polemical passion. The stance of a militant, clever, and enterprising critic always decisively dominated that of the even-tempered instructor' ('ISR' xcvii). As will be shown, in these respects the works bear a striking resemblance. As in Boileau, so too in Sumarokov 'Everything here – the principles as well as the examples – is

saturated with clear, sharp judgment. The positive side is slight, praise rare …' (xcviii). However, Sumarokov's text has less of a discernible internal arrangement than that found in Boileau.

43 Trediakovskii translated both texts into Russian. The cult of Boileau and Horace spread from Western Europe through Poland, where 'the Polish Diderot' Ignacy Krasicki even composed a fictional dialogue between the two theorists, based on late ancient moral-philosophical dialogues (Segel 221–4). Krasicki's dialogue can be found in *Oświeceni o literaturze*, ed. Kostkiewiczowa and Goliński, 85–7.

44 The translation by Segel used is in prose.

45 Describing genres as *combinatory* and *interactive*, Joseph Farrell points out that Horace's epistle exhibits the all too pervasive gap between genre theory and practice: while insisting on generic purity and essentializing generic forms, the *Ars poetica* violates generic norms. I quote the relevant fragment of Farrell's argument:

> It is Horace in his *Ars poetica* who coins the phrase 'the law of genre' [*operis lex*] and who represents this law as 'forbidding' [*vetet*] the poet to do certain things (line 135). It is he, too, who begins this poem by ridiculing … [indirectly, the combination of] elements from different genres into some monstrous whole, and thus [presenting] a forceful statement against any such practice. But Horace's clear directives regarding generic purity are complicated by the medium in which he delivers them. In the first place, the genre of the *Ars poetica* is a problem in and of itself. To us it looks like a didactic poem; but to make this decision is to assign Horace's essay on generic fundamentalism to a genre that was, as I have noted, not officially recognized by ancient critics. Not that this was Horace's first venture into ambiguous territory. The title that the *Ars poetica* bears in our medieval manuscripts is 'Letter to the Brothers Piso' (*Epistula ad Pisones*). It is indeed addressed to the Pisones (line 6), even if it does not bear the defining formal marks of a letter … Does Horace's acknowledged status as a lyric poet affect our answer to this question [of the work's genre] – that is, since Horace … has established that he is a poet, does an experiment like the *Ars poetica* also qualify as a poem, or is Horace a poet when he writes the lyric *Odes* but an essayist when he writes the *Ars*? The question may seem pedantic, but in fact Horace worked throughout his career to raise such questions ('Classical Genre in Theory and Practice,' *New Literary History* 34.3 [2003]: 394–5).

Drawing on the work of C.O. Brink, a newer study of Horace's 'poetry of criticism' casts the *Ars poetica* as the product of competing principles of design and unity – the transmission of a critical theory versus the integrity of a poetic work. Horace avoids 'technicality and the schools' language' and through this 'prevents the flow of the poem from being disturbed' (Ross S. Kilpatrick, *The Poetry of Criticism: Horace, Epistles II, and 'Ars Poetica'* [Edmonton: University of Alberta Press, 1990], 32). Another tension arises from the text's formal status as an *epistle*: a tension between 'Horace's desire to make the argument appear to flow spontaneously as in a letter to friends, while incorporating as well the kind of unity and coherence in structure that he demands' (36).

46 A.P. Sumarokov, 'Two Epistles,' in *The Literature of Eighteenth-Century Russia*, vol. 1, ed. and trans. H.B. Segel (New York: Dutton, 1967), 225. All further citations of this translation are abbreviated as 'TE.'

47 Joachim Klein calls this feature of Sumarokov's output the 'objectification of form,' distinguishing the views put forward in the second epistle from those expressed in his elegies (Joachim Klein, 'Die Vergegenständlichung der Form im russischen Klassizismus,' in *Festschrift für Herbert Bräuer zum 65. Geburtstag am 14. April 1986*, ed. Reinhold Olesch and Hans Rothe [Cologne: Böhlau, 1986], 238–44).

48 Sumarokov, 'Epistola II,' in his *Izbrannye proizvedeniia*, ed. P.N. Berkov (Leningrad: Biblioteka Poeta, 1957), 125.

49 Shtivelius is a character from a German comedy modelled on a pedantic mathematician (Reyfman 82).

50 On a comparable register is perhaps Horace's passage on language, lines 58–72.

51 I have in mind particularly those on literary language. Grinberg and Uspenskii, after such a comparison, conclude that Trediakovskii's ideas were far more thought out and put forth as a unified program (62).

52 V.K. Trediakovskii, 'Pis'mo v kotorom soderzhitsia rassuzhdenie o stikhotvorenii, ponyne v svet izdannom ot avtora dvukh od, dvukh tragedii i dvukh epistol, pisannoe ot priiatelia k priiateliu,' in *Sbornik materialov dlia istorii Imperatorskoi Akademii Nauk v XVIII veke*, vol. 2, ed. A.A. Kunik (St Petersburg: Akademiia Nauk, 1865), 435–500. All further citations of this source are abbreviated as 'PPP.'

53 A.A. Kunik, ed., *Sbornik materialov dlia istorii Imperatorskoi Akademii Nauk v XVIII veke*, vol. 2 (St Petersburg: Akademiia Nauk, 1865), 436.

54 This play is considered the first classical Russian comedy.

55 Sumarokov (unlike Lomonosov or Trediakovskii, at least until 1759, when he was dismissed) was himself not a member of the Academy.

56 N.M. Karamzin, 'Neskolko slov o russkoi literature,' in his *Izbrannye sochineniia v dvukh tomakh*, vol. 2, ed. P. Berkov (Moscow: Khudozhestvennaia Literatura, 1964), 145–56. The article was commissioned by a French-language journal and appeared originally in French.

57 For example, in 1791 he reviewed Lessing's *Emilia Galotti* (1772) for the *Moskovskii zhurnal.*

58 As Ambler explains, the words *zhurnalistika* and *publitsistika* have broader meanings than their English cognates. The former refers to periodical publications generally, the latter to publications on sociopolitical topics (184n1). The words *czasopiśmiennictwo* and *publicystyka* are their respective equivalents in contemporary Polish.

59 In the plurality of his editorial ventures and their significance for the development of literary culture, Karamzin's career parallels Mitzler's in Poland.

60 N.M. Karamzin, *Izbrannye sochineniia v dvukh tomakh,* vol. 2, ed. P. Berkov (Moscow: Khudozhestvenna Literatura, 1964), 533n.

61 N.M. Karamzin, 'A Few Words about Russian Literature: A Letter to the *Spectateur du Nord* about Russian Literature,' in *The Literature of Eighteenth-Century Russia,* vol. 1, ed. and trans. H.B. Segel (New York: Dutton, 1967), 433. All further citations are abbreviated as 'FWRL.'

62 '[I] have learned to be reserved in my judgments about the good and bad qualities of various nations' (440).

63 Karamzin's *Letters* were translated into German in 1800 and again in 1804, and into Polish in 1802.

64 Karamzin's essay (introduction plus excerpt) begins and ends with a reference to Rousseau (430, 440).

65 Reference is to Montesquieu's *The Spirit of Laws* (1752).

66 Published in *Vestnik Evropii* [Messenger of Europe] in 1802.

67 Karamzin's sycophancy to the West reveals itself in several comparisons, standard in a culture suffering from an inferiority complex, and aiming perhaps not so much at self-aggrandizement as at simple cultural translation, e.g., the mention of 'our Charles the Great' or the remark that the medieval *Slovo o polku Igoreve* [The Song of Igor's Campaign] (of then questioned authorship) 'can be compared to the best passages in Ossian' ('FWRL' 431).

68 Segel's anthology places the text in the 'literary essay' category.

69 Karamzin, *Izbrannye sochineniia* 533n. This text contains much simpler renditions than Herder's author portraits in the *Fragmente.*

70 Another instance of this: Karamzin's *Pis'ma russkovo puteshestvennika,* following the convention of European sentimentalism and neither straight fiction nor non-fiction, contains a section devoted solely to the topic of a national literature (English; it contains a brief, frank assessment of English letters, past and present), even identified by an appropriate heading ('Literature'), besides the more scattered critical remarks elsewhere in the text.

Though writing in the sentimentalist vein (in a personal and moderately emotional style), Karamzin strayed from an unadulterated 'sentimental journey' to offer *post-factum* reflections and informational content, maintained within the epistolary structure. These were based on notes and supplemented by extensive reading (Segel 393).

71 Karamzin, *Izbrannye sochineniia* 534n.

72 P. Berkov and G. Makogonenko, introduction to N.M. Karamzin, *Izbrannye sochineniia v dvukh tomakh*, vol. 1, ed. P. Berkov (Moscow: Khudozhestvenna Literatura, 1964), 17.

Conclusion

1 Casanova uses the terms *literary* and *literature* in the broadest sense of 'writing.'

2 For an overview of German forms before 1850, see for instance Hartmut Steinecke, 'Der "heilige Geist der Kritik": Zur Literaturkritik des Jungen Deutschland,' in *Literaturkritik des Jungen Deutschland: Entwicklungen – Tendenzen – Texte* (Berlin: Schmidt, 1982), 28–33. Steinecke focuses on genres disseminated by periodicals: the review, the *Charakteristik* (which ranged from biographical criticism rooted in author psychology to panoramas of the times, pulling into its orbit political and social matters), the programmatic article (*Programmartikel*), the essay, the feuilleton, and the monograph (*Einzeldarstellung*), subdivided thematically into the monograph (on genre, literary period, tendency, or current). His most interesting point concerns the generic range of *Jungdeutsche* periodicals versus traditional review publications. 'As contributors to papers edited by others, the Young Germans were compelled to curtail [the] urge' to attend to larger, more fundamental questions, and focus primarily on book reviewing (28). 'In their own journals, however, they had a free hand' (28).

A comparable sketch for Polish criticism can be found in Markiewicz's above-cited *Dopowiedzenia*, pp. 102–14. In addition to the review, the monograph, and literary history, Markiewicz lists the following written genres and subgenres: *rzecz* (speech, from *rzec*, 'to speak'; cf. Ger. *Rede*), *rys* or *zarys* (outline), *kurs* (course), (*obraz*) view, *podręcznik* (textbook), *portret literacki* (literary portrait), *charakterystyka* (characterization), *wizerunek* (image), *zarys literacki* (literary outline), *sylwetka* (profile), *szkic*, *próba* (sketch or essay, in the sense of 'attempt'), *przyczynek* (monographic article), *analiza*, *rozbiór* (analysis), *synteza* (synthesis), *uwagi* (remarks, dealing with current matters), *studium*, *studia* (study, studies, the most semantically unstable), and several literary-biographical genres (*wiadomości* [news], *pochwały* [posthumous commendations], *żywot* [life], *życie i dzieła* ['life and works'], counted among monographs). This, of course, suggests that the range of critical genres was not narrow at all. However, when one compares examples of these categories with a range of eighteenth-century examples, the *external* formal heterogeneity of the former appears to have undergone a striking reduction. For one thing, forms that were once distinct have been, because of discursive deregulation, demoted to subgenre status. The many acts of naming are, therefore, not as generative as one might expect. Another change was the specialization of critical terminology and systematization of thematic and propositional strategies for each subcategory – although this did not prevent individual styles from leaving their mark.

The genres of Russian critical texts, whose primary outlet was periodicals, did not develop as specialized a vocabulary of forms. The generic flowering one could have hoped to see in the nineteenth century was nipped in the bud. A search of my own yielded the following, more modest, list: treatise, letter, review, *razgovor* (conversation), *mysli* (thoughts; including Belinskii's *mechtaniia*, or reveries), *zamechaniia* (observations, remarks), *zametki* (notes), *rech'* (see Polish *rzecz*, above), *vopros* (question), *vzgliad* (glance, survey), *kritika* (criticism), *ocherk* (essay, study, or sketch), *stat'ia* (article), and monograph on individual authors and their works. Apart from a few longer, book-length genres, these designated creative approaches to journalistic prose.

3 As Geoffrey Hartman, defending the new discursive styles of criticism and its corresponding generic upheaval in the late 1970s and early 1980s, explained:

> literary criticism has become the last refuge of the neo-classical prohibition against mixed genres or any blurring of the demarcations between criticism and art or criticism and anything else – philosophy, religion, the social sciences ... Historically viewed, criticism played a liberal role: It set standards, but also served as the testing place and crucible for the flexible modern prose we now possess ... [I]f we are indeed in an Age of Criticism, and if a 'literature of criticism' now exists ... then criticism, too, will have to be read closely. It should not be fobbed off as a secondary activity, as a handmaiden to more 'creative' modes of thinking like poems or novels (Geoffrey H. Hartman, 'How Creative Should Literary Criticism Be?' *New York Times Book Review*, 5 April 1981: 11, 24–5).

In his manifesto a few years later, W.J.T. Mitchell took up this call, while keeping open criticism's claim to knowledge:

> Contemporary criticism is serious, experimental, encyclopedic and personal. By 'serious' I mean that it is professional, institutional, politically

engaged and cognitively ambitious (i.e. it aims at new forms of knowledge). By 'experimental' I mean that it is risky, playful, perverse, and sceptical of received forms of knowledge. By 'encyclopedic' I mean that it excludes nothing – nature, man, history, sex, politics, religion – from its attention, and refuses to confine itself to 'literature' in any traditional sense. By 'personal' I mean that it is autobiographical, self-critical and self-indulgent ...'Serious'/'Experimental'/'Encyclopedic'/'Personal': these adjectives should be understood as articulating the tension in contemporary criticism between its claim to be a scientific, methodical, rigorous discipline, and its desire to break away from discipline, science and method ... 'Experimentalism' in recent criticism therefore has a double sense. On the one hand, it suggests a scientific method of reading, which involves the testing of new hypotheses on texts – for example, that the English novel is best understood as an articulation of imperialist consciousness, or the hypothesis that every text undermines its own authority in the play of its figurative language. This mode of experimentalism produces routines and repetitious readings – we keep finding the same results in all sorts of different texts – just as a scientific experiment must be repeatable in order to be regarded as valid. 'Routinisation' and repetition are often dismissed by foes of recent criticism as a sign that it has been 'domesticated' or has lost its revolutionary potential and become simply another academic field, or that the 'human feeling' of literature is being destroyed by science. One could as easily argue that these routines are a sign of success, that they are what make contemporary criticism a teachable discipline rather than an unrepeatable miracle of genius. On the other hand, experimentalism is associated with the search for the new, the untried, the bizarre or the perverse. (W.J.T. Mitchell, 'The Golden Age of Criticism: Seven Theses and a Commentary,' *London Review of Books* 9.12 [1987]: 16, 17)

As a discourse, criticism seems to have the best of all worlds.

Selected Works Cited

Primary Sources

(1) German

Bürger, G.A. 'Herzenausguß über Volkspoesie.' In *Sturm und Drang: Kritische Schriften*, ed. E. Loewenthal, 805–11. Heidelberg: Schneider, 1972.

– 'Outpourings from the Heart on Folk Poetry.' In *Eighteenth Century German Criticism*, ed. and trans. T.J. Chamberlain, 252–7. New York: Continuum, 1994.

– 'On Popularity in Poetry.' In *Eighteenth Century German Criticism*, ed. and trans. T.J. Chamberlain, 258–61. New York: Continuum, 1994.

Goethe, J.W. von. *Literary Essays: A Selection in English*. Ed. J.E. Spingarn. New York: Harcourt Brace Jovanovich, 1921.

– 'Noten und Abhandlungen zum besseren Verständnis des West-östlichen Divans.' In *Gedenkausgabe der Werke, Briefe und Gespräche*, vol. 3, 3rd ed., 413–566. Zürich: Artemis, 1966.

– 'Literarischer Sansculottismus.' In *Goethes Werke*, vol. 12, ed. E. Trunz, 239–44. Munich: Beck, 1981.

– *Essays on Art and Literature*. Ed. J. Gearey. Trans. E. von Nardroff and E.H. von Nardroff. New York: Suhrkamp, 1986.

Gottsched, J.Ch. 'Versuch einer critischen Dichtkunst vor die Deutschen.' In *Schriften zur Literatur*, ed. H. Steinmetz, 12–196. Stuttgart: Reclam, 1982.

– 'Critical Poetics (excerpt).' In *Eighteenth Century German Criticism*, ed. and trans. T.J. Chamberlain, 3–7. New York: Continuum, 1992.

Hamann, J.G. 'Aesthetica in nuce: Eine Rhapsodie in Kabbalistischer Prose.' In *Sturm und Drang: Kritische Schriften*, ed. E. Loewenthal, 119–43. Heidelberg: Schneider, 1972.

– 'Aesthetica in nuce: A Rhapsody in Cabbalistic Prose.' Trans. J.P. Crick. In *Classic and Romantic German Aesthetics*, ed. J.M. Bernstein, 1–23. Cambridge: Cambridge University Press, 2002.

Herder, J.G. 'Über die neuere deutsche Literatur: Erste bis dritte Sammlung von Fragmenten (Auszug).' In *Sturm und Drang: Kritische Schriften*, ed. E. Loewenthal, 185–287. Heidelberg: Schneider, 1972.

– *Selected Early Works, 1764–1767: Addresses, Essays, and Drafts; Fragments on Recent German Literature*. Ed. E.A. Menze and K. Menges. Trans. Menze with M. Palma. University Park: Pennsylvania State University Press, 1992.

Lenz, J.M.R. 'Rezension des Neuen Menoza, von dem Verfasser selbst ausgesetzt.' In *Werke und Briefe*, vol. 2, ed. S. Damm, 699–704. Munich: Hanser, 1987.

Lessing, G.E. *Laocoön: An Essay on the Limits of Painting and Poetry*. Ed. and trans. E.A. McCormick. Indianapolis: Bobbs-Merrill, 1962.

– 'Siebzehnter Brief.' In *Werke und Briefe: 1758–1760*, vol. 4, ed. W. Barner, 499–501. Frankfurt: Deutscher Klassiker, 1989.

– 'Laokoon: oder über die Grenzen der Malerei und Poesie.' In *Werke und Briefe: 1766–1769*, vol. 5/2, ed. W. Barner, 11–318. Frankfurt: Deutscher Klassiker, 1990.

Möser, J. 'Über die deutsche Sprache und Literatur: Schreiben an einen Freund.' In Friedrich der Grosse, *De la littérature allemande*, ed. Ch. Gutknecht and P. Kerner, 121–41. Hamburg: Buske, 1969.

Novalis. *Werke, Briefe, Dokumente*. Ed. E. Wasmuth. Vols. 2 and 3. Heidelberg: Schneider, 1957.

– *Philosophical Writings*. Ed. and trans. M.M. Stoljar. Albany: SUNY Press, 1997.

– 'Kritik und Lesen.' In *Theorie der Romantik*, ed. H. Uerlings, 192. Stuttgart: Reclam, 2000.

– 'Dialogues.' Trans. J.P. Crick. In *Classic and Romantic German Aesthetics*, ed. J.M. Bernstein, 216–26. Cambridge: Cambridge University Press, 2002.

– *Novalis: Notes for a Romantic Encyclopaedia (Das Allgemeine Brouillon)*. Ed. and trans. David W. Wood. Albany: SUNY Press, 2007.

Schiller, F. 'On Bürger's Poems.' In *Eighteenth Century German Criticism*, ed. and trans. T.J. Chamberlain, 262–73. New York: Continuum, 1992.

– 'Über die Ästhetische Erziehung des Menschen in einer Reihe von Briefen.' In *Werke und Briefe: Theoretische Schriften*, vol. 8, ed. R. Janz, 556–676. Frankfurt: Deutscher Klassiker, 1992.

– 'Über naïve und sentimentalische Dichtung.' In *Werke und Briefe: Theoretische Schriften*, vol. 8, ed. R.-P. Janz, 706–81. Frankfurt: Deutscher Klassiker, 1992.

– 'Letters on the Aesthetic Education of Man.' In *Essays*, ed. W. Hinderer and D.O. Dahlstrom, trans. E.M. Wilkinson and L.A. Willoughby, 86–178. New York: Continuum, 2001.

Schlegel, A.W. and F. Schlegel. *Athenaeum*. Ed. C. Grützmacher. 2 vols. Munich: Rowohlt, 1969.

Schlegel, F. *Kritische Schriften*. Ed. W. Rasch. Munich: Hanser, 1956.

– *Schriften und Fragmente: Ein Gesamtbild seines Geistes*. Ed. E. Behler. Stuttgart: Krüner, 1956.

– *Dialogue on Poetry and Literary Aphorisms*. Ed. and trans. E. Behler and R. Struč. University Park: Pennsylvania State University Press, 1968.

– 'Gespräch über die Poesie.' In *Früher Idealismus und Frühromantik: Der Streit um die Grundlagen der Ästhetik (1795–1805)*, vol. 1, ed. W. Jaeschke and H. Holzey, 99–211. Hamburg: Meiner, 1990.

– *Philosophical Fragments*. Trans. P. Firchow. Foreword R. Gasché. Minneapolis: University of Minnesota Press, 1991.

– 'Über Goethes *Meister*.' In *Theorie der Romantik*, ed. H. Uerlings, 201–24. Stuttgart: Reclam, 2000.

(2) Polish

Anonymous. 'Uwagi z przyczyny "Zakusu nad zaciekami Wszechnicy Krakowskiej."' In *Ludzie Oświecenia o języku i stylu*, vol. 1, ed. M.R. Mayenowa, Z. Florczak, and L. Pszczołowska, 679–80. Warsaw: PIW, 1958.

Czartoryski, A.K. 'Przedmowa do *Kawy*.' In *Oświeceni o literaturze: Wypowiedzi pisarzy polskich 1740–1800*, ed. T. Kostkiewiczowa and Z. Goliński, 114–20. Warsaw: PWN, 1993.

– 'Przedmowa do *Panny na wydaniu*.' In *Oświeceni o literaturze*, ed. Kostkiewiczowa and Goliński, 92–114. Warsaw: PWN, 1993.

Dmochowski, F.K. *Sztuka rymotwórcza*. Wrocław: Zakład im. Ossolińskich, 1956.

Fijałkowski, M. 'O geniuszu, guście, wymowie i tłumaczeniu.' In *Oświeceni o literaturze*, ed. Kostkiewiczowa and Goliński, 431–75. Warsaw: PWN, 1993.

Golański, F.N. 'O wymowie i poezji.' In *Oświeceni o literaturze*, ed. Kostkiewiczowa and Goliński, 221–355. Warsaw: PWN, 1993.

Jabłonowski, J.A. 'Opisanie albo dysertacja pierwsza prawie o wierszach i wierszopiscach polskich wszystkich.' In *Oświeceni o literaturze*, ed. Kostkiewiczowa and Goliński, 56–8. Warsaw: PWN, 1993.

Rzewuski, W. 'O nauce wierszopiskiej.' In *Oświeceni o literaturze*, ed. Kostkiewiczowa and Goliński, 59–67. Warsaw: PWN, 1993.

Szymanowski, J. 'List o guście, czyli smaku.' In *Oświeceni o literaturze*, ed. Kostkiewiczowa and Goliński, 164–71. Warsaw: PWN, 1993.

Theatralski. 'Wystąpienie sławnego angielskiego autora Johnsona przeciw klasycystycznym rygorom w utworach teatralnych.' In *'Monitor,' 1765–1785: Wybór*, ed. E. Aleksandrowska, 119–23. Wrocław: Zakład Narodowy im. Ossolińskich, 1976.

(3) Russian

Karamzin, N.M. 'Neskol'ko slov o russkoi literature.' In *Izbrannye sochineniia v dvukh tomakh*, vol. 2, ed. P. Berkov, 145–56. Moscow: Khudozhestvennaia Literatura, 1964.

– 'Panteon rossiiskikh avtorov.' In *Izbrannye sochinieniia v dvukh tomakh*, vol. 2, ed. P. Berkov, 156–73. Moscow: Khudozhestvennaia Literatura, 1964.

– 'A Few Words about Russian Literature. A Letter to the *Spectateur du Nord* about Russian Literature.' In *The Literature of Eighteenth-Century Russia*, vol. 1, ed. and trans. H.B. Segel, 430–41. New York: Dutton, 1967.

Kheraskov, M.M. 'K satiricheskoi muze.' In *Izbrannye proizvedeniia*, ed. A.V. Zapadov, 103–5. Leningrad: Sovetskii Pisatel', 1961.

Lomonosov, M.V. 'Kratkoe rukovodstvo k krasnoriechiiu. Kniga pervaia, v kotoroi soderzhitsia ritorika, pokazuiushchaia obshchie pravila oboevo krasnoriechiia, to est' oratorii i poezii, sochinennaia v pol'zu liubiashchikh slovesnye nauki.' In *Polnoe sobranie sochinienii: Trudi po filologii, 1739–1758*, vol. 7, 89–378. Moscow: Izdatel'stvo Akademii Nauk SSSR, 1952.

– 'Pis'mo o pravilakh rossiiskogo stikhotvorstva.' In *Polnoe sobranie sochinienii: Trudi po filologii, 1739–1758*, vol. 7, 7–18. Moscow: Izdatel'stvo Akademii Nauk SSSR, 1952.

Sumarokov, A.P. 'Dve epistoly. V pervoi predlagaetsia o russkom iazyke, a vo vtoroi o stikhotvorstve.' In *Izbrannye proizvedeniia*, ed. P.N. Berkov, 112–25. Leningrad: Biblioteka Poeta, 1957.

– 'Two Epistles.' In *The Literature of Eighteenth-Century Russia*, vol. 1, ed. and trans. H.B. Segel, 224–38. New York: Dutton, 1967.

Trediakovskii, V.K. 'Pis'mo v kotorom soderzhitsia rassuzhdenie o stikhotvorenii, ponyne v svet izdannom ot avtora dvukh od, dvukh tragedii i dvukh epistol, pisannoe ot priiatelia k priiateliu.' In *Sbornik materialov dlia istorii Imperatorskoi Akademii Nauk v XVIII veke*, vol. 2, ed. A.A. Kunik, 435–500. St Petersburg: Akademiia Nauk, 1865.

– 'Novyi i kratkii sposob k slozheniiu rossiiskikh stikhov.' In *Izbrannye proizvedeniia*, ed. L.I. Timofeev, 365–85. Moscow: Sovetskii Pisatel', 1963.

Secondary Sources

General

Abrams, M.H. *A Glossary of Literary Terms*. Fort Worth: Harcourt Brace, 1993.

Althusser, L. 'Ideology and Ideological State Apparatuses (Notes towards an Investigation).' In *Lenin and Philosophy and Other Essays*, trans. B. Brewster, 127–86. London: New Left, 1971.

Bakhtin, M. 'The Problem of Speech Genres.' In *Speech Genres and Other Late Essays*, ed. C. Emerson and M. Holquist, trans. V.W. McGee, 60–102. Austin: University of Texas Press, 1986.

Bazerman, C. 'Systems of Genres and the Enactment of Social Intentions.' In *Genre and the New Rhetoric*, ed. A. Freedman and P. Medway, 79–101. London: Taylor & Francis, 1994.

– 'Letters and Social Grounding of Differentiated Genres.' In *Letter Writing as a Social Practice*, ed. D. Barton and N. Hall, 15–30. Amsterdam: Benjamins, 2000.

Beebee, T.O. *The Ideology of Genre: A Comparative Study of Generic Instability*. University Park: Pennsylvania State University Press, 1994.

Benjamin, W. 'Epistemo-Critical Prologue.' In *The Origin of German Tragic Drama*, trans. J. Osborne, 27–56. New York: New Left, 1977.

Bové, P.A. *Mastering Discourse: The Politics of Intellectual Culture*. Durham: Duke University Press, 1992.

Cain, W.E. 'Notes toward a History of Anti-Criticism.' *New Literary History* (*NLH*) 20.1 (1988): 33–48.

Casanova, P. *The World Republic of Letters*. Trans. M.B. DeBevoise. Cambridge, MA: Harvard University Press, 2004.

Cerquiglini, B. *In Praise of the Variant: A Critical History of Philology*. Trans. B. Wing. Baltimore: Johns Hopkins University Press, 1999.

Cohen, R. 'History and Genre.' *NLH* 17.2 (1986): 203–18.

Derrida, J. 'The Law of Genre.' In *Acts of Literature*, ed. D. Attridge, trans. A. Ronell, 221–52. London: Routledge, 1992.

– *Of Grammatology*. Trans. and introd. G.C. Spivak. Baltimore: Johns Hopkins University Press, 1998.

Devitt, A.J. *Writing Genres*. Carbondale: Southern Illinois University Press, 2004.

Farrell, J. 'Classical Genre in Theory and Practice.' *NLH* 34.3 (2003): 383–408.

Foucault, M. *The Archaeology of Knowledge and the Discourse on Language*. Trans. A.M. Sheridan Smith. New York: Pantheon, 1972.

– *Discipline and Punish: The Birth of the Prison*. Trans. A. Sheridan. New York: Vintage, 1979.
– 'The Order of Discourse.' Trans. I. McLeod. In *Untying the Text: A Poststructuralist Reader*, ed. R. Young, 48–78. Boston: Routledge & Kegan Paul, 1981.
– 'What Is Enlightenment?' In *The Foucault Reader*, ed. and introd. P. Rabinow, trans. C. Porter, 32–50. New York: Pantheon, 1984.
– Introduction to *The Birth of the Clinic: Archaeology of Medical Perception*, trans. A.M. Sheridan, ix–xxii. London: Routledge, 1989.
– *The History of Sexuality: An Introduction*. Trans. R. Hurley. New York: Vintage, 1990.
– *The Order of Things: An Archaeology of the Human Sciences*. New York: Vintage, 1994.
– 'The Discourse of History.' Interview by R. Bellour. In *Foucault Live: Interviews, 1961–1984*, ed. S. Lotringer, trans. L. Hochroth and J. Johnston, 19–32. New York: Semiotext[e], 1996.
– 'Nietzsche, Freud, Marx.' In *Essential Works of Foucault, 1954–84*, vol. 2, *Aesthetics, Method, and Epistemology*, ed. J.D. Faubion, trans. R. Hurley et al., 269–78. New York: New, 1998.
– 'What Is an Author?' In *Essential Works of Foucault, 1954–84*, vol. 2, *Aesthetics, Method, and Epistemology*, ed. J.D. Faubion, trans. R. Hurley et al., 205–22. New York: New Press, 1998.
Genette, G. *The Architext: An Introduction*. Trans. J.E. Lewin. Berkeley: University of California Press, 1992.
Groden, M., M. Kreiswirth, and I. Szeman, eds. *The Johns Hopkins Guide to Literary Theory and Criticism*. 2nd ed. Baltimore: Johns Hopkins University Press, 2005. Available online at http://litguide.press.jhu.edu/index.html.
Gumbrecht, H.U. *Making Sense in Life and Literature*. Trans. G. Burns. Minneapolis: University of Minnesota Press, 1992.
Hacking, I. *Historical Ontology*. Cambridge, MA: Harvard University Press, 2002.
Hartman, G.H. 'How Creative Should Literary Criticism Be?' *New York Times Book Review* (5 April 1981): 11, 24–5.
Hohendahl, P.U. 'The Scholar, the Intellectual, and the Essay: Weber, Lukács, Adorno, and Postwar Germany.' *The German Quarterly* 70 (Summer 1997): 217–32.
– *The Institution of Criticism*. Ithaca: Cornell University Press, 1982.
Jauss, H.R. *Toward an Aesthetic of Reception*. Trans. T. Bahti. Minneapolis: University of Minnesota Press, 1982.
Kennedy, G.A. 'Christianity and Criticism.' In *The Cambridge History of Literary*

Criticism, vol. 1, *Classical Criticism*, ed. Kennedy, 330–46. Cambridge: Cambridge University Press, 1990.

Kilpatrick, R.S. *The Poetry of Criticism: Horace, Epistles II, and 'Ars Poetica.'* Edmonton: University of Alberta Press, 1990.

Koselleck, R. *Critique and Crisis: Enlightenment and the Pathogenesis of Modern Society*. Oxford: Berg, 1988.

Lang, B. *Philosophy and the Art of Writing: Studies in Philosophical and Literary Style*. Lewisburg, PA: Bucknell University Press, 1983.

– *The Anatomy of Philosophical Style: Literary Philosophy and the Philosophy of Literature*. Oxford: Blackwell, 1990.

LaCapra, D. *Rethinking Intellectual History: Texts, Contexts, Language*. Ithaca: Cornell University Press, 1983.

– *History and Criticism*. Ithaca: Cornell University Press, 1985.

Lavery, J. 'Philosophical Genres and Literary Forms: A Mildly Polemical Introduction.' *Poetics Today* 28.2 (2007): 171–89.

MacDonell, D. *Theories of Discourse: An Introduction*. Oxford: Blackwell, 1986.

Maciejewski, J. *Obszary i konteksty literatury*. Warsaw: DiG, 1998.

Markiewicz, H. *Główne problemy wiedzy o literaturze*. Cracow: WL, 1965.

Miller, P.A. 'Toward a Post-Foucauldian History of Discursive Practices.' *Configurations* 7.2 (1999): 211–25.

Mills, S. *Discourse*. 2nd ed. London: Routledge, 2004.

Minnis, A., and I. Johnson. Introduction to *The Cambridge History of Literary Criticism*, vol. 2, *The Middle Ages*, ed. Minnis and Johnson, 1–12. Cambridge: Cambridge University Press, 2005.

Negt, O., and A. Kluge. *The Public Sphere and Experience: Toward an Analysis of the Bourgeois and Proletarian Public Sphere*. Trans. P. Labanyi et al. Minneapolis: University of Minnesota Press, 1993.

Opacki, I. 'Royal Genres.' Trans. D. Malcolm. In *Modern Genre Theory*, ed. D. Duff, 118–25. Essex: Pearson Education, 2000.

Quinby, L. Introduction to *Genealogy and Literature*, ed. Quinby, xi–xxix. Minneapolis: University of Minnesota Press, 1995.

Plato. 'Ion.' Trans. L. Cooper. In *The Critical Tradition: Classic Texts and Contemporary Trends*, ed. D. Richter, 17–37. New York: St Martin's, 1989.

Said, E. 'Introduction: Secular Criticism.' In *The World, the Text, and the Critic*, 1–30. Cambridge, MA: Harvard University Press, 1983.

– 'Traveling Theory.' In *The World, the Text, and the Critic*, 226–47. Cambridge, MA: Harvard University Press, 1983.

– 'Traveling Theory Reconsidered.' In *Reflections on Exile and Other Essays*, 436–52. Cambridge, MA: Harvard University Press, 2000.

Smith, D.E. 'Textually Mediated Social Organization.' In *Texts, Facts, and Femininity: Exploring the Relations of Ruling*, 209–24. London: Routledge, 1990.

Steiner, G. 'Text and Context.' In *On Difficulty and Other Essays*, 1–17. Oxford: Oxford University Press, 1978.

Tynjanov, Y., and R. Jakobson. 'Problems in the Study of Literature and Language.' Trans. H. Eagle. In *Readings in Russian Poetics*, ed. L. Matejka and K. Pomorska, 79–81. Cambridge, MA: MIT Press, 1971.

Wellek, R. *A History of Modern Criticism, 1750–1950*. Vol. 1, *The Later Eighteenth Century*. New Haven: Yale University Press, 1955.

– 'Literary Theory, Criticism, and History.' In *Concepts of Criticism*, ed. Stephen G. Nichols, Jr, 1–20. New Haven: Yale University Press, 1963.

– 'The Term and Concept of Literary Criticism.' In *Concepts of Criticism*, ed. Stephen G. Nichols, Jr, 21–33. New Haven: Yale University Press, 1963.

– *A History of Modern Criticism, 1750–1950*. Vol. 4, *The Later Nineteenth Century*. New Haven: Yale University Press, 1965.

– 'Immanuel Kant's Aesthetics and Criticism.' In *Discriminations: Further Concepts of Criticism*, 122–42. New Haven: Yale University Press, 1970.

– 'The Term and Concept of Classicism in Literary History.' In *Discriminations: Further Concepts of Criticism*, 55–89. New Haven: Yale University Press, 1970.

White, H. 'Commentary.' *NLH* 34.2 (2003): 367–76.

Ziętarska, J. *O metodzie krytyki literackiej w dobie Oświecenia*. Warsaw: WUW, 1981.

Region-Specific Studies

Ambler, E. Introduction to *Russian Journalism and Politics, 1861–1881 (The Career of Aleksei S. Suvorin)*, 13–35. Detroit: Wayne State University Press, 1972.

Anz, Th., and R. Baasner, eds. *Literaturkritik: Geschichte – Theorie – Praxis*. Munich: Beck, 2004.

Atkins, S. Introduction to *The Age of Goethe: An Anthology of German Literature*, ed. Atkins, 1–13. Boston: Houghton, 1969.

Baasner, R. ed. *Projekt Literaturkritik*. Universität Rostock. https://www.phf.uni-rostock.de/institut/igerman/forschung/litkritik/litkritik/start.htm.

Behler, E. Introduction to F. Schlegel, *Dialogue on Poetry and Literary Aphorisms*, ed. and trans. Behler and R. Struč, 3–50. University Park: Pennsylvania State University Press, 1968.

– Foreword to *German Romantic Criticism*, ed. A.L. Willson, vii–xiii. New York: Continuum, 1982.

– *Irony and the Discourse of Modernity*. Seattle: University of Washington Press, 1990.

Berghahn, K. 'From Classicist to Classical Literary Theory (1730–1806).' In *A History of German Literary Criticism, 1730–1980*, ed. P.U. Hohendahl, trans. F. Blaha, 13–98. Lincoln: University of Nebraska Press, 1988.

Berkov, P., and G. Makogonenko. Introduction to N.M. Karamzin, *Izbrannye sochineniia v dvukh tomakh*, vol. 1. ed. P. Berkov, 5–76. Moscow: Khudozhestvenna Literatura, 1964.

Berkov, P.N. *Istoriia russkoi zhurnalistiki XVIII veka*. Moscow: Izdatel'stvo Akademii Nauk SSSR, 1952.

Bernstein, J.M. Introduction to *Classic and Romantic German Aesthetics*, ed. Bernstein, vii–xxxiii. Cambridge: Cambridge University Press, 2002.

Bogner, R.G. 'Die Formationsphase der deutschsprachigen Literaturkritik.' In *Literaturkritik: Geschichte – Theorie – Praxis*, ed. Thomas Anz and Rainer Baasner, 18–19. Munich: Beck, 2004.

Bruford, W.H. *Germany in the Eighteenth Century: The Social Background of the Literary Revival*. Cambridge: Cambridge University Press, 1952.

Chamberlain, T.J., ed., trans., and introd. *Eighteenth Century German Criticism*. New York: Continuum, 1992.

Chmielowski, P. *Dzieje krytyki literackiej w Polsce*. Warsaw: Gebethner i Wolff, 1902.

Dahnke, H.-D. 'Intentionen und Resultate des Jahrgangs 1772 der *Frankfurter Gelehrten Anzeigen*.' In *Sturm und Drang: Geistiger Aufbruch 1770–1790 im Spiegel der Literatur*, ed. B. Plachta and W. Woesler, 233–47. Tübingen: Niemeyer, 1997.

Eskildsen, K.R. 'How Germany Left the Republic of Letters.' *Journal of the History of Ideas* 65.3 (2004): 421–32.

Gasché, R. Foreword to F. Schlegel, *Philosophical Fragments*, trans. P. Firchow, vii–xxxii. Minneapolis: University of Minnesota Press, 1991.

Gearey, J. Postscript to J.W. von Goethe, *Essays on Art and Literature*, ed. Gearey, trans. E. von Nardroff and E.H. von Nardroff, 229–40. New York: Suhrkamp, 1986.

Gella, A. 'The Life and Death of the Old Polish Intelligentsia.' *Slavic Review* 30.1 (1971): 1–27.

Grasshoff, H. 'Lomonosov und Gottsched: Gottscheds *Ausführliche Redekunst* und Lomonosovs *Ritorika*.' *Zeitschrift für Slawistik* 6 (1961): 498–507.

Grimm, J., and W. Grimm. *Deutsches Wörterbuch*. Leipzig: Hirzel, 1862–1951.

Grinberg, M.S., and B.A. Uspenskii. *Literaturnaia voina Trediakovskogo i Sumarokova v 1740-kh–nachale 1750-kh godov*. Chteniia po Istorii i Teorii Kul'turii. Moscow: RGGU, 2001.

Grützmacher, C. 'Zur Geschichte des "Athenaeum."' In A.W. Schlegel and F. Schlegel, *Athenaeum*, ed. Grützmacher, 250–2. Munich: Rowohlt, 1969.

Gukovskii, G. 'From "On Russian Classicism."' *Russian Literature Triquarterly* 21 (1988): 7–14.

Hammermeister, K. *The German Aesthetic Tradition*. Cambridge: Cambridge University Press, 2002.

Hombek, D. *Prasa i czasopisma polskie w XVIII wieku w perspektywie bibliologicznej*. Cracow: Universitas, 2001.

Horne, H. 'Introductory Essay: The Early Romantic Fragment and Incompleteness.' In *Theory as Practice: A Critical Anthology of Early German Romantic Writings*, ed. J. Schulte-Sasse et al., 289–313. Minneapolis: University of Minnesota Press, 1997.

Jones, G.L. 'Gottsched and the German Poets of the Seventeenth Century.' *Forum for Modern Language Studies* 7.3 (1971): 282–93.

Kästner, E. *Friedrich der Grosse und die deutsche Literatur: Die Erwiderungen auf seine Schrift 'De la littérature allemande.'* Stuttgart: Kohlhammer, 1972.

Kaleta, R. *Prekursorzy Oświecenia: 'Monitor' z roku 1763 na tle swoich czasów; Mitzler de Kolof: Redaktor i wydawca*. Wrocław: Zakład Narodowy im. Ossolińskich, 1953.

Kieffer, B. *The Storm and Stress of Language: Linguistic Catastrophe in the Early Works of Goethe, Lenz, Klinger, and Schiller*. University Park: Pennsylvania State University Press, 1986.

Klein, J. 'Die Vergegenständlichung der Form im russischen Klassizismus.' In *Festschrift für Herbert Bräuer zum 65. Geburtstag am 14. April 1986*, ed. Reinhold Olesch and Hans Rothe, 237–47. Cologne: Böhlau, 1986.

Kostkiewiczowa, T. 'Rozważania o kulturze literackiej czasów stanisławowskich.' In *Problemy kultury literackiej polskiego Oświecenia: Studia*, ed. Kostkiewiczowa, 9–32. Wrocław: Ossolineum, 1978.

– 'Krytyka literacka w Polsce w epoce Oświecenia.' In E. Sarnowska-Temeriusz and Kostkiewiczowa, *Krytyka literacka w Polsce w XVI i XVII wieku oraz w epoce Oświecenia*, 151–342. Wrocław: Zakład Narodowy im. Ossolińskich, 1990.

– 'Myśl literacka polskiego Oświecenia.' In *Oświeceni o literaturze*, ed. Kostkiewiczowa and Goliński, 7–34. Warsaw: PWN, 1993.

Kostkiewiczowa, T., and Z. Goliński, eds. *Oświeceni o literaturze: Wypowiedzi pisarzy polskich, 1740–1800*. Warsaw: PWN, 1993.

Kowalik, J.A. *The Poetics of Historical Perspectivism: Breitinger's 'Critische Dichtkunst' and the Neoclassic Tradition*. Chapel Hill: University of North Carolina Press, 1992.

Küpper, P. 'Author ad Lectorem. Vorreden im 18. Jahrhundert. Ein Forschungsvorschlag.' In *Festschrift für Rainer Gruenter*, ed. B. Fabian, 86–95. Heidelberg: Winter, 1978.

Kuleshov, V.I. *Istoriia russkoi kritiki XVIII–nachala XX vekov*. Moscow: Prozveshchenie, 1984.
Kurska, A. *Fragment Romantyczny*. Wrocław: Zakład Narodowy im. Ossolińskich, 1989.
Lacoue-Labarthe, P., and J.-L. Nancy. *The Literary Absolute: The Theory of Literature in German Romanticism*. Trans. P. Barnard and C. Lester. New York: SUNY Press, 1988.
Leventhal, R.S. *The Disciplines of Interpretation: Lessing, Herder, Schlegel, and Hermeneutics in Germany, 1750–1800*. Ed. W. Pape. Berlin: deGruyter, 1994.
Libera, Z. *Problemy polskiego Oświecenia: Kultura i styl*. Warsaw: PWN, 1969.
– *Wiek Oświecony: Studia i szkice z dziejów literatury i kultury polskiej XVIII i początków XIX wieku*. Warsaw: PIW, 1986.
Markiewicz, H. *Z dziejów polskiej wiedzy o literaturze: Prace wybrane*. Vol. 6. Cracow: Universitas, 1998.
– *Dopowiedzenia: Rozprawy i szkice z wiedzy o literaturze*. Cracow: WL, 2000.
Marmontel, J.-F. 'Critique.' In *Encyclopédie, ou dictionnaire raisonné des sciences, des arts et des métiers*, ed. D. Diderot and J. le R. d'Alembert. University of Chicago: ARTFL Encyclopédie Projet, Spring 2010 Edition, ed. R. Morrissey. http://encyclopedie.uchicago.edu/.
Mayenowa, M.R., Z. Florczak, and L. Pszczołowska, eds. *Ludzie Oświecenia o języku i stylu*. 2 vols. Warsaw: PIW, 1958.
McKenna, K.J. 'Ezhemesiachnye sochineniia.' In *Modern Encyclopedia of Russian and Soviet Literature*, vol. 7, ed. H.B. Weber, 125–6. Gulf Breeze, FL: Academic International, 1984.
Mayer, H. Introduction to *Meisterwerke deutscher Literaturkritik*. ed. Mayer. Berlin: Rütten & Loening, 1954–56.
Menze, E.A., and K. Menges. 'Commentary to the Translations.' In J.G. Herder, *Selected Early Works, 1764–1767: Addresses, Essays, and Drafts; Fragments on Recent German Literature*, ed. Menze and Menges, trans. Menze with M. Palma, 235–333. University Park: Pennsylvania State University Press, 1992.
Morozov, A.A. Introduction to M.V. Lomonosov, *Izbrannye proizvedeniia*, vol. 1, ed. Morozov, 5–58. Leningrad: Sovetskii Pisatel', 1986.
Neuhaus-Koch, A. 'Frankfurter gelehrte Anzeigen auf das Jahr 1772.' 2005. Universität Düsseldorf. 1 May 2006. http://www.phil-fak.uni-duesseldorf.de/germ2/neuhaus-koch/drang/pdf/FrankfurterAnzeigen.pdf.
Nisbet, H.B., ed. *German Aesthetic and Literary Criticism: Winckelmann, Lessing, Hamann, Herder, Schiller, Goethe*. Cambridge: Cambridge University Press, 1985.
Nisbet, H.B., and Claude Rawson, eds. *The Cambridge History of Literary Criti-*

cism, vol. 4, *The Eighteenth Century*. Cambridge: Cambridge University Press, 1997.

Nutz, M. 'Das Beispiel Goethe: Zur Konstituierung eines nationalen Klassikers.' In *Wissenschaftsgeschichte der Germanistik im 19. Jahrhundert*, ed. J. Fohrmann and W. Voßkamp, 605–37. Stuttgart: Metzler, 1994.

Paulini, H.M. *August Wilhelm Schlegel und die Vergleichende Literaturwissenschaft*. Frankfurt: Lang, 1985.

Pietraszko, S. Introduction to F.K. Dmochowski, *Sztuka rymotwórcza*, ed. Pietraszko, iii–cxcv. Wrocław: Zakład im. Ossolińskich, 1956.

– *Doktryna literacka polskiego klasycyzmu*. Wrocław: Zakład Narodowy im. Ossolińskich, 1966.

Purdy, D. 'The Whiteness of Beauty: Weimar Neo-Classicism and the Sculptural Transcendence of Color.' In *Colors 1800/1900/2000: Signs of Ethnic Difference*, ed. and introd. B. Tautz, 83–99. Amsterdam: Rodopi, 2004.

Ram, H. *The Imperial Sublime: A Russian Poetics of Empire*. Wisconsin Center for Pushkin Studies Series. Madison: University of Wisconsin Press, 2003.

Reich-Ranicki, M. 'Über den Essay und das Feuilleton.' *Der Kanon. Die Deutsche Literatur: Essays*. Frankfurt: Suhrkamp Insel, 2001.

Reyfman, I. *Vasilii Trediakovsky: The Fool of the 'New' Russian Literature*. Studies in the Harriman Institute, Columbia University. Stanford: Stanford University Press, 1990.

Rosenberg, K. 'Trediakovsky on Sumarokov: The Critical Issues,' *Russian Literature Triquarterly* 21 (1988): 49–60.

Rowland, H., and K.J. Fink, eds. *The Eighteenth-Century German Book Review*. Heidelberg: Winter, 1995.

Sarnowska-Temeriusz, E. 'Krytyka literacka w Polsce w XVI i XVII wieku.' In Sarnowska-Temeriusz and T. Kostkiewiczowa, *Krytyka literacka w Polsce w XVI i XVII wieku oraz w epoce Oświecenia*, 7–150. Wrocław: Zakład Narodowy im. Ossolińskich, 1990.

Schlaffer, H. *Poesie und Wissen: Die Entstehung des ästhetischen Bewußtseins und der philologischen Erkenntnis*. Frankfurt: Suhrkamp, 1990.

Segel, H.B., ed. *The Literature of Eighteenth-Century Russia*. Vol. 1. New York: Dutton, 1967.

Simpson, D. Introduction to *German Aesthetic and Literary Criticism: Kant, Fichte, Schelling, Schopenhauer, Hegel*, ed. Simpson, 1–24. Cambridge: Cambridge University Press, 1984.

– Introduction to *The Origins of Modern Critical Thought: German Aesthetic and Literary Criticism from Lessing to Hegel*, ed. Simpson, 1–22. Cambridge: Cambridge University Press, 1988.

Skwarczyńska, S. *Teoria listu*. Lwów: Towarzystwo Naukowe we Lwowie, 1937.

– 'Wokół teorii listu (Paradoksy).' In *Pomiędzy historią a teorią literatury*, 178–86. Warsaw: Pax, 1975.

Stacy, R.H. *Russian Literary Criticism: A Short History*. Syracuse, NY: Syracuse University Press, 1974.

Steinecke, H. 'Der "heilige Geist der Kritik": Zur Literaturkritik des Jungen Deutschland.' In *Literaturkritik des Jungen Deutschland: Entwicklungen – Tendenzen – Texte*, 16–57. Berlin: Schmidt, 1982.

Stoljar, M. *Athenaeum: A Critical Commentary*. Bern: H. Lang, 1973.

– Introduction to Novalis, *Philosophical Writings*, 1–21. Albany: SUNY Press, 1997.

Theisen, B. 'Drama in Rags: Shakespeare Reception in Eighteenth-Century Germany.' *MLN* 121.3 (2006): 505–13.

Tynianov, Y. 'The Ode as an Oratorical Genre.' Trans. A. Shukman. *NLH* 34.3 (2003): 565–96.

Van Der Laan, J. 'Nicolai's Concept of the Review Journal.' In *The Eighteenth-Century German Book Review*, ed. Herbert Rowland and Karl J. Fink, 95–112. Heidelberg: Winter, 1995.

Verweyden, T. 'Theorie und Geschichte der Parodie, Teil 3.' 20 September 1997. *Erlanger Digitale Edition: Beiträge zur Literatur- und Sprachwissenschaft*. 1 May 2006. http://www.erlangerliste.de/vorlesung/parodieIII.html.

Vinogradov, V.V. *The History of the Russian Literary Language from the Seventeenth Century to the Nineteenth*. Trans. and condensed L.L. Thomas. Madison: University of Wisconsin Press, 1969.

Walicki, A. *A History of Russian Thought from the Enlightenment to Marxism*. Trans. H. Andrews-Rusiecka. Stanford: Stanford University Press, 1979.

– *The Three Traditions in Polish Patriotism and Their Contemporary Relevance*. Bloomington: Polish Studies Center, 1988.

Ward, A. *Book Production, Fiction, and the German Reading Public, 1740–1800*. Oxford: Clarendon, 1974.

Wertz, A. 'Regenerating the Republic: The *Monitor* and Economic Reform in the Polish Enlightenment.' *CSEES Newsletter* 17.2 (2000): 13–21.

Index

www.ingramcontent.com/pod-product-compliance
Lightning Source LLC
LaVergne TN
LVHW040151080826
844660LV00014B/916/J

* 9 7 8 1 4 4 2 6 4 3 5 6 7 *